SWAB SUMMER

Transformation at the United States Coast Guard Academy

FOR THOSE WHO SERVE IN THE
United States Coast Guard

SWAB SUMMER: Transformation at the United States Coast Guard Academy

Fowler Road Press
49 Fowler Road
North Stonington, Ct 06359
Telephone: 860.535.4413

ISBN-10   0-9821685-9-4
ISBN-13   978-0-9821685-9-2

First Edition Published October, 2013
Book Design by Fowler Road Press
Photographs by Markham Starr
markhamstarrphotography.com
catboatalbum.com

Photograph of USCGC *41395* courtesy Carl Tjerandsen

SWAB SUMMER

Transformation at the United States Coast Guard Academy

MARKHAM STARR

Table of Contents

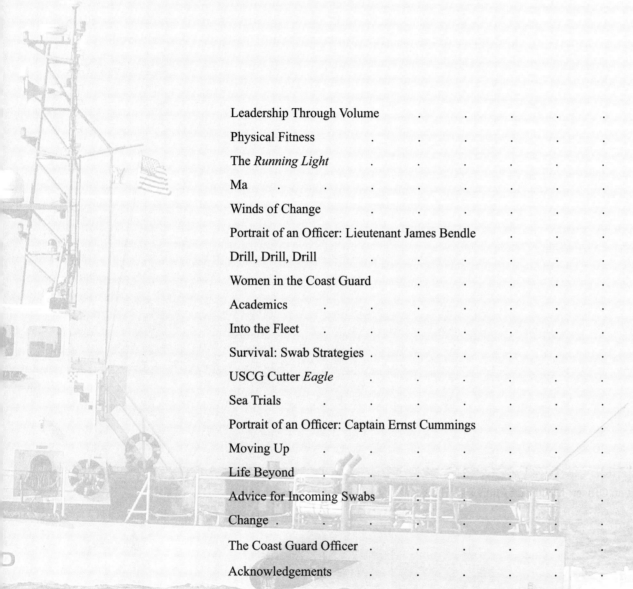

2/C Jessica Nelson leads her company's new swabs out to the parade field to begin the day's training.

Foreword

On the west shore of the Thames River stands the city of New London, Connecticut. Once an important whaling center, New London's fortunes have ebbed and flowed over the course of the last century. Traces of its former prosperity remain but fail to mask the city's current economic struggles. Those historic parts of the city that can still be found on the riverfront are drowned in a sea of commercial ventures whose prime has come and gone. At the northern end of the city proper, a pair of soaring iron structures, referred to locally as the Gold Star Bridge, links New London with the town of Groton on the opposing shore. Just north of the bridge's shadow resides the United States Coast Guard Academy. The sprawling hillside campus consists of a complex of brick buildings housing the future officers of the second-oldest continuously operating military organization in the country.

The Coast Guard is unique amongst the branches of America's armed services. Its multi-mission nature demands a level of elasticity not often found in governmental institutions. Its motto, *Semper Paratus*, or "Always Ready," is replaced jokingly in conversation with *Semper Gumby*, reflecting its need for flexibility as the world and its missions change around it.

Although America's oldest continuous seagoing service, it is perhaps the least recognized of the military's five branches. In fact, many cadets now studying at the Academy admit that they had never heard of the school before their own college searches began. The Coast Guard requires astute and flexible leadership because of the separate roles it must play in such diverse areas as search and rescue, maritime safety, environmental protection, drug and alien interdiction, and military defense of America's coastline. The foundation for building the necessary corps of leaders is laid at the Coast Guard Academy, and the first tentative steps are taken during what is known as "swab summer." Over the course of seven weeks, teenagers from diverse backgrounds undergo a profound transformation as they begin their military careers.

This book documents swab summer, the indoctrination process experienced by those choosing to serve their country by accepting an appointment to the United States Coast Guard Academy. Leaving families and friends behind, these teenagers pass through the school's gates to begin the Academy's version of boot camp, which will transform them from individuals into a cohesive group with common goals and a unified sense of purpose. They may begin the summer as teenagers, but they will end it as young men and women.

Most incoming swabs naively feel that Hollywood productions have prepared them for the experiences they will face; nearly all are shocked at the actual transition. As at every military academy, many will not make it through the summer's trials. Medical disqualifications, injuries, and plain old second thoughts will lead to several dozen departures before the summer's end. While losses seem large to those caught in the whirlwind of their first swab summer, seasoned cadets know this is but the first volley. The four years of academic, military, and athletic challenges to come will prove even more demanding. By graduation, roughly 35 percent of the incoming class will have washed away.

Swabs often feel they are the lowest of the low. Should they survive the mental and physical challenges of the following seven weeks, they will emerge from the heat of the summer's furnace as 4th class cadets. The transformation they undergo is nothing short of miraculous, yet when they emerge they are but rough forgings. It will take another four long years to fully shape and polish them into ensigns, ready to board Coast Guard cutters or aircraft around the globe. One thing is certain: they will leave New London much changed from the day they first drove through the Academy's gates.

This book follows one class of incoming swabs through the start of this long and arduous process. On Reporting-In Day, or R-Day, they begin their transition from civilians to U.S. Coast Guard officers. From day one, they will replace the words "I" and "me" with "us" and "we." The core values of the institution will permeate their thoughts. They will come to understand that the failure of one person in their company spells the failure of the company as a whole. They will end the summer with a new perspective on who they are and on what they can accomplish.

This book attempts to capture something of that transformation and of what it means to be an officer in the United States Coast Guard. Ironically, I found during my interviews that the swabs themselves are perhaps the least qualified to speak about their ongoing metamorphosis. The path ahead is much longer than the four years they will spend at the Academy or the additional five they have agreed to serve after graduation. For Coast Guard officers, growth is a lifelong endeavor, so to gain perspective on this process, I also interviewed officers with experience well beyond the Academy's gates. With an organization as large and complex as the United States Coast Guard, this book is necessarily limited in scope. Nonetheless, I hope it affords at least some understanding of the dedicated men and women protecting the nation's coastlines.

View of the United States Coast Guard Academy from across the Thames River. The first buildings at the Academy were constructed in 1932.

Introduction

Our country's history is inextricably linked to the oceans surrounding us. As early as the sixteenth century, European settlers began voyaging across the Atlantic to stake claim in this newly "discovered" land. Each newcomer's very existence depended upon the continued replenishment of supplies and settlers by sea. Over the intervening centuries, these vast bodies of water have both connected us to our allies and insulated us from our enemies. Today, they continue to provide us with food and resources and to join our commercial interests with those of other nations around the world. While we are and have been many things as a country, we will always be a seafaring nation.[1]

The United States Coast Guard is nearly as old as the nation itself. Although both a Continental Army and a Continental Navy existed during the American Revolution, they proved too costly to maintain at the war's end. Only a small portion of the Army survived congressional spending cuts, and the Navy was completely disbanded for a period of eleven years after 1783. The fledgling nation was in financial crisis, but in that crisis can be found the seeds of today's Coast Guard. Congress proposed to meet its new financial obligations by levying taxes on imported goods. Secretary of the Treasury Alexander Hamilton proposed the construction of a series of revenue cutters that would monitor shipping activity along the coast to collect the new import taxes and intercept smugglers. In 1790, Hamilton submitted a report to Congress proposing the creation of a service known as the Revenue Marine, the organization which would eventually become the modern Coast Guard. Hamilton's report states, in part: [Note: Spellings are Hamilton's.]

The following is submitted as a proper establishment for this purpose. That there be ten boats. . . . Boats of from thirty-six to forty feet keel, will answer the purpose, each having one Captain, one Lieutenant and six mariners, and armed with swivels. The first cost of one of these boats, completely equipped, may be computed at One thousand dollars. The following is an estimate of the annual expence:

10 Captains @ 40. dollars per month 4,800
10 Lieutenants @ 25. ditto per ditto 3,000
60 seamen @ 8. ditto per ditto 5,760
Provision 3,000
Wear and Tear 2,000
Dollars 18,560

The utility of an establishment of this nature must depend on the exertion, vigilance and fidelity of those, to whom the charge of the boats shall be confided. If these are not respectable characters, they will rather serve to screen, than detect fraud. To procure such, a liberal compensation must be given, and in addition to this, it will, in the opinion of the Secretary, be advisable, that they be commissioned as Officers of the Navy. This will not only induce fit men the more readily to engage, but will attach them to their duty by a nicer sense of honor.

Hamilton's 1790 cost estimates are enlightening: a cutter would cost $1,000; a lieutenant's pay, $25 per month. By the 1960s, according to one retired officer I interviewed, a lieutenant's pay had only reached $228 a month. The cost of a large cutter, on the other hand, had risen nearly a thousandfold.

Congress was, understandably, sensitive about policing its own citizens so soon after the revolution. After all, the British government's imposition of odious import taxes and its intolerable methods of collecting them had been among the factors that had driven the colonies to rebellion. Because of Congress's concerns and his

own interest in the success of this new service, Hamilton composed a letter to the captain of each new vessel slated to patrol America's waterways. The message details the qualities and temperament to be expected of every officer. Remarkably, these expectations have remained unchanged for over 200 years and appear today in the swabs' summer bible, the *Running Light*:

While I recommend in the strongest terms to the respective officers, activity, vigilance and firmness, I feel no less solicitude, that their deportment may be marked with prudence, moderation and good temper. Upon these last qualities, not less that the former, must depend the success, usefulness and consequently continuance of the establishment in which they are included. They cannot be insensible that there are some prepossessions against it, that the charge with which they are intrusted is a delicate one, and that it is easy by mismanagement, to produce serious and extensive clamour, disgust and odium. They will always keep in mind that their countrymen are freemen, and, as such, are impatient of everything that bears the least mark of a domineering spirit. They will, therefore, refrain, with the most guarded circumspection, from whatever has the semblance of haughtiness, rudeness, or insult. . . . They will endeavor to overcome difficulties, if any are experienced, by a cool and temperate perseverance in their duty—by address and moderation, rather than by vehemence or violence.

After its formation, the Revenue Marine remained the nation's only armed seagoing force until 1797, when friction developed between the young country and its old ally France. As a nation completely dependent upon foreign trade, the United States would not survive without a competent naval force protecting its interests at sea. The brewing trouble with France, along with the threat of Algerian piracy, forced Congress to act. In 1794, it authorized the construction of the first ships of what would eventually become today's modern Navy. Included in the act creating the Navy was a provision whereby the President could transfer control of the Revenue Marine's ships and men to the Department of the Navy in times of war, a provision that would put the Service's men and women in harm's way throughout the next two centuries.

As the nation developed in size and complexity, so did its maritime needs. Congress, realizing the essential role aids to navigation play in the safe conduct of trade, enacted laws to place their regulation under federal control. The Treasury Department assumed oversight in 1789, a function that would eventually be transferred to the modern Coast Guard in 1939.

The Revenue Marine's role expanded in the 1830s when Congress charged the Service with performing winter cruises to help mariners in distress. While this was the beginning of the role for which the Coast Guard is best known today, it was at the time considered simply an auxiliary function; there were already other societies dedicated to saving shipwrecked sailors along New England's coastline. It was not until 1878 that Congress believed the role important enough for federal oversight, at which time it created the U.S. Life Saving Service, another wholly separate agency that would later be combined with the Revenue Cutter Service, formally known as the Revenue Marine.

BY *Sea* AND BY *Air* ~ TO *Uphold* THE LAW, TO *Rescue* THE DISTRESSED, AND TO *Defend* THE NA

Mural depicting a breeches buoy rescue in which a canvas seat brings survivors across a line fired to the ship by a Lyle gun. This painting is in the Henriques Room in Hamilton Hall.

Throughout the nineteenth century, the Revenue Marine began to oversee other duties, beyond gathering taxes and helping distressed seamen. As long as servicemen were on patrol, Hamilton felt they should create charts to improve governmental knowledge of the waterways in which they operated. Additionally, along with the Navy, the Service worked to suppress piracy in the Caribbean and to stop the illegal importation of slaves under British and U.S. law. In 1822, servicemen began protecting timber in Florida, a material deemed essential to the construction of the nation's expanding naval fleet. Revenue Marine vessels helped fight in the Seminole Wars in the early part of the century and became the primary legal force in Alaska after its acquisition from Russia in 1867.

The Civil War split the Revenue Marine much as it had the country itself; some crews fled with their cutters south while others sailed north. The cutter *Harriet Lane*, credited with firing the first naval shot of the war off Fort Sumter, was later captured by the South, and so played a role both for and against the Union. Other Revenue cutters patrolled the seas to protect shipping or blockade harbors until the end of hostilities.

THESE SHIPS AND MEN~THE *Coast Guard* OF TODAY~STAND *Constant Watch*, READY TO PROCEED

Coast Guardsmen come ashore bearing supplies. The Henriques Room murals depict Coast Guard values as well as dramatic moments in the Coast Guard's history.

ters and the crews who operated them would finally go to the Navy, once and for all.

Despite protests by nearly all parties holding a stake in the outcome, Taft passed the bill onto Congress for approval. Given the wide controversy surrounding it, the bill stalled in Congress. In the election of 1912, Taft lost to Woodrow Wilson, who wanted instead to combine the Life Saving Service and the Revenue Cutter Service into one entity. Wilson's wish was granted, and the newly joined forces officially became the United States Coast Guard in 1915.

Almost immediately, world events would prompt rapid changes not only in the size of the institution but also in the scope of its mission. When the United States finally declared war on Germany in 1917, executive orders

The Service's role expanded throughout the next 100 years as well, both in civilian and military matters. Now known as the Revenue Cutter Service, it policed harbors around the country, protected seals in the Pribilof Islands, tracked icebergs in the North Atlantic, and secured the coastline during the Spanish American War. Despite the numerous expansions of its role over the preceding hundred years, however, the Service faced termination at the beginning of the twentieth century.

In 1911, President Taft formed the Cleveland Commission and charged it with reducing the size of the federal government. To begin with, the commission decided to combine the Life Saving and Lighthouse Services. Secondly, they would end the Revenue Cutter Service altogether and distribute its missions and assets amongst other governmental organizations. Importantly, the cut-

placed the Coast Guard fully under the Navy's control and its cutters soon began escorting convoys and patrolling European waters. Further, a massive ammunition explosion aboard a ship loading in Halifax, Nova Scotia, necessitated military control over major port operations; the office of Captain of the Port was created in response. Coast Guard officers took over security considerations, preventing accidents in four major ports during the war, a role they continue to fulfill today.

The Coast Guard had little time to rest on its laurels at the conclusion of World War I, as it now faced a new domestic problem: Prohibition. The Eighteenth Amendment to the U.S. Constitution, along with the Volstead Act of 1919, brought about a new era of Coast Guard expansion. Together, the two laws (neither of them ever popular) criminalized the production, sale, and transportation of alcohol within the borders of the United States. As the country's coastal police force, the Coast Guard tried to dam the flow of alcohol pouring into the nation along its thousands of miles of coastline. Despite dramatic increases to the numbers of Coast Guard personnel and cutters, the porous nature of the country's borders made the task nearly impossible. After fourteen long and difficult years, Congress called a halt to the effort by way of the Twenty-first Amendment. The cost to the government in its ever-expanding attempts to enforce the law, combined with the tremendous loss of potential tax revenues, had become too much to bear. Although overall the program had proved an immense failure, the Coast Guard benefited by expanding in size and capabilities.

By the mid-1930s, the Coast Guard was enforcing all maritime regulations at sea. The next major addition to its responsibilities came in 1939, when President Roosevelt brought the U.S. Lighthouse Service into its fold. In addition, the Service slowly began undertaking regulatory environmental duties. It began keeping the nation's harbors clear of ice during cold winter months and regulating the U.S. Maritime Service. The Coast Guard had always been the smallest military branch, but it was increasingly charged with a disproportionately large workload. Accordingly, in 1941, Admiral Russell Waesche increased personnel numbers with the passage of the Coast Guard Reserve and Auxiliary Act. Part of the Reserve, now separately known as the Coast Guard Auxiliary, is composed of uniformed volunteers who help regulate the recreational boating industry, and today there are over 30,000 members helping both on and off the water.

The next major challenge for the Coast Guard was, of course, World War II. Placed for a second time under the full control of the Department of the Navy, the Coast Guard again undertook its military role. Personnel oversaw port security, and cutters patrolled the Atlantic Ocean, where, among their many contributions, they sunk a dozen German U-boats. Coast Guardsmen played significant roles in amphibious landings around the globe, protected America's coastlines, and rescued service members whose ships had been sunk beneath them.

Over the course of World War II, the Coast Guard's mission list had expanded rapidly to take on the range of threats posed by Axis forces, and at the end of the war, Congress continued to add to those responsibilities. The Steamboat Inspection Service, created in 1838 to oversee safety on the new and surprisingly dangerous steam engines that were beginning to power vessels around the country, joined with the Bureau of Navigation in 1932, which oversaw aids to navigation placed in harbors, in rivers, and along the coast. This combined Bureau of Marine Inspection was itself subsumed by the Coast Guard in 1946.

As its role continued to broaden during the second half of the twentieth century, the Coast Guard modernized to fill new assignments. Though not active in Korea, the Coast Guard again took on military duties during the Vietnam War. Cutters patrolled the coasts, intercepting ships and boats bringing materials to the North. Additionally, cutters ran rivers within the country to help clear enemy forces. By 1967, the bulk of the Coast Guard's mission list was so completely removed from its initial eighteenth-century task of gathering revenues that oversight of the Coast Guard was transferred from the Treasury Department to the Department of Transportation.

Although the Coast Guard's military responsibilities tapered during the '70s and '80s, new challenges arose. Increasing amounts of its operational time became devoted to the interdiction of both drugs and illegal immigrants coming in by sea—a trend which continues today. Intercepting would-be immigrants from Cuba, Haiti, and other Caribbean nations became both a policing mission and a humanitarian one as thousands attempted the dangerous crossings in vessels that were anything but seaworthy.

During these decades, the Coast Guard's role in environmental protection also expanded. Several major oil spills, such as the *Argo Merchant* grounding off Nantucket and the *Exxon Valdez* spill in Alaska, helped solidify the Coast Guard's role not only in disaster prevention but also in environmental restoration. With the Coast Guard's help, Congress passed regulations dictating new integrity standards for ships plying American waters and gave the Service new powers to monitor them. Fearing depletion of the country's fishing stocks, Congress acted further, granting a number of agencies, including the Coast Guard, oversight of the fishing industry. While other federal departments handle the science behind these new regulations, the Coast Guard assures compliance aboard the fishing vessels themselves.

Today, the Coast Guard continues both in its military and in its civilian roles. Since the attacks of 9/11, the Service has been transferred, once again, to new oversight. Under the umbrella of the Department of Homeland Security since 2002, the Coast Guard's mission continues to evolve. Recently, personnel from the Coast Guard have taken their places in Operation Desert Shield, Desert Storm, and Operation Iraqi Freedom. Despite the lack of coastline, the Coast Guard also maintains a presence in Afghanistan.

The Coast Guard is unique among the armed services. Each of the other branches—the Army, the Navy, the Air Force, and the Marine Corps—is tasked with a narrowly defined mission, and U.S. citizens generally have a well-developed sense of what that mission is. Few, on the other hand, can list the eleven distinct missions of the Coast Guard. The Coast Guard is also unusual in that it acts on both a civilian and a military level. While the Posse Comitatus Act of 1878 prevents any of the other services from acting as a domestic police force without an act of Congress, the Coast Guard's mission in maritime law enforcement and its role as a federal regulatory agency have long required it to do exactly that.

Despite having so many missions, the Coast Guard remains the smallest of the country's armed services. In fact, with about 42,000 active and 8,000 reserve members, the Coast Guard is slightly smaller than the total number of people working for the New York City Police Department. How does the Coast Guard accomplish so much with so little? The answer, I believe, lies in the training given to each commanding officer within the Service—training that begins in New London. The United States Coast Guard Academy is a special and unique place, as are the people who pass through its gates, joining the long line of men and women who have served our country from its very beginning. R-Day is the day on which this training begins.

[1] All of the information in this chapter concerning the history of the service comes from Coast Guard *Publication 1: U.S. Coast Guard: America's Maritime Guardian*. Besides detailing the history of the Service, *Publication 1* provides an in-depth account of the role the Coast Guard plays in protecting our citizens and defending our nation.

A pair of deck guns frame the flagpole on Washington Parade Field. In the background, cadets head back to Chase Hall after a Change of Command ceremony.

R-Day

Swab summer begins on Reporting-in-Day, or R-Day, the day near the end of June when swabs take the oath of office. Most of them, newly released from their local high schools' grasps, are thrilled to leave that phase of life behind. The fortunate among them have at least been able to enjoy a few weeks of freedom. Others—those faced with late graduations—have barely had time to think about the transition they are about to make.

Swabs in the class of 2016 report from thirty-nine states and various provinces, territories, and countries. Many who are coming from great distances arrive in Connecticut well before the day they must report for duty. On Sunday, the day before R-Day, the Academy offers church services in the morning and a chance for families to view a typical swab room in Chase Hall, the imposing brick barrack that houses all cadets during their four-year stay.

Standing politely in each hallway are company officers, chiefs, and members of the cadet regimental staff, each willing to answer the thousand questions each family brings. *Are all the rooms this small? Is this building air-conditioned? How is the food here? Is swab summer as hard as we've heard?* Most questions come from parents. The incoming students, for the most part, look around nervously and offer only tentative smiles. At the Academy, even this simple opportunity to tour cadet quarters turns into a learning experience. Families who arrive late for the scheduled tour find nothing but an empty room.

That evening, families attend a buffet dinner and talk with others now in the same boat. Parents try to find their child's roommate or members from their child's company. Mothers and fathers of Academy children differ from their civilian counterparts. Seldom do parents at civilian colleges so eagerly write down the names, addresses, and e-mails of nearly everyone they meet. Parents of swabs know they will be unable to contact their child for nearly two months—two of the most challenging months of their child's life. Because of this, they search for any possible contact that may in the future lead to information on how their cadet is managing. Connections are made; alliances, quickly developed. In the weeks ahead, e-mails flash like summer lightning between them as soon as the smallest bit of information becomes available. *Swab A wrote this in a letter. Swab B wrote that.* When Swab C does not write, the worst is feared.

After dinner, families move to the Welcome Aboard reception. The reception, hosted by the Academy Parent's Association, further attempts to allay parental fears. Members of the association talk about experiences that, now less than twelve hours in the future, await the new families' children. At 2000, families pour from

A typical room in Chase Hall: A place for everything and everything in its place.

Leamy Hall into the dark evening, scattering to hotels throughout Groton and New London for a night's rest. Many will get little sleep.

The arrival times for the eight separate companies are staggered between 0700 and 0820 in an attempt to avoid morning logjams. Despite this safeguard, many families—those anxious to begin, tired of waiting, or worried about reporting late—arrive inappropriately early. Cars begin pouring through the main gate well before 0700, and there is enough excitement in the air to cause lapses in manners. Members of the cadre, the 2nd class cadets charged with the care, feeding, and training of the new swabs for the summer, stand at all possible crossroads, attempting, often unsuccessfully, to steer cars and their occupants to appropriate parking places. Several remark on the treatment they have received from drivers unwilling to follow their simple instructions. Ever disciplined, they simply bite their tongues and smile as cars drive off in the wrong direction. While the Academy is a place of rules, for outsiders, it is also one of the most polite places on earth, at times making even Disneyworld seem hostile. R-Day has begun.

R-Day. Reporting-In Day. The day when young men and women trade newly acquired teenage freedoms for an appointment to the U.S. Coast Guard Academy. Jeans and t-shirts go into long-term storage, replaced by uniforms for the foreseeable future. For swabs on R-Day, a whole world of electronic communications may as well evaporate from the face of the earth. Cell phones, tablets, computers, video games, DVD players, and headphones vanish. It is the day when 253 teenagers reach a clear demarcation in their lives, a division perhaps clearer than any they have previously experienced. On R-Day they begin their transition from a civilian to a military lifestyle. Metaphorical signs of what is to come begin rolling in from the southeast. The sky begins to blacken as a thickening storm system gathers ominously in the distance. In the hustle and excitement of getting to Leamy, few seem to notice this dark portent.

Leamy Hall takes its name from Rear Admiral Frank Leamy. The admiral, who earned a Distinguished Flying Cross for a daring rescue at sea, was also the Academy's superintendent in the late '50s and early '60s. A monumentally large and aesthetically undistinguished block of a building, Leamy houses the renowned Coast Guard band, a ballroom, a 1,280-seat auditorium, the student union, a snack bar, chaplains' offices, and a bowling alley. The building's interior architectural style is "military functional." Nothing ostentatious, nothing grand, nothing flashy. It does its job, and it does it cost-effectively. Despite its functional aesthetic, the windows on the second deck provide sweeping views of the Thames River far below, and on this day the building bursts with activity.

Swabs and their families enter through the plate-glass doors on the ground level. The entry foyer overflows with tables staffed with welcoming volunteers. From behind one of them, the Coast Guard Academy Parents Association hands out reams of paper containing helpful information. Others hawk Coast Guard memorabilia; you can buy a sweatshirt, a coffee mug, or a dozen other items emblazoned with the Coast Guard Bear or the words "U.S. Coast Guard Academy." These tables do a brisk business, and siblings of the class of 2016 run about the campus with "Property of the United States Coast Guard" stamped across their chests. Members of the cadre stand at the ready, directing incoming swabs to tables where they may sign in with their particular companies. Once done with the first floor, families move to the upper deck for the next pleasant phase of their morning.

The upper deck, or ballroom floor, covered with chairs and folding tables, hosts a continental breakfast for the new arrivals. The room buzzes with conversation as the crowd nervously awaits Alpha Company's chance to step forward and into their new lives. When they are politely ordered to the front of the hall with their bags, the mood of the room itself seems to change as parents tender one last piece of advice or encouragement. The newest members of Alpha Company form a slightly ragged line. Duffels, filled with mandated clothes, keep the formation from looking utterly shipshape.

Some students wear long pants and button down shirts. Others wear gym shorts and t-shirts, athletic logos emblazoned in brilliant hues. Fashion choices for the day seem surprisingly casual. The young women sport a remarkably uniform hairstyle: locks pulled up tightly against their heads in neat buns. If long, hair must be worn in this manner. Few girls have chosen the shoulder-length route, something they later regret when showers prove nothing more than momentary dashes beneath showerheads. In contrast, the young men have taken a variety of approaches. Knowing their fate, many have struck preemptively, buzzing their hair close, cheating the barbers across the street of the opportunity. Others have kept their hair as long as possible, their last stand as free men. The room grows quiet as a member of the cadre opens a door and Alpha Company heads through it and down a long stairwell. A string of buses idles at the bottom, waiting to shuttle them from their families and from life as they have always known it.

At this point in time, swabs begin to feel more like property of the U.S. Government. Before the Academy politely shoos the swabs' parents out the front gate, it must first transform the raw material within each bus into something presentable for the afternoon's swearing-in ceremony. This job goes to the cadre who, like the swabs themselves, have waited nervously throughout the morning. Silence reigns on the short trip up the hill to Chase Hall. Although the trip takes less than a minute, once the bus comes to a halt, swabs find themselves a world away.

Chase Hall is a massive four-story structure. Named for Abraham Lincoln's Secretary of the Treasury, it is home to more than a thousand cadets and the current crop of officer candidates attending Officer Candidate School, or OCS. It is the largest building at the Academy, a building whose true size remains concealed from the parade grounds fronting the campus. Only by circumnavigating the building can one truly appreciate its scale. Besides acting as barracks for the entire corps, Chase also holds the office of the commandant of cadets; a rifle and pistol range; the OCS wardroom, where officer candidates eat their meals; guest quarters for visiting dignitaries; and numerous support facilities such as a uniform dispensary, the Academy bookstore, a tailor shop, and a dry cleaner.

As with nearly all buildings on campus, Chase is a brick structure, punctured uniformly by double-hung windows. The imposing row of buildings lining Bear Drive, built in the 1930s, projects the solid feel of old New England.

Chase's four-story wings encase numerous quads, private outdoor areas reserved for drills and formations. The one in which the new cadets amass is perhaps the most austere of the courtyards. The day is as hot and humid as an Alabama greenhouse. The walls tower above the white squares of concrete paving the courtyard. Entering the quad from outside, swabs pass through a marble entablature held aloft by muscular Tuscan columns. Mounted in the center of the frieze is a simple plaque bearing the structure's name. Below the word "Chase," as if an afterthought, a second sign warns: "Height – 11'." Given the reception swabs receive after passing through, I begin to think Dante's inscription over the gates of hell would be more appropriate: "Abandon all hope, ye who enter here!" A thin blue line of tape leads swabs from the bus to little blue crosses neatly spaced on the bare concrete pad. Nature heightens the drama; clouds above begin swallowing the morning light, turning day into night.

The Academy's waterfront is dominated by the Seamanship Center. A cadet's first waterborne experience within the Coast Guard takes place in small sailboats.

Admissions

While the reasons for seeking an appointment are as varied as the students themselves, the Academy's goals for the Admissions Department are quite precise. The school looks to attract a very specific corps of cadets—cadets who can fulfill the Service's needs both at the Academy and throughout their careers. As with most departments, Admissions is composed of both civilian and military personnel. Coast Guard officers rotate through assignments here as they do with every other job within the Service.

While military officers bring firsthand knowledge of the organization's needs beyond graduation, their constant rotation would lead to chaos if the civilian staff did not provide some continuity over time. While not employing the cookie-cutter approach in their search for cadets, there are certain qualities they hope to find while pouring over applications.

Chris McMunn, an Academy graduate, is a lieutenant commander in the Coast Guard Reserve and now works for the Admissions Department. McMunn is the associate director of recruiting, and as such, oversees the work of his fellow Admissions officers, such as Lieutenant Commander Michael Thomas. Also a graduate of the Academy, Thomas followed a different track on his way to becoming an officer. Not financially able to complete college, he worked for the Louisville Redbirds until advised to get a degree. Thomas joined the Coast Guard and became a radioman, and a master chief took a personal interest in his abilities and encouraged him to apply to the Academy. After spending a year in the Scholar's Program with the Navy in Newport, Rhode Island, he entered the class of '96. Together, McMunn and Thomas shed light on the recruiting process from the Coast Guard's perspective.

Unlike West Point, Annapolis, or the Air Force Academy, admission to the Coast Guard Academy does not require congressional nomination. McMunn states that student choice is based on merit rather than geographic location or senatorial appointment.

We don't require the congressional nomination. I like the process here, because it seems a little cleaner; it's not who you know. Like most colleges, you send in your academic transcripts and your standardized test scores. You get a couple of your teachers to write you evaluations and letters of recommendation. You do the application, you do some essays, and the Academy gets to choose on a nationwide competition who they think will make up the best incoming class, whereas with the nomination process, in some ways, you're just competing geographically with other students from the area. I liked the concept that here, at the Coast Guard Academy, I was one of the best 300, or 320, and I was one of those best 320 nationwide, not just one of the best ten from my area. Besides that, I think our application processes are similar in terms of what we require. All the academies require an academic transcript, standardized test scores, and those instructor evaluations. We require a physical fitness test; it varies a little bit for each academy what we make them do, but it's usually pushups, sit-ups, and a mile-and-a-half run. We all require a medical exam, so they need to be found medically qualified to come on to active duty. If they fail that, we do have a medical waiver process they can try.

McMunn explains that the Coast Guard does not base its decisions on simple checklists:

The other academies are a little more formulaic in terms of how they choose, how they individually score components of their applications, where how many pull-ups you do will get you a certain number of points. Maybe you were a team captain; that might get you some more points in terms of your total candidate score at the other academies. Three years ago, we abandoned that process here at the Coast Guard Academy to go to a holistic review, which I would say is more in line with what people expect at a civilian college. They send in their things, and they're evaluated on the totality of the record. Okay, this person may have a stronger academic record, but maybe they don't have as many sports programs; those two balance each other out. We're looking at the total person and what they bring overall to the class. So I think, even if we still had that mathematically driven X number of points for this and so on, our class might not look that much different, but I think we definitely know our class much better now, because we have to really dig into the records.

We have to really appreciate what each of them brings and what they're going to contribute, and that's something I think a lot of our applicants don't always appreciate. I think they just see it as, "I've earned my appointment, right? I have 1500+ SAT scores," or, "I had straight As, and I thought I did everything I had to do." At the other academies, that may just very well get them the appointment. You total up the points, and if you have enough points you get the appointment. Here they really need to fit what we're looking to do with that class. With the smaller classes, I think it's harder here sometimes. There are just fewer spots. You can't take that model of, "All these people are deserving, let's appoint all of them." This year's class size is only about 250. Next year's class we're only taking about 230, so our class sizes are shrinking. When you need to support twenty-three varsity sports programs, about another ten club sport programs, and ten to twelve programs such as music, performing arts, and vocal clubs, in addition to everything else going on here, you really need to appreciate why each and every one of those young men and women are coming in and what they're bringing. You can't just be good and deserving of an appointment;

you really need to be coming to contribute to the Academy's community.

Given their substantially larger sizes, the other service academies have freedoms in their appointment options that are not available to the Coast Guard. West Point brought 1,193 plebes into their class of 2016; the Air Force, 1,035. The Navy started with the largest class of 2016, admitting 1,211 men and women, nearly five times as many as the Coast Guard. The only comparably sized academy is the Merchant Marine Academy at King's Point, which brought in 273 new students. According to Thomas, the size of the corps will continue to shrink in the near future:

The Service is downsizing right now. It's cyclical. This administration, probably starting around 2010, looked at it and said, "Okay, we're going to contract the military. The war is winding down in Iraq." I think sometimes people forget we get caught up in those military cuts. I'm sure, because our missions are not shrinking, we're not drawing down as much on a percentage basis, but we are drawing down, and it's probably because of the national budget. It's not a decision we made at the Academy because we can't afford it. The Service as a whole has said, "Hey, we anticipate that we need you to put out this number of officers." We have this mathematical formula, and we can tell in order to graduate this many, we need to bring in this many. So it's the Service's needs, and you could probably come back here in five to ten years and someone will tell you, "Oh yeah, we're taking 315 again."

As McMunn explains, this is not the only reason the Academy will be bringing in smaller classes:

One reason is that retention is at an all-time high, both here at the Academy and within the Service. We used to bring in 300+ to graduate 170 to 180; our graduation rates used to be 60 to 65 percent. Now our graduation rates are 75 to 80 percent, just fifteen years later, so I think they've made a lot of improvements or changes that have allowed us to retain more of our cadets. I know we've done a lot of things here to try to bring in cadets who are better prepared that we will be able to retain and, hopefully, graduate four years later. But even beyond admissions at the Academy, they've identi-

fied things within the training programs, within facilities, resources, and support programs for cadets, that have helped, as well. Cadets retain at a higher level through the four years.

It probably also doesn't hurt that the economy is what it is right now. Cadets at the Academy are probably just a little more thoughtful about it. Whereas in the past they said, "Hey, I just leave and mom and dad already told me they'd pay for college," or, "I have no issue with taking on student debt, because I know I'll get a job right after I graduate from my civilian college." Right now, I have to believe they are a little more thoughtful or realistic about where we are in the U.S., so they may decide, "Well, maybe the Coast Guard Academy isn't so bad for another year or two."

The only other thing, in addition to retention, which I think is a great thing, is that with the modernization of the Coast Guard, it just takes fewer people than it used to. Mike and I both mentioned that the ships we've been on have been decommissioned and replaced by newer cutters. I know, for example, that the 180' buoy tender that I was on, in terms of the enlisted crew, is dramatically different than our current buoy tenders. What it used to take in terms of bodies down on the deck, lugging and dragging and doing things with these huge buoys, is now done mechanically with technology. This also affects the bridge, with what the officers and crew are doing. It used to take multiple bodies to manhandle that single screw vessel; now it's somewhat like a video game. You're literally driving with a joystick. You're pushing a button when you get where you want to be, and the ship will stay put on its own. The vessels that we have now just take less people.

Most students who apply to the Academy are high achievers, but this does not necessarily make it easy to fill a class. There are a few standouts who have everything Admissions is looking for, and little thought goes into offering them an appointment. As Thomas notes:

I think it's rare, but every once and a while you get a kid and you just know. You get a kid in here who is a double 800 in critical reading and math, which is important to us with the type of school we are, and they have over 600 in writing. There are some. It's

Chris McMunn

amazing to me, because those types of cadets just fly through the system. They're very low maintenance. They pop up, they apply, and their medical is done. Maybe, if you're lucky, they call you once and ask a question. They arrive at committee and you just go, "Yeah. They're in."

The vast majority of them, however, require an agonizing amount of consideration before the decision to offer them appointments is made. He continues:

I was asked once about the toughest part of this job; it's that I say "no" over 1,200 times a year. The kid says, "Well, what's wrong with me?" I say, "Nothing. You're a great kid. I'd love to have you. I'd love to have you, but it's such a small class. Wherever you go, you're going to do great things, and if my kids are like you, I'm going to be happy."

When I came here and Chris said we read everything, I thought he was joking. I thought, "Yeah, whatever. I'll figure out my system, and I'll know who to pick." But we do; we really read everything. It's really amazing what we have to do to decide between student A and student B. Why do we take this one over that one? There's always someone at the table going, "No, I like this one." I know from my three years here there are little things that you pick up. The more you're here, the more you read, the more you're able to do that. I'll be honest; I was overwhelmed when I first got here. Out of 2,000 kids, we had to pick, I think, 290. Trying to narrow that down to 290, I said, "Hey! He's an Eagle Scout!" Someone will say from across the table, "Try to throw a rock here and not hit an Eagle Scout." "Oh, look! He's captain of three sports teams!" So are these fifty.

Then, you get the last group, and they're kids who are just reaching. In most of these cases, these students just simply aren't academically prepared for what it takes to get through here. We have a pretty good handle on what

the academics are like these days. We bring in kids who are well over 3.0s, have great SATs, and they struggle here. You take a kid who's not prepared academically, who might be a great kid in all other areas but isn't academically prepared, you know they're not going to make it. This isn't the place where you can get behind and dig out; you just dig deeper. We get a group of kids every year who want to serve their country; their parents may be military, or whatever their reasoning is, and they're great kids; they're simply just not academically prepared. Those are a little easier, and you can talk them through that. For me, the hard part is that vast middle we just don't have room for. They want to know what it was you saw that made you say no. It's sometimes hard to articulate. "There's nothing wrong. You're a great kid. If I had one more space, I'd have probably taken you."

While many top students apply, admissions officers know the game is not necessarily over once the appointments go out. In the past, perhaps, people who applied to the Academy wanted a military lifestyle. They may or may not have applied to the other service academies as well, but they were certain they wanted to serve. This is less true today, especially with all of the options now available to high-performing students. As McMunn points out, selecting candidates is just the beginning:

They are deserving of an appointment, so you appoint them, and then you start the next phase of the process of trying to yield them, to get them to accept the appointment and come to the Academy instead of all of the other places they can go. If someone is appointed here, they have undoubtedly been accepted at a lot of other great colleges or service academies.

A lot of times people will say, "Well, you guys are free, right? You don't have any tuition cost and you even pay them?" They are paid about a thousand dollars a month because they're on active duty when they're here at the

Academy, but it's that same concept. Anyone that is competitive enough to receive an appointment here probably has ROTC scholarships that are covering their tuition and giving them a stipend at a civilian school of their choosing, or they have merit-based scholarships or other types of money given to them. I think it's very rare for people to come here because they didn't have money to pay for college and we were the only option.

There are some who just sail through our process, but the vast majority are what we call fully qualified candidates. They look academically prepared to come, and they've done some extracurricular and leadership-type activities, so we think we appreciate where they would fit in and how they would contribute. They're in shape, they're medically qualified, so they meet the physical fitness and medical qualification standards. How do you pick from that big group of qualified individuals? How do you pick the ones who will make up the most diverse, dynamic, and best overall class for the Academy that year?

That can change from year to year. People may not appreciate that, but with such a small corps of cadets, if you happen to bring in a lot of female soccer players this year, for example, well, next year we're not going to focus on that as much. Hopefully, those women will continue growing, supporting, and making sure the women's soccer team remains competitive, whereas the men's baseball team did not get a lot of baseball players this year, and maybe next year we'll focus on that. These types of choices go beyond sports to cover all sorts of things. It can happen with academic majors, it can happen with extracurricular activities, it can happen with all sorts of things.

While taxpayers fund tuition at the Academy, as at all service academies, cadets must pay back this cost with five years of service after graduation. At this particular point in time, some 85 percent of the Academy's graduates re-

main in the Coast Guard beyond this requirement, indicating, in part, their satisfaction with the career path they have chosen. For teenagers with little real-life experience on which to base such an important decision, the time commitment they make is enormous. In many cases, the total commitment represents nearly half their lives. Thomas continues:

You're essentially making a nine-year commitment to us. Some will go through the process, see if they get in, and then think about it. When you're seventeen, nine years seems like a long time; some will back off. We brought in a young lady a few years ago. We

Lieutenant Commander Michael Thomas

really liked her, but she could go to MIT. When the chips fell, she chose MIT. Great school; can't blame the kid. So we're competing against those other schools. There are some kids who want to be in the military; this is what they want to do, and when we call they say yes right away and they're standing outside the gate right now, waiting for two weeks to pass so they can start. These kids have choices. I think twenty, thirty years ago, it was an easy choice. We rode in, "Do you want to come to us? We'll give you an appointment. We'll see you in a few months." I think now kids are smarter, they're more informed, they know more about the different colleges, and they make decisions differently than I may have.

Students who apply are aware that the Academy is not just another school and that the application process is extremely competitive. As McMunn says, they have many more applicants than they can use:

We're not a common-application school where they can just check a box and they've applied, so I think they have some level of interest. I think with the vast majority, we're in their top three and they want to see what happens. With some, we're definitely the number-one choice, and they're applying elsewhere as backup schools because it is a very competitive process. We yield about 80 percent of the students we appoint; your average college would love that. They're probably yielding half of the number of students they accept for their incoming class, so I think we know these students are interested. It just might take that next phase of yielding them to get them to appreciate why maybe the Coast Guard Academy, if it wasn't their first choice when they entered the application, should become the number-one choice once they have their acceptances. We never have a problem filling the class, and we never have to tender too many extra appointments. If anything, we need to be very cautious about oversubscribing the class or appointing too many people, because you never know if that yield number could spike in any given year. Although the numbers are not all done for this year, we could end up with about an 82 percent yield, which if not the highest ever, would certainly be a high, recent watermark.

In an average year, we are going to receive 2,000–2,500 completed application packages, and that's what's of most importance to us. There is a larger number above that who start our application process. They may even submit, as I mentioned, their online application and essays, their academic transcript, and standardized test scores, but never take the physical fitness test or never get the required instructor evaluations. They withdraw by not completing, or sometimes, they just call and say, "I'm not going to complete."

That number can vary greatly. Sometimes it's been as high as 6,000 people that start our process, and that leads to a higher number of completions. On average, we get about 60 percent of those who start completing the application. That's another number that we're okay with. Would we like it higher? Sure, but there are a lot of dynamics within the process that we don't have control over. We do survey on occasion those who don't complete to get an idea: Was the application process too hard? Did we not give you enough instruction? Or did you not know that you missed something and that's why you were incomplete?

I think we're doing okay, but we are always looking to improve the number of students who complete their application. That gives you the most robust applicant pool, because we only read completed applications. Some other colleges might say, "We've got 80 per-

cent of an application; they look really good!" They have other things driving their application process, such as, "They could be a full-pay, so this is someone we want to consider." This year we offered around 325 appointments to get that incoming class of 250. We need to creep up to that acceptance number, unlike other colleges, where in some regards it's "the more the merrier"; if you're paying tuition, we have a dorm room available for you, and the faculty is able to teach you. Here it's very different. You can't really go over the number the Coast Guard has given you.

As with all competitive colleges, they are not simply looking for kids who ace the SAT exams. Though that may be perhaps the easiest way to choose an incoming class, it would be unlikely to yield a robust corps. There are many intangible qualities colleges search for when creating a new class. Additionally, the Academy's mission goes far beyond the production of bachelor-of-sciences degrees. The Coast Guard must graduate officers capable of going directly into service with a particular set of skills and talents that most college graduates only develop long after leaving campus. While prized, intelligence is only one trait on a long list of qualities deemed necessary for leadership. McMunn knows they must see beyond cold numerical scores:

Even with the academic part, you're still going to get a lot of stratification between students. There is a level where students look academically qualified, but within that pool, you don't just want them to be academically qualified. We always want that, but there is definitely the student who may have to go to every peer tutoring session or spend every weekend with their academic advisor. They will have to utilize the Writing Center, they will have to go to extra academic support things to get through, but we know they have the potential to be successful here if they want to be successful here. You definitely don't want a class of them, but those students exist where everything else is so great that you want them in the class. Beyond that, there are students who will be candidates for our honors programs. These are the ones groomed to compete as Truman Scholars, Fulbright Scholars, or as a Rhodes Scholar. There are those scholars, as well, where you may see less contribution outside of the classroom. All of our cadets have to compete in two of the three athletic seasons. These can be intercompany sports or club sports. Everyone is not a Division III varsity athlete, although about 65 percent of our corps of cadets are.

There are definitely tiers within their academics we consider, but it really is the totality of their record. With academics, it's going to be harder to distinguish between the applicants. It gets easier to really know who they are once you get outside of their academics and get into what their letters of recommendation say about them. What did they write about in their essays? What do they at least identify as being important to them, and what do they value? What do they see themselves as contributing to the Academy?

Clearly, students at the Academy do not come from one mold but, as one might expect, share similarities, given their age and limited exposure to the broader world. They are also learning how competitive that world can be. While most enjoyed life as the big fish in high school, the pond in which they now hope to swim is much deeper; competitors' teeth, much sharper. McMunn tries to give applicants a realistic perspective:

I tell applicants all the time, "You might think that you are unique, or that you have done something someone else has not, but within our process it's going to be unlikely." There are some. We have a young woman coming into this year's class who is an internationally ranked competitive canoeist. She qualified for the U.S. team and had an opportunity to compete at the world championships but had opted out to come to the Academy. She's one, but for the most part, I tell them it's going to be rare. You better really use your essays, or what we call personal statements, to explain who you are, what's important to you, what you bring to the Academy, and what you're hoping to get out of this experience. The essays should never be the same. Essays are really their chance to have a voice within the process. I think we spend a lot of time trying to get to know who they are.

As with other colleges, McMunn explains, not all of the student body will come directly from high school, although most do:

The USCG Cutter *Sanibel,* a 110' Island Class Patrol Boat from Station Woods Hole, is used in search and rescue, law enforcement, and port security operations.

Seventy percent of our incoming class is coming directly from high school, so they're the vast majority. About 20 percent have gone to the prep school program, and the other 10 percent are sort of a mix. The majority of that 10 percent are coming from college, so they have one or more years of college experience, and some, although very rare, come from a nonacademic environment. They probably have college experience, but maybe they were doing a gap year of some sort, or maybe they were enlisted and they're coming directly from an enlisted community, be it Coast Guard or another branch of the military.

While the Academy has no mandated quotas, it strives to have the same level of diversity enjoyed by schools that do. Minority students made up 35 percent of those choosing to accept appointments into the class of 2016. With females representing more than 50 percent of the total U.S. population, admission officers work to bring more women in as well. As before, Thomas notes they do this as a matter of course:

The superintendent hasn't said, "You will have 20 percent women." Like every other institution, we're very conscious of that. We're a national academy; we want to represent the United States, so it is one factor among many that we consider. However, if there are no kids in, pick a state, who rise, we don't have to take them, and if there are thirty kids in Nevada that we want, we can take them, as long as we shape our class. We're a college, and we have things we have to do, but there is nothing saying we will take X number of this race, X females, X males, X people from North Dakota. We shape our class yearly.

Currently, the Coast Guard Academy has the highest percentage of females among service academies, despite the lack of any congressional pressure. In 1976, women were finally granted access to all military academies, and their presence at the Academy has been growing. The class of 2016 reached a new high with females representing 36 percent of the incoming class. Additionally, until the ban keeping women from combat roles ended in January of 2013, the Coast Guard was the only service in which women faced no limits. After graduation, women served as line officers with their male counterparts, and any avenue they chose to pursue was open to them. It remains to be seen what the restriction's end will mean for enrollment at the other service academies, but until 2013, many women chose the Coast Guard for this reason. McMunn believes, of late, the rising female population has been more organic than forced:

What I say about women in our process is that they compete very well on their own. I don't know if that's happening nationwide, but the women who apply here just seem to have done their homework, or they appreciate that they are a competitive candidate. We don't have any bonus points for gender or race, nor do I think we would have to, especially for women. I don't know why that dynamic exists, but they often seem to be emotionally committed, or they've done enough research in advance to know that "This is a school in which I'm a good fit. I seem to meet, or I'm above, their average for their profile of an incoming freshman." So it's grown steadily over the last few of years, and again, really by no design, push, quota, or anything on our side. It's been a pretty sustained 28 to 32 percent in any given year, making up about 30 percent of the total corps.

With taxpayer money in play, congressional members are certainly looking to have appointments come from their districts, whether they are from Kansas or Maine. The Coast Guard feels that it can spread appointments around the country on its own and works hard to do so. Given its small class sizes, the Academy does not want to find itself in the position of having to take cadets based simply on what congressional districts they come from. Extra work is required, however, for the Coast Guard to accomplish its goal:

This year, I think we've been sensitive to geographic diversity more than we have in the past. Congress has asked us to look at that, so that always makes you more sensitive. I think before that, when we just let it organically happen, we were probably averaging thirty-five to thirty-six states, along with a couple from the District of Columbia, Puerto Rico, and other places. It shifted year to year, so because of this congressional inquiry, within the corps of cadets, every state except South Dakota is currently represented. There's also Puerto Rico, the U.S. Virgin Islands, Guam, the Northern Marianas, and a lot of territories and other places. Additionally, we have some U.S. citizens who are living abroad, for whatever reasons: their parents are in the military, or some of them do religious, missionary, or international business-type work, so we have U.S. citizens coming from foreign countries as well.

The incoming class looks like it's going to have thirty-nine states. So even when we thought we were focusing, there is only so much you can do. People who want to come, come, and people who apply, apply. Where you solve that is not on the back end, where we say we have to take someone from Mississippi, but we don't have anyone from Mississippi we like. Rather, you recruit in those areas, and you spend time on the front end, marketing and growing your applicant pool from those areas. Because of the nomination system at the other academies, they have to take someone. Hopefully they're good, but they still have to take someone from the Iowa Second Congressional District. They have to take someone from the Mississippi senators who've nominated their folks. They definitely have all fifty states represented. So Congress asked if they needed to give us this nomination process as well, or could we solve this on our own? This is where we said, "Yes, we have a plan. Let us go out to those areas and find those folks. Let them apply and compete against everyone else, and see what happens."

Thomas continues this thought:

It's a process, but we can do it in two to three years; it's just limited resources. We went down the Ohio River and Mississippi Valley, and now we're going to go further west. It's no surprise where we get most of our kids; it's where the Coast Guard is on the coast or on the Great Lakes. Getting landlocked states is a little more difficult, but it can be done. The advantage of the Ohio or the Mississippi River Valley is the Coast Guard is on those rivers; we're not foreign to those kids. We drop down to South Dakota and they look at us and say, "Hey! You're in the Air Force!" Worst case, I've been asked to bring the car around while standing outside of a hotel! We are a foreign entity to them; they don't recognize us. We have to build our name up, let them know what it is we do. There are still places in this country where they just don't know who we are.

While class size at the Academy appeals to many students receiving appointments, the budget that goes with it poses challenges for admissions personnel. Challenges are, however, what the Coast Guard trains for, and both men enjoy the work they do. As Mc-Munn puts it:

We get great kids. I think this is a job in the Coast Guard that's often overlooked. It's fun. Busy, very busy, but a great job, and being a part of dealing with so many fine young men and women whom we bring in is very rewarding .

The class of 2016 on R-Day. While two hundred and fifty-three cadets are sworn in, it is expected that only one hundred and seventy-five will graduate after four years.

The Chosen

The students who receive appointments to the Academy are nearly as diverse as the population from which they come, representing all states, religions, and ethnic backgrounds. As might be expected, however, many have parents who themselves served in the Coast Guard or in another branch of the armed services. Swab Jake Carlton is one such student:

I've lived about half my life in Alaska now, because my dad was in the Air Force and we moved up here where he retired. The military struck me as a good idea, because you get an excellent education

and you get a good future; you don't have to worry about what you're going to do. I only applied to the Coast Guard Academy; that was really the only one that struck my fancy. I like being on the water, and I don't really have any problem with boats. I don't get seasick. My grandpa was in the Coast Guard, so that was part of the consideration.

Foxtrot Company's 2/C Jake Rendon, part of the Chase Hall Cadre, comes from a family with a very direct relationship with the Service:

I have a lot of family in the Coast Guard. My dad retired as a commander, my uncle is now an admiral, and another uncle retired as a captain. This is something I always wanted; they never pushed me at all. I knew I was going to be in the Coast Guard since I was little. Every two or three years I moved with the Coast Guard. My dad was on ships all the time, and I loved moving around: Texas, Hawaii, California, North Carolina, Virginia, and Connecticut.

One of Rendon's fellow cadre, 2/C Jennifer Patron, also belonged to a military family, although it was the Navy that inspired her interest. The impact of her father's life led her to the Coast Guard Academy:

I'm a military brat, so I traveled all over the place. I used to live in Sicily with my family and switched back and forth from there. My dad was in the Navy, and he worked in a hospital. My mom is a teacher. I was about seven years old when I became interested. My dad was a prior enlisted, so he started out in boot camp back in 1989, and I saw him progress and become a chief, and then he went to OCS in the Navy. It was really fascinating to see both sides of it—the enlisted and the officer side. I was like, "Wow, I really want to become an officer and have that leadership role."

My father was very happy for me, very proud, because it is an accomplishment, regardless of which service academy you attend. I did look into the Navy, and I applied, but in looking at both academies and what they offered, I really liked the Coast Guard; it's very much like a family. It just attracted me more, and the missions are fantastic.

2/C Joseph Trump, like Rendon, had a father as well as an uncle who served within the Coast Guard. Typical of children in military families, he also moved around the country while growing up. While he does not feel his father's career was wholly responsible for his application, he knows he may never have heard of the Academy had it not been for that:

My dad was in for five years, but he kind of regrets that now. He wishes he had stayed in longer. The first time I ever came to the Academy was when I was six months old for my dad's class reunion, and then I came back when I was five, and then when I was ten. I skipped the reunion when I was fifteen because I was doing

something. I was really interested when I was a little kid, because my dad was always telling stories that seemed really cool, especially to a little kid. The military seems fun when you are a little kid, and boats are cool. We had a boat; we lived in upper Michigan for a while on the Great Lakes. They built all the Coast Guard 225' buoy tenders across the river from the town we lived in, Marinette, Wisconsin, so I got to see six or seven of them launched, which was just amazing. For a seven-year-old, to see this huge boat built and launched into the river was cool. So I was really interested in it then, and then we moved down to Florida and I kind of went through a phase when I was twelve or thirteen when I wanted to be a lawyer, maybe an engineer, or whatever, and then probably in my sophomore year I really started to focus on the Coast Guard Academy. That's when it really started to sink in that this is where I wanted to come. I focused on that; it was my goal and it worked out. I didn't apply to any of the other academies. I have a thing for the Coast Guard because of its humanitarian mission. I wanted to be in the military—I like the discipline—but I didn't really want to kill people. I want to help people. I realize the other services help people just like we do, but the Coast Guard was a lot more appealing to me.

My dad was pretty happy about it. He never really pushed it while I was applying, because he didn't want me to pick it because he wanted me to come here. When I got the appointment, he was really excited. I was just on leave for the last three weeks, and the week before that he had a business trip to some little town in Connecticut. He was able to come by, and we hung out in Leamy for a while and talked, and he reminisced. We went to the Alumni Center and looked at the old yearbooks.

As previously stated, Chris McMunn graduated of the Academy, serving nearly a dozen years on active duty before separating from the Coast Guard to work full time in the Admissions Department. His father is a graduate of Annapolis:

I was accepted both at Annapolis and here at the Coast Guard Academy and ultimately decided this was the best fit for me. My father was really supportive. I think he figured out early on that the less he pushed me towards the military academies, the more I would naturally gravitate towards them. I'm sure at the time he would have liked me to follow in his footsteps at the Naval Academy, but I think he also knew me and that my personality fit with the Coast Guard Academy really well. I think the longer he saw me as a cadet and on active duty, he knew that it was definitely the right choice for me. I think he really appreciates what the Coast Guard does and what I've had a chance to do when I was on active duty and even now, continuing to work here at the Academy.

I went to a large high school. At the time, it was the largest high school in Virginia. My father was finishing his active-duty tour in the Navy, getting ready to retire, so he was at the Pentagon and at the State Department. It was the first time I was actually able to go to one school for more than two or three years. I went to Robinson High School in Burke, Virginia. My graduating class was 850 or almost 900 people, which is almost the entire size of the Coast Guard Academy. We have about 1,000 people in our Corps of Cadets. For me, I was looking for a smaller college experience, and when I visited here, I definitely got that feeling. When I visited Naval Academy, I felt like I did in high school—just one of thousands of people walking around.

Beyond that, we're a Division III athletic program, and the Naval Academy is Division I. I rowed crew all through high school, and I knew I wanted to do that in college. At the Naval Academy, they were like, "Yeah, you might be able to row here. Come out in the fall when you come to school, and we'll see what happens." Here it felt like I was going to be the nucleus of their program. They were super excited to have somebody with rowing experience, or at least they courted me that way, and I was able to row and be a big part of the crew team as a freshman.

But really, with all that aside, it just came down to the mission of the Coast Guard. That excited me much more. I had talked to my dad and a lot of his friends, as well as other officers in the Navy. I knew what they had done, and when I heard about folks in the Coast Guard and what they did on a day-in and a day-out basis, I was just so much more excited about being able to be active and

do my job every day instead of going through a lot of training and preparation and thinking, "Well, maybe I'll get to do my actual job." My dad told me about that when I was in the middle of the whole process. Vietnam was sort of his war. He graduated in 1970 from the Naval Academy, and his ship deployed and was in Vietnam. For the rest of his career, almost, he waited for the next time he would get to do his job. In the Coast Guard, my first ship was a buoy tender in Honolulu, Hawaii. I was there about four or five days before we deployed for our first patrol. Within a week, I was doing my job.

Perhaps the most unusual case was a cadet, recently graduated, who applied because of the profound impact rescue at sea had had on him as a child. Leaving Haiti in a tired wooden boat, his family and others had tried to reach the United States but had found themselves drifting helplessly at the current's mercy. Saved from starvation by a Coast Guard cutter that had plucked him from the ocean's desolate surface, the young man had chosen to give back to his adoptive country and help others in need by joining the Coast Guard.

Lieutenant James Bendle, now the assistant school chief for the OCS program, also met Coast Guard officers for the first time at sea, although under far less dramatic circumstances:

I enlisted in the Coast Guard in 1997. I went to college in Pennsylvania and I knew, probably in my freshman year, I wanted to be in the Coast Guard. I grew up on Long Island on the south shore in Massapequa. I'm a surfer, and I was going out on a boat with some friends. We had our boards, and we were going surfing. I don't even remember what we were doing, but we warranted a stop by the Coast Guard. Maybe with all of us and all of the boards in the boat, we attracted a little interest from the local station, and they stopped us. They were very thorough. They were real professional, but they were also very respectful. In the end, there was probably something they could have jammed us up for, but they were pretty practical about it. They said, "Look, this is where you're going, and this is what you need to do." Then, they cut us loose. They were young; they were like twenty-one, and I thought, "That's a

The cadre, responsible for indoctrinating the new swabs, graduate in 2014.

where it was pretty easy; I didn't have a waiting list or anything.

For Commander Jeffrey Haukom, interest in the Coast Guard started a little more casually. Growing up in Southern California, he spent countless hours on, in, or under water. Attending college at the University of Southern California–Riverside, he graduated with a bachelor's degree in history. Before graduating, however, he was home and sailing with his father during summer vacation:

My dad served in the Navy during Vietnam. I had an uncle who was, for a short period of time, in the Air Force. Both of my grandfathers during World War II served, one in the Army, and one in the Army Air Corps. My interest in the Coast Guard was probably born out of spending as much time as I could at the beach, body or board surfing, spearfishing, and sailing. Doing all that stuff, you'd constantly see the helicopters fly over or the cutters going out, and I always thought, "What a great job. They're helping people, they're out on a beautiful day, and they're getting paid to do it."

What really sealed the deal for me to want to actually join the Coast Guard happened when I was home for summer recess from college. It was my junior year, and I would always go home to San Diego and work at a hotel. I was a valet parking attendant—things like that. My dad worked for a commercial insurance agency, and during the summer he would take clients out sailing, and I was his crew. We were out sailing one day in San Diego Bay, and being the dad of a rising college senior, he asked, "So what are you going to do when you graduate with that history degree next year?" I said, "Well, you know, I'm not really sure yet. I guess I could teach or I could go to law school." I wasn't particularly interested in doing any of those things at the time.

While we were having this conversation, we were sailing right past a Coast Guard cutter, a large, 378' high-endurance cutter that was anchored right outside Harbor Island. I remember looking up; it's a beautiful white ship, and I can see the officers on the bridge, probably getting ready to weigh anchor and get back out to sea. Just a gorgeous day, and I'm thinking these people are out here getting paid to do it. I had always thought about the Coast Guard in the back of my mind growing up, and now that it was time to

pretty cool job, and that's a lot of responsibility for someone that age." It was probably a ten-minute process, and I thought to myself, "I would love to do that!" It's tough to actually get into the Coast Guard from Long Island because of the candidate pool, the lack of recruiters, and the talent, so I recruited out of Pennsylvania make a career decision, I thought I needed to look into it. So I was thinking about that, and my dad actually asked the question. I guess he could see me looking at the cutter, and he asked, "Have you ever thought about driving one of those big ships there?" I said, "I hadn't up until this point, but I'm going to look into it."

Haukom finished his senior year and graduated, needing the degree to apply to the Coast Guard's Officer Candidate School:

I applied. I had my interview at Air Station San Diego with three officers, and I actually met a lieutenant who was a surface operations officer at the base there, just by chance. This was pre-9/11, and security was pretty casual. He said, "You want to come see the Coast Guard base? Come on in!" There wasn't even a guard at the gate by the time I got there after hours. I walked on the base and started walking around the hangars and looking at things. Finally, somebody saw me and said, "Can I help you?" This guy, a fantastic guy, Tom Tabrah, sat me down, probably for a half an hour, an hour, and just answered every question I had about the Coast Guard and really got me excited and energized. It just solidified for me: this is what I want to do. He set up a FAM ride on a Falcon jet and a ride on a 110' cutter, so I completed the whole application process, and I heard back from them that I didn't get in. I was then determined to get in, so I applied again. At that point I had graduated, and I didn't want to commit to working at another company, because I really wanted to join the Coast Guard. So I, as a college graduate now, went back and took my old summer job as a valet parking attendant and reapplied. I reapplied and got the same answer: "Sorry, you didn't get it, but this time you're picked up as an alternate." There was some hope, and I knew the next class started on March 7. So now we're in about February, and they called me up and said, "If you can be in Yorktown, Virginia, in three weeks, we've got a spot for you." Quit my valet job, loaded up my truck, drove cross-country, and went through the seventeen-week program at the Officer Candidate School. This was 1994.

Interestingly, I would hear versions of this story repeated throughout the course of the summer: initial rejection, dogged determination, and success far beyond the initial goal of simply attaining admittance. Another case in point is that of Captain Ernie Cummings, Retired. Having lost their father at an early age, he and his two brothers all went through the Academy. For Cummings, however, acceptance to the Academy proved problematic:

My stepfather believed that the Coast Guard Academy was probably the best education around at the time, and he nurtured us—my two older brothers—to go to the Academy, and then myself. My brother Tom—he was the oldest—was in the class of '57. He had an accident and reverted to the class of '58. My other brother John was in the class of '59. I was supposed to go into the class of '61, but I flunked the entrance exam. I went to URI for a year and took the entrance exam again. I flunked again. This was when the Coast Guard Academy had its own entrance exam. Then, my father and mother sent me to a prep school in Washington, and I passed the exam the next year, so that's how I got there.

Despite his inauspicious beginnings, he went on to have a stellar career within the Service, retiring thirty years later, having handled security for President Clinton's inauguration. Of course, there are almost as many different reasons for deciding to go to the Academy as there are people attending. Many officers came to the Coast Guard later in life, having previously followed career paths that had left them unfulfilled. Another common thread is each individual's desire to serve others. 1/C Breanna Hite, leading Waterfront Cadre for the summer at the sailing center, shares this feeling with her shipmates:

I knew I wanted to serve my country. I wanted to be in the military, so I looked into the different academies. Having grown up on the water, I thought doing something on the ocean would be fitting, so I looked into both the Navy and the Coast Guard. As I thought about it more, I liked the missions of the Coast Guard better. I liked that it was smaller. To me, it's more of a family; everybody knows everybody. The one thing that really solidified it for me was: in high school, we were out sailing with my mom and her friends, and it was a pretty stormy day. We were coming back into the harbor and taking down the sails. We were in a protected harbor, and we felt safe. All of a sudden, the captain of our boat was hit in the head

26

by the boom, and she was knocked overboard. I remember looking at her in the water and seeing blood over her face. I thought she had lost an eye or something, and we called the harbor patrol, who helped us out. From that night, I decided I wanted to help save lives.

Many cadets have had relatives who have served at one point or another in time. Often, it was their great-grandparents served during the Second World War or their grandparents who served in Korea or Vietnam. For other swabs, the decision to apply may have nothing to do with family history. For example, Kyle Wood was partially steered by a childhood tragedy:

My granddad was in the Navy, and my uncle was in the Marines, and one whole side of the family was Air Force. They are excited about me coming here. I first decided to go to a military academy because one of my neighborhood friends that I grew up with committed suicide. It made me think, "I really want to do something with my life—help other people and get out there." I thought the military would help me get out there, help people, and protect the country. I first looked into the Air Force and the Navy; I didn't even know about the Coast Guard Academy until Coach Grant contacted me for baseball. I started looking into it, and I decided the Coast Guard was really where I wanted to be. It fit my personality, and they would let me play both football and baseball, so I was excited about that. I went to a small school in Tennessee, so I felt a small, closely-knit group would be better for me. I applied to the other academies, but this was my first choice.

Sheila Bertrand, the youngest swab to enter the Academy this particular summer, also felt an obligation to help others:

My mom's father was in the military, but he died when my mom was young, so I never met him. He was in the Army. I knew before anything that I wanted to be in the military. That said, I basically planned my college around the military because I knew I wanted to go to college as well. My theory is that if you are physically and mentally capable of making a difference, then you should, and I felt this was a way I could do that. I started looking into the military academies in my freshman year. Originally, I had looked at the Air

Force. In middle school, I wanted to be a pilot, and that shifted my thoughts to the Naval Academy and from there to the Coast Guard Academy. I like the water. I had never been to the Coast Guard Academy, even though it was the closest to my house, but when I came here, I could see myself here the most. It had more of what I was looking for with sports, academics, and the military life.

From Priest River, Idaho, James Hegge's reasons had more to do with establishing order in his life:

Towards the end of my senior year, I really wanted military, because I really get annoyed when people start changing up the schedule once they set it. I like my life in order, with schedules, and we figured, "Well, let's go with the military." So we started looking at military options: the academies or enlistment. I decided on the academies, and we looked at going into the Coast Guard or the Air Force. Mom really liked the idea of putting me in the Army, and if I can make her happy and still do what I want, I'm happy. I guessed helping around our borders would keep me closer to home and my family. My grandpa, whom I didn't meet until after we started applying to the academies, was in the Air Force at one point, and my cousin just enlisted in the Navy a while back. My mom's ecstatic. My dad, I don't know; he doesn't really say. At the end of my junior year and the start of my senior year, we started looking at what I wanted to do after high school. I applied to the Coast Guard, Air Force, and the Merchant Marines. Air Force said they had too many candidates and I wasn't high enough in the rankings. Coast Guard and Merchant Marines, we ended up getting the prep school option. I went with the Coast Guard. I was happy, I guess.

Swab Rheanastasia Doctolero's introduction to the Academy came at a college fair. Recruiters from various military branches were drumming up business when she came across the Coast Guard's presentation:

We had a college fair at my school, and I've seen the little booths that the military have to get kids to enlist, but enlisting was not for me. I was looking at the different types of academies. I was just passing by, and I wasn't really sure where I wanted to go or what I wanted to do. I knew I wanted to study business. I passed by the

Coast Guard booth, and I thought I should at least look. I was looking at the brochure, and the man who is our admissions officer here asked me some questions. As I told him about myself, he said, "Oh! We are interested in people like you, so why don't you come down and visit?" So I came here and visited in November, and I loved the Academy. This was the only Academy I was interested in. I'm more interested in defending the country than going out and fighting in a war. I have an uncle who was in the Air Force, and I did have an aunt who was in the Coast Guard. Another uncle was in the Army, and my grandpa was in the Army, but I'm the first to actually go to an Academy.

As with others, joining a military organization was not necessarily her lifelong dream but, rather, something that struck her as a possibility. Doctolero based her decision to apply to the Coast Guard Academy on her strong desire to help others as well. Since time immemorial, military institutions have also provided paths for those whose financial situations limit their options. While the Admissions Department strongly advises potential recruits that they should never apply to please parents or save tuition costs, the idea of a "free" education inevitably enters the decision-making process, and many swabs mention this benefit. For Scooter Finney, joining a military branch represented a path in which finances did play a role in the decision-making process:

I'm the youngest of four kids, and my parents never really had any money for us to go to school. I have one sister who's getting through community college and working, and I have a brother and another sister. Neither of them have done anything in school, so the fact that I am doing this is kind of monumental. My grandmother found the Academy on the Internet; she's the reason I heard about it. She volunteers in my school, and there was a girl going to do an ROTC Air Force scholarship, so she started looking into the military because I needed to get through college. We were look-

ing at every option. We found the military academies and all of them were essentially free; you get all the training, and when you graduate you have a job. The Coast Guard also has a humanitarian aspect, which is something I would rather do, as opposed to the Army or Navy or something like that. When I figured out all the Coast Guard does and the training I'll receive, it all made sense. I applied to a few other schools—Georgia State, University of Georgia, and North Georgia College and University—but the Coast Guard was my first choice.

Often, seemingly insignificant decisions end up altering our lives, and it is one such decision that brought Katie Brosnan to the Academy. Coming from a suburb of New York City with a host of great schools on her doorstep, she had planned to live at home and to commute to a nearby college. A military career had never entered her mind, especially having attended a Catholic school system throughout her life. When asked how she heard of the Coast Guard, she replied:

Actually, my mom was talking to a man at the bank who worked there, and she was telling him that I was interested in going to college. He said, "Oh, my stepson goes to the U.S. Coast Guard Academy. It's a really great school." He was raving about it and telling us all these wonderful things. He was like, "You should look into it." Then, I looked into it, and I really liked it. I went up for a briefing, an event the Coast Guard hosts, and I loved it. So my banker—that's how I got into it. Imagine if I didn't go to the bank that day? Pretty random! I didn't really know what to expect when I went up to the Academy, because nobody in my family is in the military, let alone the Coast Guard. I went there, and everybody was like, "My father is in the Coast Guard, and his father, and his father." I'm like, "Oh, my banker told me." I didn't apply to any of the other academies.

A change of command ceremony installs new regimental leaders before cadets disperse to their summer assignments. The cadre remain to indoctrinate incoming swabs.

You're In My Coast Guard

For the swabs on R-Day, it is but a short bus ride to Chase Hall up Hunter Liggett Drive, better known as "The Hill." Awaiting them are members of Alpha Company's Cadre I. Along with the company's chief, the cadre mill around, joking with one another and mentally rehearsing the welcoming speeches they have been preparing over the last few weeks. One cadre member's ears perk up as she hears the bus straining to come up the hill. She lets her shipmates know the bus is on its way, and all joking ends as they take their positions. They stand smartly at attention, uniforms perfectly pressed, insignia gleaming in the rapidly fading sun. Polished dress swords distinguish the two 1st class cadets, one standing at each end of the line. The four cadre between them sport blood-red slashes of braiding, which pierce their shoulder boards and wrap beneath their left arms. Their faces, which were only moments ago laughing and animated, turn to cold stone. They are, as they intend to be, an imposing sight.

Swabs leap off the bus and into the Coast Guard.

The bus turns a wide and labored arc at the top of the hill and bears down on the entrance to the quad. It pulls to a stop in front of the squared cadre, smoked glass windows obscuring its dark interior. Moments later, the driver swings open the door and the lights within snap on, illuminating the newest members of Alpha Company. Without hesitation, the most imposing member of the cadre begins marching smartly across the narrow road. Crisply turning right angles, he brings himself to the open portal. He bounds up the stairs and stands at the front of the bus, silently surveying those he has come to gather. The swabs, in turn, sit frozen in place, staring and wondering what they are expected to do. They are not left to wonder long. The cadre's first words hit them like the pressure wave from an explosion:

Get off my bus!

Each individual word shatters the silence like rifle shots. All but the driver are stunned; he has seen this performance before and faces perfectly forward to hide his grin. Astonishingly, nobody so much as blinks, let alone moves to get off the bus. They are like a flock of sheep, frozen by the sight of an approaching wolf. This, they quickly find, is unacceptable. The cadre offers further encouragement, explaining in more detail what he wants them to do:

Get off my bus! Now!

The additional clarification sends an electric shock through the group, propelling one or two swabs up and into the aisle. Almost instantly, the rest decide that they, too, *really* want to leave the bus. Unfortunately, there is limited space on such a crowded vehicle, and a tangle of recruits forms, accidentally knocking many back into their seats. Although this further displeases their new leader, he is willing to offer yet new motivation. Choosing his deepest, most booming voice, he kindly rephrases his request :

Move it! Move it! Move it!

There is little doubt now among the swabs as to what he wants. The only challenge that remains is satisfying him quickly enough. By now, the swabs are desperate to vacate the bus, and the cadre is freely offering his most helpful advice:

Stop wasting my time! Move it! Move it! Move it! Get off my bus!

Another cadre, who had been patiently waiting for the bus to empty, decides to help move things along. Addressing the stream of swabs now pouring from the bus, he offers his own encouragement:

Why are you crawling? Move with a purpose! Move with a purpose! Move it! Move it! Move it!

The swabs are beginning to catch on to the program. In their newfound haste, however, they confuse "moving with a purpose" with running. As soon as they begin to run, new orders issue from the line of cadre now stretched in warm welcome:

Stop running! There is no running! Move with a purpose! Do you think we have all day? Move it! Move it! Move it!

The line of swabs, trying to follow the blue tape leading to the center of the courtyard, lurches forward like a crazed caterpillar. Unlike Goldilocks, the swabs cannot seem to find the pace that is "just right," always moving either too slowly or too quickly to satisfy the cadre buzzing about them. The distance between swabs stretches into long gaps and collapses back into tight bunches as individual swabs try to reinterpret the orders barked in their faces. Still more cadre begin issuing new and unfamiliar guidance:

Square those corners! Stop running! Stay on the tape! Eyes in the boat! Stop looking around! What do you think this is, Disneyland? Eyes straight ahead! Stop wasting my time!

Driven by a blizzard of commands, swabs manage to find the blue crosses marking the spots on which they are to stand. The bulk of Chase Hall looms around them, suddenly less welcoming than they had remembered. Though the courtyard *appears* otherwise devoid of life, they are far from alone. Unseen, 2nd class cadets peer down from nearly every window above, recalling the day just two years earlier when they themselves stood in the swabs' shoes. For many, it seems like yesterday; for others, a lifetime ago. Smartphones in hand, they record the dramatic performance below for later review.

By now, the cadre have hit their stride. The hard brick walls amplify their voices. Each old order bounces off and mingles with a dozen new ones in the rising din. As swabs scuttle into position, they vainly try to keep their heads above the flood of orders coming from all directions. Old habits die hard, however, and each swab finds it difficult not to look at the person yelling in his or her ears. For eighteen years, they have been taught that the polite thing to do is to face the person addressing you. It now seems that their parents had been horribly misinformed:

Eyes in the boat! Stand straight! Take those sunglasses off! Chests out, shoulders back, stomach in! Do you play for the Yankees? Take that stupid hat off! Why are you touching your face? Hands by your side!

The swabs can do nothing right. The quickest among them learn it is best not to twitch a single muscle; movement only attracts unwanted attention and brings down further wrath. The others soon start to catch on. Finally, when they do all manage to settle, they can almost pass for statuary.

Suddenly, there is a brief moment of silence, and a single member

2/C Eric Ortiz encourages swabs to hurry along after leaving the bus.

of the cadre begins to stride back and forth before them. It is time for individual speeches:

Alpha Company! Welcome to the Coast Guard. Stand up straight, stop looking around, pay attention. I am 2nd Class Winters. Get a good look now. For the rest of the summer you will address me as "Miss Winters, ma'am." This is the military now. If you have a hat on your head, take it off. If you have gum in your mouth, spit it out in your hand. From now on, words like "yeah," "uh-huh," "whatever" do not exist in your vocabulary. You will answer all questions with "Yes, sir," "Yes, ma'am," or "No, sir," "No, ma'am." Is that clear?

Hoping they understand correctly, the swabs answer with their first official (if not enthusiastic):

Yes, ma'am!

Satisfied at least with their quick response, Winters continues:

You will respond to all directives with "Aye Aye, sir" or "Aye Aye, ma'am."

Of course, part of the fun for all cadre is leading swabs into traps they have not yet learned to avoid. Not realizing they have just been given another directive, the swabs fail to respond. Winters does not hesitate to pounce:

I don't think you heard what I just said! I saaaaid, you will respond to all directives with "Aye Aye, sir" or "Aye Aye, ma'am."

This time, having seen the error of their ways, they respond:

Aye Aye, ma'am!

I don't care who you are or what you did before you got here. I don't care if you finished first in your class. I don't care if you were athlete of the year. I don't care if you're the queen of the sugar plum fairies. That was then; this is now. You are in my Coast Guard now, and you will do what you are told. You will give me one hundred percent effort every single time you are asked to do something. You will not scratch an itch, you will not wipe sweat from your face, you will not blink without us telling you to do so. Is that understood?

Aye Aye, ma'am!

When she is done, a second cadre leaps in to fill the silence. He begins with his name, followed by a command to the swabs to learn it and use it each time they see him. Circling the company like a shark, he cautions them about the trials they will face over the course of the upcoming summer:

Everything you do this summer you will do as a team. There are no individuals. You either fail as a team or succeed as a team. Is that understood? You will refer to yourself as "Swab your last name here." There is no "I" in the Coast Guard. There is no "me" in the Coast Guard. You will forget those personal pronouns ever existed. Is that clear?

Aye Aye, sir!

If someone asks you a question and you don't know the answer, you will respond with, "This swab will find out, sir" or "ma'am." If you fail a task—and god forbid you do—and someone asks you why, you will respond with, "No excuses, sir," or "No excuses, ma'am." There are no excuses in the Coast Guard. Is that understood?

Aye Aye, sir!

Alpha Company! Turn around and face your cadre!

Aye Aye, sir!

After turning around to face a line of additional cadre, the swabs are instructed in the language chosen for the day—loud—to begin moving to Alpha Company's wing area, the section of Chase Hall they will call home for the summer. The cadre spring upon them again as a pack, driving them out of the quad and into the labyrinth of halls they will come to know well over the course of the next seven weeks.

Meanwhile, at the bottom of the Hill, the nervous swabs of Bravo Company begin to take their seats on a big red bus.

A swarm of cadre drive new swabs out of the courtyard and into the barracks. Once inside Chase Hall, swabs are introduced to the rest of the company's cadre,

The Challenge

The Academy faces two challenges on R-Day. The first, and most obvious, is to induct the new recruits and prepare them for the public swearing-in ceremony in the afternoon. The Coast Guard does not just want the swabs to look different from the children who left their parents at Leamy in the morning; appearing on the parade field dressed in identical uniforms will accomplish that much. Rather, it is important that the teens who arrived in the early morning hours appear transformed, that their parents see a metamorphosis they never thought possible. Parents should believe that, in the few hours the Academy has had their children, miracles have transpired. The cadre's charge is to make sure this happens, and by the time the ceremony begins, it has. Pride will brim, then spill, over parents' eyes later in the day on Washington Parade Field.

The second challenge the Academy faces on R-Day—the one parents little suspect—is to keep the parents themselves fully occupied and away from their children until the afternoon ceremony. The Coast Guard knows about idle hands and the devil's workshop, and it works hard to keep parents from meddling in what might be construed as rough treatment in Chase Hall. The Academy has not always faced this challenge. As senior officers relate, procedures were much different in the past. Captain Ernie Cummings remembers his first day at the Academy:

Swab summer was interesting, because all of the upperclassmen thought I would know a lot about it. I had two older brothers go through it, and they assumed they probably told me everything. They didn't tell me anything, and in those days, things were a little different than today; I think they're kinder these days. When you reported to the Academy then, you were dropped off at what they called the North Gate. It was almost across from Conn College, and you had your little bag, your little suitcase, with enough clothes for a couple of days, and you walked into Chase Hall. Your parents didn't even come into the Academy. I walked into Chase Hall, and as you know, they have summer ensigns, recently graduated 1st classmen who stay there to oversee the indoctrination of the new 4th class swabs. The 2nd class cadets oversaw the swabs, and the ensigns oversaw the 2nd class. Well, the one who greeted us in Chase Hall I happened to know; he was my brother. So I said, "Hi, John, how are you?" Probably the wrong thing to say, because he let me have it with every word he knew. He called me everything in the book and put me in my place, which was part of the indoctrination, I guess.

Brian Kichline, who graduated from the Academy fifty years before the incoming class will, points out another major difference between then and now:

We reported in, and then we had a week before we were sworn in. There were like 350 who came in, and they swore in something like 250. We lost something like a 100 guys just in the first week who just decided, "I don't want this garbage." When we graduated, there was 50 percent attrition in our class. We graduated a 115 out of the 300 and whatever. Part of it was academics, and part of it was people didn't like the lifestyle, and then you had guys like us

in the lower half of the class, who just really wanted it and really worked our tails off to graduate.

Times have changed, however, and parents are now allowed on campus before the class has been sworn in. As part of the morning's distractions, the superintendent of the Academy, Rear Admiral Sandra Stosz, gives a welcoming speech to the parents and families of the swabs who have been banished to Chase Hall for the morning. Following her presentation, hosts of speakers keep the audience members pinned to their seats, discussing various aspects of cadet life. The commandant of cadets talks about academic challenges and the help each student can expect to receive. The regimental commander talks about the military commitments students will fulfill. Other speakers include the dean of academics, the director of athletics, the director of admissions, cadet councilors, chaplains, and medical officers. Another block of the morning's time allows parents to meet informally with representatives to have yet more questions answered. In addition to hosting a lunch for the day's guests, the Parent's Association has scheduled bus tours of New London. Families can explore classroom buildings on campus and talk to faculty about course loads. Despite the many distractions, there are those parents who wander the campus, attempting to see how their children are engaged.

This day is as much a milestone for parents and families as it is for the swabs. Many of them, like their children, slept only fitfully the night before, spending their last few hours wondering about the path their daughters or sons have chosen. As adults, experience has undoubtedly given them a more realistic view of what it means to join a military organization. Worries about the future must cross their minds, distractions notwithstanding. Anne Brosnan, speaking with a lyrical Australian accent, had these thoughts regarding her daughter's upcoming life in the Coast Guard:

I'm getting nervous. Excited in a happy way. Nervous as a mother, of course, but it's all good. It's what Katie wants. I think the Coast Guard Academy is phenomenal. Both my husband and I came out of the first briefing we went to and looked at each other, and he actually said to me, "Now, before you say anything, I want you to think about what you really think." I said, "It's fantastic!" It's a great honor to get in, and having said that, my daughter is phenomenal. I know every mother thinks their daughter is phenomenal, but mine really is. She is everything the Coast Guard wants and more, and she doesn't even realize it. She is just so humble and just a gorgeous girl inside and out. She's going to set that place on fire. That's my opinion, although it might be slightly biased.

While parents understand that the education their children are about to receive will be extraordinary, they are often ambivalent about having their child take on a military career. At first, Anne and her husband pushed Katie toward the future the Coast Guard promised. Once Katie was offered an appointment, however, feelings changed slightly, at least for Anne:

When she got the appointment, we put the brakes on, as she said, and we told her all the drawbacks. She knew all the positives.

Swab Katie Brosnan with her brothers Owen and John on the left and her parents Owen and Anne to the right. Swabs have ten minutes to say goodbye after the class photo is taken.

Even a blind man can see all the positives, but there are things that they do give up. To be realistic about everything, you have to have the pros and cons, and is it truly a con? People say, "Well, giving back five years, wow!" But you can look at that and say, "They'll have a job as soon as they get out of college for five years." You can have your cup half empty or you can have a cup half full, depending upon how you look at things. We put her through a lot of questions: "What do you think about this?" and "You won't be able to do that!" And she came up every time. The more we gave her cons, the more she turned them into pros. Then, we knew.

Katie clearly saw the change in tone once she was offered an appointment, but if anything, her interest continued to rise:

Initially, they were very supportive. They were like, "Well, if this is what you want to do and this is going to make you happy, let's get it done." They helped me with the admission process. Whenever I wanted to go to the Academy, they were like, "Okay, let's set up a date and we'll go. Do you want to do the STEP program for women? Let's go. You want to talk to the soccer coach? Let's go." And then I got into the Academy. I actually got the appointment, and then they put the brakes on! They were like, "Okay, stop! Stop!" I was like, "Mom, this is good! Let's go! Let's go!" And she was like, "Wait! Let's think about it for a second." I was like, "What are you talking about? This is what I worked for! You brought me up to the Academy; you keep telling me how good it is." When it *came right down to it, they put the brakes on. At that point I was still full throttle. I was like, "Let's go! Let's sign the papers." Then they started telling me about all of the negatives associated with the Academy. Maybe not the negatives, but the reality: what I'm going to be missing out on if I join a service academy. Initially they told me the plus, and then they were telling me the minus, and I guess they were just trying to shake me. They asked, "Even with all this stuff, are you sure you still want to go?" And even with all that stuff, I still wanted to go. The more they said they were unsure, the more I wanted to go, and I guess it was important for them to see that. I signed, but I was seventeen when I signed, so technically I needed a guardian to sign for me. My dad signed it; my mom looked away. They're supportive of whatever makes me happy, so if the Coast Guard makes me happy, that's what they'd want me to do.*

The students who attend the Academy have a strong desire to serve their country, to belong to something larger than themselves, and to help others. Whereas some consider how they will benefit from the experience, Anne says Katie's perspective was different:

I was telling her what the Coast Guard Academy could do for her. I'd say, "Kate. This is what the Coast Guard can do for you," "This is wonderful," and all that, and she pulled me back and she said, "Mom, it's not all about me. It's about what I can give to the Coast Guard." So I was always thinking what it could do for her, and she was thinking what she could do for them. So she truly is the quintessential Coast Guard officer in the making, and I think she will go on to do great things in the Coast Guard.

Incoming swab James Hegge's mother sums up her feelings about her son's transition to Academy life in this way:

I don't think there are really words to put to it. We're pretty proud of him. I'm jealous, to be perfectly honest. What a great opportunity for these young men and women to get this experience. I think it is an opportunity to help them grow up, maybe a little more so than the kids that just go to college or something like that, because there is a little more structure, and it teaches them discipline and

that sort of thing. Some of us don't get that part of life until we're quite a bit older. I think it's a great opportunity.

While thinking about which service academy to attend, James heard a story that made his choice clear. His mother continues:

We had discussed the Army, and he had looked at the Merchant Marines, the Air Force, and the Coast Guard, but the Coast Guard was the first choice. My husband is happy about it. As a family, we all sat down and talked about it. The wrestling coach's son, a Coast Guard officer, had shared a story about a father and a nine-year-old lost at sea. They were going to call off the search, and it was this officer's choice to continue it another twelve hours or whatever it was, and they found them. They were in pretty bad shape, but James was just, you know . . . . Well, we looked at each other, and I didn't say anything, but he said what I was thinking: "Yeah, do we want to shoot and try to kill people, or do we want to save and rescue people?" It was a no-brainer.

Not surprisingly, given their interest in a military career, most students consider and apply to at least some of the other service academies. While outwardly the academies may appear much the same, the Coast Guard Academy is clearly differentiated in cadets' minds in at least two important ways. The first is the Coast Guard's overall mission. Cadets usually mention the humanitarian role the Coast Guard plays as an important factor in their decision to come to New London. The second is simply its size. Many cadets fear getting lost in an academy four times the size, whereas the Coast Guard gives them the sense of being part of an extended family. Swab Kyle Wood's mother had not even heard of the Coast Guard Academy before he began looking, but they found the size of the school attractive. She remembers:

After Coach Grant had called Kyle, I called my husband, Greg, and asked him, "Did you know there was a Coast Guard Academy?" Up to that point, we didn't even know there was an academy here, but the more we looked into it, we saw it was something that was very comparable to the other academies, on a smaller scale, and I think that was very interesting for him. He said he felt at some of the other academies, it was a little bigger business, so to speak. He thought it was a little more personable here and felt he could see himself as a student here, not just a cast member at one of the larger academies.

Brosnan also liked the size of the Academy, but that was not her only consideration:

I knew I wanted to go to a service academy; I just didn't know which one I wanted to join. I've always loved the ocean, and I've always loved the water, so I narrowed it down to Annapolis and the Coast Guard Academy. The Coast Guard Academy is smaller. I liked that smaller environment, and I didn't want to compromise when choosing a college, so I went with the Coast Guard. Also, in the Coast Guard, I can go into aviation, so that window of opportunity is also open. I didn't want to close any doors, because I'm only eighteen and it's a big decision. Being a woman, with the Academy over 30 percent female, we're not as much of a minority as in other service academies. Also, in the Coast Guard, women are not limited; I can do anything I want in the Coast Guard, and I won't be held back because of my gender. Because I'm from New York, I see the Coast Guard cutters along the Hudson River all the time. It looks exciting and sounds like an adventure to me. On the academic side, it's number one in the Northeast for baccalaureate colleges for engineering, so I will be getting an excellent education. It is tuition-free, although I will have to serve five years, but that's another adventure in itself.

Growing up, the idea of joining a military organization was on 2/C Evan Rothfeld's mind:

In junior year of high school, I looked into West Point and into the Coast Guard. The Coast Guard was smaller, and I liked that, and that it was a gritty, tough organization. I just wanted to be a part of it. Smaller was kind of a big thing for me, and I wanted to go military, big time—always wanted to. I like being a leader, or at least trying to be a leader, of a group of people. I liked doing it throughout high school, being a team captain. I like it when people are on the same page, have that same mentality, that same purpose and a goal; I enjoy trying to lead them there. Leadership is the

thing that pushed me to join the military. I'm not saying I was good at it, but I wanted to get better at it. I thought this place would be good, and it is. It's the best place I could possibly go to become a better leader.

Although 2/C Ryan Babb's parents were not in the military, many in his extended family have served in one capacity or another:

My grandfather was a Marine. He was enlisted, and my great-grandfather was a gunner's mate in the Navy. My great-uncle was in the Army; he was enlisted as well. My great-grandfather on my mother's side was a gunner's mate chief in the Navy during the Second World War. My grandfather was in Korea.

Thinking of following in his grandfather's or his great-grandfather's footsteps, he applied to the Naval Academy. While touring New England, he stopped in New London to explore what the Coast Guard might have to offer. Although the Navy remained his first choice, Babb came to the Academy for the summer's AIM program:

We got to experience a week of swab summer here, and I really enjoyed it. It was pretty rough—I wasn't really expecting the level of difficulty—but it was an eye opener, and I still enjoyed myself. I thought this might be the right place for me. I applied to the Naval Academy, the Coast Guard Academy, and three other schools for Naval ROTC. The Naval Academy answered back on April 15 of my senior year with a rejection, and I was pretty bummed out. I wasn't accepted into the Coast Guard under early admissions, but they offered me the opportunity to reapply into the general admission pool. I hadn't heard back from them, but I did get a Naval ROTC scholarship. I went to the University of Pittsburgh and was touring the Naval ROTC building, meeting with the Marine captain who was in charge. I got a call while I was meeting with him, and I asked him if I could step out of the room and take it. It was a Lieutenant JG from admissions on the phone, and she asked, "Mr. Babb, would you still like to come to the Coast Guard Academy?" I said, "Sure!" She said, "Well, we have an appointment for you. If you would like to, please let us know, and we will send your information in the mail." And so I said, "Yes, ma'am, I'd love to come."

I hung up the phone and went back to the Marine captain and said, "Sir, I'm not meant to come here. Thank you for your time. I'm going to be going to the Coast Guard." That's my whole story.

Ryan also sees the Coast Guard's humanitarian mission as a better fit:

I obviously was meant to be here. I'm doing well, and I'm loving it here. Being a Boy Scout, I practiced a lot of first aid. I was a lifeguard and things like that. It got drilled into my head that it's important to watch out for other people and put others before myself, and I found the mission of the Coast Guard really allows me to continue with that throughout the rest of my career. Its mission is humanitarian, and I can serve the people of the United States more directly. It doesn't put me in harm's way as the Navy or Marines would. I think it's a better decision in the long run to be here.

The feeling of camaraderie 2/C Cathy Durand enjoyed as part of the Junior ROTC in high school ignited her interest in the service academies:

My high school had a Junior ROTC program, and that got me looking into the Naval Academy, but I liked the humanitarian side of the Coast Guard, so I started looking here. It was probably in my junior year that I knew I wanted to come here. My grandfather was in the Navy for two years, but I didn't really know that growing up. He chose to enlist in the Navy rather than be drafted into the Army. I like the idea of serving after graduation. Having the Junior ROTC in high school, I just couldn't imagine myself not doing it after. It was a big part of me then. It was a battalion-like structure. We had a drill team, and I helped coach them with marching. We had promotions, and my senior year I was in charge of the battalion.

For 1/C Andrew Ray, the summer's regimental commander, the Coast Guard Academy was not his first choice:

This was actually my second choice. The Air Force Academy was my first pick. I got the nomination, but I wasn't picked. My dad asked if I had heard of the Coast Guard Academy. I asked, "What's that?" I had never heard of it, so I came up here for the Cadet-for-

a-Day visit, and that was an incredible experience. I attribute everything that made me want to come here from then, 2nd Class Carl Warner; he did a phenomenal job as my Cadet-for-a-Day sponsor. I thought, "This place looks pretty cool, pretty interesting. I like what it has to offer." I applied, got accepted, and I guess when I did there was no hesitation in saying this is where I'm going. For me, I wasn't a good high-school student. I was athletically involved and involved in the community and all that kind of stuff, but I didn't have any idea what I would do if I was in a normal school; I had no clue. I was interested in a lot of things, but I thought, "Can I actually make a career out of that?" So a lot of things played into my decision to come here. Once I set foot here, I thought I could see myself doing this for four years and five afterwards. I didn't get into the Air Force, which is what I wanted to do, but now that I've been here, I've never regretted it for a second. Never. Sometimes the 6:00 A.M. mornings get old, but I can't beat the friends and relationships I've made. Best thing I could ever ask for.

Captain John O'Connor, just finishing his tour as commandant of cadets at the Academy, saw the Coast Guard as a stepping stone:

I grew up in Providence, but we had a summer home in Warwick, Rhode Island, on Narragansett Bay, and I had boats as a kid. My dad was a boater, and I saw what the Coast Guard did on the water and said, "That's something I'd like to do." My original intent was to be a Rhode Island state trooper. I was going to come into the Coast Guard, get law enforcement experience, and then duck out after four years. I enlisted, but somehow I got hooked and ended up staying on. I was enlisted for twelve years, went to Officer Candidate School, and I am currently entering my thirty-sixth year of service. I am leaving here to become the sector commander in Boston, Massachusetts. It's been a great ride. I'm finishing my second year in this position. I was also chief of the Officer Candidate School for three years, which is just down the hall, and this is my fifth tour at the Academy. I have been on the faculty here as well. I'm the first commandant of cadets who isn't a product of the Academy .

A 47' Coast Guard Motor Life Boat heads back to Station Point Judith in rough weather. Self-righting, these vessels can operate in hurricane conditions.

The Rising Storm

The sky grows bleaker as company after company depart Leamy's ballroom. The process of separating parents from recruits runs like clockwork: A new company boards another bus. The bus stops in front of new cadre. The cadre herd the new group of swabs to blue tape crosses. New speeches welcome them, and soon they, too, find themselves in the depths of Chase Hall. As those inside the barrack slide windows open in futile attempts to vent the oppressive heat and humidity, snippets of the trademark one-way dialogue in which swabs and cadre engage filter out into the courtyard. Parents' expressions flicker between amusement and concern as they strain to hear what they cannot see. It seems to those on the outside that things are not going well on the inside— that within those towering brick walls, 255 people are having a very bad day. By the time the last two companies board their buses, the sun has been swallowed by the tempest now engulfing New London. When Hotel Company bolts from the last bus at 0900, it

39

feels like dusk and is, in fact, far too dark to take photos without the aid of a flash. Shortly after they hit the quad, the heavens open up, as if to signal the end of the world.

The squall outside now conceals the one inside from curious parents. The deluge sends them scrambling for cover. It rains as hard as is possible—a veritable typhoon. Not a soul stirs outside as the heavens drain. The added humidity nearly drowns the swabs as they stand stuffed in airless hallways throughout the dorm.

Companies cascade through the tasks ahead in alphabetical order, driven by energized cadre. First on Alpha Company's agenda is the traditional shaving of the heads. If you live in Annapolis, West Point, Denver, or New London on R-Day, you will see cadets being shorn on the six o'clock news.

R-Day features a single hairstyle for all male swabs. Females may have shoulder length cuts or wear longer hair in tight buns on the back of their heads.

The barbershop dates itself, retaining the look of a bygone era. Above the Formica countertop, a mirror runs the length of the room. It reflects a row of barbers at work on an unending stream of customers. The drawers are covered with simulated wood veneer, their V-shaped, chrome handles evoking a faded futurism. Each barber's station has identical equipment: a plastic bottle of Stephan's Ultrafine Talc; a glass comb jar filled with a mysterious blue fluid; a candy-striped spray bottle containing some magical elixir; and a can of Wahl Clipper Oil, which is used to keep electric shears running smoothly. The *Welcome Aboard* sign, bearing a painted lighthouse, goes unnoticed by the swabs. They have other concerns.

When I first walk in, seeking permission to take photos, I am quickly driven out by an irate, albeit polite, barber. As it happens, just before my arrival, a few wayward parents had barged in demand-ing to take pictures, which had led to a complete ban on outsiders. I find Senior Chief McDade and ask him if he might intervene on my behalf. He quickly stills the waters, and I receive a warm reception upon my return.

The five barbers happily chat through their busiest day of the year, shaving head after head for six hours running. Like the room itself, the shop's specialty harkens back to simpler times. For today at least, it is a one-haircut-fits-all operation. The barbers, quite deft with their shears, waste little time, and soon the floor is inches deep in shorn locks.

With the notable exception of the swabs, everyone involved in the activity seems to be having a good time (although cadre are careful not to let it show). The barbers are in top form. They joke with the swabs, trying to give them some sense of normalcy during their brief reprieve from the whirlwind that brought them here. They ask the young men where they are from and, more wryly, what style haircut they would like. Stunned, most can do no more than stare back with questioning eyes. One swab—out of habit, or perhaps hoping optimistically to find the day near its end—glances at his watch. The barber pounces:

Got a date? Would you like me to hurry so you can get back out there and join the fun?

Now too afraid to move or speak, the swab fails to appreciate the joke. He musters only a weak "Sir, no sir." The barber continues with what must be another standard joke, asking the young man if he would like to see the future. Regardless of the proffered answer, he takes his electric shears and shaves a swath of hair down the middle of the young man's head, leaving the balding dome of an old man. While this seems comical to others in the room, the swab sees no humor in the image he sees reflected in the hand mirror the barber raises for the occasion.

On a long bench opposite the cutting stations awaits the next row of victims, furtively peering at the mayhem from behind their raised copies of *Running Lights*, a book they will study all summer. Above them, the stuffed head of the Academy's black-bear mascot Objee opens his mouth in a snarl, perhaps angry at having been shot and stuffed. The overall impression he creates is not particularly fierce, given he is wearing red and yellow mirrored sunglasses, sports a patterned blue scarf, and holds several jackets in his forepaws, which stick out of the backboard bent at right angles.

Objee, short for Objectionable Presence, has been the Coast Guard's mascot since the turn of the twentieth century. The mascot was chosen to honor the cutter *Bear*, which spent much of its operational time in the arctic. Objee first appeared live at the Academy in 1926. Cadet Stephan Evans brought a bear cub to the campus and managed to convince the superintendent of his importance. From that day forward, a series of black bears lived on campus with the cadets. As hard as it is to believe, once it became illegal to keep wild animals in Connecticut, the last living Objee departed Academy grounds in 1984 to finish his days on a farm in upper New York State. Coast Guard historians are emphatic that this is not the same retirement farm old dogs and cats are said to roam.

The various bears taking on the role of Objee over the years wandered the halls of Chase at night, perhaps serving as extra insurance that cadets would stay in their rooms. The bears showered in cadet bathrooms and occasionally ate meals in the wardroom when well behaved. They were quartered, at one point in time, in an old observatory. One Objee was kidnapped by members of a rival sports team visiting the Academy. They managed to get him into their van, but on their drive home they quickly came to regret their rash decision. Once Objee had destroyed the interior of their vehicle, the team was more than happy to return him whence he came. Coast Guard history overflows with stories of mascots; most served their time aboard ships, but many others found stations on land. Dogs, as one might expect, were frequent companions on board, but cats, birds, live bears, and even a horse also served honorably among the ranks.

While the young men in the barbershop undoubtedly glance at the unusual coatrack above their heads, they probably think little of it. They are concentrated more on the cadre roiling up and down the hallway outside. The confining passage leading to the barbershop overflows with swabs awaiting their turns in the barbers' chairs. Though the walls are cleanly painted from truck to keel, the harsh fluorescent lighting adds little charm to the simple block construction. Swabs stand at attention, their backs to the wall, blank expressions on their faces, trying to hide behind what little cover is given by their copies of *Running Lights*. They try to blend into the very walls that are keeping them from running away, as cadre bellow at each infraction. Given the confined quarters and the abundance of hard surfaces, the volume is deafening, making it nearly impossible to determine which order is being given to whom and what it might mean. The swabs' only defense is to sound off as loudly as they can: "Yes, sir!" "No, ma'am!" or "No excuses, sir!"

Given their anxiety and the chaotic nature of the scene, swabs often confuse the gender of the cadre addressing them, placing a *Sir* where a *Ma'am* should be or a *Ma'am* where a *Sir* should be. Each such error inevitably brings forth a torrent of new questions from the mock-angry cadre: *Does Swab A not yet know the difference between a man and a woman? Does Swab A need examples? Swab A, is the person standing in front of you male or female? Does Swab A know how to address him?*

Another cadre asks the gathered company if any of them listened to her speech in the quad this morning. As nobody dares answer the question alone, having heard what happened to Swab A, a deafening silence stands as the company's response. She wonders aloud about their lack of interest in her question. Repeating it, and hoping for an answer this time, she reminds them what the only two appropriate answers can be. This time, in unison, they assure her they were listening. Sweat pours from their faces, staining their shirts a deeper blue, but they no longer respond to the glistening drops sliding along their cheeks, because they now know Coast Guard swabs never itch.

Once finished with the stylist, swabs next learn the combinations to their postal boxes and have the opportunity to test them. Many are too flustered to dial the correct combination on the first try. Beyond the double glass doors leading outside, rain continues falling in torrents, punctuated by flashes of lightning and the dull, rolling crash of thunder. When everyone's hair, or lack thereof, passes muster, and all postal boxes have been successfully opened, Alpha Company moves out to its next assigned task: weigh-in.

Weigh-in is, for the most part, quite simple. To allow for variations in body types and frame sizes, the Department of Defense has gone to using a body mass index, or BMI, to determine who does or does not meet weight standards. The process begins with a simple weight-height comparison; any swab whose weight is suspect is subjected to further tests to determine his or her actual BMI. Generally, this is a matter of formality. Teenagers applying to the Academy, as a rule, are physically fit and know the regulations regarding excess poundage. Despite this knowledge, however, the induction process abruptly ends for several incoming swabs; two girls have arrived at the Academy above weight.

How this could be is a mystery. If they were aware of the problem and thought exceptions would be made, they were mistaken. Whatever the cause—be it lack of attention to detail, miscalculation, or an unconscious escape mechanism—their careers in the Coast Guard end before they get a chance to begin. The harsh countdown to graduation begins, and there will be two fewer faces on the bleachers today when the official class portrait is snapped. All of the time, effort, and hope spent to reach this day vanishes without reward. While questions linger, the two young women head through the Academy gates for what will undoubtedly be a long and unhappy ride home. As with all titillating news at the Academy, word of the dismissal of two shipmates spreads quickly through the ranks of swabs. Every one of them is now certain there are no second chances, no extenuating circumstances. An impression has been made.

By this time, just midmorning, another disappointment has begun spreading across the campus. With the storm raging outside, the swearing-in ceremony will have to take place in a gymnasium; Washington Parade Field is under water. This news is disheartening, as the lovely green lawn, with its towering row of oaks lining Bear Drive is not only picturesque, but also far less confining. Regardless of the gymnasium's cavernous size, a hot, humid, and wet day in a room packed with a thousand people does not make for a stirring ritual. The disappointment in the air is palpable. Parents discuss this development throughout the rest of the morning, hoping the weather will clear in time to eliminate the need for the unwelcome change of plans.

As the morning progresses and additional companies join the rush to complete the assigned tasks, swabs begin to exhibit the desired uniformity. More and more sport dark blue t-shirts, their last names printed in simple block letters above the Coast Guard insignia. Dark blue shorts replace the rainbow of colored pants worn this morning. Both males and females wear white socks that nearly reach their knees. Stainless chains, from which new dog tags hang, to create reasonable facsimiles for the afternoon's performance. When these swabs next appear before their parents, they must look more martial than motley. Blocks in the schedule, simply listed as "Cadre Time," have been reserved for this phase of the day's transformation.

Cadre Time allows the new leaders to begin the indoctrination process in earnest. Those who did not have the chance to deliver personal speeches in the quad do so now, introducing themselves and listing further rules swabs must follow. These lessons, too, are conveyed in full voice. As before, every error a swab makes is quickly corrected. At this point, however, the correctional tools at the cadre's disposal are limited to: 1) shouting, and 2) shouting louder. If special emphasis is needed, two or more cadre work in stereo. As swabs have not yet been sworn in and, more importantly, have not yet had their Academy physicals, cadre cannot yet apply what is euphemistically called "incentive training."

Swabs are generally incentive trained, or IT'd, whenever they fail to achieve. The inducement to correct mistakes or improve performance comes in the form of physical exercise: pushups, sit-ups, squats, and the like. The constant threat of these "incentives" provides motivation, while the very real repetition of them builds individual physical strength within the Corps. Until every swab has been checked by Academy doctors, however, no such training is allowed. A number of high-profile incidents at various service academies, during which cadets died because of underlying medical conditions, have made everyone cautious. For the first three or four days, vocal encouragement will have to suffice.

One of the first lessons swabs learn on R-Day is the standard position of attention, which they will assume during the few fleeting moments they are not in motion this summer. When randomly asked throughout the day to repeat, verbatim, the rules of this position, swabs shout:

Ma'am—the standard position of attention is: head erect, eyes in the boat, chin in, shoulders back, chest out, stomach in, weight evenly distributed on both feet, heels together, feet forming a 45 degree angle, arms hanging naturally at the sides, palms facing inward, thumbs along trouser seams, with fingers joined in a natural curl—ma'am.

Cadre remind recruits throughout the day that there is to be no slouching, no talking, no wandering eyes. They will stand as sculpted ice, frozen until com-

Objee looks over Swab Baldwin's shoulder in the barber shop.

occasionally snake above shirt necklines. Some companies are still wearing a variety of sneakers, and others have not yet filled the empty green packs they tote, but all now appear to belong to an organization that has specific plans for their future. Of course, these are merely costuming changes, and the cadre's real work for the day has yet to begin. Though it will take all summer to build proper 4th class cadets, the cadre strive

Reporting-In Day

44

Scenes from R-Day. Left Page clockwise: Sweats pours from the face Swab Sarah Kukich, locked in a thousand-yard stare. A swab responds to a question while keeping his eyes level, and Swab Yuknat reacts to shouted commands.

Right Page clockwise: One of the cadre marches out to welcome the next bus of swabs to Chase Hall. 2/C Marco Tinari encourages swabs to move a little more quickly to the taped crosses in the courtyard, and swabs read their copies of the *Running Light* as they await their haircuts.

Morning turns to night as a storm sweeps in from the east.

manded to thaw. Intent on making a lasting first impression, cadre repeatedly emphasize that swabs will not speak unless spoken to. The consequences will be severe, they are warned, for all infractions. Swabs take this lesson immediately to heart—so much so that the cadre's success here will come to haunt them later in the day.

As the day moves forward, so does the weather system that has all but drowned the campus, not to mention the moods of the waiting parents. The sky begins to clear, and joyous news arrives with the brightening sky; the swearing-in ceremony has been moved back to the parade field. Spirits soar as preparations are made for this welcome about-face. To accommodate the requirements of the incoming class photo, an enormous set of bleachers begins to rise on the south end of the parade field. A speaker's podium is placed in front of Hamilton Hall, the broadcast system is tested, and permanent seating overlooking the parade field is wiped dry for visiting dignitaries. Several companies emerge from the darkness of Chase Hall and move onto the parade field to practice their newly acquired marching skills. The day moves on, and at precisely 1440, the newest members of the Corps gather in formation alongside the Chase Hall parking lot. Families pack the length of Bear Drive in anticipation of the moment they have waited so long to see, their cameras and cell phones ready to record the pageantry.

As if on cue, the sun breaks through the last of the clouds scudding past, and at 1500, the swearing-in ceremony begins. Officers in their finest dress uniforms line the stairs of Hamilton Hall. The Coast Guard band marches down Bear Drive and past expectant parents, filling the air with martial tunes. The Color Guard, carrying the American flag and two different Coast Guard flags, leads the procession, its standards fluttering in the brilliant light of the afternoon's sun. Eight companies of swabs swing into motion, following cadre and company regimental officers to the center of the parade field. Wearing light-blue dress shirts, navy pants, crisp, white, gold-trimmed hats, and gleaming swords, the company officers and cadre contrast nicely with the solid, deep-blue wall of swabs behind them. Each company is proceeded by its guide-on, the cadet chosen to carry the company standard.

Young men and women, in rigid block formations, quickly cover the field directly in front of Hamilton Hall. Row upon row of expectant cadets stand smartly at attention. Despite the rough day they have experienced, the swabs seem to stand a little taller, assuring their parents, or perhaps themselves, of the correctness of their decision. Speeches are delivered, congratulating cadets on their previous achievements and on the commitment they have made to put others ahead of themselves. Hints about the difficulty that lies ahead in the coming months are warmly clothed in terms of the prospects that await beyond the summer's trials. Admiral Sandra Stosz steps to the microphone to deliver the oath of office, simultaneously launching some 253 new military careers. Swabs, as instructed, raise their right hands as she delivers the oath:

Having been appointed to the rank of Cadet in the United States Coast Guard, I do solemnly swear that I will support and defend the Constitution of the United States against all enemies, foreign and domestic; that I bear true faith and allegiance to the same; and that I will well and faithfully discharge the duties of the office on which I am about to enter. So help me God.

Ironically, it is at this point the cadre's brief but effective training regimen threatens to derail the ceremony. Having been told in no uncertain terms that they shall not speak until spoken to, the new members of the Corps steadfastly remain silent. Apparently, no one told them they should answer the Admiral with an affirmative during the oath. For a brief, awkward, moment, it appears as if the entire class has changed its mind after just one rough day. Fortunately, however, Coast Guard officers are quick on their feet. Sensing the problem, and without missing a beat, Admiral Stosz adds:

The appropriate response is: "I do."

With this encouragement, the entire class snaps from its trance and shouts out, "I DO!", officially joining the ranks of the countless thousands of women and men who have served their country since the year 1790.

The class photo is the last order of business before parents get to congratulate their children on this new achievement. Though more than a mere notion, the incoming shot bears decidedly less importance than the photo that will mark the end of their time at the Academy; the graduation photo, if predictions hold, will have nearly eighty fewer faces. Before swabs begin filling the bleachers, cadre must sort them by height. Unlike a service such as the Marines, the Coast Guard has relaxed regulations concerning physical uniformity. When one imagines a platoon of the former, each stands six feet tall, and every cap seems to have been set in place with an engineer's level. This is not, however, the case with Coast Guard officers. Students enter the Academy with little

consideration given to the aesthetic ideals of parade formations. A woman can be as short as 4'10" or as tall as 6'8". A man can enter at a scant 5'. Though height will not affect a Coast Guard officer's ability to command, it does make for less tidy formations on the parade field.

Despite this variety, the sorting procedure moves along quickly, and cadets begin to flow onto the bleachers. With the sun shining brilliantly, swabs are now squinting, and the young men's scalps gleam, uncovered for the photo. With two swabs already dismissed, many must wonder which of their shipmates will not appear in the graduation photo four years hence. When all is in order, the official photo is snapped, capturing for eternity the questioning, concerned, and sometimes hopeful faces of the class of 2016.

This chore completed, the broadcast system advises parents and families that they now have a few brief moments to say farewell to their children. In exactly ten minutes, cadre will call the companies together and march them back up Bear Drive and into Chase Hall. There is a mad rush to find individual cadets amid the huge crowd now swamping the parade ground. Last-minute advice mixes with hugs, kisses, and more than a few tears. Cameras snap one or two last photos before orders to reform into companies are given. Cadets move to join their shipmates, snapping back to attention under the cadre's command. The day's visitors are politely asked to leave and head to various parking lots spread throughout the grounds. The morning tide that flooded the campus with cars now ebbs, sweeping vehicles back through the main gate and onto Interstate 95. Within the hour, the campus seems deserted. The only sounds heard are the rising and falling voices of cadre and swabs, emanating from the open windows of Chase Hall and dying in the empty courtyards.

Swabs go to Mystic Seaport Museum in full dress uniform for the Flag Day ceremony, the first chance they have to see parents and family since R-Day.

Looking Backward

The Coast Guard has a program that allows students who are thinking of applying to the Academy to experience a taste of swab summer. The Academy Introduction Mission, or AIM, takes students for one week between their junior and senior years in high school. Cadre lead and train them in a truncated version of swab summer. Though other service academies have similar programs, AIM is generally considered the most realistic experience by those kids who have participated in more than one. According to one of the Academy's latest graduates, Ensign Michael Klakring, AIM is not a summer camp:

I'm a huge fan of AIM; it's better for people to see what they're getting into and then decide it isn't for them. That's fine, because it's not for everybody, and it's not something you want to do on a whim either. AIM sealed the deal for me to come here, because I went to the summer seminars at Air Force and Navy, and they were kind of lame in comparison. They ran theirs like summer camp, and then on the last day they tried to get serious, but it didn't work, because it had been summer camp all week. AIM was the most accurate portrayal of all of them, really, and the fact that they actually did it at the Academy made me want to come here. I'm glad I did it, I'm glad I chose here.

Aimsters, as they are called, are grilled and drilled much like the swabs. Beyond the week's introduction to the military on and off the parade field, students get the chance to talk with cadets and officers about life at the Academy and beyond. The Coast Guard does, of course, use the AIM program to sell the Academy's benefits. They bring big hardware to the campus for kids to see: a black hull, the type of ship used for setting and maintaining aids to navigation; a white hull; the type used on marine patrols, on rescue operations and in law enforcement; and a Jayhawk helicopter, used in rescue missions. Students get to tour the ships and aircraft and converse with crewmembers about their particular jobs. The Academy finds AIM an effective recruitment tool, and nearly 50 percent of the kids who do well at AIM and apply to the Academy receive appointments.

A second program is the Coast Guard Academy Scholars Program, or CGAS. This program handles those students whom the Academy would like to enroll, but whose academic performance is not yet up to speed. Also called prepsters, these students come to the Academy for a three-week version of swab summer before heading off to a military academy for a preparatory year of college. Cadre 2/C Jennifer Patron, herself a CGAS graduate, explains:

It's a conditional appointment. It means they are accepted into the next year's class under the conditions they keep their grades up, that they do well militarily, and they keep in constant communication with specific people here at the Academy. That person is usually an officer, letting them know how they are doing and how they feel, because if something goes wrong at the prep school,

the Academy wouldn't know until it was too late. The preparatory schools are the equivalent of something like a community college. This year they're using Marion in Alabama, and the other one is in Georgia. They're both military schools, and the military training they receive is similar. You also have the same rigorous workload. You have to get up in the morning and go to formation, wear a uniform, and all that stuff. I went to an Army prep school, so everything was Army-based. Everyone was saying, "Huah!" I was like, "I don't know what that means. I'm a little Coastie. I don't know what's going on." That was funny. The whole purpose is to prepare students academically, so regardless of where you are, as long as you're getting the curriculum done, that's what's important. Learning Army lingo was fun, but I also learned I didn't want to be in the Army. I'm much happier in the Coast Guard.

The program is for kids who need to boost their academics, who need to work on something like their math or their English. They send them to these prep schools, and they take the same basic courses that any freshman would take here at the Academy. They take calculus, chemistry, physics, and things like that. It helps them prepare, and they know exactly what they need to work on. It's that extra little push so that once they're at the Academy, they're not struggling to make it through. They can ease into their classes.

If candidates successfully complete their Prep year, they are enrolled into the next year's class as swabs with everyone else. These students often have an easier time with swab summer because of their military training during Prep year and their shortened swab-summer experience the year before. Despite working to prepare herself, Patron still experienced butterflies on R-Day:

I was very nervous. I did a lot of things to prepare to come to the Academy. I did the AIM program, I did CGAS, so by the time I got to swab summer I was already, "All right, I know what to expect." The summer was a little different, because it was longer than the CGAS program. The CGAS program was more compact; everything the swabs learned in seven weeks, we were fire-hosed with in three. We learned things very quickly in swab summer, but it was a different dynamic. I was very nervous both times, because, obviously, you're going into something you're not really sure of. But I knew the Academy was going to take care of me and that my peers were all going through the same thing, so that gave me some comfort.

I showed up with my parents. There's all these people, and your adrenaline is going. You're excited, but you're nervous. It's very nerve-racking, so I had my family with me. Working up to that point, we were all very proud. I was proud of myself for getting through Prep school, and my parents, my sister, and my brother were all sitting there in Leamy Hall. We're sitting there, waiting and waiting. They give you a specific time to report in. With my last name Patron, it took a while. They finally called our section, and my dad was like, "All right, this is what you've been working for. This is just the start of it, but you've already worked hard to get here." I am very close with my family, so we gave each other hugs. When we lived in Italy, we all picked up Italian. My mom speaks the best Italian, and the rest of us speak something like Spangtalian, but there is a word called forza, which means something like "go onward," a type of encouragement they use. So both my mom and my dad say, "Forza! Go onward! Do great things!" So I gave them my packet, stood at attention, and that's how it started.

Patron's fellow cadre 2/C Joseph Trump recalls only too well his introduction to the Academy:

I remember the day before, the Sunday, where swabs and their parents can come in and see where their room is going to be and meet the other swabs. That day was really exciting, and I wasn't nervous at all that day. I saw where my room was, and I met my roommate, which was good, and we walked around the campus. I had seen the campus before, but my dad was shocked: "What is this? They have air-conditioning?" We looked at the honor wall, took some pictures, and met my company.

On R-Day, I woke up probably around four o'clock in the morning. We were staying over in Groton, because we had driven up from Florida. Me and my dad went to breakfast at a twenty-four-hour diner because it was four-thirty in the morning. We figured I

should be well nourished for the first day, because we didn't know what was going to happen. We went to breakfast, then back to the hotel to pick up my mom, and then we drove across the bridge. That's when I started to get a little nervous. I was wearing a plain white t-shirt and athletic shorts, because I knew they would probably make us change pretty fast. I really had no idea, because my dad was here in '77, and it could have been completely different. We went to Leamy Hall, and I stopped being nervous while I was still with my parents and everybody was milling around. I went up to sign in, and then I walked out through the doors to the balcony of Leamy. I got pretty nervous after that.

I got out there, and we were all standing on the wall; the sun was right in our eyes, and there was one firstie from our company, the executive officer, and he had a sword and all that stuff. He was standing in front of us, and I dropped my passport out of the folder I was carrying. He just told me, "Pick it up, and get back in line." That's when I really got pretty nervous. After that, it was all pretty much a blur. I remember the bus ride, and then I don't remember anything specific after the bus ride before meeting with the parents again a couple of hours later. You get your haircut, somehow you learn how to march a little bit, and you get some uniform items. Looking back on it, I don't even know how you get all that stuff so fast. I guess they have maybe six hours or so to teach you to look okay in a uniform and how to march. It all seems pretty crazy to me, and it doesn't seem like I've been here for two years at all.

4/C Kyneesha Womack had also gone through the CGAS program and was therefore able to help her fellow swabs who had less experience. Despite her preparation, she still found the first day shocking:

The first day was kind of rough, but I'm a prepster and I was here last year, so the initial shock wasn't as bad as most people's, but it was still a pretty difficult day. It was a perfectly stormy day, with all the rain and getting yelled at. I think the worst part of the first day was probably getting off the bus. You're still kind of relaxed, and you're not really in military mode yet, but the moment they stop the bus is when it all hits you. They just start screaming, "Get off the bus! Get off the bus!" You have to put your game face on right then and there. You don't want to, but it's something you have to do to get through it. It was shocking. You don't really expect it.

It was rough just getting back into the military mode. I was able to help some of the others; they didn't really know what to expect. When they get here, they're scared, and they don't think they want to be here. Most of them really want to leave, so your job is to say, "Hey, it's not that bad." If I'm on my A game all the time, then it's going to make them want to reach that standard as well, so that's pretty much what I've been doing. I mainly get to talk to the females, because when we have head and water breaks we have three minutes. We try to give them pointers during the break. During some trainings, they'll give us time to talk to each other, so all the prepsters give everyone tips and hints on how to do things. With the little time we do have, we use it wisely. Time management is a huge part; that's what they say is going to help us throughout the year, so that's why we practice time management every day.

Swab Rheanastasia Doctolero did not have the benefit of going through either preparatory program. She prepared herself as best she could before R-Day but still found the first week difficult:

I'm doing a little better than the first day; the first day was crazy. I'm a little tired. I'm not used to the little bit of sleep that I get now, but everything else is pretty good. I'm doing pretty well compared to a lot of people who actually didn't prepare at all. A lot of people have been falling out and passing out. In our company alone, we've lost four people on sick call—passed out and taken to the hospital. But they've come back, so that's good. Preparing has helped me a lot.

The first day was extremely long. I've never had such a long day in my life. Never. It felt like eight days in one. Each day now is still long, but they're shorter than the last. They say

Regimental Commander 1/C Andrew Ray on Flag Day. As commander, Ray is tasked with the smooth operation of swab summer at the cadet level.

AIM students inspect a Sikorsky HH-60 Jayhawk. Helicopters and a variety of ships are brought to the Academy during the summer to further entice prospective cadets.

the weeks go by quickly and the days go by slowly, and it's actually really true. Now I understand what it means. I'm surprised this week is already done, but the days are really long.

For many, by the end of their first semester, R-Day has already faded into the past. 4/C Jake Carlton remembers only the highlights:

R-Day is now just a blur in the past really. I remember getting here, relaxing, and getting a chance to look around, but once we signed in, our companies got called and it was pretty much: "Hit the wall, stare out." Then, straight from the bus, it was all yelling and "Go, go, go!" The first day sucked. One way to cope with it, though, was to be a million miles away. You don't really have the time to think about anything, because they keep you so busy that you don't have any free time to think by yourself. When you go to bed at night, you're usually so tired that you pass out like a light. I

looked forward to the sleep, because it was nice to get to sleep, but then of course we had to wake up at 0530 every morning to go to cals, which was tiring, too.

2/C Ryan Babb, now enjoying his turn as cadre, remembers much of his first day:

I was pretty nervous. I pretty much knew what was going to happen because of the AIM program. That prepared me really well for R-Day. I was really nervous, and saying goodbye to your family and friends, knowing that you're not going to come back the same person, was as weird feeling. The night before R-Day, I was in a hotel in Groton, and I couldn't sleep. R-Day was a blur, but I do remember coming through the check-in line, standing against the bulkhead waiting for the bus, them rushing us onto the bus and driving us to the archways where we got out. We had a little bit of

52

marching and maneuvering practice, but not a whole bunch. We got our operational dress-uniform pants and a blue Coast Guard Academy shirt, a canteen belt, and a ball cap. That's about it; from then on it's a blur, until I took my oath on Washington Parade Field. I got to say goodbye to my parents for ten minutes, but I was pretty tired because I hadn't gotten that much sleep the night before. I was calm; I wouldn't say relaxed, but I was calm, and I told them that it was going to be a rough summer and that I couldn't wait to see them on Labor Day weekend—a fifty-day stint. I can't remember anything else.

1/C Andrew Ray, now four years past his introduction to the Academy and in charge of swab summer at the cadet level, clearly recalls the cadre and the impression they made:

I guess they're ensigns now, my cadre. First thing I remember is the quad speech. When they came out, there was this one humongous guy, John Stimmel, and I thought to myself, "Who is this guy?" He turned out to be a phenomenal guy—really, really, nice and personable. During the summer, everyone has their own little persona, and you can never really read the cadre—who they are and what they're like. As a swab, you see them as perfect; they know everything. They almost seem robotic, and you almost see them as not being human. Once the swab summer experience ends, you can finally speak with them and find out who they really are—get to know them. It's great. The cadre are perfect, and they look at you like you're down here, not because you're the scum of the earth, but because you know nothing about this place and they know everything. That's something my mom said. She came up here last year for R-Day when I was a cadre and said, "It's not that you guys look older or are bigger, it's the way you carry yourselves, the way you're squared away, and the fact that you know everything and that you have to teach them."

Koachar Mohammad's experience on his first day was, in many ways, typical of what most swabs report. Beyond the sudden and shocking loss of freedom, there was another and more profound realization:

I saw my mother crying, but I was still okay. I thought that it was going to be all right, but I also remember thinking, "What did I get myself into?" I thought it was going to be a lot easier than it actually was. The first day we didn't really do anything physical, especially because the parents were still there. A lot of it they could still see, and I think that's one of the parts they don't want to see and the Coast Guard doesn't want to show.

I think the most shocking part about the first day was when we swore in, where we said we would uphold and defend the Constitution of the United States of America. I thought that was a little bit shocking; I don't think I assessed the gravity of what I was getting into and the responsibility that, as a commissioned officer, you will protect the United States of America. I think I still didn't realize it when I said, "I do", but I think as I've matured here at the Academy, I now know the gravity of that oath, how important that is, and what a big decision it was I made.

Up until the swearing-in ceremony, the path to the Academy has perhaps felt more a game to many swabs, a challenge to see if they can make the grade: finish the paperwork, pass the tests, measure up. The reality of what they have done comes on R-Day, and with it, many doubts. The concept of defending the country against all enemies becomes solidly concrete. For nearly all, misgivings felt throughout the summer are simple jitters—an internal line of questioning which fades as confidence builds and shock dissipates. For a small handful, however, the doubts will do more than linger. Continuing to grow, they will eventually overwhelm them. Realizing the military lifestyle is not what they have imagined or hoped, they will ask to resign, quickly finding themselves bobbing in the wake as their shipmates steam into the future.

All eight companies of cadets stand at attention on the parade field. The Guidons have earned the honor of carrying the company standard, a swallow-tailed guidon.

Portrait of an Officer

According to Nicholas Mynuk, the instructional system specialist for the Academy's Cadet Training Department, the Coast Guard's relatively small size sets it apart from the other armed services. The Coast Guard, in particular, cannot afford to have narrowly specialized officers:

In the Marine Corps, every marine is a rifleman. Every Coastie, prior to their first fleet assignment, has been exposed to firearms and has the opportunity to qualify, so if that time does come, there may only be a need for some refresher training to bring that person online to fulfill their new mission. But that's one thing with the Coast Guard; they're very multi-faceted. There are not enough

54

people to do the jobs. You can't be that specialized. When you do that, you not only limit the promotion opportunities, you limit the Service.

To confirm that this is true, one need only ask career officers what positions they have held. Although the average citizen may work for a half a dozen companies over his or her lifetime, the job positions themselves are, for the most part, much the same from one employer to the next. Bankers seldom become sports writers or start building houses. Coast Guard officers, on the other hand, may always work for the same company, but their résumés read more like job-description catalogues. Duty rotations, which come generally three years apart, consistently point them toward new horizons. To ensure success, officers head back to school to acquire the specialized knowledge they need to complete new tasks. These schools may be Coast Guard operations, private universities, or other military academies. An officer may train to lead boarding parties at sea or may earn a PhD in advanced statistical analysis. Having well-rounded officers allows the Coast Guard to tackle new situations in a rapidly changing world.

While at the Academy for the summer, I spoke with many officers holding a variety of positions within the school's hierarchy. For the most part, I did not single out particular officers; I simply asked any I bumped into during my wanderings whether they would be willing to chat. I typically began the conversations by asking why they had joined the Coast Guard and what route had brought them to New London. Their careers were, in a word, astounding. For Coast Guard officers, the one constant seems to be change. Captain John O'Connor serves as one example. While there may be no typical career, O'Connor's accomplishments demonstrate the flexibility that is demanded of all career officers.

Captain John O'Connor, Commandant of Cadets

Captain John O'Connor, at the time of the interview, was the commandant of cadets at the Academy, a position comparable to that of the dean of students at a civilian college. Although he did not come from a military family, O'Connor had an uncle who served

two tours in Vietnam. Growing up in Rhode Island, O'Connor had planned to enlist for one four-year tour before becoming a police officer. He described his circuitous path to the position of commandant of cadets after enlistment:

I graduated from boot camp in Cape May. I was a typical Rhode Islander, where if you go to Connecticut, you pack a lunch; you go to Massachusetts, you pack a lunch. I'd never even been on a plane before I enlisted and went to boot camp. After Cape May, I got orders to Honolulu. I came home for a few days' leave and then got on a plane and flew out to Hawaii. I was on the Coast Guard cutter MALLOW, which was a 180' buoy tender. We worked the South Pacific and the Hawaiian Island chain for aids to navigation. Was on board there for about a year, and then got orders to Quartermaster and Signalman A School (we don't have either of those ratings anymore). I finished those schools, made 3rd class petty officer, and went on independent duty to the WHITE LUPINE, which was a 133' buoy tender out of Rockland, Maine, so I learned how to navigate in the Gulf of Maine. That was a great tour. I learned a lot; you had to mature quickly.

I finished that job and went to the Captain of the Port, Providence, Rhode Island, where I was in charge of the Marine Environmental Response Desk: oil spills, hazardous chemical releases, that sort of thing. I made chief petty officer in 1983 and went to the Coast Guard cutter BIBB out of New Bedford, Massachusetts, which was a 327' high-endurance cutter, and now a reef in Key Largo. After decommissioning that ship, I went to the Coast Guard cutter EVERGREEN out of New London, so I was back in New London. On both of those ships, I was the underway OOD, in-port OOD, boarding officer, boarding-team member, and assistant navigator—that sort of thing.

Then, I came here to the Academy to be the drug-and-alcohol-education specialist. That was something I was really looking forward to—not so much to be the drug-and-alcohol-education specialist, but to have contact with cadets. At that time, we didn't have company chiefs, so there was limited exposure of cadets to senior enlisted people. It was an opportunity for me to be a role model to them as to what they could expect from senior enlisted people. I did that, and I made senior chief while I was here. I only had eleven years of service, so I said, "Okay, now what? I'm going to hang out, make master chief, and retire?" I was at the top of the pyramid, if you will, in the enlisted community. So I applied to Officer Candidate School, got accepted, and graduated in December of 1989.

I went to my fifth ship, which was the CAMPBELL, a 270' cutter out of New Bedford, Massachusetts. I was first lieutenant on her, and she was the first ship I had been on built after 1942, and the first ship I had been on that had a flight deck, so those were a couple of things that made it interesting. I left there to come back here to teach in professional maritime studies. I taught nautical science over in Yeaton Hall—did that for two and a half years—and then we stood up a leadership program, and I was asked by the commandant of cadets to move over and be part of that, so I did that for another couple of years. I was selected for lieutenant, and command of Station New London, right down the river, and did that for three years. Then, I was selected for graduate school, to come back to the Academy to serve in the faculty in the Department of Humanities. I went to Harvard University and finished a master's in education, a certificate of advanced studies in human development and psychology, and my doctorate in human development and psychology. I wrote my dissertation while I was here.

Left here in three years and went to be aide-de-camp to the commandant in Washington, DC, and was there when we made the transition from the Department of Transportation to the Department of Homeland Security. I served in that position for two full years and then went up to assume command of Group Boston. I was the group commander there for a year, was part of the sectorization process, and became the deputy sector commander in Boston for a year before coming back here to become the chief of the Officer Candidate School from 2006 to 2009.

I was then selected to go to senior service school at the Naval War College and ended up with another master's degree in national security and strategic studies. After that, I came back here again

to be the commandant of cadets. I've been here two years now, and I'll head up to Boston to be the sector commander next.

There being frequent turnover of military staff at the Academy, I asked O'Connor about continuity problems and the reasoning behind short deployments. He had this to say:

It's nice to have corporate knowledge, and that corporate knowledge typically resides within our civilian population in the Coast Guard. I think the rotations keep it fresh, keep new ideas coming in. It allows officers to retool. For example, my job is the equivalent of a vice president of student affairs—dean of students—at any other college or university, but I'm also in charge of the professional development of the cadets, so if I don't have recent operational experience, then I'm probably less prepared to do that well. The idea is to rotate, get some operational experience, and then come back into the training environment or staff positions. You can't serve any of those positions well if you don't really know what's happening at the pointy end of the spear.

Whereas a civilian college may stagnate with professors whose entire careers have taken place within the institution, the Academy has never had that problem. Continual change is generally considered beneficial from the military's viewpoint. Lieutenant Kehlenbach notes, however, that the Academy does routinely employ civilians in those positions where constant turnover would prove disruptive:

There are some civilian faculty—like the dean is a civilian. Some of the people who are the course writers or curriculum writers are civilians. All the secretarial staff and administrative support staff are civilians. That's true of the Coast Guard in general. There's 30 percent turnover every year, so in the command centers, they've civilianized a couple of the search-and-rescue-coordinator positions to maintain that continuity. The Coast Guard has a tendency to put people in a position to see one, do one, teach one. So the first time around you would observe, the second time you would execute, the third time you would be training your relief. So the first year I came in, I was observing, asking questions: "Why do we do it that way?" Not being an Academy grad, I didn't know what all the traditions were. Asking a lot of questions: "What's the relevancy? Why are we doing it? Are we doing it because it's always been done that way, or are we doing it with a purpose?" That is how I came into it, but the person who is actually running it has had that experience of seeing it a year before, at a minimum.

The concept Kehlenbach describes ("see one, do one, teach one") is a major component in the Academy's training program for cadets, as well. Swabs move from the bottom of the cadet ladder to the top over the course of four years at the Academy, then start climbing a new ladder as ensigns when they join the fleet. Although his duties were soon to change, O'Connor described his then-current role at the Academy:

I'm responsible for the wellness, professional development, and good order and discipline of the corps of cadets. I oversee their cadet activities, club activities, and social activities, as well as their professional development, whether it's on the waterfront or on the range with rifles and pistols. It can be navigation or military customs, courtesies, and traditions—those sorts of things. That's all in my purview, as well as their leadership development. We do that in a number of different ways, and that's a shared responsibility across all members of the United States Coast Guard Academy.

What we really provide in the commandant of cadets division is practicums. They learn some things in the classroom, then they bring it back to Chase Hall, and we put them in leadership positions where they practice that leadership responsibility they have. It could be in the simulator, where you're the conning officer of a ship, or you may be the navigator, the nav-plotter, or what have you—again, practicums with regard to what the expectations are—standing the watch on the quarter deck, standing the watch in the wing area, being in charge of colors in the morning, or being part of the colors detail and what your responsibilities are in contributing to that team. So it's all about first providing theoretical background, providing the information that people need in order to carry out a task, and then providing practicums to allow people to practice them. Then, of course, there is a reflective pro-

Captain John O'Connor

cess: How well did that go? What refinements do I need to make? Then, we try it all over again.

It's all about creating a foundation on which to build more complex tasks, so we want that foundation to be solid, recognizing that as you become more senior in the corps of cadets, and then more senior as an officer in the Coast Guard, bigger things are going to be required of you. Are you ready to answer the call, and are you ready to step up and be able to do those things well? That's why the foundational piece is so important. As a developmental psychologist, which is what I am by education, this is all about transformation, it's all about development, it's all about providing those opportunities for growth and development.

Cadets, assuming they survive their four years at the Academy, will graduate as ensigns. In most cases, they will board ships to serve their first tours of duty as part of the working Coast Guard. O'Connor points out, however, that this pattern has changed somewhat in recent years:

Most all go to ships, and if we could still send all to ships, we would. Two thousand four was the first year where we had to deviate from that, and it's really because of the number of graduates we have and minimally manned ships. With the new cutters coming out, we need fewer people to operate them. There isn't always enough space on the ships we have to put all of our graduates on board. If we could, we would, and that was a mandate from the commandant, to maximize that exposure. That said, we've had to allow some individuals to go directly to flight school. That is not the preference. The preference would be to have someone have a two-year float experience before going to flight school, and that's what we did in the past.

We also have a few who will go directly to sectors right out of the Academy. The vast majority, about 85 percent, will go to ships. That doesn't close any doors. If you go to a ship right out of the Academy, all doors remain open. If you do something different, doors start to close. One of the things we always talk to young people about, when making those decisions, is keeping all doors open as long as they can. Somebody may know that they really don't want to go to sea. If they really know they don't want to go to sea, then they probably should pursue something else. If they don't know if they want to go to sea, than they should go, because they may find out that they love it, and often do.

They may end up anywhere. You can stay on ships your whole career, if that's what you want to do, but people make different decisions. There are a lot of opportunities, so people find, after a ship tour, they can go to another ship tour, whether it's becoming an

executive officer or a commanding officer of a patrol boat. They could be an operations officer on a large cutter, or an engineer on a larger ship, so there are a lot of opportunities to stay afloat if that's what you want for your career track. People also end up going to staff positions and sometimes, in those staff positions, they find some other passion they want to follow. The aviation piece may be something that they want to do, so they go and do that later on. Individuals can go into the sector community, so they can be response officers in a sector, or they can be prevention officers. A lot of our engineers could go and be marine inspectors, for example, in the marine-safety field, and those are all really rewarding and viable career tracks.

Grad-school opportunities—sometimes that will dictate where you go. For example, if you get an MBA, you may end up in the finance world. Again, the best way to remain promotable is to have a solid operational track which interests you, whether it's afloat, in-sector, or aviation, and you need to do that as a touchstone as you do other things. You need to keep going back to be re-inoculated, if you will, to get some recency of experience in operations, and then go back and do some of those other things for which you have a passion. If you do that well, then you can have a very long and successful career.

You get a little bit more versatility than you might in some of the other services—in education, for one. In the Navy, you need to stay in operations. If you're not in operations, you're not doing the things you need to do to remain promotable. We in the Coast Guard really value education, so it is not a knock on your career to go to graduate school and get advanced degrees, which can allow you to serve whatever unit you're trying to serve better. We see that as a very positive thing in our organization. You're able to do joint tours, you're able to do the operational tours. It tends to be very rewarding for individuals who want to pursue advanced graduate work.

When asked if Coast Guard officers differ much from their counterparts in other branches, O'Connor had this to say:

I think they look the same. At the core, there are more similarities than differences. Our missions are different, so when I talk to young people about whether or not they should come to the Coast Guard Academy, if this should be their choice for a college education, one of the things I talk about is the fact that you can get a great education at any of the federal service academies—a great education, bar none—and it's going to serve you well for the rest of your life. The bottom line is, when you graduate: Is that service doing the missions that you are interested in? If you want to fly, then there are a lot of options. If you want to sail submarines, then there is only one option. Do you want to do what the Army does? Then go to West Point. Do you want to do what the Navy does? Then go to Annapolis. Do you want what the Air Force does? Then go to the Air Force Academy. Many of those things the Coast Guard also does, and there's a lot of other things the Coast Guard does that the other Services don't. What young people need to really think about is: What does the Service do? I'm going to get a great education no matter where I go, but what does the Service do, and is that what I want to do when I graduate? That's the way to make the decision, but at the core, more similarities than differences across the Services.

Looking back over his career so far, O'Connor had no regrets:

It's been a great ride. It's been absolutely wonderful, and I think that's the thing that keeps you interested. If I were in the same job for any long period of time, I think it would bore the heck out of me. You're ready after three years to move on, to do the next thing, and I think that's what keeps you interested.

Cadre are trained during 100ᵗʰ Week by instructors from the Coast Guard's Cape May facility. These instructors train all personnel entering the ranks of the enlisted.

The Cadre

Cadre\ 'kad-rē\ n. 1) Frame, framework. 2) The nucleus of trained professional officers or service members, able to assume control and forming the basis for the training of new units or other military expansion.

Despite receiving top billing in the title chosen for the summer's drama, swabs comprise just half of the players on the stage. It may be called swab summer, but the training that occurs is just as important for the cadre. The cadre's first leadership experience is as vital to them as the indoctrination is to the swabs. It takes the participation of both groups to make the summer a success—one group playing the role of leaders; the other, of followers. To Lieutenant LuAnn Kehlenbach, the goal for both parties is clear:

For the swabs, it's to be indoctrinated into the Coast Guard. At the end of their training period, they are ready to be a 4th class cadet and a member of the corps. For the cadre, it's an opportunity for them to practice their leadership skills and to be both a mentor and a role model, and it's their job to make sure those swabs are ready to become 4th class.

Although clearly defined goals exist, Senior Chief McDade points out that not everyone may fully understand or appreciate them:

The goal is that they reach all their training milestones. The milestones are set week by week, but it's basic military indoctrination. For cadre, it's: "Don't expect them to show up and know everything." If they knew everything that was in the RUNNING LIGHT—which is essentially their goal—if they knew all those things, we wouldn't need that program. For each week, it's outlined how much of that swabs are supposed to know. They are inundated with knowledge and put into a stressful situation where they have to use that knowledge, much like being an officer in the military. Eventually, if they become the CO of a ship and can't regurgitate that information in a stressful environment, they're going to fail. That's the reasoning behind it; that's the background. You need to be able to perform in a high-stress environment, and swab summer is definitely high stress, at least for most. Everybody has a different stress threshold, and as company chiefs, we see the full gamut. There are many swabs who didn't really know what to expect. I've talked to swabs after the summer who had no idea. They thought it was: "Oh, I'll just go and sit in a class, they'll teach me about uniforms and rank, and then I'm going to start school and everything is going to be rainbows and unicorns." Then, you have those who really have a good idea of what's going to happen, and there is less of a shock factor for them. It might still be intense, but they knew it was coming.

Indoctrination techniques may have changed over the years, but as the commandant of cadets, Captain John O'Connor, sees it, the objectives have remained the same:

Things have changed over the years. I went through boot camp in the seventies and society was different, the military was different, the concept of training and development was different. The similarity in the goal is the same, and that is to transition people out of civilian life to military life. So, really, what you do is you train to the lowest common denominator. For example, in boot camp, we had individuals who had prior service, but you don't train to those individuals. You have to train to the individual who is brand-new, just out of high school, who has no exposure to the military at all, and then you hope that some of those individuals who had prior service are there to help mentor the others along. They will jell as a team more quickly and then move together in a positive way in the right direction in terms of their development. So that's similar, because you end up with individuals here with prior enlisted experience, and those individuals become part of a class that comes through the Academy. And, really, that swab summer experience, like the boot camp experience, is to take individuals—raw material coming out of civilian life—and in just a few short weeks, make them ready to join the corps of cadets when they return in the fall.

Senior Chief McDade is the enlisted officer in charge of Alpha Company.

It's the military focus: understanding what our core values are, how to wear the uniform properly, having a sense of pride in the heritage of the United States Coast Guard and its history so they feel like a member. When the corps comes back, the swabs are on stage. They need to perform—show the upperclassmen they're worthy of joining the corps of cadets. That's really the emphasis, and it's the same emphasis in boot camp. You're not coming out of there with any real proficiency, and you don't come out of swab summer with any real proficiency, other than wearing the uniform well, maybe doing some military customs and courtesies, that type of thing. It's really building the foundation on which to build more complex tasks as they mature through their cadet career. This is the same as an individual who's coming out of boot camp, now going to a unit where he or she is going to be expected to do the Coast Guard mission. When they're doing the Coast Guard mission, they can't be worried about how to wear the uniform.

One of the things I talk to my staff about all the time is that swab summer is not the hard part. The hard part is when you're going to have to do academics on top of all the military things that were required of you all summer. That's the hard part. So learning it well enough, not having to worry about it when you're actually in the midst of the academic semester, is really the goal. After swab summer, the military part tails off quite a bit. Of course you get squaring of meals, bracing up, no talking in the passageway; those sorts of things that were there in swab summer are the same sorts of things that go into the academic year. It's a very difficult, emotional, physical, and academic year as a 4th class as well, but if it were easy, everybody would do it. It is a badge of honor, if you will, as you move through the cadet system and the officer corps; it's a common experience that you have endured with your classmates and share with other Academy graduates.

As banners around the campus remind both visitors and cadets, the Academy creates leaders. O'Connor continues:

We say in some of our literature the idea is to educate, develop, train, and inspire leaders of character, and that's really what we're trying to do from day one, and we do that in many different ways.

That begins to happen as soon as they get off the bus and start their indoctrination process. The haircut, the uniform issue, all of those things are meant to build pride in individuals. It's the education, training, development, and inspiration of leaders of character. It's a transformational process. It looks more transactional in the summer, where people feel like, "I need to do this to avoid punishment or do this to get rewarded," but I think that's necessary at the infancy of someone's career in order to make that transition from being a civilian to being in the military.

For O'Connor, success comes as cadets move beyond the transactional:

That said, after swab summer, this can be much more transformational, and the idea there is to make sure we are instilling the core values in the individual. We want individuals to be intrinsically motivated to do things because they understand it is the right thing to do, instead of doing it because of the fear of consequence, or even because of consequence. The consequences may be good, and if that's your motivator, then that's not really where we're trying to go either. We want them to act in a certain way because they understand it's the right thing to do. So part of what we do, and we have the luxury of doing this in a training environment, is to explain the why of what it is we want them to do; to give them a sense of why this is important so they can begin to internalize those values.

You can't always do that in an operational environment, because sometimes it's an emergency and you just need to respond. But what people need to understand is that if there is time to explain the why, people are typically going to explain the why, and when they are demanding something of you up front, it's probably because it's an emergency. They understand they need to respond immediately and the explanation will come later. At the Academy, we have the luxury of explaining the why up front in a training environment and we take advantage of that.

Swab summer is just the beginning of a very long process, a process that does not necessarily end after four years in New London.

Commander Haukom, who oversees cadet military training, discusses the process of character development at the Academy:

I have to make sure they get this now in addition to all the other things we have to do (teach them how to march, how to follow orders, how to wear a uniform, and all that). We gradually build it up from there into the professional training, the leadership training. Honor is the thing we're really starting to focus on this week. Honor training, ethics training—it's a gradual process. With the 4th class we start off with basic stuff: What does honor mean? What does it mean to us as military officers? It's more than just not lying, cheating, or attempting to deceive. It's certainly that, but there's a little bit more to it as well, so let's talk about what else honor means to a military officer. We lay the foundation, and we build up from there. This leadership development training progresses over the 200-week continuum, and my piece is just a small part. They get this on the academic side, they get it on the professional development side, and within the Cadet Division in the military training realm, we have our own piece of character and leadership development to work on. So it's a progressive curriculum that culminates during their 1st class year when they are holding leadership positions within the corps. We take them right up to that point. You started off as a teenager, not knowing how to put your uniform on, and now here we are four years later, and you've led the corps of cadets, and you're about to receive your commission and head to an operational Coast Guard unit and lead real Coast Guard members.

As in all military organizations, there is a distinct chain of command. Links high on the chain are responsible for and oversee the links below them. Oversight is critical, and swab summer is no exception. Captain John O'Connor explains:

Swab summer is for both the swabs and the cadre, and I think it's critically important to the development of both. The cadre—and they take their positions very, very seriously—know that they have

the responsibility to develop the incoming class. They also recognize that it's an opportunity for them, as a practicum, to practice the leadership techniques they've learned over time and bring those to bear in the development of these young people, so it's crucial to both. Now, there is oversight of course. You get 1st class cadets and a regimental staff that have oversight. We have company chiefs for every company that have oversight above them, and then senior staff who are involved in that process as well. So they are practicums with practicum supervisors. The swabs are supervised by the cadre; cadre, supervised by 1st class; 1st class, supervised by the C-Division staff; and it's a growth opportunity for all.

As O'Connor implies, cadre may represent a discrete link in the chain of supervision, but the leadership training they receive begins well before the swabs' arrival on R-Day. Whether they realize it or not, cadre have been preparing for their new position since their very own bus rides up the Hill to Chase. Likewise, the moment cadre begin indoctrinating the new swabs, they begin shaping the swabs' own ideas about how they, in turn, will lead as cadre in two years' time. Each class is preparing to assume the duties and responsibilities of the one above while simultaneously molding those below. Nor does this process end on graduation day.

Life for Coast Guard officers is a set of continuously expanding circles, like the ripples created when one tosses a rock into a pond. Just as each ripple encircles a greater area as it emanates away from its singular point of origin, each new assignment in an officer's career should introduce new skill sets, widen responsibilities, and build overall knowledge. Should these circles cease to expand, the officer's career is often considered to be over.

Cadre march to the beat of the same drummer, casting harsh shadows along Bear Drive beneath an unfiltered sun.

Polished Boots

Lacking personal exposure to the military process, I questioned officers about the effectiveness of having inexperienced 2nd class cadets indoctrinate swabs. My initial mistake was in thinking the summer is exclusively about these new recruits. As I quickly learned, it is as much about the personal growth and training of cadre. As is often stated, the most effective way to learn a job is to do the job, and this philosophy saturates Coast Guard practice throughout the ranks. Cadets have to begin leading at some point, and where better to begin than in a controlled, non-operational environment under the watchful eyes of experience? Swab summer effectively kills two birds with a single stone. Bringing in professionals, such as the company commanders from Cape May, might very well produce the best possible results in the shortest period of time, but it would also eliminate the first real leadership test cadets have the opportunity to face. And although cadre might not be able to mold incoming swabs quite as effectively as would enlisted personnel, this is only the first seven weeks of the cadets' 200-week training program. The goals set for each experience are necessarily different, and both work well.

Beginning with R-Day, every experience at the Academy has been carefully designed to prepare cadets for the leadership positions they will later assume. The sophistication of this design may go unnoticed by the casual observer, but it should not come as a surprise. After all, military academies have been creating officers for hundreds of years. They have had time to both study and perfect the process, and while many things have changed over the centuries, the basic principles remain much the same. Placing 2nd class cadets in charge of the incoming class is an obvious example of a preparatory experience, but more subtle leadership opportunities abound. Outwardly, it may seem that swabs do nothing more than follow orders during the indoctrination process. For the first few days, this may even be true; they spend the majority of their time learning to follow, not lead. Embedded within the most mundane tasks of a swab's day, however, lie opportunities. Take, for instance, the polishing of boots.

If, like me, you have polished shoes perhaps a dozen or so times in your life, you might consider the action too trivial to note. Spit and polish beautify military formations, but do they win battles? Perhaps they do. The quickest way to make someone feel like part of something larger is to hand him a uniform, be it the operational dress uniform of a Coast Guard cadet or the shredded jeans and t-shirts of a New London youth. It undoubtedly takes more than a cotton uniform and leather footwear to make an officer, but a well-polished boot makes for a good first step.

Glistening boots lend troops a feeling of precision and competence, and uniformity enhances the sense of belonging to an elite group. The experience of polishing boots together promotes camaraderie between bunkmates, among classmates, and throughout the Corps. Moreover, teaching cadets to take pride in their work, regardless of any particular task's importance, yields further benefits down the road. After all, losing a ship for want of a simple plug is as bad as, if not worse than, losing it for want of a working engine.

Most swabs have no idea how to polish a boot to military standards, but there are the few among them who do. They may have learned from their parents or in their high schools' Junior ROTC programs. Cadre take advantage of this small window of opportunity, as 2/C Paul Delesola from Golf Company explains:

We always look to give the high-performing swabs leadership roles. If we have one swab who's good at shining boondockers, I expect the entire division's boondockers to look that good. That swab now leads others in the company; we really put that type of pressure on the high-performing swabs. If someone is not performing well, we'll pair them up as roommates. We'll put a high-performing swab and a low-performing swab together, and if the low-performing swab messes up, we'll go to the high-performing swab and ask, "Why didn't you help him out? He's your roommate. Why didn't you check his uniform before he came out of the room?" If someone is really high-performing, we don't just praise them for being a high-performer. We go to them and ask, "Why isn't everyone like you? Why aren't you helping everyone else out? This is a team, and if you don't succeed as a team, you also fail as individuals." That's the biggest thing I think swab summer teaches them, and I think that so far, Golf Company has done a great job. There are a lot of really high-performing swabs, and we make it very clear to them we expect them to help their shipmates and that there is a different weight on their shoulders. I think a lot of them understand that process and understand the importance of it. They're really starting to come together.

Delesola notes that they apply these same lessons to nearly all tasks:

We did rack remedials, where we had them all take their sheets off their beds and then gave them a certain amount of time to make their racks. After they made their racks, we went around and

65

we picked the best room we could find and we said, "Every rack should look this good. If one person in the company can do it, there is no excuse for everyone in the company not being able to do it. That one person should be showing all of the other swabs how to do it." I think they began to realize that during the school year this will make a really big difference. Everything we teach them they are going to need to get through the next year.

Swabs receive small leadership opportunities on the ropes course, in math class, and even during IT sessions throughout the summer. When they themselves become cadre, they are expected to pass their accumulated experience on to the new group of swabs. Despite its seeming insignificance, the first step along the road to becoming an admiral begins in a polished boot.

Commander Haukom related a story concerning his indoctrination process at OCS. He had forgotten to shave before heading out the door for the morning's inspection. His roommate, perfectly shaven, was torn apart by their commanding officer and IT'd. Haukom was ordered to stand by and watch his shipmate suffer the consequences of his own failure. Although Haukom himself had erred, the commanding officer saw the greater offense in one shipmate's neglect of another. It was a lesson Haukom never forgot, a mistake he never repeated. This method was used to train 2/C Stephanie Jocis as a swab, and she uses the same lesson to train her swabs, telling them:

Always be looking out for each other. If you can do something more quickly than someone else, go help them. If you're done changing, help your shipmates with their canteen belt. If someone messes up and has to hold out their water bottle, another swab will put their hand underneath to help hold it up. You can see them supporting each other a lot more than before. That's the biggest thing in the Coast Guard; it's all teamwork, it's all supporting one another. Everyone is going to need help. Everyone has different strengths, different weaknesses, and it's learning how to work with others and make the organization better altogether. Helping their shipmates get on the same page gives them a leadership role amongst themselves. That's been really effective.

Lieutenant Commander Michael Thomas had already served in the Coast Guard as enlisted before enrolling in the Academy. Because of his age and experience, he often knew more than the cadre; his only choice was to bite his tongue. Although sometimes frustrated, he used his previous experience to help his shipmates navigate unfamiliar waters. They, in turn, reciprocated:

As far as making the rack, shining the shoes, doing the pushups, that wasn't as big an issue for me. It was more the mental side I think for me. I remember it was hot and humid. They helped me with the memory techniques, remembering all of the indoc stuff you had to remember, and I would help check their uniforms before they went out, make sure they were all lined up, could help make beds, teach them the tricks I'd learned for shining shoes over the years. It was kind of a barter system: you help me get ready for the indoc test, and I'll help you get your room ready for inspection. There were a lot more of us priors coming through at one time then there are now.

You kind of took it upon yourself to take the heat. One of us would be, "Okay, I'll go down the hallway and find out what's on the schedule next." That's the game; a freshman goes down the hallway, and everyone wants to stop him. So you took it upon yourself to do it. Or you go down one way, and while everyone yells at you, the others run the other way. I think the cadre expect you to set an example when you're older and you've been through this. I'd like to say all of us were mature about this and we handled it well, but that's not the truth. There's some of us that probably brought more hate and discontent with our mouths than we probably should have. When I came through, there were thirteen of us that were around here for swab summer, and we were a cross-section. There were some of us who were locked on. They knew it was a game, and treated it like a game, and it didn't bother them to do a hundred pushups a day.

Life at the Academy, indeed life as a Coast Guard officer, centers around responsibility. Individuals are accountable for their own actions and are held responsible both to and for the larger community. In the first few days of the summer, swabs struggle to keep

Soon to be leading swabs as members of the cadre, 3/C Cadets Bishop, Harvey, and Lowary attend classes taught by the Leadership Development Center.

their own heads above water. They learn to answer all questions and follow all commands. They learn to wear their uniforms correctly and to keep their eyes in the boat at all times. Within a few short days, however, many begin to take on responsibility for their roommates: Is her bed made properly? Did he grab his cover as he headed out the door? Do they know the meals for the day?

Cadets' primary concern may be to follow others during their first academic year, but they also learn to operate as a team and to help their shipmates. Even as 4th class, they have significant responsi-

bilities. Civilians typically take on what they feel they can handle; cadets are given more than they possibly could. The differences between college life and cadet life are growing more stark. According to the National Center for Education Statistics, nearly 60 percent of all full-time students in bachelor's-degree programs now take six years to complete their college educations. The enormous amount of trust and responsibility cadets are given is well illustrated by the cadre's role during the summer. To further prepare them, cadre participate in something called 100th Week.

Company Commander Chase, a Cape May drill instructor, practices his one-armed pushups while simultaneously correcting 3/C Jennifer Patron's technique.

100th Week

There is no question that cadets receive informal leadership training at every opportunity, but in no way does their preparation end there. They also take prescribed leadership classes and train formally throughout their time in New London. One such formal training comes toward the end of the cadets' 3rd class, or sophomore, year. It is called "100th Week."

100th Week takes place over the course of five days (namely, the students' hundredth week at the Academy), during which time the Academy is said to "train the trainers." It is an intensive refresher course, a review of all of the leadership skills they have learned over the past two years. A few short weeks later, their second academic year will end and they will rise from 3rd class to 2nd class cadets, assuming their first duties as cadre.

Nicholas Mynuk, who retired as a chief warrant officer after twenty-one years of service, worked as a Department of Defense contractor before coming to the Academy to assume his new role:

I am the instructional system specialist—capturing cadet military training, in a standardized, Coast Guard format. That's my first task, and then we'll go through updating and streamlining the material, making it a little more measurable in the end. Hopefully, we'll have a product that can be certified for military-science credits on the backside when the students graduate. Along with their academic degree, they may also have so many credits towards a military-science degree as well. That would place value on their time marching out on the parade field, gathering those skills in leadership in credits.

Mynuk explains 100th Week as follows:

Our 100th Week program is our main focus this time of year. We split the corps of cadets, and we have our 2nd class cadets go off to their summer programs, and our 3rd class cadets transitioning into 2nd class cadets, whom we call the cadre. They basically run our swab summer. The entire class is part of the cadre, but not all cadre deal with the swabs here at the Academy. There are five different cadre groups, such as Waterfront Cadre, Chase Hall Cadre, EAGLE Cadre, CGAS, and AIM Cadre—which is a program where high-school students spend a few days here at the Academy and get a little taste of swab summer—and a couple of others. So they are broken up into different types of cadre, but all of those cadre receive similar training during the 100th Week transition program.

The 100th Week program this year follows a three-prong approach. We have five days of military training: we do two days of leadership-and-management refresher training here at the Academy, which focuses on communications, peer leadership, and team-building skills, and then they move to a hands-on application of the skills at a nearby National Guard military reservation. Here, they apply these skills in three different areas. We start with a leaders' reaction course. This is basically a cinder-block building with open walls and open ceilings. Students work out physical chal-

lenges where they must get people and objects from one side of a barrier to another without touching the ground, by only using this pipe or that two-by-four to solve the problem. They are evaluated in their changing roles as leaders or as followers.

Secondly, we have a land-navigation course. We set scenarios where the students are following maps within a specific time limit, from one place to another, using back roads out in the woods in Niantic. They may come across an injured person. They will have to address the person's needs. They've all been trained in first aid, and they'll have to transport that person to a specific location. There may be a drug-interdiction scenario, where they'll find a substance they need to test, take custody of, and move to another location. This is all happening while successfully transitioning these back roads. This helps them put some of their navigational, map-reading, and leadership skills into play. It's also a good way for us to get a group of people from one place to another without wasting time.

That's when they'll start on their third challenge, the events-confidence course. This is essentially an obstacle course. It's there for them to overcome their fears and to work as a team, letting those dynamics come out. All three of these are part of the final two days of the 100th Week training, actually putting what they have learned as a student in a leadership class to use in the field. That's what we want them to get out of it.

Elite instructors from the Coast Guard's main training facility in Cape May, New Jersey, come to the Academy to train the cadre. The classic Hollywood drill sergeant is modeled after just such men and women. They are the living embodiment of spit and polish, and even the "Smokey the Bear" covers they wear, slanting forward over their eyes, bristle with attitude. Back in Cape May, their job is to convert recruits entering the Service as enlisted personnel into operationally effective seamen who will be ready for their first assignments in eight weeks. Mynuk continues:

These company commanders are the cream of the crop, and they come here to rekindle military attitudes. Sitting in a college class-

room, with two years between being a swab themselves and taking on this central training role, they may have become rusty on a few things: how to stand up straight, how to march properly, and other manners of military dress. We have these company commanders come up and train the trainers. First, they're going to spark their interest with some spirited interactions. After those interactions, they are going to work through other areas: rekindling military attitudes, inspections, and close-order drill, which is marching and the manual of arms with rifles. Then they will go over the Academy's incentive training, which is a tool that is used here and in Cape May to get people focused. Those are our main goals for that week. At the end of the week, students will transition from a red collar device to a white collar device, which essentially transitions them to 2ⁿᵈ class cadets, ready to take on their duties and responsibilities. A big part of swab summer is boot camp, and who do you want running boot camp? You want our professionals who train to the military standards of the United States Marine Corps. We try to tie back all that we do to a reference that is rock-solid, that can't be disputed.

Our main focus is to get the cadre ready. They are in a difficult position, because they are not cadre yet and the swabs are not 4ᵗʰ class cadets. After swab summer, swabs transition to 4ᵗʰ class— green collar devices, no stripes on their shoulder boards. They are the focus. Everybody needs to lead them, but 3ʳᵈ class folks already know what they need to do and they're just going through their paces. But you move up to your 2ⁿᵈ class, and they're doing all the leading, primarily with the 4ᵗʰ class. Of course, your firsties, the seniors, with blue on their collars, they're already focusing on the future; they're going to be graduating in May. We're moving those 3ʳᵈ class to 2ⁿᵈ class to build their leadership skills, to be able to effectively administer swab summer, and to begin the transition into corps leaders.

Of course, the new cadre are not left entirely on their own. Regardless of rank, high or low, there is always oversight. Mynuk describes it this way:

It's like the man- or woman-behind-the-curtain thing. We have barracks personnel, company chiefs, who oversee their companies. They are present at all times during those ramped up, heavy-duty periods of training in the advisor position and for safety. They assure adherence to policy if some of the cadre start veering from established standards. We do prepare cadre, but Academy staff are in charge of their companies and make sure things go right, according to policy. They address any issues right then and there, well before they get out of hand.

Although most cadre relish the idea of finally being in charge, many approach the task with some trepidation. Despite the formal and informal training they have received over two years, cadre may initially feel unequal to the task. In most cases, however, any lingering doubts soon vanish. Collin Shembry, now an ensign heading to flight school, remembers his initial apprehension very well:

We had a lot of trainings in the weeks leading into swab summer, but many of us still had those doubts: Were we ready? I was in Cadre II , so the swabs had a full week with the first cadre section before we came in, and we were able to learn from their mistakes. I was still a little apprehensive about whether or not I was ready and if I could do everything the way it was supposed to be done while appearing to be perfect. That apprehension was gone probably within ten minutes of actually being out there. I remember being shaky as we were about to go out and do our cadre relief in front of the swabs and give our little speeches. I was nervous for that, but then we sent them to their rooms and made them do something, and the switch was on. What had happened ten minutes ago was completely forgotten—totally into it. It's something where you don't really think about how much you already do know about things. Of course, what makes it easy is that the swabs know nothing and you have all the answers to their simple questions.

For 2/C Joseph Trump, it was not until after 100ᵗʰ Week that he began to feel more comfortable with his upcoming role as a leader:

Before 100th Week, I felt like I had no idea at all. I was completely in the dark; I had no clue about anything I was going to have to do. After 100th Week, I definitely felt a lot more prepared, and that goes fully to the Cape May company commanders. They taught us as much as they possibly could in the short amount of time we had with them. They are just incredible: how much they know and how much they taught us. It was really surprising to me how much better I felt as a leader just within that one week. I don't know if I am a better leader, but I feel like I have a lot more resources and knowledge than I did before. I would say that I'm still not completely prepared, because I've never been in a situation like this before, but I probably have all the general tools I'll need to develop more in order to be successful. I'm not the first cadre; I'm in the second cadre section, so I'll have a little bit more time. I'll also be here for range week and T-boats week before I actually start, so I'll be able to watch my classmates for a little bit. I'll be able to see what they do before I actually have to do it, so that will probably help. In the evening, if the first cadre aren't with the swabs, I can probably talk to them about it. They will have to tell us what they're doing before we transition; there is a really significant pass-down of information regarding the company and the swabs and all that. The more we can talk to them, the better prepared we'll be.

2/C Cathy Durand, who was also part of Cadre II, had this to say:

The way it works this year is the first group has them for two weeks, and then we come in. I think it's going to be interesting. I know I want to be a certain way, and a lot of the people who are in my group and will be cadre with me feel the same way I do, but then you always hear the people that say, "I just want to wreck kids! I just want to tear them apart!" That has a place but shouldn't be the only thing you're thinking about. It's up to others to pull them back a little bit. Ideally, there is a lot of communication. I know my cadre told us stories afterwards; they communicated a lot, but I feel like it's easy to just be into it and ignore everyone else. Ideally, there is a lot of communication.

Until the very end of her 3rd class year, Durand also felt unprepared:

Throughout the year, in every large brief we have, they say: "In nine more months, you'll be cadre." "In five more months, you'll be cadre." They keep bringing it up, but they don't do anything about it until 100th Week. All of a sudden, it's like, "You need to know this now!" But we have prep week, which is two weeks from now, and that, I heard, will have a few more trainings for us. They've given us an SOP online, and they've given us some trainings, but we still don't know a lot of things. I was talking with my roommate last night about how there is still confusion on what certain rules mean; they've never been explained to us. I guess a lot of it is learning on the job, but hopefully a lot of it gets cleared up. There are restrictions on things like IT'ing kids. There are conflicting rules, and we don't know which one is right or what certain rules mean—what are we allowed to do to them, and what we are not allowed to do. In my mind, if it doesn't say you can't do it, then you can. But in other people's minds, if it doesn't say you can, then you can't do it. So no one really knows about that middle ground. I felt more prepared after 100th Week. I think that did help a lot, but I'm still nervous.

Whereas Durand felt uncertain about many of the details, 2/C Ryan Babb had no significant qualms:

I feel like I'm definitely prepared. The Academy prepared us pretty well, but I'm not going to lie; I'm still pretty nervous. Pretty nervous. I have a direct effect on the future of the Coast Guard by training the class of 2016. Thankfully, I don't have to do it individually. I'm going to be working with a lot of great people in my cadre section and within my class, but it's a huge job. I'm Chase Hall Cadre. I'll have from Reporting-In Day until July 8, at which point, in the evening, the cadre will switch off. At that point, I go on leave and come back July 29. At noon, we will take over again and finish that last week, where the swabs will go into sea trials, the culminating event of swab summer, and then onto EAGLE.

100th Week: Training the Trainers

Clockwise: Some "spirited interaction" between Cape May Company Commander Chase and one of the summer's cadre. The first day of 100th Week gives the cadre a quick reminder of what swab summer feels like to the incoming class. The rest of the week is used to refresh leadership skills cadets have been learning over the course of the past two years.

Teamwork is an essential part of Coast Guard training, and cadre are given a number of problems to solve together. In this exercise, the class finds itself on one side of a small tarp. Their task is to stand on the other side without ever touching the ground.

Cape May staff put cadre through the same exercises they will give swabs in the coming months, teaching them proper techniques and showing them how to improve the performance of their newest company members.

Clockwise: A Cape May drill instructor conducts a group review of the morning's training. Cape May staff are masters at delivering pressure without heat, turning trainer personas on and off at will. This emotional detachment is something the cadre often struggle with over the course of the summer.

A member of the cadre rejoins her company as they polish their techniques while practicing the standard manual of arms. Two years since they themselves were swabs, the finer points of many precision drill maneuvers may have dulled.

3/C Carter Schlank stands at attention in a Chase Hall courtyard under a cloudless sky. After 100th Week, most cadre feel better prepared to handle their upcoming leadership roles. The proper indoctrination of the incoming class of cadets is left in their hands.

The last two days of 100th Week involve training at a local National Guard base. Cadets are challenged individually on this obstacle course before moving on to the Leadership Reaction Course. The reaction course tests their ability to lead their peers and work as a team to accomplish specific goals. On that course, tests usually revolve around moving a group of eight to ten people from one side of an open room to the other and across physical obstacles using only a few simple tools. The third part of their training here requires cadets to navigate through densely wooded terrain and solve problems they encounter along the way, such as caring for a wounded comrade or taking custody of a stash of illegal drugs. All of their tasks are designed to refresh what they have already learned as cadets.

Clockwise: Cadre climb up and over another physical obstacle on their way to R-Day.

Using two pipes and a length of rope, cadre must get themselves and an ammunition box across this obstacle without touching the ground along the way.

Instructors from the Leadership Development Center explain the next obstacle to the cadet charged with leading her shipmates. Cadre are graded on how well they work as either team members or leaders.

A Connecticut National Guard camp provides new challenges for Coast Guard cadets seeing it all for the first time. The sounds of heavy machine gun fire and explosions from detonated mines are heard throughout the day as National Guard soldiers continue to run their own training programs. One of the cadre, while navigating through the woods, inadvertently walked into an ambush set by National Guardsmen, giving her a bit of a scare while undoubtedly amusing the soldiers.

Clockwise: 3/C Phillips works his way along the monkey bars. While these cadets are still in their 3rd class year during 100th Week, they earn their white lapel pins and become rising 2nd class cadets and cadre at the end of the spring semester.

A cadet swings herself over a log hurdle in the woods of Niantic. Many shorter cadets face additional challenges with obstacles built for taller soldiers. One cadet could walk upright beneath a log hurdle she was supposed to vault.

A group of cadets hop over the low hurdles as they race towards the end of the obstacle course.

Clockwise: 3/C Brandon Foy and fellow cadre drilling with rifles.

A cadet leads her fellow cadre members under the watchful eyes of a Cape May company commander.

Cadre also receive leadership training in the classroom during 100th Week.

I'd say the most important thing for the cadre is that they invest the time and effort into their swabs they would either have had gotten from their cadre or would have hoped to have their cadre give them. My goal, personally, is to make sure that I'm creating a better cadet than I am. That's not to say I'm a bad cadet, but I'd like to make cadets who will succeed at the Academy and make it with flying colors.

Each cadre has a unique perspective on the proper approach to the indoctrination process—a perspective which has been shaped by his or her own swab-summer experience and their own training over the intervening years. They all experienced good and bad cadre when they first arrived, and they talk about what they learned from each. Although the best way to assimilate past cadres' approaches may seem cut and dry—take the good and toss the rest—this year's cadre were strangely ambivalent about a number of the methods that they had not liked as swabs. In a surprisingly honest way, they often confessed that they would probably do many of the very same things that they themselves had not liked—doing unto others as was done unto them.

For some, the temptation to abuse their new power proves too great—just look at the number of cadre who lose their voices over the course of the summer. But yelling is easy; leading effectively is much more difficult. There is no doubt that indoctrination is, in part, about getting recruits to understand that they must do, unquestioningly, as they are told. But the Academy needs cadre to move beyond the thrill of having people jump on command, at least when there is no underlying objective. In the end, proper leadership is about driving people to achieve specific goals, not wielding power for power's sake.

Although most cadre do have a bit of fun with their newfound status, the majority quickly move on to the serious business of indoctrination. 2/C Jake Rendon believes he was able to transform his own negative swab-summer experiences into positive action as Foxtrot Cadre:

I learned from my cadre. I took the good things I saw and the bad things I saw and tried to put the good into effect. I wouldn't say

I'm doing things very differently; it's just I'm picking and choosing what I want to do. Being a swab is definitely a learning experience that goes into becoming a cadre. Sometimes your best leaders are the ones who show you what not to do. I definitely remember my experiences, and I'm trying to be the best cadre for them I can. I'm with a very good group and I'm happy with it. We never argue; we all listen to each other. We have our Taps meeting at 2200. The swabs all get to bed, and we go to the day room and read all of their thoughts of the day. We discuss the day—what went right, what went wrong, and what we can do better the next day. We'll then plan the next day: What did or didn't work? What swabs do we need to pay attention to, or what do we need to fix? We have that meeting every night to discuss it.

Each of the eight companies is led by a chief or a senior chief. These enlisted personnel are all noncommissioned officers, or NCOs. Their long journeys to reach this status began years ago at the boot camp in Cape May. Entering as seaman recruits, they rose through the ranks of seaman apprentice, seaman, and petty officer 3rd, 2nd, and 1st class before finally becoming chief petty officers. Because the competition is fierce, the real-life experience they bring to the Academy is immeasurable.

Many chiefs further their careers by leaving the ranks of the enlisted and attending the Academy's Officer Candidate School, graduating as commissioned officers. Lieutenant LuAnn Kehlenbach is one such example. Kehlenbach is the swab summer practicum officer, supervising all eight companies. Whereas a chief oversees an individual company, the lieutenant oversees the work of all eight chiefs.

As an advanced high-school student, Kehlenbach began taking college classes before her senior exams. She struggled, however, with her first attempt at college life, and she did not give it another try until after her parents retired and moved to Texas. Although her performance improved the second time around, she still had trouble staying motivated. When a classmate suggested that she look into the Coast Guard, Kehlenbach saw something she liked and enlisted. From then on, her problems staying focused vanished:

I enlisted in the Coast Guard in '94 and I graduated from boot camp in October; that was at Cape May. Since I was a little bit older—I was twenty, as opposed to the seventeen- and eighteen-year-olds who were my shipmates—I found their maturity level to be a little low. Instead of worrying about the training, they were worried about which boys were cute, and I found that a little challenging, just to get them to focus on the training. Overall, it was good training. They take you from not knowing anything to being fleet-ready in eight weeks, so it's quite a transformation.

My first unit was South Padre Island, Texas, in Port Isabelle, which is right on the border with Mexico. From there, I was selected to be the admiral's driver in District 8 , which is in New Orleans, so I spent some time driving the admiral around. It offered me some unique opportunities, such as going to the Bob Bondurant School of High Performance Driving for executive protection. All in all, it was a good tour. From there I went to Petaluma, California, for dental-assistant A-School, which is the basic training for dental techs. Back then, you had to first become a nationally registered EMT, so I had to do that as part of my training. Got orders to Cape May, New Jersey, where I spent two years helping with dental exams and dental procedures on recruits who came through Cape May. As a dental tech, you can't make E-5. There was no room for promotion or advancement, so I had to go back to Petaluma for another A-School, and that time it was for HS, or health services technician, so I learned a new trade and they gave me new orders right back to Cape May. So all told, I spent five years in Cape May working at the clinic in various capacities.

Kehlenbach's drive, ambition, and desire to progress kept her moving forward, and she obtained her master's degree along the way. Talent and hard work are usually rewarded in the Coast Guard; wishing to move from the NCO side of the equation, Kehlenbach made her next move:

From Cape May, I was fortunate enough to be selected for Officer Candidate School, which is here in New London. I came here for the seventeen weeks of basic officer training and graduated in the summer of 2002. Got orders to Group Portland, Maine, and spent

Lieutenant LuAnn Kehlenbach.

twenty-four months in Portland. From there I was transferred to Yorktown, Virginia, to the National Search and Rescue School. I spent two years teaching at the Search and Rescue School, and my last year there I was on the Command Center Standardization Team. The team travels throughout the Coast Guard going to command centers, ensuring that they're following commandant policy as far as how the center operates. From there, I spent three years in Anchorage, Alaska, standing up their sector. The Coast Guard transitioned after 9/11. They combined units that did operations and others that did marine safety into sectors. District 17, which is Alaska, didn't have any legacy groups, so it was standing up a sector where there had only been marine safety. It was quite a challenge standing up a command center from scratch, but after three years, I can say I left it better than I found it. I've been stationed here at the Academy for the last two years.

Whereas the cadre may have questions about their summer's mission and goals, the Academy does not; it measures cadre performance by swab progress. Kehlenbach elaborates:

Prior to 100th Week, the cadre have classes in leadership and organizational behavior, and they've lived it as well. For the summer, they are given weekly goals; at the end of the first week, it might be that the swabs are able to recite three meals in a row, be able to do basic facing movements, or recite the Coast Guard mission. So they have a set of objectives. That's how they move through the seven weeks. Are they meeting all those goals? The swabs are also given indoctrination quizzes to check their knowledge, so there are benchmarks along the way. There is a forty-nine day training schedule broken down by company and by what's going on. It's basically a spreadsheet, and it has each company's activities listed for every hour of the day, from the time they wake up to the time they go to bed. It's very standardized. The swabs spend a lot of their day in class, so it's not just the running around here doing the military stuff. They're getting courses on honor, respect, and devotion to duty. They're getting some summer math and actual classroom training. In addition, they're getting training in areas such as first aid, swimming, and strength workouts with the gym staff, so it's not just boot camp.

As the saying goes, practice makes perfect, and Commander Haukom notes cadre are even given the opportunity to practice R-Day:

What's really fun is to watch the cadre during their prep week before R-Day; they practice on themselves. They'll break up fifty-fifty,

and then they'll role-play. Half are swabs, half are cadre, and it's funny because the cadre who are role-playing as swabs remember all the silly things and act out. It takes place out there, and I watch them and laugh; it's like watching a comedy to see the cadre and their reactions to their challenge. It must be difficult for them not to break out into laughter as classmates, but to their credit, they do a really good job of maintaining their roles. Then, of course, they swap positions. They prepare well and it's fun to watch. Then, you watch the real thing happen when the real swabs show up, and the swabs do just what the cadre had said. They maintain their character very well, and they work on it. Overall, I think we have a solid program.

When asked whether he worries about the prospect of overzealous cadre, Haukom had this to say:

We have the benefit of being a little bit smaller, and I think that contributes to the tight-knit community we have here, given our size in relation to the other service academies. I think we're in a better position to focus on the individual. That's one of the things we constantly remind our cadre: "Yes, they're swabs, and yes, we have to transform civilians into military members, but they're also someone's son and daughter and brother and sister. We are going to get them to do what we want them to do, and it's not always going to be pleasant for them, but we are going to treat them with respect. There will be no hazing, and we're not ever going to put their safety in jeopardy of any kind." We have a layered defense against that ever happening. We have people watching the cadre, and then people watching them, and so we've been successful in that regard.

One of those people watching the cadre is Senior Chief Tony Mc-Dade. As the head of Alpha Company, he supervises both swabs and cadre throughout the year:

During swab summer, I serve as the practicum supervisor, as do all the other company chiefs. In that role, I provide oversight, guidance, and mentoring to both the cadre, who are training the incoming swabs, as well as to the swabs themselves. I also fill the role as the senior company chief. There are eight company chiefs and one serves as the senior company chief. My role there is as the voice of the company chiefs to the command and vice versa, and I am the company chief of Alpha Company. Each company has either a lieutenant or a lieutenant commander, as well as a senior enlisted—either a chief or a senior chief. Some things we do overlap, but there are clear differences.

McDade's path into the Coast Guard was circuitous, as are many. Both of his grandfathers served in the Army in World War II, and he always had an interest in the military as a youth. With little Coast Guard presence in New Mexico, McDade went into the Army Reserves. When trouble arose in the Gulf, he was called to active duty for Desert Storm and went to Saudi Arabia. Upon his return, he decided he wanted to remain on active duty, but not with the Army:

I had always thought about the Coast Guard, but now that I was going active duty, I looked into it. Essentially, they allowed me to be released from my obligated service to the Army Reserves to go active duty in another service. I then enlisted in the Coast Guard, which was initially going to be for four years, and that was about twenty years ago. My time in the Army was very short. The active-duty time was for training, and operation time was for Desert Storm, so it was a pretty short period. But immediately upon coming into the Coast Guard, I felt it was the right service for me.

There is no one particular skill set the Academy looks for when selecting company chiefs. Instead, it looks for personnel with significant service experience. McDade's training is in pollution response, foreign-vessel exams, facility inspections, and other such related matters. While waiting to get into A-School to learn these trades, he went to a small-boat unit:

I enjoyed the small-boat station, and then the school started putting more people through. You put your name on a list, and when you're up, you're up. I then went to A-School, which is in Yorktown, Virginia. I was then assigned to the icebreaker POLAR STAR, and then to MSO [Marine Safety Office] Puget Sound, which is now Sector Seattle. From there I went to Philadelphia. MSOs/sectors are my background. They don't have MSOs anymore; they're

called sectors. Went to LA, back to Yorktown as an instructor, and then worked as the assistant school chief at the MST School. [Marine Science Technician.] I was interested in a special assignment, just to be doing something different, and I looked at a lot of them. I didn't know much about this job, I guess, because you could argue by Coast Guard standards, it's relatively new. It's been around for about eight years now. I heard about it from someone who had been stationed here and was in my unit, and I started looking into it and made the decision to apply. I came here in the summer of 2009, one week before swab summer. It's a four-year rotation. When I was selected, I was an E-7; I was a chief. Between the time that I was selected for the position—we receive our orders basically a year in advance—and that time, I advanced to senior chief, but my detail at headquarters allowed me to fill it, even though I was advancing.

As McDade mentions, eight years earlier, the Coast Guard had seen a clear need to increase cadet exposure to enlisted personnel before graduation. To McDade, the reasons were obvious:

Cadets are what I call the soon-to-be officers. I call them that because—the reality is—those who got here when I got here are going to leave here when I leave here, and they're going to outrank me; they're going to be officers. But prior to having the company chiefs here, cadet day-to-day interaction with enlisted, and specifically senior enlisted, was minimal. And one of the things officers need to realize is they're going to have to rely on their senior enlisted in order to succeed, as are their senior enlisted going to have to rely on them. So one of the things this does is it fosters what that relationship should be and how it works so that when they go out in the fleet, it shortens the learning curve.

A lot of what we do is leadership mentoring. While some of us may have degrees, none of us went through this institution. However, as far as years of experience in leadership, it is pretty significant. I think the most junior chief here has about twelve or fourteen years of experience. So in a nutshell, that's what our role is: we help mentor the cadets. During swab summer, it's getting new swabs up to speed as well as helping the cadre shape and hone their

Cadets work together to cross a "water hazard" with an ammunition box.

leadership skills. Swab summer is the closest thing they have to boot camp—a basic, military type indoctrination—and it's done by very junior, very young men and women whose average age is probably—I don't know—twenty-one or twenty-two, if that, for the cadre. So they have a tremendous amount of responsibility. Part of what we're here for is to help guide them, mentor them, and make sure they succeed.

Needless to say, the hope is for individual learning curves to trend upward from day one; a small subset, however, will not. Of course, cadre do glean valuable lessons from their failures, so determining when, exactly, intervention is needed is a balancing act with which each chief wrestles:

The amount of oversight we give them varies. Some days, there is virtually none. Some days, it's just standing back and watching everything run. And some days, it's, "Okay, we're hitting speed bumps." If there is a problem, where is that problem? Is that prob-

lem with the swab? Is that problem with the cad-re? Is that problem in communication between the two? I personally try to stand back and allow them to figure it out, because I believe in experiential learning, unless there is a safety issue or a gross violation of SOP [standard operating procedure] or anything like that. Up until then, we stand back. A lot of times, it's after the fact. You'll see something unravel. I can see that it's heading south, but sometimes, dependent upon the person—and each person learns differently—sometimes it's good for them to make those mistakes. We're talking about maybe choosing the wrong leadership style, maybe taking the wrong course. We're not talking about violating an SOP or a safety thing; if there is a safety issue, it's time-out, immediately.

It's interesting, because there's definitely individual personalities, and then you put those individuals together as a group, and that group has a personality of its own. It's not always necessarily what you would predict: "Okay, I know these individuals. I know these particular 3rd classmen; I've had interactions with them. I think I know their strengths and their weaknesses, so if you add X, Y, and Z together, it's going to equal whatever." That's not always how it pans out. And that's one of the things it's important for them to learn, because in the Service, you don't get to pick your team. Despite that, you're still expected to perform; you're expected to accomplish your mission.

The Coast Guard looks to maximize growth opportunities, and each cadet has his or her own strengths and weaknesses. As is natural, cadets may seek to avoid certain situations that make them uncomfortable. Commanding officers are always encouraging students to address their fears, but swab summer serves as a particularly good opportunity to put students into situations they might not choose.

We try to balance what they want with what they need. Sometimes what they want is not necessarily what they need as far as lead-

ership development goes. In a utopian world, each cadet puts in for the position that will challenge them, which they're slightly uncomfortable with, but that's not always the case.

McDade is clearly impressed by the program the Academy uses to create officers, although he did have some initial misgivings when first assigned to New London:

I have to say I don't subscribe to the cookie-cutter model. I see the whole gamut of cadets, and I think they all bring something to the organization. My goal, if you ask me—and this is not the Academy talking—is to have officers who leave here with drive, motivation, a high degree of integrity, character, and an eagerness to learn. I think those are critical things. If it is an officer whose technical skills perhaps aren't quite where they should be, they're going to get there if they have that drive and that integrity, and I think we do a damned good job. Seeing what they go through blows my mind. Coming here, I was thinking, "Okay, I've got twenty- to twenty-two-year-olds, who, for the lack of a better description, are going to be filling the role of a Cape May company commander with swabs, and they're being entrusted with the care, feeding, and everything." It amazes me how they step up and really do a phenomenal job. It still blows my mind, the amount of maturity they display.

I think part of that is if you give them the responsibility, and let them run with it, they're going to surprise you in more instances than not. It doesn't mean they won't make mistakes; they're not perfect, they're learning. The cadre learn a lot about themselves, because it's the first time they're in a real leadership position. At first, for some, there is the novelty of, "I'm in charge and I'm running the show!" And then, for them, soon to follow that reality is the second perception that, "Wow, I'm in charge, and guess what? The buck stops with me!" It amazes me to see the growth that occurs. They can always go to somebody if there is an issue, but they are really in a position where they have to make decisions. Just day to day: "There is a glitch here. Something's wrong with the training schedule, or whatever the case may be, and we've got to think and address it." Each group is different. I've had them come to

me immediately, "Oh, we've got a problem." If it's something I'm confident they're going to handle, that maybe they just don't have the confidence to handle, I'll say, "Wow! You do have a problem! Let me know how that works out for you." It depends on the group, and part of my job is to gauge where they are, get them into the mode of, "Let's see if I can't find the answer within, or if I can't solve the problem within, then I'll go elsewhere." This is what they are going to have to do as officers.

In keeping with the Academy's goal of placing ever-increasing amounts of responsibility on cadets' shoulders, there is a chain of command among the cadets themselves. Swabs, of course, are the lowest links in the chain. The top link held by a cadet is the regimental commander. 1/C Andrew Ray, who holds that position this swab summer, explains the organizational hierarchy within the corps of cadets:

From reg. staff, you get the eight companies, Alpha through Hotel. There is a company commander who is a 1st class, and they're four stripes. Each company has a specific responsibility within the corps. Alpha Company is health and wellness. They're planning ICs—the medical things and things like that. They facilitate that within the company, with specific divisions within the company taking care of certain responsibilities. Bravo is training, Charlie is honor, Delta is drill and ceremonies, and so on, so everything that happens here at the Academy gets broken up into eight parts. Those company commanders are responsible for making sure the tasks, goals, and missions that fall to their company are always taken care of. Second in charge is the company executive officer. They're like the XO, the right-hand man. They're making sure company operations are going smoothly, especially during the swab-summer training period. They make sure the 2nd class are doing their job—they're attending their trainings, they're at formations—making sure accountability is being taken. The company commander is really the oversight, where the XO is almost the enforcer to a degree, making sure things are getting done. Within that, for the summer training period, you have all the 2nd class that are left. The XO makes sure they are going to their weekly trainings, whether they're at the range, active cadre, AIM Cadre, T-boats, or anything like that. The corps shrinks drastically during the summer as cadets not involved directly in swab summer head into the fleet. So there is the company commander, the XO, the remaining staff, and the cadets who are in that company that are here.

During the school year, you have other 1st class cadets that are department heads and division officers that have other responsibilities that help the company. You might be regimental nutrition division. You have a 4th, 3rd, 2nd, and one 1st class leading it, and you get everything done. There's the regimental blood drive division, so they're organizing blood drives throughout the school year, and they have underclass to lean on for the work as well. The breakdown can get thin at times, depending on who is here, but it's always just working down the chain, down the ladder, getting things done. You need to rely on people, build that trust. They have to want to work for you, otherwise your company is going to sink.

Because his parents worked for the Department of Defense, Ray was raised in Australia, but he now calls Maryland his home. Although he never had any specific connection with the Coast Guard, he did have relatives who served in the Air Force and in the Navy. His active lifestyle and love of the outdoors boosted his interest in joining the Service. Now in his last year at the Academy, he has advanced into the highest leadership position cadets achieve:

As the regimental commander, I oversee everything cadets do here—from summer school, the swab summer program, and the Scholars Program for the prepsters to random events that happen at the Academy—although swab summer is my main priority. It's everything from what I mentioned to cadets that get into trouble and are investigated, overseeing their punishments, to making sure that duties are stood by those cadets who have them. I also make sure hazing or anything of that nature doesn't exist, that everyone's abiding by the rules and regulations. I take care of anything that comes down from the officers on the Quarterdeck that needs to go to the corps. My XO and myself are the middlemen for ideas from the Quarterdeck. We facilitate them within the corps, making sure

everyone is on the same page and in agreement. My chief of staff assists; she really looks over all of the programs with a fine-tooth comb, keeping an eye on them to make sure they are successful.

Beginning on R-Day, the cadre put into practice all that they have learned in their first two years. 2/C Joseph Trump reflects back on a film he saw before coming to the Academy and describes his experience re-watching the same film after his 100th Week training:

I watched a show when I was on leave about the Marine Corps's boot camp. I had seen that same show years ago when I was in high school. I was sitting on my couch watching the show, and I was thinking about how this show looked to me now, having been through something similar, compared to what it looked like when I was a kid watching the same show. When I was a kid, it looked like complete chaos, and I didn't understand a thing. I didn't understand the words they were using, I didn't understand why they were doing what they were doing—I didn't understand anything. It seemed like they were just yelling, and that was it. Now when I watched that show, I understood, especially after 100th Week. I was watching how the drill instructors were acting instead of how the recruits were acting, which is what I think I was watching when I was little. It was really important to see how significant every single, little, thing they do is. That's what I think is going to be important now as I go into this.

Trump believes his swabs find themselves in that same boat, not completely able to fathom the process:

As far as the goal, I don't think the swabs understand it, although they might think they know what they're getting into. I think the goal for them, as far as the Coast Guard is concerned, is to get them into the mindset that they're not civilians anymore and they need to act as such; they need to act like they are in the military. Even the first time I went home on leave as a 4th class, it's so ingrained in you to carry your cover a certain way, look a certain way, and speak to others a certain way, that it almost comes across to other people as a little bit strange. When I'm in the airport as a 4th class going on leave in my uniform and I go to a McDonald's, and there's someone behind the counter that is probably not old enough to be called sir, I call them sir or ma'am. It's probably not what everybody does; it's what the Coast Guard wants us to do—to get in that habit, to get in that mindset. I should act with them with the same civility as I would with a captain. I think it is really important. I'd say that's the Coast Guard's goal for swab summer, and I think it works, mostly.

The cadre's job does not end on the parade field or in the class-room. Responsible for their company's newest members, they must document all significant daily activities:

There is what is called the Wiki. It's online, and it has the SOP, the standard operating procedures, and all the expectations, all the rules, and everything we're supposed to accomplish. It has places for us to enter information: if a swab gets hurt or goes to the clinic, or if they do something good or something bad. We're supposed to write down every single significant thing a swab does and everything we do with the company. So every time we IT them, give them motivational training, or whatever, we put it all in the Wiki so it's documented. This makes it easy for the regimental staff to see what's going on and for the officers who are involved to see what's going on and see how each company is progressing.

The statistics and information on the Wiki serve as one record of swab progress, and thus cadre effectiveness, Trump feels the final measure of success lies elsewhere. For him, it is not enough to say his swabs survived the summer:

I don't know if my success can really be measured at the end of the summer as a cadre. I would like to see my swabs graduate, because that's the point. Just becoming a cadet is good, and it's an important step, but the overall goal of swab summer is to begin getting them ready to graduate. At least that's how I feel about it, so I won't feel that my job as a cadre for those swabs will be complete until they graduate. Just like Julia Harwood, the cadre I spoke with, the company commander; she e-mailed me just out of nowhere. I would love to have that opportunity with my swabs. I talked to one of my other cadre, Leslie Stincamp, all the time

last year when I saw her around. She would talk about how she couldn't believe I was about to be cadre and she an ensign. She's really proud of us, her swabs, and she wants to see us succeed. I feel like that. I won't be completely done, because there's still a lot I can teach them, which is even more important if they come and ask me for help. They'll have other people they can ask, but I think the relationship between swabs and cadre is something that's unique. It will always be there, and there will always be a mentor feeling, regardless of what their actual relationship is to you in the future.

2/C Rendon, watching his swabs work a group problem on the ropes course, explains how he sees his role as part of Cadre II:

The first cadre gave the initial shock—a lot of yelling, a lot of screaming. "You're in the military now!" And now we're transitioning into that learning period where we're not so much about yelling and screaming but teaching. We're teaching them things that will be beneficial to them during the school year and towards becoming an officer. This is where it all starts, so we switch into that teaching mode. This part is interesting, to see where they start. We have them for three weeks. We're in our last week now, so it's

Cadre run to the next obstacle ahead at Camp Niantic.

been exciting to see that growth. The biggest growth I've seen with this group is with the teamwork aspect, especially in these specific obstacles. The first time we did this with them, they were bickering and yelling—too many people talking. You can see the change right now; the teamwork is unbelievable, and I can see their motivation. They actually want to be here now.

I think they're doing very well, and they've done a great job. They have their slip-ups, of course, as every group does. Some days, they're moving a little slow or they're not really motivated, but I had that as a swab, too. As a whole, they're really motivated. Their hustle is always there, so I think they want to be here. By this point, the ones who didn't want to be here are already gone. You always get those few—their parents force them to join or they came for the wrong reasons. But now we have the kids who really want to be here. There are a few where the whole military lifestyle is still a bit of a shock, and now we have to convey the point that it's all worth it.

They have it made at this place; they really do. I always try to get the point across that there are kids around the country dying to be in their position, and in the end, it's all worth it. Even though you've got to wake up early and you're not getting summer break, it's definitely worth it. We try to get that point across, make them realize that all the military, all the order, all the yelling is worth it in the end. They may not see it now, but it is. I love it here. I would never want anything different, and I try to convey that to them.

2/C Rothfeld, who also took over two weeks after R-Day, sees his mission in this way:

We have an overall goal. Obviously, it's to get them from being just a swab to being fully prepared for their 4th class year. In the 4th class year, they are followers. Being a follower, you just need to know the basics. We wanted to make sure swabs learn and, if they do things right, obviously, tell them what they're doing right and, if they're wrong, tell them what they're doing wrong. Some people might take IT, some people might take yelling, some people might take a different approach, and we all understood that. We met as a group and talked about our overall goal.

We have to yell at them sometimes when they're having a slow day; maybe they're just not motivated or they're tired. They need to know: in real life, maybe you can afford to have those days when you're tired, but in the military, you can't wake up and say, "I'll just do this with half motivation, without a positive attitude." So we have to yell at them sometimes. Some do well with yelling; a certain number of them don't. There are times when we don't yell at them; we just talk to them and try to use different tones of voice. If you just stay with a monotone, they don't really listen. If someone is yelling, maybe it's good the next person doesn't yell. Some days you can be jumping up and down screaming, and some days they're already moving, they're already doing well. They woke up, and they're ready to go, so it's more like being a catalyst, cheering and pushing them to go, go, go. They're all pretty positive.

They all have certain days where they feel negative and it's just a matter of us being positive with them. We never think that they can't do it, and they all feel they can make it. They have some bad days where maybe they feel as if they regret their decision, but that's normal. I haven't had anyone say they want out. I've pulled some of them aside and asked, "Hey, what's wrong?" There are some people that have bad days, really bad days, so I ask them what's going on. They're just not there at the moment, so I try to get them back into the swing of things and usually that works. Sometimes it doesn't, but individual attention helps a lot.

When asked if there were many differences to contend with between males and females regarding the physical activities of the summer, Rothfeld felt there were none that really mattered in the long run:

There are differences. Guys, for the most part, are stronger, but you just have to keep in mind that there are some girls who can work out just as hard as the guys. There are some girls that can't work that hard, but they hold their position. Maybe it's a plank, maybe it's a pushup, and you can see they're working. It's almost palpable. You can also see when they're just mentally giving up; you can see it. That's when you get a little angry and you tell them, "Hey, look." If they can't do many pushups, that's a physical thing;

they'll get better. But there's the mental part. We need to get them to keep pushing, keep pushing. It goes beyond just the physical workout. It's building perseverance, which is definitely required at this school, especially at 0530 when they're working out. We have to keep pushing them and they'll be all right.

For Rothfeld, preparing the swabs for their first and most difficult academic year was something he wished they could do more:

I understand they're swabs, but I really want them to get a feel for the 4th class year, especially academically, because a lot of kids are getting kicked out for academics because they just can't keep performing. When I was a swab, our cadre would scare us with what the school was going to be like, and once you got into it, it really wasn't that hard. I wish there was a class that would mentally prepare them—let them know what they have to do academically, as well. You obviously have to work hard, but it's also their mentality. You have to say to yourself, first of all, that you like the subjects. I remember taking chemistry, and people would say, "Chemistry stinks." But it's really an interesting class, and anything can be really interesting if you approach it that way. Some of them lose that sense. I would try to implement a class that would help them with this, bringing in officers that have done well academically to talk to them. A lot of people feel you're here, yes, to become an officer, but you're also here to learn; it's still a school. To be an officer, you have to be well rounded and you have to know a lot about many different things. It's just a matter of, "Are you going to enjoy the classes, or are you going to sleep through them?" They get into the military mindset and forget this is a school.

2/C Jennifer Patron, one of Rothfeld's fellow cadre, also feels the summer's mission is about much more than getting swabs safely to the end:

For the swabs, it goes back to the mission. The goal is still to graduate young men and women with sound bodies, stout hearts and alert minds. It's to prepare them to be cadets and to get through the Academy. The Academy is just a training period before you go into the fleet, so the overall mission is to create the sound officer who knows right from wrong and who is a very confident leader. That's the goal; once you get into the fleet, you are in charge of leading people. They expect you to be confident leaders. Confident, competent, and humble leaders.

You go back to the core values. That's a very funny thing, too. You go to the Academy, and it's very intimidating. You see all these people with very high GPAs, very smart, very structured. They look like nearly perfect people, and you're like, "Oh my goodness!" You can be as smart as you want, but the bottom line is still having to be a good person. Obviously, they want you to be smart, but like everyone has said, and what I really believe is, it has to do with integrity, being humble, and being respectful. If you don't have those qualities as a base, no one is going to listen to you, no one is going to take you seriously. You can be the smartest person ever, but if you don't have the people skills and you can't associate and communicate with them, then there is no point to it.

During the academic year, your 3rd class year, you have a course in leadership and organizational behavior. A lot of the classes are straightforward academics, the STEM classes, but you also have classes in morals, ethics, and things like that. I think a lot of our development happens during the summer as well, because you really start to get to know yourself through interactions with other people. That's when you really start to understand, and that's really important; there is only so much you can learn in a classroom. We also have an ethics week here at the Academy. You listen to people who tell you why it's important to do this, why it's important to have this kind of character. That's one week, but they have things throughout the year. People will come in and talk to us corps-wide; they remind you what this is all about.

Lieutenant Greg Batchelder

Portrait of an Officer

The Personnel Officer for swab summer is Lieutenant Greg Batchelder. As such, he deals with numerous problems cadre and swabs face throughout the training period. While he is company officer for Foxtrot, he leaves the daily task of running the company to his chief.

I personally don't have a whole lot of daily interaction with the cadre; he does the day-to-day mentoring and coaching. My chief will come by and brief me two to three times a day on issues—things that are going well, things that aren't going so well. If I see something, I'll bring it up to him or the cadre, so it's a little different. I'm in charge of overseeing all the personnel issues of swab summer: all the DQs [disqualifications], all the people who want to leave, all the medical issues, all the mishaps and people getting hurt—big picture stuff. I track all of that, so I have the pulse of what's going on. For common injuries, we have the medical staff. There is a request-to-leave process we follow with some of them. There are exceptions to the process; like if they're a disruption to the company, we'll take them out. So all of the issues that have bubbled to the surface are the ones I deal with all the time, but the day-to-day interaction, knowing how things are going, I rely on my chief. Whenever I do have a free moment, I like to go out and watch—especially my company—to see what's going on, see how everything is going, and get some feedback on the training program.

Originally from Connecticut, Batchelder received an appointment to the Academy during his senior year in high school, but he turned it down, believing he was not quite ready for regimentation. He briefly attended first Penn State then St. Lawrence College in Upstate New York, but was ultimately unhappy with both experiences. He decided it was time to reapply to the Academy, and he soon found himself in New London. Although he knew little about the Coast Guard when he arrived, he learned to love being part of the Service. After graduation, he went south to his first assignment:

First tour out of here I went to the DAUNTLESS, a 210' medium-endurance cutter in Galveston, Texas. We were doing a lot of drug patrols, migrants, all that good stuff. Being in Texas, except for three patrols, we mostly handled migrants. We did two drug patrols and one fisheries patrol. Pretty much with every patrol, the first thing we did was go down to Key West, to the Florida Straits, to resupply and either stayed there or went further. We had migrants on every patrol; we always interdicted someone. Some patrols, from the first day until the day you leave, you have migrants on board.

Most migrant and drug patrols concentrate on the Caribbean Sea, the Gulf of Mexico, and the US-Mexican border. As Batchedler explains, migrant interdiction is a complicated process:

I was on big ships. The 210' was a medium-endurance cutter, and then there are the smaller 110' and 87' patrol boats—they're the main inter-

ceptors, if you will—and then there's always a holding platform. They'll drop them off with us, and we'll process them. They'll get interviewed, and we'll get clearance through the State Department through the sector to send them back. We'll take them back and repatriate them, or, if they decide to put them through further screening processes, we'll take them to Guantanamo Bay to figure out what to do with them. We may have them on the ship anywhere from five days to a couple of weeks, depending on how quickly the paperwork goes through. If there are any errors in the spelling of the names, which happens occasionally, they could be on longer. It's a pretty constant flow, and we can have multiple groups on board at any given time. One group will get cleared to go back, and we'll keep the other groups. Then, we'll have another group come in, and then, one of the oldest groups will get cleared to go back, so it's a constant flow of groups of people coming in and going out.

Batchelder started out as a deck watch and a ship's communication officer, responsible for all incoming and outgoing communications. After serving a year, a change in responsibilities accompanied his promotion to first lieutenant:

As the first lieutenant, you're responsible for the exterior of the ship: all the painting, maintenance, and the two small boats. You're responsible for the operation of the small boats that get launched. Maintenance for these boats takes place on the engineering side, but you're responsible for all the deck pieces: life preservers, fire extinguishers, all that good stuff. We also have to train the crew, have all the boarding teams ready to go. We're also responsible for all of the helicopter operations, and that was the biggest division on the ship. I had twenty-one people in my division. I had one chief who worked for me, a handful of petty officers, and sixteen non-rates, so we were pretty busy. There were about seventy-five people on board altogether.

Batchelder's next deployment took him to the black hull *Cyprus*, a 225′ buoy tender in Mobile, Alabama. This assignment exposed him to yet a different mission—maintenance of crucial aids to navigation along our coasts and throughout our waterways:

The main mission on a 225′ is aids to navigation, so our AOR [area of responsibility] ran from the Florida Panhandle all the way to the Texas-Mexico border. We had channels and buoys scattered throughout, although most of them ran to Mobile, Pensacola, and the Mississippi River area. Any time there is a discrepancy that can't be fixed by a smaller unit—a hurricane, a commercial vessel hits a buoy, a buoy sinks or gets pulled off-station—we would go out and take care of it. We had just over a hundred aids we were responsible for. We'll work a channel and we'll know everything is on-station—it's where it should be, it looks good, all the lights are working properly. Sometimes, commercial pilots or commercial vessels will call problems in, because they run the channels all the time. They'll say, "Hey, number seven looks like it's in the channel a little bit. Can you go out there and take a look at it?" Once they report that discrepancy, there is a work sheet we go through. We work up a point total, based on the type of discrepancy, the class of the aid, how critical it is, if there are other discrepancies in the area, and a bunch of other factors. How soon you have to respond depends on that point total. It could be immediate—as soon as possible, weather permitting—or it can be deferred until later. Multiple discrepancies in the area makes it a bigger deal. A major aid is a bigger deal. There are smaller aids to navigation units who will go out to check them first. To get the giant ship underway for one small discrepancy, even if it is a critical aid, is expensive, so the smaller unit can go out if it is something like a light's been extinguished. If it's off-station, sunk, or missing, then we'll respond as soon as we can, get out there, and put it back on station. I wouldn't say these things happen daily, but they happen on a weekly basis.

The Coast Guard's fleet is relatively small when one considers its diverse mission list, so very few cutters serve a single purpose. Larger black-hulled vessels, although designed first and foremost to tend buoys, are especially versatile:

On the CYPRUS, we also did migrant patrols. We did 500 hours. The two different types of cutters operate on different schedules and cycles. A medium-endurance cutter operates on days away from home port every year. When I was there, it was 185 days away from home port per year, and the 225' buoy tender was 2,100 hours of operations per year. Operations are broken down by district. They give you different blocks of time to cover different missions, such as A-time, public affairs, living marine resources, and the fisheries. We assisted NOAA [the National Oceanic Atmospheric Administration] and tended their buoys as well, so there was a chunk of time for that. Also, being down in the Gulf of Mexico, we got 500 hours per year for migrant work, so we would go to Key West and operate as the holding platform for migrants.

While there are similarities between the large, white-hulled and black-hulled vessels, Batchelder notes that their differences are more numerous:

It's hard to say which one I liked better. They're different; it's a different atmosphere on both. On a big white hull, there are a lot of perceptions of what it's like working on a smaller unit, say a small patrol boat, or a black hull, a buoy tender. They are quite a bit different. The 225', a black-hulled buoy tender, is run more like a smaller unit. It has a much smaller crew; there were about fifty-five people on board, and we had one of the bigger crews of the 225' fleet. It's a different mission, so you know the crew differently. You have an actual work schedule on the buoy tender, and you're going out most of the time with something to accomplish. You work hard, and then you go back home. It's totally different from a white hull, where you go out and you're gone for six weeks, regardless if you find anything or not. So it's hard to say which one I prefer.

I wouldn't mind going back to either. Hopefully, after this tour, I'm going to go back to a patrol boat—a 110' patrol boat or one of the new fast response cutters. If I don't get one of those, I definitely want to go back to the 225's as the XO. I'm looking to skip another ride right now on one of those big white boats. It depends on what they offer me, but I'll pretty much take anything. Different things on each of them are fun. The interdictions and the high-paced operations on the big white hulls are fun, but the really exciting ones happen few and far between. When I was a cadet, I thought I would never want to go to a buoy tender; I would never want to see one,

and I didn't even know why the Coast Guard did that mission. My chief, who came in when I was on the 210', was a buoy tender sailor the majority of his career. He was like, "They're awesome. You anchor every night. You go out, and you have a work schedule, and when you're done working, you go back in. The crew is a lot smaller." The 225'—going out, working buoys, driving, coaching the junior officers, and breaking in those learning how to drive—is a lot of fun, too, so both have their merits.

The Coast Guard assigns a high priority to the education of its officers, both on and off the water. Following his two-year stint on the Cyprus, Batchelder enrolled in graduate school:

I went to the Eisenhower Leadership Development Program, a joint program between West Point and Columbia. West Point needs so many more company officers (they're called TAC officers there)—roughly twenty people per year—so the Coast Guard tags along on that program. We've been doing it for a few years. I was the sixth cohort to go through that Columbia program, and your degree is from the university. A lot of the Columbia professors come up and teach at West Point, and some of the classes are taught by West Point professors. It's basically a two-year program in organizational psychology, or at least civilians get two years. For us, it's crammed into eleven months, so we're taking six or seven graduate classes at a time. I did that, got my master's degree, and I came here in the summer of 2011 to be a company officer.

Because of rapid turnover in the military staff at the Academy, it was difficult to obtain information on how Academy policies have evolved over time; each officer can speak to only a few years' history at most. That is not to say, of course, that everything at the Academy changes with each rotation. On the contrary, the Coast Guard has a sophisticated system in place that allows for personnel fluctuations while simultaneously minimizing disruption to ongoing programs. Information is passed to incoming replacements both verbally and via reams of SOPs. Any actual change at the Academy, as at most military institutions, occurs at a stately pace.

From most cadets' perspective, life at the Academy has remained forever the same. When commenting on the school's operation, they often state, as though from personal experience, "It's always been this way!" In the whirlwind of swab summer, however, a number of cadre become convinced that the incoming class is somehow inferior to all those who have come before—particularly their own. When Batchelder was examining the cadre experience as part of his graduate work, he found this aspect particularly amusing; other aspects left him more troubled:

It's funny you mention some of the cadre saying, "This is the worst class ever; they're terrible." Every year that happens—every year I've been here at least. "These are the worst swabs: they don't listen, they don't know what's going on, they don't know anything." In reality, they're the same as every other year. What I've seen in the past is swabs turning into cadre. The cadre who say, "These are horrible swabs!"—if you look back through the trackers, they're the ones who were listed as the horrible swabs. They had issues, they couldn't memorize things, and they were not fit for full duty all the time. They are the same ones who say, "Oh, so and so is never fit for full duty." How soon they forget what they went through! One thing they say is, "It was done to me, so I'm going to do it to them." That's a common thread. If it's not specifically prohibited in the SOP, they say, "It was done to me, so it's okay, right?" That's probably not the best training tool. We fight a lot of those battles, when they can't articulate the purpose behind their actions.

Batchelder has been through six swab summers, and he notes many similarities among them. Cadre inevitably go through the same process, year after year, while wrestling with their introduction to leadership:

They first start by doing what was done to them, and that's the biggest challenge we have. We have to make sure they're following the SOP, doing what they should be doing, and meeting the training objectives. Ideally, that's what we want them to do, but we're still fighting that battle of, "We're doing what was done to me." They want to put their own mark on swab summer; they've had these great ideas that have been stewing in their heads for two years. They're like, "This is going to be awesome. We're going to do this." Well, there may be no training value in what they want to do.

It takes them about a week, a week and a half, to figure out that the stuff they're doing doesn't get them results. They're frustrated with the swabs: they can't remember names, they can't square, they're not good at drill, they're late everywhere, they're not working as a team, their uniforms don't look good, and their rooms don't look

USCG Cutter *Ida Lewis* is a black-hulled, 175' Keeper Class buoy tender.

good. "Everything is wrong! They're terrible swabs! These are the worst swabs ever!"

But some of them realize sooner than others, at the week-and-a-half mark or so, "Okay, what we're doing is probably not working. All the stuff they've trained us on and what is in the SOP is there for a reason. Perhaps we should follow it more closely rather than do what we think is right." That's when you see some transition in their development. Screaming at swabs doesn't work. If they can't square and you just keep screaming at them, it's probably not going to make them square any better. You probably need to take a step back and go over the basic steps of how to square—have them learn in a different environment than the intense, six-people-screaming-in-your-face method you're using. They're not going to learn anything that way. I think they figure that out later on in the summer.

The big transition is when that first set of cadre come back, having left them after the first two weeks. Now, however, the swabs are in their sixth or seventh week of training. They're no longer two-week swabs, but the cadre will come in and try to treat them like they're week-two swabs. It'll be hard. There will be a lot of head-butting between the cadre and the swabs. We'll hear, "They're treating us unfairly. They're being too mean. They're not giving us enough time." And the cadre will be saying, "They're not respecting us. They're questioning us."

Although on-the-job training is sometimes awkward or painful, many of these lessons cannot be taught in the classroom:

I think eventually they'll reflect and realize what they've learned about themselves and training. When the cadre first get them, they want to indoctrinate swabs and make the experience intense, part of what's gone on here forever. One thing—at least, in Foxtrot, the point chief and I try to drive home—is you can at first raise your voice and try to get that command presence up front (the yelling part, I'm sure, has been here for a long, long time), but we want them to understand that they can't do that in the fleet. This is just part of the training here. When you go out on your summer next year, when someone who works for you doesn't listen, you can't just start yelling at him. Well, you could, but you're not going to get the results you want. That's what they need to really figure out: How do you get the results using different methods? That's what we harp on in Foxtrot. Some of them get it, and others, it's in one ear and out the other.

Four members of the cadre talk amongst themselves before beginning the next phase of training with their swabs.

Oversight

Just as cadre are training swabs to follow, company officers are training cadre to lead. Keeping the cadre on task and operating within Coast Guard guidelines is a major task for company chiefs and lieutenants throughout the summer. When swabs do begin to run off course, Lieutenant Kehlenbach encourages cadre to figure out, first and foremost, why the swabs have strayed:

That would be part of the cadre using some trained initiative to find out, to inquire what's going on with the swab. They need to ask the question, "You were a good performer, and now you're not—what happened?" Often there is some underlying condition: there's a problem with a family member at home, they're concerned their mom is ill, or some other problem. We can help them work through that problem, and typically, their performance rebounds. If it isn't an issue with that, sometimes it's not what they wanted, so they've given up. Again, the cadre has to step in and give them that pep talk, remind them why they joined, so they can help them through that doubt and remind them they joined for a reason. Everybody's reason is different, but get them to focus on whatever that reason was so that they can continue on.

When it is cadre who veer off course, intervention from the officer level is handled very carefully. Kehlenbach knows that they, too, must learn as much from their mistakes as from their successes:

As observers, if we see the cadre starting to do something that's not in accordance with the standard operating procedures and there is potential there for someone to be injured, then we would take immediate action. But if they're doing something that isn't in accordance with policy that can be easily corrected, we might wait for the evolution to finish before pulling them aside. We try not to do anything that will diminish their credibility in front of the swabs, so we typically would not intervene in front of them. Errors are part of the learning process, and that's when you would come back and say, "Let's talk about what you did, why you decided to do it that way." Maybe let them know how it could be perceived, and then they can think about it. Normally, every night at 2200, the cadre come together as a group to debrief the day, discuss how it went. It's called a Taps meeting, and that's a time where they can talk about things that went well and things that went badly. Again, it's a team. They should be looking out for each other, and they will typically intervene on each other's behalf; it doesn't normally need to be one of the staff who has to step in. If they see their shipmates starting to go down a wrong path, they'll fix it.

Every day there is a particular cadre in charge, and it's their responsibility on that day to ensure the plan of the day is carried out by the company. Obviously, everything we do is teamwork, so they have to rely on their team to get it done. In some of the other trainings the 2ⁿᵈ class receive over the summer, like the coastal sail training program, they work with their peers and they work at being in charge. They can work on conflict resolution and how they

approach things. They learn that it is much nicer to ask someone to do something than to tell them. So some of it is just them learning how to work as a team.

Every group of cadre is a little bit different. Some of them, who haven't built the confidence yet, will do it by groupthink, and others will be very set and say, "We're going to do it this way," and maybe it works and maybe it doesn't. They learn from that: maybe they shouldn't go into it quite as strongly with their opinions. Every group is a little bit different in how they work together, and sometimes the first week it doesn't go well, and they learn as much from what doesn't go well as what does. There is a lot of change over the summer with the cadre. Taking ownership and setting an example is a nice transition to see. You really see a shift, not only physically, but in their mental approach to things as well.

Cadre are often aware of their own developmental progress, even as it is happening. 2/C Jake Rendon reveals just such an awareness:

I really have started to develop my leadership style. This is the first time I've been put into a leadership position at this place. The first year, it's all just following orders; basically, you do what you're told. The second year, you're still following orders but also mentoring the new kids. It is a lot of work being a cadre. Planning, making sure everybody is there, making sure they're where they need to be. It's more planning than I expected. They get up at 0530. I'm usually up at about 0520. There are three people who take them to cals every morning: me, Mr. Ashley, and Mr. Berringer. We get up about ten minutes earlier, take them to cals, and bring them back. We usually get to bed around 2300 because of the Taps meeting, but we're used to it. This is actually sometimes more sleep than we get during the school year. This is the first leadership position that we've had to hold, and it's really been a learning experience for me. My growth as a leader has really improved this summer, just being in this position, learning what I like and what I don't like as a leader. I've enjoyed it. I've loved my summer experience so far; it's been a great time.

As regimental commander, 1/C Ray is experiencing his third swab summer, and each iteration has given him a different perspective. He distinguishes two major leadership styles:

There's something that I've learned in my time here: transactional and transformational leadership. When they screw up transactionally, you punish them immediately. You make them do pushups, some kind of physical training. You get in their face; you make them do some type of remedial instruction. That only goes so far, and I think by week three or four, when they finally learn the ropes and can finally march themselves to lectures or some training they have, it becomes more transformational. They want to please the cadre. They're doing it because they want to succeed. They want to earn Honor Company. I'm sure being punished is in the back of their minds, but as the weeks progress, you are going to do that less and less as they perform to higher standards simply because they want to. They're looking to succeed, and then, of course, they have EAGLE some time in the last three weeks. It's that break where they take a deep breath. Then, they come back, and they say, "We only have two weeks, one week left. Let's just knock it out." Then, they're done.

There is a noticeable change from the middle of the summer on, where swabs get in the habit of getting up early. Their brains begin functioning, memorizing information faster, and retaining it. Things like that. I think it's just three to four weeks and everyone gets a hold of it. Obviously, some are a lot faster than others. Since nobody knows anybody in the group, it's very weird to see who steps up from the company. They usually are the preps. The prepsters have already done a year at a prep school and gone through a modified swab summer the year before, so they have a much easier time, because they know what to expect. Those are the leaders within the swab companies that immediately emerge; you notice that right off the bat. Not only are they squared away, but they are helping everyone else. We'll leave their rooms a complete mess, and they'll go help someone else, because they know they will all be much better off. They have the experience, and people

look to them like, "You know how to shine your shoes that much better; you've been doing it for a year." They go to see them. It's immediately noticeable, just in how they carry themselves. If they have a swab-only session, just the thirty of them in the classroom, they hash out whatever's going on internally with the company chief. The prepsters are the ones who will speak up, write on the whiteboard, collect information and pass it along, and propose new ideas.

Just as there are incoming cadets each summer who excel, there are a number who struggle well beyond the first few weeks. Ray continues:

At the same time, you see the few who might not have the support at home. They write letters and don't get them all back, or they're homesick—not traumatic, but it's exceptionally new for them. You see those who always drag; they always look miserable. From the cadre point of view, it's exceptionally hard to motivate them, and I can imagine from the swab's point of view how hard it is to get motivated. There can come a point where there is only so much you can do; they've already made up their minds, and you can only push them so far. That happens all the way from day one until the last week.

Swabs do a thought of the day every day. They put that on the outside of their door, so when the cadre come in, they know what's going on in their heads. When I was a swab, the very first day, I turned to my roommate, and I said, "Hey, man, are you ready to put our thoughts of the day outside?" And he was just bawling and crying. At first I thought I had done something to him, that I had been mean, kind of a jerk. The next day, he went to talk to somebody, and I didn't see him again, so it can happen that fast. Or at week six, they realize, "I've done this for this long. I don't want to do this anymore." It's that close, and the school year is about to start. I don't think there has ever been a group of three people that say, "Let's quit together." I don't think that happens; it's very much an individual choice. Some don't necessarily get accepted within the company, which is always a shame. You never know by the end

The cadre shoulder tremendous responsibility, and the summer can be just as stressful for them as it is for the swabs. Ray describes both groups' outlooks:

As a swab, you see the cadre, and they seem perfect. They know everything. They're always correcting you, because there's always something wrong. They're not just making stuff up just to yell at you; there are always things they can find. As a cadre, you find it hard not to laugh when they do funny things. If you need to laugh, you step around the corner or step into a room, but you find it exceptionally stressful when they continually mess up or do something wrong. You wonder, "How in the world am I going to fix this, all the while staying within the guidelines of the standard operation procedures?" When it gets to the point beyond frustration, what do you do?

Beyond dealing with recalcitrant swabs, the cadre must also learn to work with their own peers—peers with whom they often find themselves at loggerheads:

Granted, you know everybody, because there are only 250 people in your class here, but your styles are different; you want to do different things with them. Something happened to you in your swab summer that you thought was good, but the same thing happened to them and they thought it was awful. It's a group of eight, but getting along with all of them is very stressful. You get tired of seeing one another very quickly. The days are long, 0500 to 2300.

There is a lead cadre, and that position rotates each day. One of the 2ⁿᵈ class in the cadre is the lead; it's their show for the day, but everyone has their input. No one is on a different level except for the 1ˢᵗ class cadets overseeing them. They're all on the same playing field but have different styles, expectations, or even personalities. When I was a cadre, one of my good friends and I were always in your face. We were jerks. We were very mean, all the time, and some of our fellow cadre didn't like that. They always thought we were way too abrasive, in your face, and blah, blah, blah. And that's just personalities. Our approach might have been effective; theirs might have been effective. It's just style, and that's

A member of the cadre records the team's goals for the upcoming summer.

of the summer how they will make out during the school year or over the course of the next four years.

something I think the cadre's summer is truly all about. It's finding your style, finding out what works for you and fits your personality, without taking you out of your element. While we didn't always agree, a lot of times you have to put your differences aside and say, "Look, this isn't going to change our friendship; this isn't going to change the outcome of the summer." Swallow your pride. My company, Foxtrot Company, was Honor Company for the summer, and that was the greatest thing. Not only were we effective as leaders, our swabs followed us, they trusted us, they did what we asked. They performed highly and won. And winning is big for me; I love winning.

My progression went something like this: During my swab summer, I told myself I would be the guy who would never yell. I'd be like, "Whatever, just do what you want," because I realized how frustrating it was for me during swab summer. But then, the Academy gets to you throughout the next two years, and you realize what it's about and why it has to be done. I went from being somebody who thought I was going to do nothing, just hang out all of the time and take an easy, three-week vacation, to realizing the importance of it. That's why I became more in your face, always serious, and loud. I also got that from John Stimmel, who I thought was an absolute animal of a cadre. He was always in your face, always ready to go, but could tone it down immediately. He was very cool.

Ray admits to having been overly abrasive as cadre, but he has since reflected upon the experience. When asked whether he would change his approach were he to do it all over again, he had this to say:

I think—and this is just my personal opinion—I think for swab summer, having that time—that in-your-face, loud, demanding, exceptionally particular time—is good, as long as you know when to tone it down. The first few weeks, I ran into the problem of not knowing when to tone it down, but I finally learned it for the last week. When they do mess up and they mess up big, get all over them. If it's a small thing, that's when you can TOPS them. You need to bridge the gap to the school year. During the school year,

you're not going to scream at them. You're not going to make them do something like physical activity. There are other things during the school year that exist, but you're never going to get what you want by constantly yelling 24/7. You have to finally turn it back. So if I was to do it again, I certainly would.

Ray's real turning point came when cadre from another company asked for help with a swab who was not performing:

This one company had a swab who wasn't doing very well, or they didn't think he was doing very well, so they had him come and sit at our table, thinking maybe fresh faces will get through to him. My friend and I were all ready to just rip into this kid to figure out what was going on. Instead, we just started talking to him, and we got through to this kid by just talking to him like a normal human being. That was one of the best things I had done all summer. We talked to him like a human being at dinner. We didn't ask him any indoc questions or knowledge. We just talked about what he wanted to do, and we saw his performance change immediately. That was exceptionally rewarding as a cadre: knowing this worked, especially for him. While this is always on a case-by-case basis, knowing that this was successful was huge. There's always that balance in leadership styles that has to be worked out. You need to learn to balance it all and figure out what's going to be successful for your summer.

2/C Ben Mckeethan, as part of Chase Hall Cadre II, realized in the swabs' third week that he needed to adopt a more subtle leadership style:

The yelling is effective for the first couple of days, but right now, we're more in a teaching role. At this point in the summer, it's gotten to be that simply acting disappointed in them whenever they mess up is more effective than yelling at them, because they've come to respect us, and they don't want to let us down. And that's done on purpose. Part of that comes from letting them know when they're doing things well or acting legitimately indignant when they don't. That's more effective than yelling at this point. A couple of days ago, they had a pretty good day, so we were like, "If they're doing what they need to do, let's have some fun with them, joke around a little bit, as long as they're still able to get everything done." We adjust styles accordingly. Usually, they'll get into moods. They'll have a few really good days, and then they'll go into a slump. But then we work to build them back up and get them to where they need to be.

As with most, Mckeethan tries to draw from his own experience:

Most of us try to emulate the styles we saw in our cadre, because your cadre are some of the most influential people you encounter in the eighteen or twenty years you've been alive. I definitely draw upon some of the styles and attitudes my cadre had, and only in the good sense. Some of the things I now realize they shouldn't have done help guard me against doing the same things. One good thing is we debrief after everything. Even after my swab summer, my cadre asked us, "Okay, how did we do? What do you think we could have done better?" Some of that information we kept and I remember still. I try to avoid things they said they should have avoided.

Mckeethan clearly sees the benefits of giving this leadership opportunity to 2nd class cadets:

It's been a great learning experience. I'd argue it's as much or more for us than it is for the swabs. Most of the stuff we're learning to do is going to be useful to us when we're out in the fleet. We're going to be in the officers' position where we're actually leading people. Right now, swabs are learning how to do basic tasks, how to function in the military, whereas the whole point of the Academy is to develop that leadership role within us. The military part is just the way they go about doing it. I feel it's been a great experience, because we're getting time to lead them around. Their whole schedule is dependent upon us. We're in charge of getting them to medical appointments and all of those things. We have to coordinate how to do that on time, making sure everyone gets to where they need to be. It's been a great leadership experience.

There were definitely some nerves to begin with, but I think that kind of goes with this being the first major leadership experience

we've had. We've been in positions where we've led groups of our peers, but not in positions where we were in charge of our subordinates. So there were nerves, but I feel that going through swab summer ourselves, and then the 100th Week program, really helped to prepare us for this. You're never going to feel 100 percent prepared, but that's kind of the whole point of this program. You get into a rhythm. It only took about a day and a half to get into the rhythm of how to talk to them and how to get things done.

When McKeethan encounters problems he can not handle alone, he looks to his superiors for guidance:

We have Senior Chief McDade above us. He's kind of the mentor for this whole summer program, and for the school year as well. He's been a lot of help; he's our guide through the whole thing. If we have any questions about how we should handle anything, we go to him. That's also why we have the 1st class, the company commander and the XO, but senior chief has done a great job of guiding us through situations, and he also meets with the swabs if they need to talk about things. We meet with him as needed, although we usually talk to him every day. We see him in the hall, and he asks us how things are going. If we have any issues, we talk about them right then. His door is always open, so if he's in his office and we need to talk to him about something, he's always there for us. We schedule weekly meetings to talk about the company as a whole, and he can gauge how things are going.

As Mckeethan explains, cadre rarely need to refer to their daily performance logs to measure their swabs' progress:

We generally know how everyone in the company is doing, because we spend sixteen hours a day with them; we can gauge how well they're doing. At times, we will look online if things are really going wrong and we need to talk to them, or if they need to go to a different program to get motivated. But generally, we don't use the online documentation for much in our meetings. Different people respond to different things. We'll try negative reinforcement, making them do pushups or something, and we'll try positive reinforcement—all the different types of training we learned during 100th Week or at the Academy—and if things still aren't working out, we start going to other people. We would go to our senior chief and ask him, we would go to our firsties and ask them. Eventually, there are different programs we can use to try to get them moving along.

Over time, each company develops its own personality, based on the individual command styles of those leading it. 2/C Trump elaborates:

It's very dependent upon how the company officer wants to run his company. The company officer is responsible for that company—every single thing that goes on. There is a cadet chain of command—a company commander, and a company executive officer, and all of the different divisions—but eventually, it's that officer's responsibility. In my company—I'm in Foxtrot now—our company officer is Lieutenant Batchelder, and he is very hands-off. He gives a lot of responsibility to the company commander. He said he'll be there if we need him; he just wants us to run it the way we are going to run it. He has an overall command philosophy where as long as we're getting done what needs to get done—like our rooms look good, our uniforms look good, people are showing up to formation—he has no problem letting us do it our way. He has given the company commander the power to grant longs and shorts for the weekend and grant late racks for people to use. That's kind of unheard of, as far as the rest of the corps. Most company officers don't give the company commanders that kind of responsibility. But I think it is really, really good. I think if you can have that much responsibility in an environment where it's not that big a deal, it teaches that you can make mistakes and it's okay, instead of being thrust into it as an actual officer out in the fleet without that experience. The company officer can be right on top of things and really get into the details if they want to. It's really up to them, but it can be either way.

Clockwise: 2/C Kate Compagnoni leads her company's walking wounded back to the barracks. Swabs sustain all types of injuries throughout the summer's training, from twisted ankles to sprained wrists. The wristbands issued by Academy doctors let cadre know which swabs are excused from certain activities until again deemed fit for full duty.

Swab Kyneesha Womack drills with her company.

Swabs attend classes throughout the summer. Due to physical exhaustion from constant motion, it is often difficult for them to stay awake once off the field and seated comfortably. Swabs who fear they may dose can stand during class without giving offense.

Clockwise: Swab Jake Carlton listens to the next set of instructions.

Companies gather in a courtyard just before lunch begins. Never losing an opportunity, cadre quiz swabs on their indoc material, and mistakes often result in added physical exercise.

The ropes course involves physical puzzles swabs must solve as a team. In this problem, the company must cross a bridge without touching the lawn, something many groups never accomplished.

101

Drilling with rifles on the Washington Parade Field.

Through the Eyes of the Cadre

In some ways, cadre and swabs are like the yin and yang of Chinese philosophy. Although the relationship between leader and follower often seems antagonistic, each ultimately complements and edifies the other. As 2/C Sam Birchee discovered, however, benefits from the pairing do not necessarily come easily:

It's a little frustrating. You see them beginning to pick up on some of the smaller things. It is interesting to see the new AIM students every week. You're reminded that's how the swabs looked when they came in, so you do see the difference, and that's nice to be able to see, "Oh, now I remember what they were like on R-Day!" There are times when you get frustrated when they can't grasp something you've been harping on for a whole week. You keep telling them, "Eyes in the boat," and they just can't get it. But then you look at AIM students, and you remember that was them on the first day, so they actually have come a longer way than you sometimes realize. I think when you get to become cadre, you always think you were a better swab than you were. You've got to remember that you weren't that amazing swab when you started. You have to try to change some of their habits, get them to understand they can't do the things the way they've always done them. It's different here. Even if society is one way, that doesn't mean we get to stop respecting authority or having honor. It's frustrating sometimes, but at the same time, you've got to just keep going. It's hard to break eighteen years of habit.

You have to remember that everyone comes from different backgrounds and places, so everyone has their own issues. Some kid can't pick up indoc that quickly, or the pressure gets to him. Another kid does everything great but has an attitude that he's better than everybody else. It depends on how they were raised, where they are from, and what kind of person they are. Somehow, you have to take that and keep it but still form them in the same general mold of a cadet at the United States Coast Guard Academy. It takes different approaches with different kids. Sometimes, one cadre just doesn't get through to a kid, so we take another aside and say, "You try to get through to him." I think the biggest thing is that we have so many different cadre, and everyone has a different personality, different ideas, and different ways they can try to get through. It's really good to be able to work off one another.

It's definitely challenging. It's challenging for me, too, you know? A lot of these kids come in and they've been team captains, they've been the top of their class, and everything, and here they come in even with everyone else, and they come in at the bottom of the corps. It's something that's hard to grasp for a lot of people. It was hard for me. I remember in my swab summer, when we had team building exercises, everyone would try to take control, because everyone was used to being in charge. That's something we have to help them with: how to become a follower, when to lead, and when to follow. That's something they are also going to have to

learn partially on their own. We'll give them the opportunities, but I can't tell them, "You're going to lead this, and you're not going to lead that."

Working with Birchee is shipmate 2/C Stephanie Jocis. She sees progress hidden amid the frustration:

I think we can definitely see a change. Hotel Company is definitely coming together more as a team. I just came in on Sunday, and they seem to be bonding a lot more than they were. For the cadre, it's a hard balance to acknowledge the kids who are making changes and moving in the right direction while dealing with the kids who aren't. It's really hard to make that balance, because we stress teamwork. We follow the Navy saying: The weakest link is going to bring everyone down. We're trying to motivate them to want to be better, to want to be a team, and to want to help one another succeed. We're all here; we care about them, we respect them, and that's why we're out here all day. They need to get these small things down in order to do well, both in the school year and in the Coast Guard.

The cadre engage in a variety of training missions over the course of the summer. Before the swabs even arrive, they spend a week finalizing their leadership plans and reviewing what they have learned during 100th Week and throughout their first two years at the Academy. At some point during the summer, they will spend a week on the range, qualifying with the standard service pistol. They will learn to drive one of the three T-Boats [training boats] berthed along the Academy's waterfront. They will be exposed to basic ship handling and shipboard engineering aboard the three old Navy tugs *Honor*, *Respect*, and *Duty*. They will spend two weeks at sea as part of a coastal sailing program. They will take ROTR, a class in which they learn the "rules of the road" for vessels at sea. They will spend perhaps their favorite week of the summer in the Cadet Aviation Training Program, or CATP, where they will be introduced to aviation, both in flight simulators and aboard working aircraft. And, of course, they will spend three weeks honing their leadership skills as cadre.

2/C Paul Delesola of Golf Company came to the role of cadre straight from the pistol range and had no time to first observe his fellow students in action. When asked how he and his shipmates go about creating a cohesive team spirit among swabs, he had this to say:

We've been doing things where they cannot possibly succeed as individuals. We'll make it necessary for them to work as a team, and we give them little hints along the way. We'll tell them, "This is how you succeed as a team." There is a fine line; you want to give them enough information to succeed, but you also need to hold back some information to the point where they fail a couple of times and realize what they have to do as a team. That's what's great about this for us, the cadre; it's such a hands-on leadership opportunity. You go from being in charge of one or two 4th class cadets in your division the entire year, and then you get a bunch of training, and they throw thirty-two swabs at you and your classmates, and you are entrusted with their care. You're with them from 0530 in the morning until 2200, and then there's a two-hour debrief after that. You get an intensely involved leadership experience.

In our division, we have a couple of high-performing swabs with regards to indoc and a couple who are not high-performing. I make my expectations very clear in each formation as to what they need to know. If those expectations aren't met as a whole, as a team, I'll explain to them that I don't care if one swab is light-years beyond everyone else and is ahead of the game. If one other swab does not know their indoc, then the whole division fails and the whole division gets IT'd. That goes for everything.

Delesola is clearly enjoying his experience as cadre. He sees the role lasting far beyond the three weeks he is in charge:

You definitely get attached, and you enjoy being able to interact with them and have such an instrumental part in their growth. It's definitely a great experience, and I'm really glad I got to do swab summer, especially because I'm going to see them when they are inducted as 4th class, throughout the school year, and out in the fleet in a couple of years. My goal for swab summer was to develop

a relationship with the swabs, where if they need anything in the future, they can come to the 2nd class—whether it's during their first academic year or it's twenty years down the road and they're wondering what they should do about their next promotion. That's the kind of relationship you want, and the cadre-swab bond is really strong, because you're the first person they see in the military with few exceptions. You're the first person they see, and that means a lot to them, because you basically instill within them the knowledge that will help them get through their first year. It's been a really, really good experience.

Although there is no shortage of obligatory yelling throughout the summer, many cadre find it difficult to play bad cop. Delesola believes it is necessary, but he also tempers his actions:

It's really hard in general to be that mean to people, but you have to realize that it's something that has to be done. It's not really inhumane in the sense that you're really trying to help them. A lot of times, if I'm really harping on someone because they're messing up, I'll pull them aside. I do this with everyone; I'll pull them aside afterwards and tell them that I believe in them and that all of the other cadre believe in them, that each day is a new slate. And it really is. We really do want to see them succeed. They can swing from up to down so quickly. For instance, yesterday, they wanted ICs, and they were all super-excited, so we gave them extra time to shower and get their uniforms ready, and then they missed that time, completely flipping a positive into a negative. Sometimes, you give them a little bit of slack and everything gets taken away. It's a give-and-take—definitely a give-and-take.

I'm sure it will get a little more frustrating and tiring as the weeks go on, but it is nice to see them progress. When we took over, there was a formal room-and-wing inspection, an intensive cleaning of the barracks. Every little nitpicky thing we saw we tore them apart for. Most of the rooms looked decent; some of them looked pretty bad. They didn't really realize how serious the formal room-and-wing is. But this week, it's going to be a completely different experience, because they now know all the things we're looking for—things as small as: We don't want any water in your iron. We don't want a drop of water in your canteen. Your nametag can't be off by a quarter of an inch. They seem like nitpicky things, but we want them to know that during the school year, these are the kind of things they are going to have to worry about. It's these little things that will add up into big things. They need to realize attention to detail isn't something that's just for the Academy; more importantly, it's for the fleet, as well. If you are off a degree or two on your course heading when you're trying to find somebody in the water, it really can mean the difference between life and death. Building swabs up during the summer is about letting them know they can do it.

Ensign Shembry, whose own cadre experience is now two years in the past, remembers one event that was particularly frustrating:

We took over on the first Sunday they were here, so they had only been here for seven days. They had gotten a lot of the basic stuff down, but they still had a long way to go. There were times when we were frustrated. We didn't get frustrated over the little things, like bracing up or eyes out of the boat—those kinds of things—but when they didn't get honor or the core values right, it was frustrating. When we did a shower drill, we would post someone out in the quad where we could see their windows. They are supposed to close their blinds. We would see the lights go on and record which blinds weren't closed, so we knew who hadn't closed their blinds, and we'd go back up and say, "Hey, stick out your paw if you didn't close your blinds." When the person who didn't will not admit it, it's very frustrating. You keep giving him a chance, and you think to yourself, "Please do the right thing! Just tell us the truth!" When they just wouldn't do it, that was really frustrating. That one really got a lot of us angry, so that was not a fun night for him. With the other stuff, you could get frustrated if it was one kid repeatedly messing up and you had spent a lot of time with him and he just wouldn't get it, but most of the time you just tried to find a new way to present the material or whatever it was he needed to do.

Because each swab responds best to a different combination of leadership styles, cadre find themselves playing different roles, de-

Swabs line the passageway in Chase Hall as cadre introduce themselves.

pending on which shipmates are at their side. Shembry found he could easily adapt to varying situations:

There were five of us in the cadre section—two guys, both very, very, physically fit and aggressive. They were hard as far as the physical stuff, but they were more likely to relax and goof around with the kids. When I was paired up with them, I would take the more accountable position—try to get them to do their job better with less of the joking around, leaving the IT to them. When I was with two women cadre, one of them was extremely intense in every aspect, and the other one was very nice, the motherly type, the one soft cadre you need. So I was the one who filled the gap for what was needed. Everyone else had a very defined role of who they were, and my personality changed depending upon the day. I could be hot or cold. It wasn't that I would enforce something one day and not the other, it was just how I did it, whether I was kinder about it or it was straight to IT.

As Shembry explains, cadre learn during their 100th Week training to look for signs that swabs have reached their limits:

We get training by the Cape May company commanders. They do this professionally for four years, for every new recruit who comes into the Coast Guard, so they are truly experts at this, and they know what to look for. They give you the warning signs—what to look for. The swabs will kind of go blank; they will lock their knees out and start shaking. That's where kids will pass out. You could tell when your training wasn't effective; you'd start to get different responses out of them. They may be trying really hard to do everything you want them to do, or they may just be trying to make everything stop. You can see the shift. It is a personal judgment, but the lead cadre every day provides oversight and, as a safety observer, makes sure everything is going well. Everyone assumes that role at some point during the summer, but if you're the one yelling and you're the one who's in that swab's face, someone needs to be watching you. With every IT session, someone is doing the exercises with them, but there's also someone who's watching to make sure no one is about to pass out or hurt themselves. That's what standard operating procedures are for. We have a binder with the SOP, which says what the time limits are, how often you have to give them water, and other such things, trying to mitigate any of those dangers.

Shembry recalls one particularly harsh remedial technique:

There was a kind of action they used to have, but has now been banned, called "wolf-packing" a swab. I remember it happening to me when I was a swab. You'd have one cadre yelling at you on one side, and then, all of a sudden, there would be another cadre on the other side yelling at you, and then one behind you. You've got three extremely loud people, all screaming in your face, and you have no idea what they want. Once there are too many of them, you tune everything out. You're just, "Yes, sir! Aye aye, sir! Yes, sir! Yes, sir! Yes, sir! Yes, sir!" You're not even responding to what they're doing; it's just too much. They stopped doing that, and I think it was for the best, because it didn't serve any real purpose.

Although wolf-packing may have been officially banned, similar (albeit milder) techniques persist. However, many continue to question their proper place, if any, in the overall training scheme.

Margaret Bowen is the etiquette instructor at the Academy. Her mission is to refine cadets' behavior as they journey through the Academy. She remains in contact with them throughout their four years, affording her the opportunity to witness and monitor their growth and development. According to Bowen, cadre take their summer's work very seriously:

Sometimes, it's important that they yell, that they get that person's attention. It's like when you yell at your children, you know? Part of it is frustration, and part of it is getting their attention. I'll never forget walking down the passageway in Chase Hall. Of course, I knew most of the cadre really, really well, but I don't say anything. When I walk through there, I might as well be a stranger, but I noticed one cadre in particular. His name was Frank, and he was the biggest goofball. I just loved him to death; he was terrific. He was just a great kid, and now he was cadre, and they do take this very seriously. The cadets were lined up in the hallway with their backs against the wall and their chins tucked in, waiting for something. The cadre were pacing back and forth, and Frank was right there in this cadet's face, right up to his ear. He was talking to him in a very low, very serious voice. I wasn't listening to what he said, but I didn't have to. It was in that tone of voice, and I thought, "Holy cow, this is Frank?" It gave me the chills, and I thought, "This kid is serious."

One young lady I remember, one of my kids, was a hoot. She stopped my car in the middle of the road. She was cadre, and she said, "This whole cadre thing is really something. All of a sudden, I really understand I have these kids in my hand and whatever I tell them they're going to believe. You have to be very careful about what you say!" They know that the way these swabs are taught is going to stay with them for the rest of their lives. They have a lot of responsibility; they truly do. But it's fun to watch them grow, and I do see them grow. I see them get here first day swab summer: their hair is short now, they're skinny, they're scared, some of them with baby fat and round faces. They look so young, and after their first year, they come back from their summer on EAGLE, and you can see they're changing. They're developing these personalities, and they're starting to come out of their shells a little bit. They're physically changing, and when they come in for their 2nd class year as cadre, you see they're now young men and women. Their bodies have changed. They get a more defined jawline, the men are shaving a little bit more, the women are slimming down. You look at them and go, "Wow!" And then, when they come back as seniors, they're men and women; they truly are, and they have all this responsibility. When they come back and they're officers, and I knew them as cadets, the new cadets ask, "What was the lieutenant like when he was a cadet?" I say, "He was stellar, he was awesome, he was great!" And of course, I remember him as not so stellar, not so awesome, and not so great, but they're glad I don't tell secrets.

Transformation is what the Academy is all about and provokes some of the most rewarding feelings for all involved. Dr. Wingrove-Haugland feels much the same as Bowen:

Huge changes. It's really good to see some of the cadets you've been working with take on leadership positions and perform really well. I sailed on EAGLE for a week, and there was this cadet who was now a 2nd class, and I had taught her as a 4th class. She was so shy, meek, and retiring that I couldn't help but think, "How in the world is she going to develop a command presence?" I just couldn't see it. And there she was, on the bridge of EAGLE, barking out orders. "You have the con?" "Aye!" And boy, she did. A year and a half previous to that, there was no way she could have done that. It was really something to see, someone excelling in a role that just a year and a half earlier would have no chance of even playing that role. It's very rewarding to watch.

Senior Chief McDade admits that he had many doubts when he first accepted his position at the Academy. Could these young women and men handle the responsibilities they have been given? As with others, he was quickly impressed:

I think the transformation is phenomenal, not just for the civilians who come in as swabs, but for the cadre. You watch this 3rd class, kind of wide-eyed, go from, "I just had to keep myself squared away and serve as a good role model to the 4th class below me, and everything was good," to all of a sudden, "Not only do I have to role-model it, I have to make sure that: 1) I'm taking care of those I'm charged with taking care of, all the swabs, and 2) that I am making sure that they are up to speed, because if they are failing, what am I doing? What am I doing to fix that, or am I part of the problem?" So it is a critical part of development, not just for the swabs, but the cadre as well. I think it's a big eye-opener for them.

I'm consistently, overwhelmingly proud, overall, of the remarkable job the cadets do. It's easy to get caught up in some of the conduct stuff and all the other stuff that occurs, but the vast majority of the corps of cadets is doing a phenomenal job all the time. When I first came here, I saw how much control, autonomy, and the amount of responsibility the cadre have, and I was concerned. Actually, I was worried. And now, I'm still vigilant, but just from watching them, I have a lot of faith in them. I've caught myself at times micromanaging and getting into things, when, for the most part, nine times out of ten, it's like, "Wow!"

Lieutenant Andrew Norberg

Portrait of an Officer

Cadets have both civilian and military professors at the Academy. Most military subjects are taught by officers who have both academic and field experience. Civilian instructors generally teach in areas where no special military knowledge is required, such as chemistry, math, English, or history.

Lieutenant Andrew Norberg, an Academy graduate, is currently a military navigational instructor. When I spoke with

him, he had only recently been assigned to duty in New London, but he knows his alma mater well. Norberg comes from a military family, but like many former and current cadets, he knew little of the Coast Guard before actually applying:

I'm an army brat. I was born in Germany and lived two places there. We moved to Colorado for two years, then to Oklahoma, Pennsylvania, and finally to Virginia, where my dad retired. I say I'm from Alaska, because I was stationed there and plan on retiring there. That's where I'm going to try to set my roots down. My original plan was to graduate from the Naval Academy and be a helicopter pilot. I actually found out about the Academy when I was applying for colleges. Rowing was my sport, and I had a friend whom I rowed with whose dad was familiar with New England. He took us up here to look at schools, as rowing is a big sport in New England. He used to be a submariner, so he knew about the Coast Guard. He said, "While we're up here, let's give the Coast Guard Academy a try." I knew nothing about it other than they had a crew team. I met with the crew coach, and he told me what was available in terms of getting here, so I just filled out an early application and received early acceptance. At that point, I still didn't really know a whole lot, other than they were interested in me. I came in June of 2004, so I graduated in 2008. I was a marine and environmental science major, and I focused in physical and biological oceanography.

After graduation, Norberg spent his first tour aboard ship on the frigid waters of the arctic:

I was assigned to cutter ALEX HALEY, which is in Kodiak, Alaska—spent two years there as a deck watch officer and a boarding officer. She was a medium-endurance cutter. It's kind of an oddball. It's not one of the 210's or the 270's; it's 282' long—an old Navy salvage ship that was converted to Coast Guard use. They put a flight deck and a hangar on it and started using it for Coast Guard missions. I did four patrols up in the Bering Sea in the arctic and would board fishing vessels, checking their safety equipment, their nets, and their catch. Drug running, since the Coast Guard has been up north, really hasn't been an issue. Immigrants aren't an issue; it's mostly fisheries stuff. The fisheries are very highly regulated in Alaska. The vessel owners up there have been in the business for a while and are well respected. They know there is a lot to lose, so they don't tolerate drug use or alcohol abuse. It tends to be very clean. They're very tough, and there were very few violations, at least when I was there.

With the training he had received, Norberg felt comfortable with his first assignment:

It was pretty much what I expected. I had never been to Alaska before, so that was something new. When I got there, the ship was in dry dock, so that was interesting, too. There's still a steep learning curve, because you're actually the ensign, you're actually the officer, so it's still a little bit different than seeing it as a 1st class cadet. But it was easy, because I talked the language at that point. Learning isn't the problem; it's just the fact that you have to. It was a new ship for me, so I had to learn where everything was, but at least I knew what that symbol meant on a piece of paper, so I could find it—or I had seen a firefighting system very similar to it, so I could guess where this piece of equipment was. I had already dealt with this type of engine on another ship, so re-qualifying was a piece of cake. It's not terrible, but there's definitely a learning curve. Then, there's all the stuff that goes into being on a ship that you don't get to learn here as a cadet, such as with law enforcement—for instance, how to be a boarding officer. I had to qualify with the pistol and then go to boarding-officer school. There's an infinite number of things you have to go through. If you went to a buoy tender, you'd have to go to these aids to navigation schools. We don't get into dealing with buoys or aids to navigation at all here. We know what they are, but in terms of how to clean one, how to pull it out of the water, and other things like that, we learn later. I still don't have any of that experience. Guys who go to icebreakers have to learn how to deal with ice, so there are a considerable number of things we aren't taught here. When I was here, through all four years, there was always something new the Academy had to feed you; it's pretty hard to run dry on things to work on while here.

The Coast Guard's mission often overlaps with the Navy's, and the two branches share many responsibilities. Familiarity among their officers is essential if they are to work together effectively. Accordingly, the two branches exchange personnel on a regular basis to promote inter-service cooperation and understanding. Lieutenant Norberg's next assignment was just such an exchange:

From there I went to the USS FITZGERALD, a Navy destroyer in Japan. I spent two years there on exchange with the Navy as a navigator. The Coast Guard, as a whole, ends up doing a lot of missions with the Navy. The Navy helps out a great deal with interdicting drugs. We have teams that utilize Navy ships because they can go faster and have longer legs; that is to say, they can go out farther. We'll do boardings off of the Navy ships. We work in the same space, and it helps if the branches work together. We have shared knowledge, and because of that program, we have people in the Coast Guard who understand the Navy. Still, most people in the Coast Guard have certain stereotypes, usually not the best, of the Navy. I think the Coast Guard is better than the Navy, and I am glad I'm part of the Coast Guard now that I've spent two years with them. That said, the Navy is great at what they do, but it is different from what's expected from the Coast Guard, and they do many things we often cannot, as Coasties, appreciate.

Throughout the summer, I had the chance to meet a number of prospective students and their families. Three fathers stood out in particular, as each wore the uniform of another service branch. Poking fun, I asked if they were betraying their respective services by touring the Coast Guard Academy. Their responses were enlightening. Each of the three men had served on a joint base where the Coast Guard had a presence, and each went to great lengths to praise the Coast Guard's performance. In fact, there was consensus among the fathers that the Coast Guard was invariably the most squared-away outfit on location. With Coast Guard officers, the answer to any request was an unwavering "Yes, sir, we can do that"—in contrast to the responses they sometimes received from their own less-cooperative peers. It was evident that Coast Guard officers had made an immediate and lasting impression on these men, and each told me he would be proud to have his child attend the Academy.

My own experience at the Academy was no different. This eagerness to go above and beyond was common to every single officer and cadet with whom I had contact. It is simply part of the Coast Guard culture, and it is something that Lieutenant Norberg believes sets his service apart:

The one thing I've noticed throughout the Coast Guard, especially here, and one of the reasons I came back to the Academy, was how people are treated. The Navy is such a huge organization that you don't get the personal touch you do in the Coast Guard. When you go on a cutter, you get lots of focused attention. The crews get that focused attention. The command structure, even all the way up to the commandant, can be very personal, whereas in the Navy, it's very distant. The tendency is to treat subordinates with less respect. Not treating them as human is a lot easier to do, and that tendency spreads. In the Coast Guard, it doesn't. It is a very close, very tight-knit group. That's one thing I appreciate about the Coast Guard: the fact that it is that intimate and that close. The Navy is so big that they focus people on one specific task. In the Coast Guard, when I came here, you didn't just focus on being the best at something; you focused on being the most well-rounded person you could so you could attack any issue that came up when you left here. You may not be the best ship driver, you may not be the best navigator, but you will be the best leader, because you can handle any number of things, whether it is a personnel or an equipment issue. You can at least think through the issue and resolve it. The Navy, I feel, is not the same, because so much depends on excelling in their specialty.

Fresh off his years on the Navy destroyer, Norberg came right back to the Academy:

Nautical Science III is the course I'll be teaching, so I'll be teaching the 2nd class cadets. This class is focused on advanced ship handling and navigation, so we'll be spending a lot of time in the simulators we have and learning how to communicate with radios. There's a certain language that you use on a radio that you don't use when talking to friends. For these instructor positions, there's no checklist that says you know this, this, and this, because it's assumed that in the years I've spent in the Coast Guard and the two years I've spent as a navigator in the Navy, I am going to

be well-versed in what I'll be teaching. Nautical science is the one subject in which Coast Guard officers are expected to be well-versed, whereas, if I was going to teach a science or an engineering course, I would have to go get a master's or a doctorate degree in that field.

Swabs and 3rd class cadets both spend portions of their summers aboard the *Eagle*, the Coast Guard's sail training vessel. Norberg had this to say about the ship:

In the 3rd class summer, they spend half of the time on the EAGLE, and the other half they spend on a cutter somewhere in the fleet. The EAGLE feels like an extension of the Academy, because you go there as a class. I took it like a vacation. You're still learning, and you're training, but you get to see really cool places, and there are receptions. It's a different classroom—one you don't get during the school year. I really enjoyed EAGLE, but some of my classmates didn't. Some people just see it as having to clean dishes and putting up with seasickness, which it is as well. The other half of the summer you're placed at active units for five or six weeks, which will be all over the country. When I was in Alaska, we had cadets who flew up there to meet us, while others went all the way down to Florida. They are integrated into the crew as a junior enlisted person would be on a ship. They don't start off with an officer role; they're still learning how to take orders. They will go on boardings, and ride in the small boats and helicopters. They're part of the tie-down crews for helicopters, they're in the engine rooms; whatever a regular crew member does, they get a chance to do.

There's a grace period they have when they come on board as they get used to the ship, and the crew has to get used to them as well. As they come on during the summer, you may have to reiterate proper protocol between the crew and cadets. They're still training to become officers, and the crew has to treat them as such. It's kind of confusing at some points, but overall, integration really isn't an issue. They jump right in with the crew and learn as much as they can. There's a PQS, a performance qualification standard, they get for the summer, and they have to fill out so many of these blocks to come back to the Academy and get a performance evalu-

ation. Things like drawing out the firefighting system aboard the ship: where all the valves are located, how the water flows, where the pumps are, and how much pressure is in the system. That's just for one system; then there's the fuel system, the electrical system, and the sewage system. That's just part of the engineering side. They have to learn topside as well. They can get qualified as a quartermaster of the watch up on the bridge, with the charts where they plot the ship's location. They will practice dead reckoning, where the ship is going to go, taking fixes, writing in the logs, and all that stuff. On the supply side, they have to learn how to fill out procurement requests and things like that. Throughout the whole ship, there are little tests like those the crewmembers have to master. It's not like you have to learn to do everything; you're given a little booklet of like a hundred tasks, and you have to do maybe eighty-five of them.

After four years in New London, Lieutenant Norberg will be transferred to his next assignment. He hopes to assume command of a ship:

When one swab forgets his cover, or hat, the whole company is reminded to check their shipmate's uniforms before inspection after having to wear their hands for the afternoon.

There's a screening process. The Coast Guard says, "Okay, this person is suitable for commanding a ship." I did the screening three years ago and applied to get command for my second assignment on an 87' patrol boat. I didn't pass it then, but I did this time to get command of a 110' patrol boat. I passed the screening, but the billets weren't available. Out of forty people who screened, thirty people were considered acceptable, and then there were only twenty billets available, so not everybody who screened got to go. I was a very junior lieutenant, and I was competing with people who had been a lieutenant for four years while I had been one for just a few months. So that was my first choice, but I didn't get the opportunity to go; this was my second choice. I'm hoping that once my four years here are done, I'll get a chance to command. I think the Coast Guard does a really great job of performance-based assignments, so if you perform really well, they'll put you at the top of the list.

A rack of lowly mops, or swabs, aboard the USCG Cutter *Eagle*.

Swabs

Swab: *Noun*   1) A nautical term for a yarn mop.
2) A useless or contemptible person.
3) A low ranking sailor.

At the end of R-Day, after the swabs' parents and families have finally departed, the Academy seems deserted. Any cadets who remain on campus for the summer have been instructed to stay out of sight as much as possible; swabs are to be left alone with their tormentors. At 1650, swabs are led to Dimick Hall, where Captain O'Connor welcomes them to the Academy. Named after a long-serving mathematics teacher, Dimick is a modern, circular auditorium set into the hillside on Hunter Liggett Drive, just below the Academy's library, and serves as a meeting and lecture space for large groups. After the welcoming speech comes a presentation on the school's academic curriculum. Companies then head back to Chase for their first formation, and then to the dining hall, or wardroom as it is known, for their first evening meal. If swabs had hoped that dinner would afford them an opportunity to quietly reflect on the events of the day, they were, once again, sadly mistaken.

Meals are just like all other swab summer activities: loud, rushed struggles for survival. Whether they are also nutritional is less certain. That is not to say there is anything wrong with the food itself; cadets speak quite highly of Academy meals. Rather, swabs are in a constant race against the clock—a race they often lose.

The wardroom is, in a word, cacophonous. Cadre eat up much of the swabs' time with quizzes: What is the mission of the United States Coast Guard? What are the nine Academy rules? What is the proper position of attention? As always, questions and answers are delivered at maximum volume, making genteel conversation downright impossible. During the summer, while waiting for lunch to end, I often sat on benches near the Honor Wall, well below Chase Hall. Even at that distance, the noise was enough to stop visitors in their tracks. Certain that a fight had broken out among the entire corps, they would look at me as though I were crazy when I told them that they were merely hearing lunch.

Despite this chaos, swabs do eventually learn to ingest enough food to get them to their next meal. As Swab Sheila Bertrand describes, however, there are a number of difficulties to surmount:

The food is good. It's hard to eat. It tastes good, but the first three days I didn't hardly eat anything, because you have the whole squaring thing and the way you have to sit, one fist from here, one fist there, your feet at a 45-degree angle, your heels together on the ground, and then they're indoc'ing you at the beginning of your meal. You have to wait until one plate gets all the way around and then somebody asks for permission to bring the food aboard to begin eating. By that time, you probably have ten minutes to cut each little piece, and you can only chew three times for every piece of food you eat, and then you have to swallow it, because you only have three seconds to respond if they were to command or ask a question of you. So that's hard, and then you have to leave at will.

There's a 180 seconds, and you have to scream for 180 seconds. Usually you have to do that two, three, or four times. Based on that, they say, "You're dismissed; you are excused," and you have ten minutes from the time leave-at-will begins, minus the three minutes, so seven minutes to get from the screaming point to the third deck, brush your teeth, change your shirt if you need to, and anything else. I can't wait for the day we get off for the three hours with our family, to go out to dinner and eat like a human being. It's like seventeen more days.

Despite the imposed difficulties, Swab Rheanastasia Doctolero finds she still must rely on her own self-discipline:

The food here is really good. I actually have to tell myself not to eat so much, not to overindulge, because there's always enough sweets. I'm always starving. What I try to do to get myself to eat better is I take two fruits, and I eat them before I begin my meal, so I'm kind of half-way full. When I do get my meal, I eat enough, but I'm not stuffed. I used to stuff myself. The first two days, I was like, "Oh my gosh! Look at all this food!" And they were like, "You can have as much as you want." So I used to stuff myself, and I would feel bad, but I'm teaching myself that even though the brownies are good, just have one!

As a swab, Katie Brosnan found dining at the Academy to be a new experience in more ways than one:

You know, when you come to the Academy, one of the biggest things the kids say is, "Oh, the sense of community—that's why I like the Academy. It's really family-oriented here." They really take care of you here. Yes, they're screaming in your face all the time, but when it comes down to it, they take care of you. Even at breakfast, they give you cereal, and one of my cadre, Mr. Kahl—he's my division officer—if there's cereal we don't want, he will actually go back and get the cereal we want; he gets me two boxes of Lucky Charms every day! It sounds so little, you know? But he'll go check other tables to try to get your cereal. Not all cadre are like that. Some of them are like, "It's just Golden Grahams. Eat it." The thing is, if we were in a regular environment, I would be so appreciative. "Oh, thanks!" Because it's cadre and swabs, you can't really be grateful. It's just, "Thank you, sir." But you can't even say thank you, because they get mad. They say, "Don't say thank you; I'm just doing my job." That was hard for me, not saying thank you. With Cadre I, I got yelled at a lot for being polite; I didn't understand. But with Cadre II, it's different, because Cadre II, they say thank you, and they say please, so I guess depends on the person. With Cadre I, I think they're just trying to shock you; that's their job.

You go in on day one just thinking, "Okay, just take it day by day—just day by day and I'll be fine." Then, by day three, you figure, "No, just take it meal by meal. Just got to make it to breakfast. Just got to make it to lunch. Just got to make it to dinner." It's meal by meal. It's not sad or depressing or anything like that; it's just your day is so jam-packed that the time between meals would normally be a regular day; it would be jam-packed with enough activities for a regular day for a regular person, so in every day, there's essentially three. That's how much you're doing and how everything is arranged. First, you're going to the waterfront, sail-boating, and then all of a sudden you're at Survival at Sea, jumping off the diving board in a pitch-black room. Then you have swimming lessons, IC sports where you're playing other companies' teams, getting trainings on everything from weapons to being honorable, and having math class. It's really busy; it's a lot going on. It's good though; it's good.

What really makes eating interesting for swabs, however, is the "eyes in the boat" policy, which is enforced through their entire 4th class year. Swabs may not look at anything that is not directly in front of them and at eye level. Their heads do not turn, nor do their eyes swivel—at least not when cadre are nearby. This is much harder than it sounds. Try simply staring ahead as you go about two minutes of your day, and you will immediately appreciate how difficult this can be. While we derive much enjoyment from simply gazing about, our eyes also scan the surrounding environment for danger, an instinctual behavior. We naturally direct our attention to loud noises or sudden movements, and we learn from an early age to initiate and maintain eye contact. Swabs however,

must overcome eighteen years of training and habit. Cadre Ryan Babb explains the basic rules governing swab behavior:

Your head is completely straight forward, and your eyes never move. You can't look to the side or turn your head to see something. You have to square all your corners, stay in the middle of the passageway, and you can't talk to anybody except upperclass in the passageway. The big thing people always get caught for is looking around with their eyes. That's one of the big learning curves; you need to always look forward, never look around. Squaring your meal is also really hard. You can look down to cut your food or glance down to see what you are putting on your fork, but other than that, you have to keep your eyes straight and square your movements, even while eating. They have to do these things the whole first year. When you're outside or in a common area, you don't have to be braced up, but when you are in the passageways in Chase Hall, you have to keep your eyes in the boat, square your corners, and greet people. Every upperclassman you pass is, "Good afternoon, sir" or "ma'am," and if you know them, it's, "Good afternoon, Mr. Babb, sir." It's really interesting when you try to get to know the people in your company without looking at them, because you are required to know them. The first couple of weeks, if you don't know them, they'll let you slide, but you really need to know them.

According to the cadre, the "eyes in the boat" policy provides invaluable training; it teaches swabs to stay focused under even the most extreme circumstances. The example invariably used to illustrate the benefits of the policy is this: they may find themselves in a rescue operation at sea, surrounded by a maelstrom of hectic activity, and charged with keeping their eyes on a victim bobbing among the waves. Faced with this situation, they must be able to focus on their task and ignore all other stimuli. A now retired Captain Carl Tjerandsen explained that cadets face increasing amounts of stress and pressure throughout their four years at the Academy. This exposure has a ratcheting effect, eventually creating officers who, even when at sea, in a storm, exhausted and ill, will roll out of their bunks and stand watch without complaint.

While eating, swabs are simply not allowed to look at the food on their plates. As can be imagined, this makes for situations that can be either difficult or humorous, depending on your perspective. Swabs do, however, adapt quickly to this novel challenge. Commander Haukom remembers this part of his boot camp experience well:

Couldn't look at my food. I remember I learned very quickly: Don't get peas on your plate, because they'll fall off, or if you do, get mashed potatoes and mix them together, because they'll stick together. You have to square your meals, and you only have five minutes to do it.

Swab Rheanastasia Doctolero learned to work through the handicap and is now relatively confident she will be able to get enough calories this summer:

I'm actually getting pretty good at it. It depends on the food. Sometimes the food isn't exactly recognizable. I remember one time, I thought we were having macaroni, but it was really cauliflower. I made a mistake when I picked it up and tried to square, and I dropped it on myself, but overall I'm pretty good at squaring. I'm pretty quick with it. What I do is: I pick up my plate, and I memorize where everything is, so after that, I'm like bam, bam, bam, so I can get it done and start studying my RUNNING LIGHT.

Sometimes, I just don't feel like talking, because I'm trying so hard not to spill stuff on my shirt, because you can't look at it. Like soup, I love to eat the soup, but it's just so hard. And the worst part is, you're walking around greeting people, and you go to your room and you see all this stuff on your shirt, and you're like, "Oh my God! I've been walking around with all these stains? I'm so embarrassed!" I hate that so much. I'll be walking around, and when I get to my room, there is a blob of oatmeal on my shirt. I'm like, "What? When did that happen?"

After the first week, 4/C Kyle Wood decided simply to abandon table etiquette in favor of consumption:

I've learned tricks like eating with a spoon, pile it all on with my hand—don't be afraid to get your left hand dirty and pack it onto the spoon. I'm getting used to it, so I'm getting more food down. I've still lost over twelve pounds, but I guess it's good for me. I'm in shape more.

When companies are marching or running about the campus, cadre often employ chants beyond the standard "Left . . . Left . . . Left, Right, Left"—both to improve morale and to provide extra material that swabs must absorb. While one popular ditty expresses swabs' desire to go home, another jokes about the food quality:

They say that in the Coast Guard, the chow is mighty fine;
A chicken jumped off the table and started marking time.

They say that in the Coast Guard, the coffee's mighty fine;
It looks like muddy water and tastes like turpentine.

They say that in the Coast Guard, the biscuits are mighty fine;
One rolled right off the table and killed a friend of mine.

At 1840, their twenty-minute R-Day dinner complete, swabs move on to their next activity—a medical service brief and the chance to fill out additional paperwork, which adds a few more hours to their already-long day. Then, before they are allowed the reprieve of sleep, they must do one more thing. Because Chase Hall houses over a thousand cadets, fire drills are essential, so swabs must learn evacuation procedures for the barracks and perform a full walkthrough before the day ends. With this final task complete, swabs may at last return to their rooms. The mournful sound of taps echoes through the darkened halls, lights blink off, and a wonderful silence covers the campus as the cadre assemble to discuss the next day's schedule. Although swabs are beyond exhausted, most report getting little sleep this first night.

Foxtrot Company waits for orders on Bear Drive after a grueling round of morning calisthenics.

In-Processing

Most of Week One is devoted to what is called "in-processing," a military term that encompasses all of the unavoidable paperwork and physical exams. Before the real work of indoctrination can begin, students must undergo a complete physical with Academy doctors. Roughly half of the students who leave the Academy before graduation do so during swab summer, and a sizable portion of those leave for medical reasons. As Admiral Sandra Stosz, the Academy's current superintendent explains, every service academy has been working to improve graduation rates over the years:

I came in '78, and all of the service academies had a higher attrition rate in those days. Speaking for ours, in particular, we had about 50 percent for many years. When my class came in, they came in with something like 312 people, and we graduated 156,

116

and that's about 50 percent. We came in with thirty women and graduated ten, so women were a two-thirds attrition rate. Now we have about 80 percent retention; all the academies are about that now. The retention has come up over time for many reasons; certainly our society has become much more of a society where you intervene to try to make people successful.

There are a number of reasons why young people attrit out of here, and first and foremost is medical. It's gotten a lot better with DOD-MERB, the Department of Defense Medical Examination Review Board. They are the medical assessing facility for all young people entering service academies. They've gotten really good, but still, when some youngsters present here, some of them will be color-blind and somehow have passed that test. There are always a number who attrit because they aren't medically fit when they get here. Then, there are a number that attrit, too, during swab summer, when it doesn't meet their expectations. Some of those end up being slightly medical; people start spending their time in the ward because they want to get away from the barracks. They don't want to be here, but they don't want to quit because of parental pressure. Unfortunately, with the bad economy, we can tell this is becoming a factor. My assistant commandant of cadets tells me that last summer, all the young people she interviewed who dropped on request were here because their parents had made them come for the free education.

In the summertime, we lose about 10 percent of our cadets, so out of the 20 percent attrition, as much as 7–10 percent comes during swab summer. A lot of that is medical or that initial coming-to-Jesus moment kids have as they realize whether or not this is the place they want to be. Almost all of them who drop on request were here because parents pushed them or they thought they were doing what their parents wanted them to do. During the school year, it becomes academic failure, honor failure, athletic failure, or weight failure. Right now, I've got some 1st class cadets getting ready to graduate who aren't meeting weight or physical-fitness standards. There are different criteria they just have to meet; we have to have standards for commissioning. If they can't get the

academics, despite the intrusive interventions we have nowadays, it's truly because they aren't able to.

The cadre are fully unleashed on Friday, once swabs have cleared their medical exams. Although every swab was examined before arriving at the Academy, a surprising number of them will fail the in-house testing program. For those whose problems are not chronic, there exist a number of options. Many with only minor, temporary problems receive medical chits; they wear wristbands, limiting their participation in specific areas of physical endeavor. These black bands come and go from swabs' wrists throughout the seven weeks. A sprained ankle may keep a swab from running or jumping on the obstacle course. A severe cold may allow the swab to respond to questions without yelling. Once the physical problem has been corrected, the chit disappears and training resumes at the normal pace. For Ensign Shembry, a medical problem he had as a child almost entirely derailed his plans to become an officer:

I remember being excited and a little nervous because I received a conditional appointment. I had a little medical hang-up, based on the fact I had asthma way back when I was five or six. They informed me they wanted me, but I had to go through another battery of tests. That was a little scary, because they put me in a box and gave me an asthma attack. I passed that test and they said, "Okay, you're good to go."

Both swabs and cadre report that the Academy takes very good care of their health. There is a well-staffed clinic to deal with any physical problems that may arise during the summer or school year. If they so choose, cadets may also meet with counselors for emotional and psychological support—be they military officers, civilian doctors, clergymen or others.

In some cases, a medical problem may be serious enough to jeopardize a swab's enrollment. If the condition is expected to vanish over the course of the next year, as in a case of appendicitis, the swab may choose to leave and return the following summer. In the worst cases, however, such as the discovery of a previously undetected heart condition, the medical problem permanently disqualifies the student from ever becoming a cadet. These are the most heartbreaking disenrollments, as the swabs have done nothing wrong and are not choosing to leave of their own accord. Finally, swabs may injure themselves so severely during summer training that disenrollment becomes the only option. The losses reported by 4/C Koachar Mohammad of Echo Company are typical:

We lost three people over the summer. One was right in the beginning—a girl, for weight. She was over the weight standard. One of them, after the medical inspections, determined he was colorblind, but he stuck around for a couple of weeks, so he left about the third week. Another one had completed about two weeks, two and a half weeks, and then he decided to drop, because I believe—his words—he said that he was doing it for his parents, not for himself, and it wasn't right for him. It had some effect on our company. The guy that left, the one who said he was doing it for his parents, wrote a letter. It was a very emotional letter, and he gave everybody a boost to go on. For the most part, they were early on, but it was upsetting, especially to see the one who left because of his color blindness, because he really wanted to be here, and the only reason he left was because of medical.

Perhaps the saddest case, however, involved a 4th class cadet. According to Mohammad:

There was one girl in my chemistry class who, after the first week of school, got kicked out because she had asthma. She made the whole swab summer. She was my lab partner, and one day I asked, "Where is she?" Here at the Academy, you can't miss class. If somebody is missing, there has to be a reason. The whole swab summer with asthma, and then the first week of school she gets kicked out. It was terrible. I felt bad for her.

Ensign Shembry recalls that the cadre used one swab's summer disenrollment as a motivational tool:

As a swab, we only lost one in my company, and he was in the first week due to medical reasons. He had some sort of a heart problem, and they used that against us pretty well. Anytime we weren't performing, they would tell us, "That kid is still bracing up in the ward and wants desperately to come back with us. Even with his heart problem, he has more heart than any one of you."

Ensign Klakring remembers students washing out not only during swab summer, but throughout his four years at the Academy:

There was this one kid who came around and was offering everyone cookies. He said, "Want a cookie? I'm leaving tomorrow." "Yes. What?" There were also a couple of people who left for medical stuff but actually came back the next year, which was nice to see. I think there were a couple of people who left just after R-Day. We all look at our pictures of R-Day, and we say, "Who's that person?" They left after a couple of days—don't even remember them. We definitely lost the most during swab summer, but then we certainly lost a lot during 4th class year, and last year we had a few—a good number of people who decided they didn't want to do it or were kicked out for various reasons. There's always this sense of uncertainty, a kind of thin ice. You need to be on your best behavior and do your thing, stay out of trouble, and eventually graduate. I don't think it was ever shocking with the ones who left. You could see they didn't like it. Some of them decided to enlist—get out and enlist—and others decided they wanted to do something else with their lives. It's rather unfortunate they took the spot of somebody who really wanted to get in and didn't, but it is nice they at least gave it full effort through swab summer and 4th class year. I think people get scared during the summer and the 4th class year, but once you cross that barrier, it gets so much easier; it's a whole different world. Everything combined in that first year is extremely difficult.

Medical problems are not, of course, the only cause for departure; some leave by choice. These are students who conclude that they can no longer see themselves living a military lifestyle for the next nine years. When they first request disenrollment, they are offered counseling; if they remain committed to the idea, the long process of disenrollment begins. They will be sent to Zulu Company, a company of ghosts, and kept separate from their shipmates. They will then have to wait several long weeks as a second volume of paperwork is processed.

Although half of all disenrollments happen during swab summer, cadets will continue to wash out throughout the four academic years. Senior Chief McDade explains some of the reasons:

Physically, if they wash out, it's going to be because of the PFE, the Physical Fitness Exam. Academically, it's going to be through an academic review board. In some cases, they're afforded an extension. Instead of doing it in four years, they might do four years and a semester, or even a whole extra year. I think the system does a pretty good job. Yes, you can have somebody who's great academically, but if he can't pass the PFE, he won't make it. The bottom line, as an officer in the Coast Guard, is it has to be the full deal. You can't say, "I'm great academically, but militarily I'm just going to take a pass." It's all important. You have some who are academic superstars and militarily will be sent home, and vice versa. You'll have cadets who are militarily and even physically great, but if they don't cut it academically, they're going home, too. Now, it's not cut and dry, and I've seen plenty of exceptions. Okay, we've got a very solid military performer, solid physical fitness, but they're struggling academically, so they might get an extension. They're given all the tools to succeed. Obviously, the onus rests on them to make it happen, and that's what the company chiefs are here for: to make sure they're aware of the tools and use them. We lead the horses to water—can't make them drink.

Lieutenant Batchelder oversees the discharge process. He tallies the summer's mounting losses after the first three weeks:

We've had six depart so far, but there are sixteen waiting to depart in various stages, so there are quite a few. It's a big process to get them out. The numbers, though, are pretty average. Last year was the lowest ever, so a lot of people remember just last year and don't think about previous years. But if you go all the way back to summer 2006, you'll see we're right in the middle of the averages. It's not the most we've ever had, and it's not the least. Last year, we had extremely low numbers across the board for everything. We lost only four or five people that wanted to leave on their own. This year, we're up to thirteen already. So what's the big difference? Last year's class was an anomaly.

Given the tough climate in which these teenagers find themselves, the number of cadets who choose to leave is surprisingly small. Indeed, retention rates at military service academies mirror, or even beat, those at civilian colleges, despite the added challenges their students face. According to U.S. News & World Report's annual survey of 1,219 ranked colleges, only 40 percent of full-time first-year students who enrolled in 2005 graduated within four years. Although disenrollment is certainly a tough reality at the Academy, Captain O'Connor notes that once students pass the initial hurdles, the retention rate is quite high:

Right now, we're retaining about 70 percent of a class across the four years. Typically, we get people into the academic year, and they start developing a sense for who we are and what we do, and it keeps people here. People get excited about what it is they're doing, what they're preparing for, and they stay. The retention once they graduate is really high. We do better than most of the other DOD services. One of the things they talk about in DOD is: You love your academy and hate your service. At the Coast Guard Academy—and I hope it's changed—sometimes, they would say they hate their academy but love their service. This is a difficult way to get an education, so it's not the most pleasant thing all the time, but I think the people who stay take a lot of satisfaction out of being successful here. Then, when they get out into the Service and are actually doing the mission, the people are incredible. The mission is incredible, and people are steeped with pride. They want to do this for a living, and they do.

That's what really hooks people: understanding our history, understanding our tradition, understanding the legacy of which they are becoming a part, along with the core values of the organization. They understand they have a responsibility to that history, to that tradition, to that legacy in the way they conduct themselves in uniform as members of the United States Coast Guard. That's a large part of what we do during swab summer. I think people find it very rewarding.

Swabs rise at 0530—though the word "rise" is an understatement. More accurately, they are blasted from their racks. They hit the

Clockwise: Swab Barrameda crawls along a rope upside-down on the Academy's obstacle course.

2/C Victoria Phillips is the day's chosen leader. To keep cadre from deadlocking on decisions with their peers, a daily leader is able to make the final decision. Each of the cadre leads at some point, and all learn to follow during the course of the summer.

Swabs work another physical problem inside Billard Hall. The group, along with a beachball, must cross the gym floor without touching it. They land on the triangular beams by utilizing a rope swing.

Clockwise: Swabs Adam Kline and Shane Rainey discuss how they will solve a problem on the ropes course. Learning to work together or follow another is a significant challenge for a group of students chosen for their leadership qualities.

Cadre members Ashley and Trump discuss the day's routine.

Swab Ardy Effendi helps his fellow shipmate Jeremy Tyrrell as he works to improve the number of sit-ups he can do in a two minute period.

deck running, bound not to rest until taps is played. Once dressed, each company begins its assigned tasks, maintaining a schedule that literally accounts for every minute of the day. During their in-processing week, all swabs take a urinalysis test, undergo a physical exam, and complete a math assessment quiz to determine their academic placement in the upcoming school year. All swabs take the same summer math class; they must keep their analytical skills honed, as the first academic year is heavily weighted toward science, technology, engineering, and math. Time is allotted for swabs to learn about counseling options, to receive uniforms and swimsuits, and to undergo an "impact test"—a test which helps the Coast Guard determine a baseline from which to measure possible concussions in the future. Alpha and Bravo Company will also meet with their company chiefs for a mandatory lecture on sexual harassment.

The events after lunch are much the same, with each company rotating through until 1630. At that time, all companies report to Leamy, where the Academy's senior chaplain addresses the class. The Coast Guard Academy, like all military academies, accommodates differing religious needs within the community. If particular services are not available on campus, students are allowed to attend local services in New London or Groton. Interestingly, chaplains throughout the Coast Guard are actually Navy officers, although they wear Coast Guard uniforms when working as Coast Guard chaplains. Captain Finch, the senior chaplain at the Academy and on his third tour with the Coast Guard, explains:

The Coast Guard utilizes Navy chaplains. There are about forty Navy chaplains who are part of the Coast Guard. The Coast Guard pays for the billets, and we come on board and we serve the Coast Guard. We actually serve four of the maritime services: we serve at the Merchant Marine Academy, the Coast Guard Academy and the operational Coast Guard, the Marine Corps, and the Navy. We're allowed to wear the uniform in the forty billets the Coast Guard has. They take Navy chaplains and assign them within the Coast Guard. It works out really well. For the billets that they buy, we serve them both as reservists and active components.

According to Finch, surveys show that nearly half of all Academy cadets become involved with the chaplains or their programs at one point or another. This involvement does not necessarily have religious overtones:

We meet a lot of cadets who don't want a lot of religious counseling. I've helped students that are atheists or agnostics, that simply want to talk and don't want a clinician. They just really need a spiritual life coach, which is really a lot of what the chaplain ends up doing.

When asked how he accounted for such high numbers, Finch had these thoughts:

When you look at this millennial generation, or Generation Y, it is very committed to things—very different from the boomers, Generation X, and others when it comes to institutions. They actually trust institutions: government, churches, and such. They very much mirror the hero generation, the generation that fought World War II. Among other things, three or four million of them have been raised by their grandparents. A lot of people don't realize that. These kids have a tremendous admiration for that generation; they fought wars and have a big impact, even today.

Part of it may be the demographic of the higher income, where faith has been more of a component, or if from the military, faith certainly plays a larger part. But also, too, this generation has been faced with few opportunities. There are no jobs. This is the worst recession since the Great Depression, and we've had a two-front war that's been going on ten, eleven years. Then, throw in 9/11 and a whole slew of other things in between, and they haven't really been given a whole lot. So I think they tend to be hyper-pragmatic, even when it comes to issues of faith. They're looking for traditional things that have been tested by time. They tend to like things that work, that are inclusive, that build groups, teams, and communities, and they tend to stick closely together.

After this session, the entire corps marches to a lecture at Dimick concerning Coast Guard regulations, followed by evening formation and supper. Then, they return to Leamy for a discussion on the

Cadet Oath and the core values they will hear so much about over the next seven weeks—honor, respect, and devotion to duty. The last hour of their second day they spend with the cadre in the company wing area. The cadre cannot yet IT swabs, but rest assured: they find other ways to keep them occupied.

Summers along the Connecticut shoreline can be both hot and humid, and this particular summer was notably both. In fact, it was one of the hottest in the state's recorded history, making swab life all the more difficult. Many days, the combined temperature-humidity index climbed above the Academy's safety mark for personnel, requiring the curtailment of heavy, physical activity. Swabs carried their canteens with them at all times, guzzling water when needed or when under direct orders to "hydrate" (the maximum time allowed between swab water breaks is engraved in the SOP).

The giant block of masonry that serves as the cadets' barracks gathers and traps energy from the sun throughout the day. When swabs are finally allowed to hit their racks, they feel as if they are sleeping in ovens. Although a small portion of Chase is air-conditioned, most is not. Each room's solitary window draws breath with only the help of a box fan, offering minimal relief. Swabs coming from states such as Florida, Alabama, or Mississippi feel at home, joking about the cool New England climate. Others, from northern states, are less complimentary. Regardless of their tastes in weather, most sleep fitfully for the first few days, boiling over with excess adrenaline. By the end of the following week, how-

ever, physical exhaustion will begin to trump nervous anxiety. Despite her upbringing in the south, Swab Rheanastasia Doctolero has had trouble adjusting:

It's been really hot. I'm kind of used to it coming from Florida, so it's not that bad during the day, but sleeping is terrible. I'm not used to sleeping so hot; I usually have AC. There is no air-conditioning here, and it's weird; you go to bed hot, hot, hot, hot, and you're on top of your covers. I usually wake up in the middle of the night—because I don't really sleep well here yet—but I'll wake up in the middle of the night around twelve, one o'clock, and it'll be freezing. I'll be freezing, so I'll get under my covers, and I'll wake up, and it's hot again. It's really weird.

By the time swabs hit their racks, they have little energy left. Swab Kyle Wood might enjoy more time to chat with his roommate, but sleep is too critical to survival:

Most of the time, me and my roommate, Swab Winter, we just go straight to bed. There's been a night or two that we have stayed up and talked to learn a little bit about each other, and that's been a good experience to get to know him and get closer to him. When we have calisthenics, we get up at 0530, and then every other morning, it's 0600. Lights-out are at 2200. If we go straight to bed, we get at least eight hours. We don't have air-conditioning, but it's not bad. Coming from Tennessee, where it's warm and humid, I almost get cold late at night, so it's not bad.

Honor, *Respect*, and *Duty* are used in ship handling classes cadets receive at the Academy. The navy tugs take their names from the Academy's core values.

Core Values

Throughout the summer, swabs attend a series of classroom military trainings, beginning with An Introduction to the Core Value of Honor. Dr. Erik Wingrove-Haugland, a civilian professor, conducts these trainings. Although he did not choose a military career for himself, his father served in the Navy in WWII, as did all but two of his father's classmates. He also notes, with evident pride, that his son is an Army combat medic who served in Iraq. Dr. Erik, as he is known, received his PhD in philosophy from Vanderbilt University and taught at both the high-school and college levels before coming to the Academy:

I came here and had a great interview. I loved it, and it was clear they liked me, so they offered me the job. My wife was a little skeptical—a military academy? I thought I'd come for a year or two and go back on the job market, and now it's fifteen years later. I had been worried about intellectual freedom in a military academy, and when I got here, it wasn't that they just gave me the freedom to do, it was like, "You've got the whole ball." My colleagues in the department are just great, and the students are excellent—all kinds of luxuries, like everyone's in class every day. Ninety percent of them have done the reading, and the ten percent who haven't are embarrassed about it, as opposed to the place I had been teaching, where a third of the class is missing on a particular day, and the next day they're there for the second day of Kant and ask, "Well, can you fill us in on . . . ?" and it's, "No, I can't. Sorry. Of course you don't understand this now." But the students here are very good, by and large. I really enjoy it quite a lot.

They brought me in to teach the main ethics course, and I've taught that every semester since I've been here. I get to teach usually one other course per year in addition; that's an elective course. Lately, that's been the Islam course, but next semester, I'm doing an Asian philosophy course. I try to do things I think the cadets might be interested in, but also, the courses are just really different from everything else they're taking. Mainly, it's been the ethics course, which I designed and now we use my custom textbook for. It's a required course, so all of the cadets take it.

When they take it is kind of a hot-button issue for me right now, because originally, they were taking it 4th class year as freshmen, and my read was it was way too early. Freshmen are very idealistic, and so they loved the class. I loved them, and everybody was happy. However, we know the cadets get cynical during their time here, and my fear was that a lot of our material was probably going by the wayside along with their idealism. Also, they weren't quite ready for it, intellectually or emotionally. I don't know of any other college in the country that has a required ethics course they teach freshmen. Almost everybody else has it sophomore or junior year. In the other service academies, it's mostly as sophomores or juniors, so we moved the ethics course about ten years ago.

Although cadets now take the ethics course later in their academic careers, Dr. Erik still feels it is not perfectly placed. However, he has been happy to see better results with older students:

I get challenged in class a lot more. The 4th class was happy with whatever I said. It's a much more challenging group to teach. The 4th class have really not seen the Coast Guard. At least the 3rd class

has done a tour; they've been afloat for a couple of months. The 2nd class have had the cadre experience, which is a very important developmental time for them, so now they have a little more realistic view of things. I think it's the right move, but I really don't want it to become a 1st class course. It's just too late. You really want 1st class courses to be very directly relevant to what they're going to be doing, otherwise they just won't put in the effort. Maritime law enforcement—that's a great 1st class course, whereas the ethics course is more indirectly relevant. But they don't see that, especially once they get their billet in March. They're only interested in things that are relevant to what they're about to be doing.

Instilling the first core value—honor—presents a significant challenge for the Academy. The world in which today's youths mature is quite different from the one in which their grandparents were raised. Finding public role models who can withstand close scrutiny often seems an impossible task. Athletes, entertainers, financial titans, and elected officials frequently populate exposés on the evening news. Current polling of both high-school and college students finds that over 75 percent casually admit to having cheated in school. Worse, most believe their behavior is justified—nothing more than the means to get ahead. Dr. Erik sees societal problems reflected in our children's behavior:

My sense is—and I think this is borne out by a lot of empirical data—that the students we're getting out of high school are less committed to honor and more willing to lie and cheat, so I think we have a more difficult challenge every year because of that. I like to think that what I'm doing is effective, but at the same time, we had a 1st class cadet last year who was dismissed after, I believe, 107 cases of theft.

The extreme case Dr. Erik describes is an anomaly, but minor cases do arise with some frequency. After all, the Coast Guard draws its students from the same general population as does every other institution, and the Admissions Department has no magic crystal ball. What sets a military institution apart from its civilian counterparts, however, is its response to those infractions it does discover. A poll of civilian-college administrators found that 34 percent no longer consider cheating a problem worth addressing. In contrast, with very few exceptions, honor-code violations at military institutions generally bring forth swift punishment. Indeed, the Coast Guard Academy has discharged students within mere months of graduation for even minor violations. Dr. Erik feels that incoming cadets' mindsets simply mirror national trends:

They are a little self-selecting, because they want to go into the military. At one time, there was a thought that if you wanted to go into the military, you were a pretty virtuous, upright person of good character. I just don't think that's true anymore. I don't think you can take for granted that the people entering the military have the kind of values that they probably did take for granted fifty years ago. They're still kids, and every once and a while, they do something to remind you of that. Even some of our top cadets have engaged in really questionable behavior, but, you know, they're still twenty-one-, twenty-two-year-olds, and that just comes with the territory. West Point and the Naval Academy have had their share of cheating scandals, and other things as well. As a matter of fact, it was the West Point scandal in '91 that probably was responsible for creating this course. The commandant of the Coast Guard said, "We need an ethics course."

What is different at the Academy, however, is the conviction that cadets must rise to a higher standard:

We have a different feeling about honor, I think, than civilian colleges, for two reasons. One is taxpayers are paying for this, and the other is we hire 100 percent of our graduates; 100 percent of our graduates go into the Coast Guard, and it's a big deal. For an officer to engage in dishonorable behavior would just be terrible.

It may never be possible to eliminate all instances of honor-code violations, but it must be remembered that they are few and far between. When a problem arises at a service academy, the media jump onto the story as if they have uncovered something entirely unknown to American society, ignoring the 75 percent of civilian-college students who openly admit to engaging in the very same behavior. There is no doubt that integrity is critically important at

our service academies, but the moral outrage following each such story can ultimately seem a little disingenuous. The question is not whether scoundrels exist, but what is done with whose who are discovered. In today's world, politicians simply apologize on national TV, promise to seek counseling, and begin their next election campaigns. Sports heroes with multi-million-dollar contracts pay fifty-thousand-dollar penalties and watch a few games from the sidelines. Cadets, on the other hand, are disenrolled; their careers, over.

In the end, the Academy graduates only those young women and men who possess the high character the Coast Guard requires. The institution is a difficult place to get through—for countless reasons—and it would be highly suspicious if everyone who entered proved able to pass such a rigorous test. The system is designed to fully test the physical, mental, and ethical integrity of each individual cadet, to remove those who fail to pass muster, and to graduate only those who may be trusted with command.

Dr. Erik's core-value classes provide welcome relief from the daily summer routine. They get swabs off the drill field, out of the sun, and, most importantly, away from the cadre. Classes are held in Hamilton Hall, which is named for Alexander Hamilton, the man who brought the Revenue Marine to life in 1790. Built in 1932, Hamilton Hall is one in a long line of buildings facing Bear Drive. Most of the building is devoted to academic offices, but it also holds the Hall of Graduates, a room displaying the name of every Academy alum. Core-value training takes place in the Henriques Room, certainly the most beautiful and appropriate chamber on the campus.

Henriques originally housed the school's library, and it retains the library's lofty ceilings and glass-fronted bookcases. The windows above the bookcases illuminate the room's most unique feature—a series of murals depicting memorable Coast Guard actions throughout history. The scenes were painted by a Yale Art School graduate, Aldis Brown, as a part of Roosevelt's New Deal that put unemployed artists to work enhancing government facilities during the Great Depression. Brown's wonderful murals instill in new students not only an appreciation for the institution's historical importance, but also a deep sense of pride in their service's traditions.

The core-value classes are not lectures (which have literally put exhausted swabs to sleep in the past). Rather, they are interactive discussions, which stand in stark contrast to the military trainings that occupy most of the swabs' time. These classes are some of the only occasions during the long summer months when swabs are allowed—encouraged, even—to voice their opinions. Needless to say, swabs readily welcome the experience.

When Dr. Erik first arrived as a new professor, he reviewed the effectiveness of honor training at the Academy:

My first summer here, they asked me to sit in on two trainings they were doing and write a report, making observations and recommendations. One was the cadre training. The cadre get a weeklong training period, and it was pretty good. There were a few

Banners hung along Bear Drive remind cadets of the Academy's overall mission.

things where I had some suggestions. It was all taught by instructors at the Academy, and it was taught to small groups with a lot of interaction—pretty effective. The swab-summer honor class I observed was taught by a 1st class cadet. At the time, it was taught to companies, and that was when we had three companies (nine platoons), so a company was a hundred—a hundred swabs. They packed them into Dimick Hall, turned the lights out, and showed a PowerPoint slideshow. The 1st class cadet would read the slides, like the swabs couldn't read or something. It was naptime, and it was all a "see this, don't do it" approach—no interaction, no case studies, no examples of what it's really like. Not surprisingly, we were having a lot of problems with honor issues. I wrote, "This is a really ineffective training. You've got to get experienced instructors, small groups, and you've got to have materials that are directly relevant to them. You've got to use case studies. You've got to get them talking and make it an interactive experience so it's not

just a check-the-box, "We've told you not to do this" kind of training. It has to be a "We really mean this, and it's hard. We expect you to live up to the standard."

As with a lot of things in the Coast Guard, if you've identified a problem and found a solution, the response is often, "Go ahead! It's all you!" I didn't really see myself that first summer as making a pitch for me doing this, but that's how the Coast Guard looked at it. "Well, who should implement this? Well, the guy who made the recommendations." So I've been teaching it most summers. I'd guess I've taught it about twelve summers. I think it's relatively effective. I know it's more effective than packing a hundred swabs into a dark room and reading PowerPoint slides to them.

The classes are just an introduction, but they clearly outline the very cut-and-dry nature of the Academy's honor system: either you are honorable or you are not. Swabs are given real-life examples to study before each class discussion. In one such example, a cadet lends a friend her notebook without realizing that a paper she had written is tucked inside. Her friend does not immediately return the paper upon discovering the mistake. Both are found guilty of honor violations: he, for not reporting her oversight; she, for the oversight itself. Of course, this scenario strikes students as highly unfair; they clearly see the friend's error, but hers seems

Helping hands pull a shipmate over a wooden wall on the O-Course.

an honest mistake. For future Coast Guard officers, however, responsibility means just that—taking full responsibility for all of their actions. It was the young lady's duty to know what she was handing her friend. In the Academy's conception, honor comes in only two shades—black and white. The discussions that follow show how unprepared many swabs feel for this new challenge to their worldview.

The Coast Guard, like any military service, worries about the damage that dishonorable officers can cause, both directly to their shipmates and indirectly to the reputation of the Service as a whole. It is vitally important that the civilian population can trust the men and women we arm. Dr. Erik explains a fundamental distinction, however, between officers who are dishonorable and those who are merely inept:

The Coast Guard really does believe its core values. It's not just lip service, and that makes a big difference. The system is set up to deal with incompetent officers, and the system does a pretty good job of weeding them out. But a dishonorable officer can sneak by; they can hide it. It's hard to hide incompetence, but dishonorable people can get away with it. You can't question yourself until you have honor and integrity. It's like trying to play chess with yourself; you win every time. If you're not being honest with yourself: "Well, am I doing this correctly? Yes, of course! Move on." A dishonorable officer can do a tremendous amount of damage to a service, because nobody is watching them; their job is to watch other people. The buck has to stop there, so it's absolutely vital they're honorable.

Commander Haukom is the cadet training officer at the Academy. Having attended a public university before entering the Coast Guard, he has seen the issue from both sides:

Working with the cadets here and thinking back to my own experiences, I remember going through college, and if you could find a shortcut, hey, why not take it? Of course, that wasn't everybody, but I knew a lot of people who had the mindset: "Well, what's wrong with it? It's a shortcut; take advantage of it." To me, it didn't seem quite right, and when I questioned them, the response was often: "Well, that's reality; that's the way the world is." Unfortunately, there's probably some truth to that, but here, shortcuts are a big deal. If you think you want to take one, you better be prepared to pay the consequence, because even a seemingly insignificant shortcut could be the end of your time here, and we see it all the time. That's why we put so much stock in honor.

Any offense can be raised to that level. Did you just screw up there? Did you just have a mind-lapse? Did you just make a mistake? People make mistakes; that's fine. You're going to pay a little bit of a consequence. But if we prove through investigation, through an honor board convening, that it wasn't just a momentary lapse of reason—you knew exactly what you were doing, you knew why you were doing it, it was an honor offense—then we're taking that to the next level. So you do see people dismissed for what on paper, in a normal civilian university, would be like, "Are you kidding? They kicked him out for whispering an answer to his friend on a test?" Here, yes. It's an honor offense, and one of our core values is honor. If you can't act honorably all the time and in a situation that demands honor, how can we expect you to stand a watch on a ship? So it's a big deal here, and when cadets see their classmates disenrolled for what, in their opinion, may seem like a minor offense, I think they start to realize the gravity of this thing we call honor, and how it is at the core of everything we do. If you don't have that honor foundation, we don't need your services.

During swab summer, lessons about something as abstract as honor could easily get lost in the fray. According to 4/C Jake Carlton, though, these lessons still managed to make an impact:

Honor, respect, and devotion to duty—the three core values. They did a pretty good job of instilling them into us, what each of them means. We had the honor trainings. Most of the time, we were dead tired when they happened, because it was the middle of swab summer. We were all physically drained, and a lot of us didn't eat a whole lot because we are afraid of puking once we got IT'd, so there was that aspect, but they did a good job of instilling those values in you and what they mean. We had one person who had two cell phones and only turned in one at the beginning of the summer. That showed us a little bit about honor, honesty, and respecting the lessons they were trying to teach us. He ended up sitting for an entire week at the head table, the command table where the company commanders sat, where all they did was yell at him. He

barely got to eat, and they would just constantly watch him for the littlest infraction and yell at him about it. It was kind of like, "Oh crap! Just for something stupid like that!"

4/C Scooter Finney feels that the introduction to core values laid a clear path to future success:

I do think it was effective. You hear the three words, and you hear them over and over again, and after you get through the summer and you've put that much work into them, it starts to mean something. I take it very seriously. I would say there are some people here to this day who don't take it entirely seriously, but the biggest thing is probably that I've put this much work into the core values. Honor, respect, and devotion to duty are essentially the simple guidelines for performing well. If you just do that, then you'll perform. They do mean something different after the summer.

4/C Rheanastasia Doctolero candidly admits that, like most kids, she never thought deeply about the concept of honor while she was growing up:

I guess I really didn't think of honor. I didn't really think about it; it wasn't part of my life. I can see things that people would do in the past, like copying homework. In the past I might have been like, "Oh, if everyone does it, it's nothing." But now I see it's not an honorable thing to do. It really isn't. If it isn't something that upholds me to the standard where I should be, I just won't do it. It's more than just yourself now; you're representing the entire Coast Guard. You have to hold yourself to the highest standard. The trainings really do help. Honor, respect, devotion to duty—they really come into play. If I didn't come here, I probably never would have thought of those things. I didn't really think about it until I got here, and now it's like, "Oh, it's not the honorable thing to do."

Not all swabs, however, come to the Academy without having considered these concepts at a deeper level. To 4/C Katie Brosnan, a highly introspective young woman, the meaning of the word honor always seemed obvious. Brosnan's father is a New York City police detective, and she attended Catholic schools throughout her life. For her, honor, respect, and devotion have always been a way of life. The core values of the Academy were simply a given, a perfect match for the way she already viewed the world and her place within it. Swab summer did not make her question her own conceptions of honor, respect, and devotion to duty, but it did make her question what those concepts meant to some of her fellow cadets. Indeed, she learned some of her greatest lessons from the errors of her cadre:

Hmmm. Honor, respect, and devotion to duty. Cadre throw around that word honor a lot. You know when you say a word so much it really has no meaning? Honor is one of those words they use so much they lose track of what it means. I hardly know what it means anymore. How can you yell at people like they did? I'm not talking about yelling at them because they did something wrong, or yelling at them because you're cadre and you're supposed to, but viciously and rabidly yelling at people while preaching respect at the same time.

Honor. You come into the school year, it's not swab summer anymore, and people just get kicked out left and right. Honor offense. Honor offense. Honor offense. Four of my cadre got kicked out over swab summer. I didn't know one of them, because he was AIM Cadre, but the other three of them, I respected them so much. I thought they were such good leaders.

Like many of her shipmates, Brosnan entered the summer brimming with idealism. Particularly hard on her was a realization she soon had about honor and respect: those who demand to be treated with honor and respect are not always honorable and respectful themselves. For Brosnan, the shock and disillusionment that accompanied this realization were painful:

Honor used to be a positive. "Yeah! Honor!" I have my sense of honor, you know—doing the right thing no matter what, having integrity. Honor is not a bad thing. I know it is a positive, and I know you want honor. Over swab summer, I realized that it means a lot. It's a heavy word. It's a really heavy word; it's not something that can be thrown around.

Despite her negative experiences, she came away with perhaps the most important lesson the Academy could teach:

What I like when the Academy talks about honor is that you own your own honor. You're the one who gives it away, and you're the one who keeps it. You're the one that protects it. I like that a lot, because honor is something that's unique to all of us. I like how they stress it's yours. You can taint it, or you can protect it. They got that part straight about honor, in my eyes anyway.

Swab Shane Rainey takes a gulp of water from his canteen. Unusually hot and humid summer weather added to the swab's difficulties.

Leadership Through Volume:

The cadre have as much to learn about leading as the swabs do about following. Many will only realize the important lessons they have learned long after the summer has faded. During the summer, there are cadre who, clearly, are in control of their emotions and comfortable in their command roles. And then there are those who, just as clearly, are not. Many swabs I interviewed spoke of this contrast between high- and low-performing cadre. 4/C Rheanastasia Doctolero gave her take:

The whole angry-at-everything style did not teach me anything at all. It got to the point where whatever he said, we knew he was just saying it because he was mad. You shut them off. As soon as they started talking, you just didn't want to listen to them, because they

131

were always angry. You feel like no matter what you do, they're going to get mad, so whether you try to do your best or you don't do it at all, you're going to get the same reaction. So definitely not that. The whole "I'm going to be mad at the world" didn't help us at all; it just annoyed us, and we had to get IT'd like eight million times. We also had a cadre who had this bored-with-the-world mentality. That didn't really help us either. It just seemed like he didn't care. I found the most effective cadre to be those that don't get mad too often, but when they do get mad, you know you messed up. There were three of them that, if they got mad, we were like, "Oh crap!" We felt bad, and we tried to be on our best behavior after that. I want to be that kind of a person, because when you respect the cadre like that, you learn so much more and you develop a better relationship.

4/C Katie Brosnan had similar experiences with cadre who mistook rage for effective leadership:

You see the veins popping out of their head and their faces were red. I had some cadre like that, and when you see them like that, it's like, "Is this leadership? Do I want to follow you? No!" They were just angry people. We are going to mess up. Okay. We mess up all the time; we're swabs. Some of them were angry all the time, and you knew it wasn't about you. Sometimes, you could tell it was personal, even though they were saying, "No, it's strictly professional; don't worry." "No, you're yelling in my face for thirty minutes. You're mad."

It's weird, because they don't even know you. What bothered me a lot was like, okay, you don't shine your shoes, you don't shine your belt enough, and you don't get your uniform right—that's what they're here to teach you. What I wasn't prepared for, I think, was when they tap into your personal traits: "You're not honorable. You have no integrity." When they say things like that, it's like, "You don't know me at all. This is me at swab summer. I'm out of my home, I'm out of my family, I don't really know what I'm doing, I don't know what you're going to do to me, and you're like, "You have no honor. You have no integrity." That sentence—when you say that to someone, that's personal. It's not "You can't run; you're

holding up the team!" It's not something like paying attention to detail. It's personal when you call out someone's character and personality and you don't even know them.

The immense stress that comes with the cadres' assigned task undoubtedly explains at least some of the anger swabs encounter. Fortunately for the swabs, those cadre who are perpetually lost in anger are only part of a larger, diverse set of personalities. Anger and fear can be motivational tools when used judiciously, but swabs learn simply to ignore them over time. For 4/C Jake Carlton, as for most, positive reinforcement ended up being more effective in the long run:

Once you get through that yelling phase, most people just get tired of it and it doesn't affect them anymore. That's when positive encouragement is a lot more helpful. I had a couple of cadre who were like that, who were more positive in their encouragement with me, and it helped me a lot. Whenever they were with me, doing some of the IT and stuff, I would push myself a little more than when they just yelled at me to do it.

The irony of the situation is that cadre are learning the exact same lessons that swabs are learning, just from the opposite end of the experience. They, too, figure out that screaming's effectiveness quickly wears off and that screaming louder bears even smaller fruit. Ideally, they learn these lessons early enough to try new approaches. 4/C Kyle Wood noticed that swabs and cadre ultimately come to the same realizations:

I think they're starting to understand how to motivate us with something other than yelling. With yelling, some people feel it makes them want to do worse, because they feel they're not doing anything right. Most cadre are now teaching and uplifting, congratulating, and that really makes some people want to work harder, because they feel like, "Yeah! I'm getting close! I got this! I'm going to keep going!"

And then there are the exceptional cadre—those who not only practice the proper balance of positive and negative reinforcement, but who truly embody the Coast Guard ideal of taking care of their subordinates at all times. Wood was fortunate enough to have one such cadre in his company:

I remember during the summer one instance, when I wasn't doing that well, or I wasn't performing to their expectations, there was one of the cadre who stood out. He actually pulled me aside from everything else, and he talked to me. He was like, "Relax. What's going on?" He just talked to me. I'm on the football team, and there were two cadre who were football players. One of my fellow shipmates from my company and I got sent to PEP, the performance-enhancing platoon. That's really hard and physically demanding, and when we got back, these two football guys gave us a bag of chips and a Gatorade. They put it in our rooms, obviously not telling anybody. I'm pretty sure they didn't tell the other cadre, but that was nice of them to do that.

For others with CGAS experience, like 4/C Kyneesha Womack, the cadre were as expected:

I really do like my cadre. My cadre, even though they're mean to us when they have to be, they're really nice people. They really care about what they're doing, they really care about us, and they really care about doing their job. I see exactly why they have to scream at us. They never scream at us for a random reason. They never IT'd anybody for a random reason. There's always a reason behind everything that they do. They have a job to do, and they're learning just as much from this experience as we are.

4/C Sheila Bertrand found that the quiet voice often spoke the loudest:

There was always the one cadre who wouldn't yell and the rest of the cadre who would scream in your face. We had a cadre, Miss Nelson, who one day—I don't even remember what we did—but she never yelled at us; she just walked up and down the hallway as we were lined up against the bulkhead, and she just said, "I am so disappointed in you, Delta Company." It hit us more than getting yelled at. We had other cadre who would just scream in your face.

Fortunately, the cadre whom the swabs find ineffective stand out precisely because they are exceptions to the rule. Most, given their

first opportunity to lead, rise to the occasion. For 4/C Katie Brosnan, this was as big a lesson:

You'll have some cadre who are really inspirational. They'll talk to you, and you can tell they really mean what they're saying. They're trying to inspire you. They'll say, "Look, I know it sucks right now, but you're going to be an officer one day, and this is why you need to do all the stupid little things, because one day you're going to earn the privilege of saving someone's life. You need to really want this." Those cadre were my favorite. I never cried during swab summer, except when they would give those inspirational talks. I never cried out of sadness or because I can't do these pushups, but I would tear up during the inspirational talks.

She ended the summer with an appreciation for many of the qualities that go into true leadership. Overall, she felt they did well:

As a whole, I thought my cadre did a really good job. Looking at the other companies, I think my cadre were some of the best. Obviously, I didn't go through swab summer with all the other cadre, but I respected my cadre a lot. You also have to know that it's their first time really doing this. Some are really into it, and some are not into it at all. I definitely have a lot of respect for them. It must be tough, and they have a lot of work to do. They have a lot of work to do.

Without exception, every swab complained about the so-called "rabid" cadre—the ones who would yell for no apparent reason. However, when asked whether they would eliminate this problem if given the chance, their answers were surprising. 4/C Rheanastasia Doctolero, looking back on the summer from the distance of an academic semester, had this to say:

I honestly think it should remain as is. Even in the fleet, you're going to deal with people who aren't perfect. You're going to deal with people who are tough and stubborn, and you're just going to have to deal with it. You're only on the boat for so long—four months—and then you move. It's definitely about learning to work with people. You're not going to have it where everybody's perfect and happy and they're all perfect cadre or all perfect captains. So

Swabs drill with fixed bayonets on the parade field.

they are teaching you everything. You take what they did right, what they did wrong, and you put that in your pocket, thinking, "Well, when I'm cadre, I'm going to do this and not that." I think that's where it starts, along with the leadership examples you notice along the way. I think my class will do pretty well, after seeing my peers switch it on and off during 100th Week. The way they act and the way they carry themselves gives me confidence. I know a lot of my good friends are going to be very levelheaded, very sincere about what they do. That's something that I picked up from my swab and my CGAS summer: you really need to be sincere.

After day three, the real work of summer begins. For swabs, the most significant development is the addition of IT to the cadre's arsenal. Cadre 2/C Durand explains this new tool:

You spend a lot of time in Chase Hall learning how to put on uniforms and learning how to do things. You have drill on the fields, you have trainings, learning Coast Guard customs, and swab summer math. There are a lot of things that go on during the day. If they mess up anywhere, for any reason, the only way you can punish them physically is with what's called IT—incentive training. These are pushups, sit-ups, squats, and that kind of thing. It can last up to five minutes, I think, and it's a minute on and then thirty seconds rest. You can only do that five times during the day. They don't really know that; they think it lasts all day. They don't know the restrictions we have with them, so it seems awful. In the morning, there are calisthenics, too. Some of the physical work is to get them in shape, and then there's some that's considered punishment. There are a lot of rules for swab summer they have to follow. They have to greet everyone they see. If they didn't greet, you can drop them right there. If they're carrying something wrong, if they don't square, if they take their eyes out of the boat—any little thing becomes a big deal. Outside of the context of swab summer, you wouldn't ever get

I definitely feel swab summer teaches you to deal with these different types of people and to listen to authority—not try to undermine it and get in trouble for it, you know? I'm glad I didn't have all perfect cadre. I think having the mix of cadre actually does help us out. You realize you're not going to have all perfect officers above you when you go out there. Some people are going to undermine you, and some people are going to build you up. You've got to learn to deal with what you're given.

As a member of the cadre, 2/C Jennifer Patron has enough experience to know that the good is mixed in with the bad. The important thing is to absorb the good and move forward:

100th Week was pretty much the official kickoff for cadre preparation, but I honestly believe it starts during your own swab summer, because when you're in your swab summer, you see these people, your cadre, and you hold them up to such a high standard, because in trouble for it. Over the summer, you can get dropped for pretty much anything.

Some swabs mistakenly believe that there are no limits imposed on incentive training—and why would cadre correct them? In reality, cadre must follow strict rules and are accountable for every physical incentive they administer. 4/C Fred Higgins did notice restraint, even as a swab:

It was really controlled. I even noticed that with every exercise they gave, there was somebody timing them. This was me taking my eyes out of the boat, but the timer would be giving them the thumbs-up or something to tell them they needed to stop, rest them, and give them water, so nothing really ever got carried away. But I could tell the cadre really wanted to take it farther than they could.

Incentive training is used throughout the summer to correct both large and small errors. 4/C Koachar Mohammad jokingly reminisces about a simpler time when the word incentive was used less euphemistically:

When things weren't really working—like, for example, not making a time—all I can remember is them basically IT'ing and yelling at us. There were instances where I remember that they offered incentives for us to succeed. As incentives, they would make it easier for us or have fun with us. For example, during meals, if we won the IC games (the intercompany games), they'd offer us chocolate milk during meals. So there were definitely incentives. Or say, for example, when we were lagging behind, they would tell us the punishment before they gave it to us. That was something that would really help. It was punishment we would normally receive; it's just they would tell us what it was going to be ahead of time. It was "Okay, if you guys fail, you're going to have to do this." It's kind of like training a dog. Now that we knew what was going to happen if we failed, we tried even harder to make that goal, and most of the time we would make it. When we knew, we tried a little bit harder.

Humor has its place even in incentive training. One day during the summer, swabs had the choice of playing one of two different intercompany games. When one particular swab chose volleyball, a cadre, frustrated at losing such a good soccer player, shouted, "Swab X, if we lose this game because you decided to play volleyball, I'm going to IT you into the ground!" He stuck to his guns and played volleyball. He has not been seen since.

Pushups are used throughout the summer as incentive to do better while simultaneously building upper body strength.

Physical Fitness

As a military institution, the Academy must concern itself with its students' physical fitness level. Accordingly, sports generally play a major role in the cadets' lives. Like all colleges, the Academy has a large staff of athletic coaches. They field twenty-three sports teams, which is no easy task, given the relatively small student population.

Chris Parsons is one of the athletic coaches at the Academy. After graduating from Middlebury College with a degree in economics, he went to work on Wall Street until his passion for athletics drew him back onto the field. After earning his master's degree in sports management, he worked at various colleges before coming to New London:

This is the beginning of my eleventh year here. If you look at the length of stay of a typical physical-education coach here, it's pretty lengthy. We have the longest-serving faculty member here, Steve Eldridge, who's been working here for forty-six years, which is as old as I am. When I came here eleven years ago, Jeff Cardinale, who was the department head, was just finishing his fortieth year. I replaced Ray Cieplik, who was here for forty years, and now we have a core of us who are all between probably nine and fifteen years. The job is very unique from a coaching point of view; it has so many positive outcomes and challenges—things that really make you enjoy what you do.

Swabs remain in motion for the better part of each day. Cadre lead them through many of their physical tasks, but the permanent coaching staff also plays a major role:

The physical-education staff works with the swabs throughout the whole course of the summer. The first thing we do with them is the physical fitness exam on Thursday of the first week. There is a set standard they need to meet. It is the first time they are doing the exam with phys-ed faculty overseeing the exam. This PFE [physical fitness exam] is the same physical exam they will be doing twice a year for the next four years. This sets standards they need to meet and a final commissioning standard they need to pass during their senior year or they won't be commissioned. Most of the kids have taken it with a high-school coach—the Academy asks them to take it before they come as part of their application process—and I can imagine the nerves during that first exam they take. I find it uplifting, the way they encourage one another. It's only four days into their time here, but they are starting to come together as a company and begin that teamwork. You see it that quickly, and you see it at both ends. You see it with the kids who are really performing, and you see it with the kids who are underperforming, pulled along by their shipmates. That was what struck me the first swab summer I was here—that in five days, they start to come together and pull each other through.

The coaching staff oversees training on the obstacle course, on the ropes course, in the gymnasium, and in the pool—all areas where swabs can easily hurt themselves without professional guidance. These are also areas in which swabs progress developmentally as

teams. Whereas the obstacle course is aimed primarily at improving individual performance, the ropes course focus is squarely on group effort. Without help from shipmates, the physical puzzles cannot be solved. Parsons elaborates:

One of the largest components we have is the obstacle course, in conjunction with our ropes course. The ropes course develops teamwork and leadership, while the obstacle course is just that— can we get them through the different obstacles we've set forth? One of the most challenging is the twenty-five-foot rope climb. If they can't successfully do this rope climb, then they can't go up in the rigging on EAGLE. It's tough for some kids to pull themselves up twenty-five feet, and there is also a little bit of a fear factor. We time the courses, looking to see which company can perform the best on the obstacle course. On the ropes course, the cadre can't say anything, because they've all done each element. If you've done the element before and you know how to solve the problem, you must remain mute. But they are allowed to encourage swabs quite a bit on the obstacle course; you hope the competitive drive comes through there.

Coaches strive to make physical fitness a lifelong commitment among cadets, not just some bothersome summer requirement. Training goes far beyond pushups, sit-ups, and running endless circles around the track:

There are kids who come here who just need coaching in terms of physical fitness. That student may offer something to the Academy that allows Admissions to say, "You know what? We're going to work with this student a little bit more on the athletic side, because they offer this or that." Swab summer also encourages a learning process from the physical-education point of view. We also have in their 4th class year, their very first year, two classes they take: Principals of Fitness and Wellness, 1 and 2. They instill the mindset that fitness and wellness are both important. That, combined with the physical fitness exam, is how we try to get them to where they need to go. Not every person who comes to the Academy is going to be a star athlete, but getting them through the physical-fitness part is important. We have a fitness circuit-training component, where we see them twice a week, and we put each company through physical circuit training, as we call it, and also through strength training. We introduce them to different kinds of weight training in the lower weight room. Some of the kids who come here have never been in a weight room. Some kids come and they are avid lifters already. We introduce them to that world and try to get them to understand the importance of strength training and physical fitness.

Cadets, it goes without saying, must also feel at home in the water:

Obviously, as the Coast Guard, we have a swimming component. When they get here, the first thing we do is to figure out how well they swim. They need to tread water for a certain period of time in the Roland pool. In the Ballard pool, there's a jump. They need to cross and cover and jump off into the pool. Some of the kids who come are not strong swimmers; they'll go through remedial swimming for the course of the summer, and if they need to, they'll stay in the remedial swim class for the fall. The others will be placed accordingly. There are kids who come who can't swim, and it's a challenge, especially when you get to the point where you're eighteen years old and you don't know how. There is a Survival at Sea component that happens right in the beginning of swab summer. It's the basics: they'll put them in their ODUs [operational dress uniforms] and teach them how to inflate a shirt and a pair of pants to stay afloat, teach them about hypothermia, and things like that. In their 3rd class year, there is a class called The Professional Rescuer that every cadet needs to take, and that is an ADCPR first-aid and lifeguard certification. The lifeguarding is the American Red Cross–certified course, along with what we feel they need in addition. The American Red Cross is equipment-oriented, and we do a number of saves where you don't use anything, as if you were on a boat and somebody falls off and you need to go get them. My guess is that about 85 percent of the cadets are passing the lifeguarding portion; 100 percent pass the ADCPR first-aid portion. We make sure they do that. That's the goal. They are trained lifesavers in terms of the water, and they are able to survive at sea when they

leave here. And really, for some of their summer assignments, they need to know that before they leave here.

Knowing that Academy graduates are unlikely to be headed to careers in professional sports, I was curious about rationale behind the emphasis on athletics. After all, no matter your strength, you still use hydraulics, not biceps, to lift a three-ton buoy. Of course, I was being nearsighted. Parsons reminded me that cadets hone more than just their physiques on the playing field:

From our point of view, where do people get leadership experience at the high-school level? Through athletics and extracurricular activities. Athletics, Boy Scouts, Junior ROTC, and different clubs within their school. They're not looking for the student who is a double-800 on the SAT and a 4.0 student who doesn't take part in anything other than academics. That person is not the well-rounded person they're looking for. They're looking for the person who achieves academically, who also has some strong leadership skills—the captains of their high-school teams, the presidents of their student council, the Boy Scout who achieved the rank of Eagle Scout, the company leader for the Junior ROTC, or something like that. Those activities play a pretty vital role when they look at kids. There is an area academically these kids need to fit, but we get a ton of kids who apply from that area. Now what makes them stand out and makes us offer them an appointment? Well, being a potential member of one of our teams is definitely going to do that. Being a musician and part of the jazz band is definitely going to do that. We are this very interesting school with a lot of different offerings, and we need to fill them. They are also going to get some of their leadership training being a part of those things while they're here.

Ideally, when they go out into the Coast Guard, they are able to work as an officer and as a team. The Admissions Department is looking to yield well-rounded individuals. We are looking to be competitively successful here at the Coast Guard Academy. We're a niche. We are the United States Coast Guard Academy. We have had, at various times, some phenomenal athletes. We have a fe-

male softball pitcher who just graduated who is one of the most decorated Division III pitchers in the history of the sport. We are unique, and we offer something a lot of places can't—an education that is phenomenal, a guaranteed job for five years, free education, and really, whether you stay for five or twenty years, you set yourself up for a lot of success in the private sector when you're done. I would have to believe that most companies, if they interview somebody who has gone through a service academy, put that resumé close to the top of the pile.

In reality, athletics at the Coast Guard Academy is the best leadership laboratory. You have a team of twenty-four players the upperclass are going to lead. They're going to mentor the younger players. You have to deal with success, and you have to deal with failure. Our teams have to play a certain way in terms of how we compete. Within every sport, there are boundaries that get stretched in terms of the ethics of the sport. Because of who we are, it is demanded of us that we instill in them the right way to play: fair, clean, all those different things. Dealing with that as an athlete, when you're playing against a team that might be doing some things we would consider unethical, raises challenges from a coaching standpoint.

The Academy constantly places leadership opportunities in the paths of cadets. These can be as simple as organizing blood drives in local communities or as complex as filling the role of regimental commander for the entire corps. Sports offer another route:

Captains of each team wear a pin on their uniform; everybody knows who they are. I think striving to be a captain of an athletic team here is one of the ultimate leadership positions—that and some of the command positions within their company. You find some really strong kids who are both. There are those who are militarily squared away, great leaders on their team, really leading the corps, and I think athletics has really helped them get to those positions on the military side because there is so much teamwork and communication. In sports you get the opportunity, if you're the captain or a leader, not only to communicate with your

Swab Kaitlin Dickson struggles to climb the 20' rope on the obstacle course.

team and the younger players, but with the coaching staff as well. You need to be able to get the needs of the team to the coaches.

139

This page, clockwise: 2/C Anna Ruth goes one-on-one with Swab Mason Totri after pulling him from the larger formation.

Eight companies of swabs march along Mystic Seaport's waterfront during the Mystic Flag Day ceremony.

Swabs enjoy a laugh down on the waterfront. Beyond learning to sail, short periods of normalcy go far in the repair of frayed nerves.

Opposite page, clockwise: Swabs practice their marching skills on the parade field.

Swab Michael Shermot stands at attention.

Lunch at the Academy. Swabs must keep their eyes straight ahead and square corners when eating.

Swabs running laps on the track by the river.

It's similar in many ways to what being a young officer would be doing—managing people, the boat, and dealing with staff above you. It's obviously all about communication in the end.

From a coaching point of view, the most satisfying part of the job is graduation and finding out what your former players are doing in the Service. It instills a real sense of pride, that you've have a real impact on them, and I think coaches have a huge impact on their athletes being successful and getting through the place. There are some you don't have to guide too much, and there are others that you spent a lot of time with, and when they graduate, you really feel great.

While their teams seldom make national news, coaches take great pride in the accomplishments of their athletes. The changes they witness over only four years are remarkable, as Parsons describes:

From my perspective, the growth is amazing between the time they get here and the time they leave. The first four weeks of swab summer you definitely see fear; you see them questioning their decision. They're always braced up, and the personality that you knew, especially for the ones you personally recruited as players, tends to go away in those first four weeks, and it's really hard to get it to come back out. As swab summer starts to come to a close, you really begin to see the confidence come back. Then, the school year starts, and the freshman year is a long, hard year. Swab summer is over, but now starts the academic year. They put the most credits on the 4th class. They are trying to manage their academics, the military requirements, and their athletics. Sixty-five percent of them play a varsity sport, so it's a challenge. You see growth, but it's pretty slow during the 4th class year. During their 3rd class year, they're at ease, but they are waiting to lead; they're still a little stunted in their growth. They've got some 4th class cadets they need to manage, and they're getting ready to really take off from a leadership point of view. In between their 3rd class and their 2nd class year, the cadre experience is what really gets them moving forward. They've also gotten through the two most difficult academic years. They've gotten through chemistry, physics, all the math requirements, and they are getting into their electives. Now, they're academically at ease. They've figured it out, and you start to see their grades improve, because they are within their major. Their confidence increases, and their performance as athletes really starts to improve. The teams that have strong numbers in junior and senior classes here are successful. It's a very difficult place to be successful if you have a young team. There is just so much affecting their minds that it's hard for them to focus, but by the time they're seniors, it's generally smooth sailing. They're leading up in the barracks, they're leading the sports teams, and they're getting ready to leave.

Swabs study the *Running Light* whenever time and opportunity allows. Considered their bible, they carry it with them in their socks throughout the summer.

The *Running Light*

Uniform, rifle, and water bottle aside, every swab's most essential piece of gear is a personal copy of the *Running Light*. This 114-page basic summer handbook must be carried at all times. Three inches wide and under five inches tall, it is designed to fit in a swab's sock, along with a pen for making notes. Any time not devoted to mandated activities is to be spent memorizing its contents. When read, it is held out at face height, arm level and squared at the elbow. With text less than one-sixteenth of an inch in height, only young eyes can read it without aid (I, personally, needed prescription glasses and a magnifying glass.) It is tantamount to high treason to be caught without it during the summer, and no swab ever forgets it twice.

Swab Kyle Wood

hearts, and alert minds, with a liking for the sea and its lore, and with that high sense of honor, loyalty and obedience which goes with trained initiative and leadership; well-grounded in seamanship, the sciences, and the amenities, and strong in the resolve to be worthy of the traditions of commissioned officers in the United States Coast Guard in service of their country and humanity.

The *Running Light* is available for purchase before R-Day, but few swabs seem to take advantage of the opportunity. Had they done so, the first half-dozen pages may have given them pause. The second page contains, in all its gravitas, the oath of office to which all military personnel must swear. Page four continues with an ominous "welcome" letter from the cadre:

Swab summer is a seven-week basic Coast Guard indoctrination program that will test your resolve and perseverance in times of great adversity. Your summer experience can be summarized in one word: intensity. You will be pushed to both physical and mental limits you never knew existed. The experience you will have will forever be ingrained into your memory as one of the most challenging experiences of your life.

The letter goes on to emphasize that the most important lesson swabs will learn is that teamwork is the key to success. This idea is the bedrock upon which the Coast Guard rests. Swabs will need to work with and support their shipmates, valuing others' well-being above their own. The letter concludes with an explanation of the cadre's role in their immediate future. The cadre, it states, will prepare them to join the ranks of their fellow cadets, making sure they have the skills required to succeed both at the Academy and within the operational Coast Guard.

The weightiest material, however, fills page six. There, swabs will find the Code of Conduct they must swear to uphold. Most cadets cite the Coast Guard's humanitarian mission as their reason for choosing this particular Academy. The Code of Conduct provokes the stark realization that their careers will involve more than rescue operations. Of the six articles comprising the Code, the first mentions the possible need to give one's life in the course of duty, and four detail the behavior expected of military personnel who are taken as prisoners of war—heady stuff for teenagers who have not yet learned to live outside their parents'

This little blue book, with its embossed gold lettering, begins with the first thing swabs must commit to memory—the mission of the U.S. Coast Guard. Originally written in 1929 by Vice Admiral Harry Hamlet, the Academy's superintendent at the time, the statement was modified in the 1970s to reflect the Academy's admission of women. It now reads:

The mission of the United States Coast Guard Academy is to graduate young men and women of sound bodies, stout homes. The Code mentions nothing of saving lives on tempestuous seas.

The first six pages of the *Running Light* are undoubtedly the most sobering. But there is another page, page seven, that will also play a leading role in their new lives. It is devoted entirely to the Academy's three core values—honor, respect, and devotion to duty. At first glance, the page appears merely to present a list of easily applied rules. The reality, however, is quite different.

When questioned about the first core value—honor—swabs regurgitate a brief chant that states they will not lie, cheat, steal, nor attempt to deceive. The concept goes well beyond this simple mantra:

The Honor Concept is a higher standard of conduct that can neither be delineated by laws nor defined by regulations. It is epitomized by an individual who places loyalty to duty above loyalty to personal friendship or to selfish desire.

Respect, the second of the three core values, permeates the campus. Visitors strolling the grounds are warmly greeted by every uniformed person they pass. Cadets do not wander with bowed heads, preoccupied with iPods or cell phones. Rather, they look you in the eye and greet you before you can say hello. Manners are learned responses, and while many cadets have been taught this element of respect at the Academy, it still is wonderful to experience in this day and age.

The final core value, devotion to duty, means more than simply staying fifteen minutes past quitting time to finish a letter. There is a legendary saying recorded in Coast Guard annals about duty. According to Coast Guard historians, the statement was uttered by Patrick Etheridge, the captain of a life-saving station on Cape Hatteras. A ship, having struck Diamond Shoals in a storm, was breaking up in the heavy surf. Etheridge gave the command to launch the station's lifeboat in an attempt to save the ship's crew. When a crewmember from the station remarked that although getting to the sinking ship might be possible, a return trip was doubtful, Etheridge is said to have replied:

The Blue Book says we've got to go out, and it doesn't say a damn thing about having to come back.

This quote reflects the same general standard Coast Guardsmen hold today; any in doubt need only turn to the hundreds of transcripts of rescues performed under extreme circumstances. The word duty connotes more to a military officer than it does to the average civilian. The *Running Light* provides swabs with the Coast Guard's version of the concept:

Devotion to duty is the measure of the unique devotion a cadet, through the sworn Oath of the Armed Forces, bears to the nation. Duty is the moral obligation to place the accomplishment of assigned tasks before the needs, considerations, and advancements of any other ideal, organization, or individual. This often entails personal sacrifice, which must supersede any other loyalties in order to preserve the highest standards within the organization. Duty requires loyalty to ideals much greater than ourselves: the Coast Guard, the Constitution, and ultimately the wellbeing of the nation and humanity. Though duty may be simple or hard, mundane or extraordinary, in each given task lays the inherent burden of choice. By virtue of your choice and unique position, this choice cannot be avoided.

The balance of the *Running Light* is filled with concerns that are more mundane: rules and regulations, etiquette, and mission statements, as well as facts and statistics that become part of a cadet's knowledge base over the course of the summer and 4th class year. Flashcard pages provide a photo and a technical description of each type of ship and aircraft the Coast Guard deploys in its missions. There are seven pages alone devoted to the insignias found on uniforms, identifying not only the ranks of Coast Guard officers, but also the ranks of Army, Navy, and Marine Corps personnel. Swabs must memorize signal flags, Coast Guard sector maps, and an overview of the history and traditions of the Service. There are songs to be sung, traditions to be learned, and diagrams depicting which articles of clothing go in which drawer in a properly stowed room.

Swabs must commit much of the *Running Light* to memory by the end of the summer, and all of it by the end of the first academic year. Most of what swabs must memorize is useful and edifying. Some of it, however, is whimsical nonsense known as "spewage." Cadre 2/C Durand explains:

Indoc is all of the rules they have to memorize. Each week, they are supposed to know different things, and there are tests throughout the summer. That's another thing they can get IT'd for. You can go up to them and say, "Give me the fifth Academy rule!" and they have to tell you right away. There are a lot of things in the RUNNING LIGHT they have to memorize word for word. Some of it is actually stuff you need to know later. A lot of it is rules of the road, like what I'm doing now as part of my summer training, or things we will use out in the fleet. There are silly things in there, too, like "How's the Cow?" You can ask any swab this question just for the fun of it, and they will respond:

She walks, she talks, she's full of chalk. The lacteal fluid extracted from the female of the bovine species is highly prolific to the nth degree, ma'am.

As Senior Chief McDade points out, spewage is just another tool for honing swabs' skills:

When they're on the bridge of the ship, there is going to be data that they are just going to have to memorize. If they are in a sector dealing with a major incident, they are going to have to be able to give briefs and retain large amounts of data, and they're going to have to do that in stressful situations. The data, as random as some of it may be, is to get them used to being able to memorize and retain knowledge in stressful situations. You do get better at it. You are able to detach yourself from the stress and get the job done. 4th class year is still very stressful, as lax as it seems when compared to swab summer. Now, they're doing what's called clocks, but it's still memorizing data—memorizing what the next meal is or the next two meals. It's memorizing data and being able to recite that. Then, they have what is called 4th Class Boards, which is a lot of indoctrination stuff, and they have to sit in front of a board and answer questions. There may only be ten questions, but the volume of stuff you must study is enormous, so that, in and of itself, adds a degree of stress.

Swabs must recite another ancient bit of doggerel when they cannot answer a question posed by a superior:

Ma'am, my cranium, consisting of Vermont marble, volcanic lava, and African ivory, covered with a thick layer of case-hardened steel, forms an impenetrable barrier to all that seeks to impress itself upon the ashen tissues of my brain. Hence, the effulgent and ostentatiously effervescent phrases just directed and reiterated for my comprehension have failed to penetrate and permeate the somniferous forces of my atrocious intelligence, ma'am.

For Ensign Shembry, questioning swabs on how long they have been in the Coast Guard is always entertaining:

There's always one fun piece of indoc. The fun pieces are their response to a lot of the standard questions, like "How long have you been in the Coast Guard?" Ask a swab that question, and they will put on their heartiest pirate voice and say:

All me bloomin' life, sir. My father was King Neptune, me mother was a mermaid. I was born on de crest of a wave and rocked in de cradle of de deep. Me eyes is stars, me teeth is spars, me hair is hemp and seaweed, and when I spits, I spits tar. I's tough, I is, I am, I are, sir.

The *Running Light* is not, of course, the definitive manual for actual Coast Guard officers. That distinction goes to a much weightier tome, *The Coast Guardsman's Manual*. Unlike the *Running Light*, though, it will not fit into a swab's sock.

Margaret Bowen

MA

The summer is, of course, just the beginning of the transformative process, and a thousand critical steps lie ahead. One such step is facilitated by Margaret Bowen, the Academy's director of social development. Academy graduates, when not searching for survivors on storm-tossed seas or apprehending go-fast boats smuggling drugs into the country, may find themselves attending formal dinners at embassies or testifying at congressional hearings.

To assure that officers are as at ease in a formal setting as they are on the rolling deck of a ship, cadets receive specialized training. Bowen is the Academy's version of Miss Manners, although in informal situations with cadets, she is simply called Ma. Originally from northern New England, she attended the University of Maine and has been married to a Coastie for over forty years. Her husband, a retired agent with the Coast Guard Investigative Service, or CGIS, was stationed at the Academy, so the entire family was exposed to cadet life. Their oldest son, in fact, liked the Academy well enough to attend, graduating in 1993. She discusses how her position in Academy life has evolved:

I had been so involved in cadet life, starting with my son's classmates. It was like a fraternity at our house on the weekends where the kids would just show up. After a while, it got to be that my husband Bill and I were out shopping, and when we got home there would be cadets doing laundry at our house. Sometimes I knew them and sometimes I didn't, depending upon whom my son gave a key to. One time we came home and a couple of his classmates were there that we knew very, very well. We had, more or less, adopted them as sponsor parents. We walked in and they were doing laundry, and one was doing dishes or something. I looked at them, they were seniors at this point, and said, "Guys, the doors were locked. How did you get in?" They said, "Well, we had to tear a little corner of your screen in order to sneak in through the bathroom." I said, "So you broke into the house? What would you have done if the police had come by?" They said, "We would have pointed to our pictures right there on the wall and said, 'See, we belong here! These are our parents!'"

Bowen initially began working at the Academy in the athletic department and in the chapel program:

When this position opened years ago, I hadn't even thought about it to tell you the truth, but a number of people here at the Academy asked, "Why don't you apply?" because they knew I was already involved with cadet life through athletics, the chapel program, and as a sponsor parent. So I did, and I got the position. From there I was certified by the Protocol School of Washington as a business-etiquette consultant, a dining-etiquette expert, and as a public speaker. I've been here ever since. I developed the program; it was kind of bare-bones at the time, but it's really expanded. It not only involves etiquette training, but every social event we have here is designed with their development and their social skills in mind, whether it's movie night, the activities fair, a formal, a dinner dance, or dinner theater. We have all kinds of things going on, and they don't even realize what they're learning. If you can make it fun for them, it's like anything else; they're being taught without realizing it, and they're more open to it.

As junior officers, when they get to their units, they're going to be hit with "Oh, guess what? We are going to have a change of command and you are in charge," or "We have a visiting VIP." They may have to handle visits by a congressional representative, a senator, a foreign ambassador, or they are going to go to foreign countries and they're going to have receptions, and they need to know how to plan these things. A big part of their training as seniors, as 1ˢᵗ class, is on event management protocol. By that time, they've had three years of etiquette, so they pretty well know what they're supposed to do, but when it comes to event management protocol, that's something new. I give them lists and resources, so when they go out there, they are fairly comfortable with it, and, of course, I'm always at the other end of the Internet or the telephone with whatever they need.

Cadets receive training in all aspects of their future lives as officers, and Bowen sees her role as adding the final touch:

When they come here, they're taught military professionalism, they're taught academics, they're taught physical fitness, teamwork, and athletics. Their spiritual side is taken care of. They're all put together. We take that whole package, and we put polish on it. When they walk out the door, they're a polished, military officer. It's so important. We've all seen people who know their stuff but have the social skills of an eggplant. It's very, very important that they know how to speak to people, they know how to shake hands, they know how to look people in the eye, they know what not to say, they know what's appropriate and what's inappropriate, they

know how to dress in military attire because they wear uniforms. Their entire professional career is going to be uniforms, except for those times when it's not. When they're told, "The attire for this event is civilian informal," they look around and ask, "Well, what does that mean?" What is civilian informal in Key West or Kodiak, Alaska, may be different from what is civilian informal in Washington, D.C., or even Los Angeles.

The affection Bowen feels for cadets is obvious, and she is amazed at each generation's ability to handle the rigors of Academy life:

I have a lot of confidence in this generation. It's just they all start out pretty much the same. You look at them, and you think, "Oh my gosh!" And the older you get, the younger they look; their parents are starting to look younger! I start to talk to them, and I get to know them, and nine times out of ten, you know there's a heart there that's really willing to give to their country and to get through the Academy. This is a very tough school—very tough. I see what they go through. The toughest thing they have to go through is time management the first year. They just can't do everything they want to do, they just can't be involved in everything they want to be involved in, and they find that out. We let them know that there is stuff out there if they want to pick and choose, and nobody tells them they shouldn't be in this or that, unless their grades start to suffer. That's the focus. You're not going to graduate here and be in the World Cup. You're not going to graduate from here and be a movie star. You're going to be an officer in the United States Coast Guard, and you'll have your degree. From that point on, the world's your oyster. They don't always see it that way, especially as cadets. I know when I was that age, I wanted it yesterday, too.

Not an officer herself, Bowen allows the one-on-one relationships she cultivates with her students to be relatively informal. Needless to say, cadets find this a welcome change:

I'm in a whole different environment from the professors or the officers. When they see me, it's "Hi, Mom!" I get to know and see a different side of them that others don't see around here. We talk about their families, if they're having problems at home, because they know I'm not going to say anything. My husband and I got the nicknames Mom and Dad way back when we started first working here. It wasn't something we asked for; it was just something they started. Then, one year, this big ol' Texan started calling us Ma and Pa. I'm a Maine girl. I'd never heard Ma and Pa before, and all of a sudden we were Ma and Pa and have been ever since. They just have to call me Mrs. Bowen when they're in front of officers. A lot of them are just so precious, although sometimes you just want to shake some sense into some of them, but that's true with any kid, even your own. For the most part, they're just amazing young men and women.

According to Bowen, training men is no different from training women; neither sex wants to be embarrassed in social situations. How much work she has to do with any individual is dependent more upon their upbringing:

I think a lot of it goes back to how they were raised. If mom and dad made it a priority to know how to hold that fork and knife, to stand up when an older person comes into the room, to shake hands correctly, if those were priorities, then you're not going to have problems with either one of them. But in either case, if the only time they've ever eaten a dinner was on a TV tray in front of the TV with their hands, regardless of gender, that's all they're going to know when they get here.

I can tell when somebody needs a little more help. The fall semester of their 4th class year I conduct an etiquette training dinner at the officers' club. They dress in their good uniforms, and I have a training session with them. I discuss how to hold the fork and knife, and then I walk around as they're eating and gently coach them. That's a really interesting evening. That's their big introduction. I don't cover much of that during swab summer, because they all look at me like deer caught in the headlights. They're scared, they're hot, they're sweaty, they're tired, and then they sit in an air-conditioned classroom and all of a sudden, their heads start bobbing, so it's not a very long class during swab summer.

During the summer, it's the basics. I have two sessions with them. The first part is about shaking hands and its importance. I mostly

stress why we have this kind of training in the corps of cadets, why it's important. In this session, I get them ready for the superintendent's reception. The admiral hosts a reception for them in Crown Park, behind the chapel, and it is usually the Monday of what we call CAP week, or Cadet Administrative Processing. It's the add/drop week, and it's their very first military social event. They also get their shoulder boards that day, so it's a very cool day for them. They go up to Crown Park and go through a receiving line; I teach them how to do it correctly. They have punch, and they're taught how to engage the faculty in conversation, how to walk around, how to drink punch and eat cookies and still talk and shake hands. It's very, very important that they have this introduction to the social graces; they realize they're not going to fall apart; it's not going to be hard, and I will lead them through it every step of the way. They also get to learn that the admiral and officers are also people; they're not going to bite their heads off.

Bowen is generally pressed for time with cadets, given their demanding schedules:

The classes I have with them are somewhat sporadic. The majority of their classes are done during their freshman year. I take the topics we briefly covered during swab summer and I break them down. For instance, I'll have one class that covers nothing but introductions and handshakes. I'll have another class that does nothing but cover the topic of being a welcomed guest, being a considerate host, or how to write social correspondence—thank-you notes and things like that. We'll have an entire class where they have a writing exercise. Then, I'll do a Jeopardy game with them, or anything that I can do to engage them. They are such a competitive group that during a Jeopardy game, they're hootin' and hollerin' and going on, but by gosh, they're awake, so some of it is sinking in. I'll give them an online quiz, or I'll have a couple of senior officers come in and talk about the wardroom, what it's like on ships they've been on, and what to expect. Then, we have what we call just-in-time training. Just before their first formal, the Holiday Ball at the beginning of December, they have their dining-etiquette classes, because it's a dinner dance. In the spring, the up-

perclass will have their civilian-attire training. In the early fall, for the upperclass, we have a dress-for-success night. We work with a couple of local stores in the area, men's and women's clothing stores, and they help us put it on.

With technology rapidly transforming our lives, there are new challenges for Bowen as she works her piece of the puzzle. During class-wide lectures in Dimick, she occasionally sees the glow of computer screens or cell phones at the back of the hall. She does not let the irony of the situation pass:

Hello! This is an etiquette class! So I have noticed a lot of changes with the advent of technology, but you have to deal with that and make it work. You need to train them how to use it correctly. I tell them, "I can give you the tools you need to succeed, but I am not your mother, and I'm not going to walk around behind you with a stick." They have to choose to do it, and they eventually do. It's just being aware: Say hello to people on the street. When you meet your professors, say good morning. How do you speak to people?

Look them in the eye, engage them. That's what engagement is all about. They learn. I see them develop, and they learn to carry on a conversation. By the time they're seniors, they're something else.

Most encouraging to Bowen is that cadets, at their core, are in the game for all the right reasons:

The cadets are wonderful people to work with. They're young, and they keep you on your toes. They have great heart. I saw that when I was sick and going through chemo—how wonderful they were, how caring they were. Cadets would ask, "Can we come over to the house and do homework?" They wouldn't do homework. They just wanted to sit in the living room with me. They just wanted to be with me, and we would watch TV together, or they would just stick their head in the door just to say, "Hi! How are you doing?" That's the kind of heart these kids have. They had their own lives, but they didn't forget. I saw that side of them. You could see it coming during their 4th class year. They develop. They are an awesome bunch.

For many swabs, the waterfront sailing program is their first exposure to sailing. Most thoroughly enjoy the experience and the break it provides from the daily grind.

Winds of Change

The Coast Guard's identity is permanently linked to the sea. Although Coast Guardsmen are seen on land, inspecting ship construction, and airborne, in brilliantly colored helicopters and airplanes, the majority of their work transpires on the open sea.

Because of this maritime focus, the Academy finds time for the swabs to spend part of their summer on the water, despite countless competing demands.

The swabs' sail training begins right at home on the Thames River. The waterfront sailing program takes place at the Seamanship Center, which is built on top of what is known as Jacob's Rock.

In addition to housing classrooms, this facility provides docking space for the fleet of sailboats the Academy uses to teach basic maritime skills in a hands-on environment. Swabs begin in boats known as Vanguard 420s and Flying Juniors, two similar classes of dinghies often used competitively in collegiate sailing programs. The Academy maintains a fleet of larger boats for sail-training purposes, but the best way to hone sailing skills is in dinghies, boats that react quickly to the slightest change in helm or trim—the smaller the boat, the greater effect any individual has on its performance. The fast-moving 420s are just under 14' in length and 180 pounds in weight, so a sailor's actions have immediate consequences, and they are sailed by a team of two, providing another chance for cadets to work together to accomplish specific goals.

Cadets graduate to larger boats after swab summer. Part of the cadre's summer, for instance, is spent on Colgate 26s. At nearly twice the length of the 420s and displacing 2,600 pounds, the Colgates offer a different sailing experience. Initially, cadets sail these boats, too, right in front of the Academy, but they begin to stray from the river's protective banks as their skills develop. The mouth of the Thames lies within Long Island Sound, which offers some protection from the winds and swells of the Atlantic Ocean. As cadets take these more-imposing boats out into deeper waters, they learn to interact with larger weather patterns and oceangoing traffic, further broadening their experience. Although the Colgates have proven useful trainers over the years, they are slowly being replaced by the beautiful Leadership 44s that are now joining the fleet. As their name implies, the Leaderships are just over 44' in length and weigh in at nearly 25,000 pounds, allowing cadets to cruise New England waters for extended periods with larger crews.

The summer before her senior year, 1/C Breanna Hite assumed the highest cadet leadership role on the waterfront. Her job was to oversee the cadre as they taught the swabs to sail. Originally from Laguna Beach, California, Hite started sailing when she was eight years old. She explains the sail training that cadets receive over their four years at the Academy:

During their swab summer, they'll sail down here in the dinghies—the 420s and the Flying Juniors—and then they also do one week on EAGLE. During their 3rd class summer, the majority of them are on EAGLE for six weeks, a big increase in sailing time. In your 2nd class summer, in addition to all of the trainings you have throughout the summer and your role as cadre for three weeks, you get a chance to sail on the new Leadership 44s as part of the Coastal Sail

Chief Moore and 1/C Breanna Hite.

Training Program. That is a two-week program. For that time, they are underway and they sail along the coast and pull into a different port every night.

In a world powered by fossil fuels, many wonder about the need for sail training. Hite chimes in:

The sailing program, as with a lot of things in swab summer, puts you outside of your comfort level. This is something that maybe a lot of them thought they would never do. We are looking for transformation, and now they can do things they didn't think they could. Another thing is the communication and teamwork required. They see how important it is for the crew and the skipper to communicate in order to do things successfully. Additionally, I think it's healthy for them to come down here once a week and be in a relaxed environment where they can smile. I think it's emotionally and mentally healthy for them.

It's nice to see one confident person ask somebody who's not as confident to be their partner and take them under their wing. A lot of times, if there are sailors in the company, they'll take somebody that doesn't know what they're doing and help them out a little bit. There are definitely people who express nervousness about being in a boat, but there's never been anybody who said, "I won't do it." They always get out, and perhaps they're not the most successful boat out on the water, but for the most part, they'll come back to the dock, and they'll say they learned something. They'll take away something every time.

Hite hastens to add that the sailing skills themselves can and do come in handy:

For the majority of your 1ˢᵗ class summer, you go to an operational unit. It's actually pretty cool: I just heard about a 1ˢᵗ class cadet on her boat right now. She's on a 110' cutter and went out on a SAR [search and rescue] mission to rescue a sailboat that had run out of food and water and everything else. For some reason, they couldn't tow the sailboat back. The cadet was the only one on the cutter who knew how to sail, so they put her and one other crewmember onto the sailboat and they sailed the boat back to the harbor, so you never know when your sailing knowledge can help you.

Just as the Chase Hall Cadre command swabs on the Hill, Waterfront Cadre command swabs once they hit the docks. The training environment is much different once swabs leave land, as these cadre are more relaxed. Military discipline is maintained, of course, on the docks, but it is brought down a notch in the interest of safety; swabs must be able to look around to sail a boat or to avoid waterfront hazards. Senior Chief McDade explains:

It's a different type of environment. I wouldn't say it's less demanding; it's just less of a high-stress environment. It makes me think of the Army and when you went to the range. In Army basic training, they were on you all the time. When you went to the range, they dropped it down a key, because safety was the biggest concern. You were obviously in a higher-risk environment, so you want to make sure people understand what's going on. It's the same with the sailing program.

Some Waterfront Cadre worry that they are missing out on the action up on the Hill. Hite was not one of them:

I was Waterfront Cadre. I don't think I missed anything by not being Chase Hall Cadre. This summer, there are a lot of Waterfront Cadre down here who have approached me and said, "You know, I really want to be involved in Chase Hall, too." I let them know that I was actually really involved as cadre up in Chase Hall, as well. There are ways to make it work, even though you're down here all day. You still have mornings up there; you still have evenings up there. It's exhausting, and I think the Chase Hall Cadre don't realize how hard the Waterfront Cadre work, but there are definitely ways to be involved and play a part in forming those swabs.

In relation to Chase Hall Cadre, Waterfront Cadre have fewer opportunities to spend time with individual swabs. Because of this, Hite feels the waterfront staff does not get to witness quite the same amount of personal growth:

I guess I don't see as much change down here as you would up in Chase Hall from day one—not knowing how to square properly or how to sound off—but it's an amazing feeling to see the transformation of these people on the water. The majority of them have never been in or rigged their own boat before. For instance, yesterday we had Charlie and Golf Companies down here. It was a windy day and only their second time being out on the river by themselves. Not a single person capsized. It was really cool to watch from here. There were boats that were about to capsize, but they knew what to do, so that's a huge transformation—from not knowing how to tie a simple figure-eight stopper knot to knowing how to rig and sail a boat by themselves.

Ensign Michael Klakring enjoyed being part of the Waterfront Cadre when he was a 2nd class cadet:

I was Waterfront Cadre, but I tried to spend as much time as I could up the Hill with the swabs and the rest of the cadre, too. I'm pretty sarcastic, and I joke around a lot, and I don't think that works very effectively. You can joke around too much, and then it's tough to get serious and get swabs to follow along. It was also tough, not being around for a lot of the day, to come back in the evening to the barracks. I might have had a great day at the waterfront, and I go up to Hotel Company, and they're having a terrible day, and it's hard to make the transition. I could be in a pretty good mood, but then I get up there and the rest of the cadre up there are just hating it; they just can't understand what's wrong with all of the swabs. You take it for granted—that's for sure—what you did and did not know at those points in Academy life. Being Waterfront Cadre is nice; it's a good deal. I did wish I could have spent more time with my company—specifically, with the swabs—and gone through all the daily routines with them, but it was nice to see everybody down here. You get to see all of the companies, and it's a good time. You can see the transition. They get more confident, more comfortable with each other and with the whole routine by the end of the summer.

For 2/C Sam Birchee, being Waterfront Cadre was a learning experience in more ways than one:

I didn't grow up on the water—not that I don't enjoy it. I've really learned to appreciate it, and I've enjoyed sailing on the waterfront. It's been interesting for me, not being a sailor, so I've had to learn everything and also teach the swabs. I've really enjoyed it. It's been pretty rewarding to be able to learn it and then teach it, and it has helped me a lot. Even though I'm not a sailor on the sailing team, I think it's really cool to be able to learn how to sail. It's a skillset most people don't have, and now I can say, "Yeah, I know how to sail!" I've really enjoyed it.

When not leading swabs, the cadre spend time learning how to sail the larger Colgate 26s as part of their own training in team-

work and leadership. As Ensign Shembry points out, they, too, are taught by leaders above them in the chain of command:

The ensigns, except for Mr. Lloyd, are all down here teaching the 26' Colgates. It's the small keel-boat sail-training program. Basically, we get a group of 2nd class cadets every week while they are not doing cadre work. This will teach them the basics of sailing and small-boat handling. If you're a boarding officer on a 210' cutter, you're going to be boarding small boats, and it's good to understand what limitations they might have. Everyone's not on a 210' cutter with two radars, a GPS, and a whole bunch of charts. We go out there, and we don't have a radar, we don't have a GPS. We have a radio, and we navigate by where the buoys are. These boats represent the kind of vessel you're boarding where the owner's knowledge isn't as extensive as a professional mariner's might be. It's a very enjoyable program. For the first two days, we stay up here, north of the bridge, because we do a lot of classroom time. Wednesday, we take them south of the bridge, near the beach, so they can see what it's like near the channel dealing with other vessels. On Thursday, we'll take them to Fisher's Island; that's a destination sail, and that's good fun. It's similar to the L-44s; they are side-by-side programs, so you get one or the other. When they get all of the new L-44s in, the Colgate summer program will go away. On the 44s, they go out for two weeks and stay in a different port every night; they just hop around. It's a very good way to train them.

While the principles of sailing a dinghy or a Leadership 44 are theoretically the same, in practice, there are significant differences in what can be accomplished on either boat. Leadership 44s offer a chance for cadets to learn to work with each other in tight quarters at sea over an extended period. Six cadets, as well as a safety officer, head out for New England waters on these larger boats. Commander Haukom is enthusiastic about the training potential of the 44s:

It's reason enough to join the Coast Guard Academy by itself, but it's more than just a pleasure sail. It is a structured environment where responsibilities rotate. Every day, there is a new cadet leader

A fleet of Vanguard 420s rigged and ready to go. Racing dinghies such as these quickly sharpen sailing skills, reacting as they do to the slightest change in wind or the crew's actions. Built to be sailed by two, the boats also foster teamwork and camaraderie.

On the Waterfront

Clockwise: Swab Samantha Corcoran enjoying time on the water. Smiling is frowned upon over the course of the summer, but inevitable when swabs find themselves once again in control of a small part of their day.

Cadets first learn to right their boats after a capsize before they are set free in the 420s.

A look of doubt crosses Swab Nicholas Trefonides' face as he and his ship-mate, Marie Navetta, approach their first landing on the Seamanship Center's docks. Swabs are quick learners, and most feel at home after a few sessions on the water.

Clockwise: Swabs learning to rig their 420s. While many have sailed, most are completely unfamiliar with the terminology associated with sailing and its complicated gear.

Because dinghies respond so rapidly to change, they make the best platforms for teaching the art of sailing.

Stormy Petrel heads out onto the Thames River with crew of 2nd class cadets. When not fulfilling their roles as cadre, cadets are assigned to other programs throughout the summer months. These Leadership 44s give cadre a chance to go to sea for a week, having planned every aspect of their voyage with their shipmates.

Clockwise: Capsizing a boat makes many swabs nervous the first time though the exercise.

A member of the waterfront cadre instructs swabs as they rig their boats.

A company of swabs listens to the long list of rules governing the waterfront.

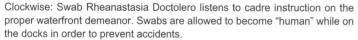

Clockwise: Swab Rheanastasia Doctolero listens to cadre instruction on the proper waterfront demeanor. Swabs are allowed to become "human" while on the docks in order to prevent accidents.

By land, sea or air, Swab Frederick Higgins demonstrates the Coast Guard's flexibility.

Three Colgate 26s converge on the Thames River as cadre improve their sailing skills. These boats are being replaced with Leadership 44s.

of the day, watch captain, as well as navigator, boatswain's mate, engineer, helmsman, and cook, and they rotate through each position. They have a budget, so they plan meals, they go shopping, and they make sure the boat is topped off with fresh water and fuel. They work on safety and man overboard drills. They navigate. They do time-distance equations: "If we want to sail, do we have enough wind to sail? How much speed are we likely to make in the three knots of wind here? We need to be here by sunset. Plan it out." The safety officer is overseeing all of this, and they have to tell him or her what the plan is. The safety officers are just that; they are there for safety. The cadets do it all. It starts off with some structured guidance and suggestions: "Look, you people know how to do this. You've been through nautical science. You know how to navigate. Think about it. Talk about it. Work as a team. Watch captain, you're gonna make the final decision and report to me." The safety officers will give them enough rope. If they make bad decisions, they're going to get in very late, and they're going to be very tired and wet. The officer won't let them do anything unsafe, obviously.

As Haukom stresses, what they learn goes far beyond basic sail-handling:

It's remarkable to get underway on day one, when they're still bumping into each other (literally) as they're trying to navigate and maneuver and tack and jibe. On the last day, the safety officer is not saying a word, the cadets are giving all the right commands; it's like a choreographed ballet. This is one of the most rewarding things I've seen in the training-officer capacity since I've been here, in terms of witnessing a real transformation in such a short period of time. It's hard to describe, really. They're bringing all the fundamentals of navigation and seamanship to bear—line commands, when to tack or jibe, keeping the vessel clearly away from shoal water—and all the while meeting deadlines and waypoints and whatnot. It's great to see the peer leadership involved there; the designated watch captain of the day formulates a plan with the people who are reporting to him or her and executes it. Sometimes, it means making tough decisions and telling your classmates

things they don't necessarily want to hear. And oh, by the way, that classmate may be the watch captain the next day.

I have not seen, since I've been underway on these vessels, anything other than teamwork. I think the cadets get it. Sure, I read reports about cadets who did not do exceptionally well, but for the most part, they get it. They say, "Okay, we're going to use your plan; you're the watch captain. Maybe I'll try something different tomorrow." It's wonderful to see them come together and work as a team in this leadership environment; they all know that one person is making the final decision, and it works. It just works. The transformation in them is even more remarkable because some of these people don't even know how to sail on the first day. Maybe they got a week of it during swab summer in dinghies, but now they're going to spend a week and a half on board this sailboat with five of their best friends (or not), and they're going to have to make it work. I remember going out on a sortie on day one, and the cadets were asking very, very basic questions, like "What's this line? What's this for?" I had to point out some very basic things. I re-joined them at the very end on their last leg, and I remember having a conversation with a particular cadet on day one, and having another conversation on the final day where she was teaching me things. That transformation was just awesome.

Swab reaction to the waterfront sailing program is generally favorable. Even for those who do not enjoy the training itself, the waterfront at least offers a reprieve from the Chase Hall Cadre's incessant haranguing. Other than having to mind their manners and address cadre appropriately while on the docks, swabs can relax, or, as they often say, act like human beings. The change in swabs' demeanor is quite striking. Although the stated purpose of the relaxed attitude is to keep swabs from walking off docks or being knocked unconscious by booms as they tack or jibe, the smiling, joking, and laughing seemed therapeutic as well. As for the cadre, it was clear that many preferred the relaxed nature of the waterfront to the rigidity of Chase Hall. Although some Chase Hall Cadre enjoyed wielding authoritarian control over swabs, most confessed that perpetually intimidating people whom they liked was a difficult and draining task. Cadre on the waterfront were able to maintain discipline while simultaneously showing swabs their human side—something swabs periodically need throughout the summer. As a swab, 4/C Sheila Bertrand found the experience was memorable, if not exactly her cup of tea:

I'm not a big fan of sailing. I flipped the boat three times, and I think we were on the water for maybe an hour or so. You're in the water and you're tired, and you have to flip the boat back. You have to climb up the side and lean on it. I didn't enjoy it. Some people thought it was a nice break. I thought it was a nice break away from the cadre; you didn't have to square, you could look around, and you're on the water. I'm just not a big sailor. But other than that, it was a good break.

4/C Scooter Finney enjoyed the program wholeheartedly:

The waterfront was really fun. It was really funny, because our cadre just yell at us and they seem very coarse, but we got down there, and they were smiling, and it made us realize they are actually people. I got to sail a little bit. I had the tiller, so I was controlling the boat, and I turned around a buoy. That was really fun. We had the most wind of anyone, so that was cool. The Academy has a sailing team, and I want to do that. I've never sailed in my life, but I'm pretty set on being on the sailing team. That's what I want to do.

Lieutenant James Bendle

Portrait of an Officer

The path that led Lieutenant James Bendle to become a Coast Guard officer began long after high school. As a teenager, he suspected he did not have the grades to apply directly to the Academy, so he instead attended a civilian college in Pennsylvania and then enlisted:

I figured I would just get some experience and see if I would really like the Coast Guard as much as I thought I would, and I did. Four years into my first enlistment, I put in my first package to go to OCS here in New London, and I got picked up. I went in May and graduated in September. I had seventeen weeks of training here at the Academy, and my first unit was Group Woods Hole, which is now Sector Southeast New England. It was a great unit, an unbelievable place to serve. At the time, I was the Homeland Security liaison. We did fisheries law enforcement, a short assay for transit ferries, and ran aids to navigation teams we were responsible for,

along with maritime domain awareness. I think we had nine stations at that time.

It was a two-year tour, and I was immersed in various aspects of Coast Guard operations. I worked as a search-and-rescue controller, organizing SAR. We had a station on Nantucket, almost twenty miles offshore. That was a pretty wild unit to work with. There was a senior chief there who ran a tight ship, but there were a lot of things going on out there. I was part of a team that worked with the Secret Service when Laura Bush spent four days out on the Vineyard. That was one of the first missions I had as an officer. I remember sending a picture home to my mom; we were on an 80' yacht, and there were five Coast Guard enlisted folks, me, and Laura Bush. I thought, "This is what I signed up for. This is so cool!" I was working with the Secret Service, establishing security zones around the boat and ensuring the safe transit of the president's wife.

One of the eleven core missions of the Coast Guard is oversight of the fishing industry within the territorial waters of the United States. Although the Service does not make the rules regarding which fish are caught, when, and in what quantities, it oversees compliance with those laws. As with all specialties, Coast Guard officers receive focused training before they board their first fishing vessel. Bendle spent part of his career at one of these training centers:

I was the second in command of the fisheries training center on Cape Cod for three years. It's a law-enforcement training command on the Otis Air National Guard Base called the Northeast Regional Fisheries Training Center. There are five training centers in the Coast Guard that teach fisheries regulations. I taught, and I was second in command, so I did a lot of administrative personnel stuff. We did a lot of boardings. I got out on cutters. I got out on stations to go do boardings and law enforcement. We worked with the National Marine Fisheries and local and federal law-enforcement agencies, like CBP, ICE, and all those folks who do law enforcement. That was a cool job—very rewarding—and I learned a lot in that one, too.

Always advancing, Bendle turned south for his next deployment:

After that, I transferred down to Louisiana, where I was commanding officer of a small-boat station—semi-isolated duty—and that was a wild ride. Station Grand Isle: it's one of the four to seven least-requested small-boat stations in the Coast Guard. I requested it. There are very few Coast Guard stations that can be commanded by a lieutenant. I think there are twelve of them, so they are sought after, and there are some nice ones like the Channel Islands, Monterey, Cape May, and Atlantic City. I would say that Grand Isle is not the Cadillac of that group, but I was proud to get it and I really enjoyed it. I was down there for three years, and we were destroyed by a hurricane during my second year, with something like five or six million dollars in damage. I was the only Coast Guard officer within, I'd say, fifty miles. The sector I worked for was almost three hours away, so I was alone as a commissioned officer on the edge of the fray. I was out there and got to deal with a lot of wild things. It was a very interesting tour. Going to Louisiana from New York, as you can imagine, was a bit of a cultural shift, too, but it was very rewarding. It's a massive facility—twenty-six acres—with sixty-five active-duty Coast Guard members, plus family, so there were 110 people living and working on this base. We had a cutter tied up there, and it was practically at the end of the earth. The last telephone pole in the state of Louisiana was right at the gate of the station.

Although the hurricane that leveled his base certainly tested his unit's mettle, an even greater challenge lay in store for the Coast Guard as a whole:

Just three months before I transferred came the Deepwater Horizon disaster. There were two stations, Venice and Grand Isle, equidistant from where the explosion happened. We towed back one of the rescue rafts that was exploded off the top of the rig. The president came to the unit, and I have a picture of the president and me. Our unit was heavily involved; we were in charge of the boat response to Deepwater Horizon as far as safety, security, and increased patrols, and that's how I finished up my tour in Louisiana. It was good now that it is over, but it was pretty wild when

it was going on. It was tough, because we really worked hard on our base to forward the reputation of the Coast Guard throughout our history in the area. We had a great working relationship with everyone in the town and with the people who dealt directly with the Coast Guard in southern Louisiana. Things went south as far as their opinion of the Coast Guard in the middle of that. I realize that history will judge us on how we handled that incident. I know things still show up in the papers about once a month on things that are still happening in Louisiana, but that was an unprecedented event. The amount of support, the number of hours, the manpower directed towards that was incredible. Just incredible.

I'm sure there are lessons learned, and I am somewhat proud to have been part of it, but I prefer not to have to do something like that again. We certainly answered the call, but it was very challenging. A lot of folks served on that end; in some communities, they're welcomed, and in others, they are not. You're affecting people's livelihood—the fisheries and recreation—and at the bottom of my mind is the thought that all Coast Guard personnel leave. We all transfer, so as bad as it is, orders will eventually come to move on. For those folks who live there, there are no transfers; they're always going to be there, so it's tough. Great people though. I never thought I would love it as much as I did. It's an amazing place. After that, I came back here.

It was my first pick to come back to OCS. When I left the OCS, I knew right away that I wanted to come back, eventually, because of the caliber of officers who trained me and the culture of the school. There is no place like the Coast Guard Academy. There is nothing like this. I went to Cape May when I enlisted—that's our entry point for the enlisted folks—and I went down there again to sponsor a recruit company a year ago, and I was like, "Wow, it just doesn't look right. It just doesn't look that good." I realized that nothing looks quite like this. Cape May is an incredible facility, and the grounds are immaculate. It's a massive facility, with everyone looking sharp and bustling around doing their thing, but it doesn't look like the Coast Guard Academy. This is the epicenter for the Coast Guard in regards to officership and professionalism.

This is a very special place. I remember when I checked in. I was coming off this tour, and I was thinking, "I'm pretty tight. I got it!" There was a lieutenant right across from me, and she was checking in. We were doing our paperwork, and I asked her where she was coming from. She said school and asked where I was coming from. I said Grand Isle. I asked her what school she was coming from, and she said Yale, and I was like, "Oh . . . what did you do there?" She answered physics, and I'm thinking, "I've got to get out of here. They wouldn't let me buy a T-shirt at Yale." The caliber of the people coming through those doors is incredible. That was a real eye-opener into the type of people I would be serving with, and that hasn't changed in two years. Everyone who comes here has this amazing background and history.

Returning to the school that had made him an officer, Bendle felt right at home helping others climb the chain of command:

I'm the assistant school chief of OCS. I'm second in command of the Officer Candidate School. OCS is a seventeen-week program, and it's basically for college graduates or enlisted members who have some college credit. They arrive here and enter the Service as commissioned officers seventeen weeks later. I had a bachelor's degree and four years of service when I went into this program. We also do a three-week Reserve Officer Candidate School, which graduates people who will be officers in the reserves, serving one weekend a month and two weeks out of the year. We do that once a year, and then we have a Direct Commissioned Officer School, too. We have a class on board right now. This is a four- or five-week class, depending upon how much experience they have. They will spend four weeks on heavy academics. They are already commissioned, but they're commissioned from another source. They're coming from the Army, the Navy, or they are Kings Point maritime grads with specific skillsets the Coast Guard is looking for, or from private schools. They will be commissioned without having to go through the seventeen-week or a four-year program here at the Academy. We have two OCS classes a year— one in August and one in January. Add that on top of an ROC class and three DCO

classes, and I think it comes down to six or seven weeks out of the calendar year we do not have a class on board.

OCS provides those who wish to become officers a path to their goals other than through the Academy. Qualifications vary with the training and experience each person brings to the table:

For enlisted personnel, it's four years of active-duty service and a certain number of college credits or a bachelor's degree. You can also apply for OCS with a bachelor's degree as a civilian right off the street, and right now the selection rate for that is 4 percent, so that's very, very difficult. I think the selection rate for enlisted members trying to get into OCS is about 17 percent. They are here for the seventeen weeks, and it's a rigorous and comprehensive program. You're up at 0500 in the morning, and you go to bed at taps at 2200. You're doing physical exercise—marching, motivation. It's a boot-camp atmosphere, similar to what the swabs go through for the first couple of weeks, and then it tapers off into a mentoring model later in the program. During that, they will do two weeks on EAGLE, a number of outreach field trips to different units, and go to the wet trainer or firefighting school in Newport. The wet trainer is the SS BUTTECUP; it's a boat that's designed to flood to train them in damage control. They've been going to the fisheries training center on Cape Cod for law-enforcement training day, and they have a lot of academics. It's a pretty aggressive schedule. In recruiting them, they are looking for candidates with a STEM background: science, technology, engineering, and math. Those are the folks picked up directly from civilian life. They may be coming right out of college, or some of them have some work experience. We've had some pretty impressive folks.

Enlisted personnel who want to follow this path, as Bendle did, have additional hurdles to clear:

They have a job, and that's the tough part for them. It's harder for them to get those types of college credits. They get ACE accreditation for going to Coast Guard schools, and a lot of them do distance learning and do what they can to apply. Many of them went

Men and women enrolled in the Officer Candidate School at the Academy march past swabs training near the flagpole. OCS provides another path for those wishing to become officers. Many of these candidates are experienced enlisted personnel who want to further their careers in the Coast Guard.

Clockwise: Officer candidates spend some of their time on the drill field, but most come from a military background and require little training there. More of their time is spent in classrooms or on trips in the field.

Officer Candidate Oropeza stands at attention for a formal inspection of her company.

Candidates in the OCS program come from all walks of life and backgrounds. They may come from the Coast Guard, other military branches, or directly from civilian life if they have very specific talents the Coast Guard requires.

to college, did a year and a half or so, and enlisted in the Coast Guard. They did a few online credits and put them together to get an associate's or a bachelor's degree. In this day and age, you have people going to boot camp with bachelor's degrees—that's standard fare—and in some cases, they have master's degrees and are enlisting in the Coast Guard with the hope of going OCS. If after four years they don't get picked up, they leave.

Like any demanding program, OCS sees its fair share of dropouts:

Over the course of a year, I'd say our attrition rate is about 10 percent. We may not lose anybody in a particular class, and in the next class lose seven. You never know. It's medical, injury, weight, or core values. Some people have an honor incident. Seventeen weeks is a really short time, and we can't have any doubt of your ability to serve as a commissioned officer. We've only had one of those since I've been here that resulted in disenrollment.

Military academies pride themselves on the quality of their graduates, often engendering an elitist attitude between grads and those who work their way up through the ranks. Bendle feels those attitudes are now long past, at least within the Coast Guard:

I think many years ago, there was the mentality of us and them. Many years ago, OCS was sort of designed as a patch to quickly get a few more officers into the corps, but that's really no longer the case. The big difference is probably the candidates' initial maturity. The folks coming into the Academy are incredibly brilliant and talented, but they're twenty-two when they're commissioned, and our folks are twenty-six or twenty-seven on average, so they are a little more mature; they have a little more life experience. The upper age limit is thirty-four for an OCS candidate. I've served

alongside Academy graduates and OCS ensigns, and in reality, there is little difference. There might be for that first six months, because sometimes the Academy folks will stick together and the OCS will stick together, but the units in which they are assigned will see those things going on and break those cliques up pretty quickly to get them tracking: "We have a job to do. This is not high school." I haven't really seen that, which is a good thing. An officer is an officer is an officer. You're either one or you are not.

The ensigns from OCS start out with a little more technical and a little more life experience, but the Academy does a great job getting the cadets out to experience some of these things during their summer months. Going to the Academy is a tremendous sacrifice. I remember what my college experience was versus what these folks go through. No one yelled at me. They should have, but they didn't. The discipline, the number of hours, and the amount of community service requirements that are involved—it's very, very impressive. You realize these are some of the best young Americans. The folks who come through our doors are just a little bit older. We had two rescue swimmers in the last class. One was a chief with twelve years of service before he came to OCS. That's one of the most impressive rates in the Coast Guard. If you want to talk about attrition rates, you don't make it through that program and the Coast Guard unless you're incredible. While you have to be physically incredible, the leadership stuff is weighted just as heavily. Those guys and gals are very impressive, and to think that they would hang up their wings or flippers to become an officer is pretty impressive. That is tough—earning your anchors, becoming a chief, and turning them in to come to OCS. We have at least two coming on Thursday as well.

Quite literally, every single minute of a swab's day is scheduled, so much of the summer is spent running from one task to the next.

Drill, Drill, Drill

Swab summer is all about indoctrination, and the first commandment handed down to new cadets is: Thou shalt obey every order unquestioningly. Unbeknownst to swabs, however, that last word is not exactly etched in stone once they become officers. In reality, there do exist procedures that allow new ideas to percolate up from within the ranks. Lieutenant Kehlenbach explains:

There is a system in place where individuals can route ideas up the chain of command. If there is a particular regulation that they disagree with and they think there may be a better way to do it—a commonsense approach—we encourage that, and we forward

168

those initiatives up the chain of command for approval. But there is a degree. We are a military organization, and Admiral Papp, the commandant, speaks often of selective obedience. He has been quoted as saying that selective obedience breeds selective obedience. If you set an environment where you're not following the rules, those below you will believe it's okay for them to pick and choose, and that's not good for a military organization. Taking away the selective obedience would really be the goal—that you wear the uniform the way it's supposed to be worn because that's the way it is; but if you want to recommend a better way, please route that up; but in the meantime, continue to follow the rules.

There is no question that the effectiveness of military organizations depends upon its members' strict obedience and rigorous adherence to standard operating procedures, but officers do occasionally find themselves in situations where rigid compliance proves impossible. Coast Guardsmen are no exception, so the Service makes allowances for officers in the field who find themselves in unique circumstances. Asked when Coast Guard personnel may deviate from the SOP, Kehlenbach had this to say:

The Coast Guard puts officers in charge they trust to make decisions and take some risks. It's each commanding officer's responsibility to weigh the risk versus gain. So if there were the need to (in order to save someone's life) do something that's outside of standard operational procedures, they would be empowered to take that risk, but then there's also in place a procedure for case studies to be done where those discrepancies can be documented. Lessons can be learned, and the rest of the fleet can learn from the action. Then, if a policy needs to be changed, there is some background there on why. There is discussion about this here, but once they leave the Academy, there is something called Team Coordination Training, and it talks about that risk management and how every person on a team has a voice. Just because the rank might be different, everybody has a voice in it. If someone sees a safety hazard, they need to bring it up. So these problems are discussed, and that's part of the 2nd class training. In the Coastal Sail Training Program, there is a lot of opportunity for them to make split deci-

sions because of the weather. There is always a safety observer on board (an "adult") with them that can, if it went well, talk about why that decision went well and, if it went badly, talk about that decision too. We spend a lot of time talking about why they did the things they did, what they would do differently, and what they learned from the situation.

Although officers can occasionally diverge from the tried and true, Lieutenant Bendle emphasizes that officers must never place their crews in peril without reason:

Our first responders certainly have a lot of freedom. They're trained, and we prepare them. I was a boat coxswain for three and a half years, and we trained for everything. But when you're in five-, six-foot seas with zero visibility and trying to pull someone out of the water, you act accordingly. As long as you have proper justification, which in a lot of cases is just letting people know what you're doing up the chain of command, you're usually okay. It's a hazardous business, but we have to mitigate risk. We are still doing some incredible rescues, and you can't always follow the policy. That said, you're not going to put our folks in mortal danger for a boat with no one on it; that's the type of situation where policies rule.

The majority of the commands that cadre issue and that swabs must obey are quite basic. They may simply require dropping and doing twenty-five pushups or running two miles around an oval track. These tasks are not particularly complicated, yet they effectively breed obedience in the swabs. They also serve at least one other important function: ensuring swabs are fit enough to pass the first of eight physical fitness exams, or PFEs, they must take while at the Academy. Cadets are given several chances to pass each test, but continued failure will result in expulsion. Senior Chief Tony McDade explains:

The PFE is arguably different from sports. Regardless of what sport you are participating in— whether you're doing ICs, which is a non-varsity sport to get your sport credit, or if you are a softball player, a baseball player, a wrestler, or whatever—you have to take the physical fitness exam. It's the mile-and-a-half run, it's pushups, and it's sit-ups, and cadets are expected to maintain that physical fitness. There are trainers and coaches here to help them. I tell my cadets, "If you can't do it here, you're certainly not going to be able to do it in the fleet." The tools and resources are all here. They're given classes in strength training. They're given classes in cardio conditioning. So it's not just "Hey, you have to pass this." That's one of the things the chiefs help facilitate. If we have a cadet who's struggling with a PFE, it's not like you fail it once and you go home; that's not how it works. For just about anything they can fail, there's typically some type of probationary status, depending on the severity. Some of them, you're going home. Even with the athletic or physical fitness, there are tools. We catch them and put them in a probationary status. The probationary status is not punishment, but it is to get them up to speed. There are class standards, and there are graduation standards, and it's incremental. As a 4th class, the class standard is lower than a 1st class. We'd like to have them all meeting the graduation standard, but the reality is that it just doesn't happen, and so it's tiered. There is an emphasis on it during swab summer, and a lot of the training they get is geared towards that. When you finish swab summer, there aren't going to be people making you do pushups, unless for your sport they have you doing them, but you're going to have to make the time to work out and take care of that.

As 2/C Cathy Durand notes, the Academy takes the PFE seriously:

Most people can pass pretty easily, but there are always people who are remedial. You can get kicked out. Right before graduation, I think one or two kids got kicked out for not being able to pass. Then there are weight standards too. Even if you pass the PFE, you still have to pass your weight standard. Most people don't have a problem, but it can be a big deal.

When asked whether she had physically trained for swab summer before arriving at the Academy, Durand's answer was somewhat typical:

Probably not as much as I should have. I tried to start running—because the only sport I had in high school was dance, and that's not very physical—so I tried to run, but getting closer to my summer was also closer to my graduation, so I let it go a little bit. I definitely could have been in better shape coming in, but at the same time, I didn't really have a problem. The first week, you can't do anything physical, but the next week you can. So that second week, where we could start running and stuff, was really hard for me, but I got in shape during that week, and then the rest of the summer was fine.

Many students entering the Academy feel that their participation in high-school sports has prepared them for the physical challenges ahead. What they overlook is the fact that nearly all their classmates were also selected based at least in part on their athletic abilities. The bar on day one is simply set that much higher. 4/C Sheila Bertrand had felt confident about her physical abilities as R-Day was still approaching:

They tell you to get in shape. I play varsity sports during the school year, so I can get in shape pretty quickly. For me, I think, I can let it hit me, and I don't think it will be as bad as for someone who doesn't play any sports. I'm going to let it hit me, more or less. I'm constantly outside playing sports. I haven't been sleeping for the past few weeks, but I haven't been going to the gym and doing four-hour-long workouts, either. I know what to expect, physically.

With swab summer over, she admits that there may have been some difficulties:

I'd say the hardest part would probably be—and this is going to sound funny—the obstacle course. It took me like three tries before I could do every single obstacle, and you're physically, mentally, and emotionally drained when you get there. Physically, that was the hardest thing I did. Some people did it perfectly the first time. That was the hardest thing. However, by like maybe the third or the fourth time, I was going through it—obviously tired, but I made it. The first time I went through that, I thought I was dying. The wall was probably the obstacle that took me the longest to get, but once *you hit the wall and you get up and you're on top and climbing over, you have the best feeling in the world, and you know you only have three more hurdles and a low crawl under some wire to go. You can't help but turn everything now, looking back, into a positive situation; you see how it benefited you.*

4/C Katie Brosnan recalls taking the Coast Guard's recommendations seriously and beginning her training for swab summer long before high-school graduation. During the initial application process, teenagers must pass a version of the PFE administered by a high-school coach. Brosnan remembers taking her test under less than optimal conditions:

There is something called the physical fitness exam, and to get into the Academy, you have to score at least 130 or 160—something like that. I think 130 is acceptable, but they want you to be 160 by swab summer, and they want you to be at 200 when you're a cadet. You have to pass that test to be considered for the Coast Guard Academy, so I had my gym teacher administer it for me. It was kind of funny, because I live in New York City. You can do the pushups and the sit-ups in the gym, right? No big deal. But you have to run a mile and a half, so I end up going to Central Park and running around the Great Lawn. I'm jumping over baby carriages and pedestrians, and I'm trying to get a good time, because I want to get into the Academy. I'm sprinting, and he's like, "Keep going! Keep going!" Of course, I don't want to hit anyone, so my time probably wasn't the fastest. It was pouring rain that day, too—pouring rain in Central Park. That was an experience, but I did pass, so that was good.

That was when I applied—around October, November—but since I've graduated, I've been trying to do the physical fitness exam every day. I'll run a mile and a half or two miles every day, and then I'll try to do as many sit-ups and as many pushups as I can in two minutes. Just because I said I do it doesn't mean I do it well; it just means I try. I also play soccer, so I can't try too hard when I'm doing the physical fitness exam—because I don't want to pull anything or tire myself out before I have a soccer game—but I am

The morning begins with a grueling round of exercises, just as the sun begins to rise across the river.

playing soccer, so I am training in that respect. I was talking to my friend who goes to West Point, and she was saying it was good to practice running, because you will run everywhere. But when it comes down to it, running is easy. You should work on pushups and building your arm strength. I guess, being a female, our arms aren't as strong, so I really have to focus on my doing pushups.

Although she certainly found the summer physically challenging, Brosnan felt she was able to keep up with her shipmates:

It's boot camp. It's swab summer, so you are going to do some pushups, you're going to do some sit-ups, and you're going to run for a long time. It's going to stink, because it's hot; it's summer, so that's inevitable. I wasn't worried about running. If anything, I was like, "Oh, cool! I'm going to get in shape!" I passed everything, but it definitely was hard, you know? I wasn't the fastest kid in my company, by any means, but I wasn't the slowest, either. What they do during swab summer is keep up with the slowest in your company. So as long as I wasn't the slowest, I didn't feel too bad about it. But you could see some of the kids in our company—especially the athletes and a lot of the guys who really wanted to work out—could get a little uneasy and ticked off, because they had to literally jog so all the kids could keep up. But the whole point of it is that you're a team, and you fail and you succeed as a team.

2/C Hunko reminds swabs there is only one way for them to respond.

4/C Fred Higgins thought the physical training was made all the more difficult by the added stress brought on by the cadre:

It was difficult mainly because it was so mental. I'm pretty sure that if we did the exact same workout but I was in control of it, I could have done it easily. But when somebody is yelling at you and saying how bad you are, it really gets you down, so that made it difficult.

4/C Kyle Wood took it all in stride, although he stops short of calling the summer enjoyable:

It was pretty hard all the way through. I lost a lot of weight over the summer, but it was good for me. It was hard, but it was fun in the end. Well, I don't know about fun, but it helped me get in shape physically, so that was a good thing. Mentally, it can get hard with not much sleep and so much physical activity, but I always tried to keep a good attitude, and that helped me a lot. I didn't ever really get down, so that was good. I never questioned my decision.

4/C Jake Carlton echoes Wood's feelings:

The days are long, but the weeks are going by pretty quickly. I'm surprised they went by as quickly as that. There's a lot of ups and downs, and it's very stressful. You get physically and mentally very tired, because there's so much indoc to learn, and once the physical training starts, you're pretty much physically worn out by the end of every day. Regardless, they expect you to keep moving while fatigued and dead tired. I wasn't very in-shape when I came. I was in better shape than a few people but not that great compared to a few others, and that's kind of the thing I regretted not doing—getting better at my pushups and sit-ups. It wasn't fun the first couple of weeks, but eventually I got stronger. I didn't eat very well the first couple of weeks, which didn't help any, so I had no energy. They spent a lot of the time quizzing us on indoc and yelling at us during meals. But I think they're changing that for next year, where, during meals, they're not yelling at them anymore, they're letting them eat—which is a good idea, because you need the food energy, especially with how many calories you burn each day. I remember at the end of swab summer, I had lost a lot of weight; my pants were really loose on me. As soon as swab summer ended and I started getting that food in me, I gained it all right back.

4/C Rheanastasia Doctolero struggled initially but soon began to notice the positive effects the training regimen was having:

It's getting better. I'm getting into the routine of things, so it's not like I'm surprised by anything anymore. Physically, I can feel myself getting stronger. Before, I would do two pushups, and I'd be dying. Now, I'm getting twenty before I start to wear away. Even the obstacle course—the first time we did it, I couldn't get up the rope. It was so weird. The second time we were going, I was like, "I hate this obstacle course. I'm never going to finish it." I got on the rope, and it was like, "Man, this is really easy." I got to the top, and I couldn't believe it. I could feel myself getting stronger, and that made me happy. I did the best time in my company for girls, and I'm aiming for the record; I want to be number one.

There are those swabs who sail through the summer's physical challenges without undue strain. But far fewer escape the psychological stress of the mental game they are forced to play. It seems as though cadre anticipate their every move, pounce on their every mistake. Swabs manage to vent some of their inevitable frustration with this marching ditty:

Cadre Everywhere I Go

Everywhere I go
There's a cadre standin' there
Everywhere I go
There's a cadre standin' there
Why won't they lemme alone?
Why don't they ever go home?
When I'm eatin' my chow
And I can't figure how,
Everywhere I go
There's a cadre standin' there.

2/C Ryan Babb, looking back to his time as a swab, remembers what it was like for him:

I would say pretty rough; it was an eye-opener. There were a lot of tough days—and a lot of days where it technically wasn't tough but mentally it was tough due to the fact that we were just dead tired. I'd say the Academy is physically challenging, but I think it's mentally more challenging. If you can maintain your mental stamina and tell yourself, "You're going to be fine, you're going to be fine," you'll make it through. I remember during the first week, I knew I wanted to be here, but I had to tell myself, "Just make it to the next meal. Make it to the next meal." I just kept doing that, and then after the first week, I was dead set on making it through. I knew I wasn't going to go home.

Before arriving, 4/C Scooter Finney had been more concerned about the physical hurdles in store than the mental ones. He concludes his worries had been misplaced:

The physical part was doable. I think anyone should have been able to do it, anyone could do it. There were people who, during

A swab receives special attention for underperforming during morning calisthenics. This special session is euphemistically known as going to the "hurt locker".

Adrenaline wears off and exhaustion sets in by mid-summer. While swab Scooter Finney appears to be napping, he probably just blinked at the right time.

ing able to smile, not being able to look around, not being able to act crazy. I feel like the summer made me appreciate all of that a lot more. It made me appreciate sleep more. It made me appreciate time more, especially, and even simple things like being able to smile or look at your food. I noticed a lot of things I took for granted, which I think was really good.

For a number of swabs, this is their first real time away from home. As nearly all lines of communication with parents, siblings, and friends are severed for the length of the summer, many cadets find this forced separation to be one of the greatest challenges to overcome. 4/C Koachar Mohammad was among them:

For me, what I thought about a lot was my family, and for some reason, the summer made me feel worse about my family than I did about me. It's kind of ironic, because my family was at home, and, of course, they were fine. For some reason, during the summer, I thought because I was having such a bad time, maybe they were, too. I was really worried about them. I don't really know why. It was mentally difficult, not having control over my own actions, especially coming from an environment where I had never experienced this. Even being an athlete on several teams, where coaches are constantly yelling, this was completely different.

4/C Jake Carlton also missed being with his family, a continent away in Alaska:

It was mainly homesickness that affected me. I had no problem with yelling; it doesn't really faze me. I know it's part of what's happening; just get it done. It doesn't really bother me. It's more being homesick and across country and knowing that some people, during the Mystic Flag Ceremony, got to see their families because they live nearby. Or during EAGLE, a couple of the people I knew had their families at the ports to see them. I like the liberty they gave us, but I don't like the fact it was more beneficial for people who live nearby; they get to see their families, while others don't. At least they let you have your cell phone to call home, which was nice. You get your cell phone on EAGLE, and you get your cell phone during the Mystic Flag Ceremony.

the summer, couldn't keep up, but I felt I was somewhere in the middle of the pack. The hardest part mentally for me was not be-

4/C Doctolero felt her most notable pangs of homesickness when she missed, for the first time in her life, her sister's birthday. Beyond that, general psychological strain was the toughest part of the summer:

It was mentally draining. I feel like you didn't have time to recuperate from the day before, so it was a continuous mind-drag. You can't think or focus on anything. It was very, very mentally tiring—going through the day, knowing, "Dang, I have eight hours to go before I can go back to sleep." Your thought for the whole day was: "Oh my gosh, why isn't this time going faster?" The physical part, it was always there, but it was little things you could overcome. It's easier to overcome a physical challenge than a mental challenge. It was just hard. You can't really control the mental aspects. When you wake up and you're waiting for the time to go back to bed, you can't make time go faster, so you're just thinking about it the whole day. If we're doing pushups and I decide to slack them down on the floor, then that's my break, but there's no real mental break, you know?

Lieutenant Commander Chris McMunn, looking back over the many years since his initiation, remembers how valuable the entire experience proved in the long run:

Swab summer was definitely challenging. They always talk about it being the most challenging thing you'll ever do, and I'd say that's probably true, maybe because of the duration of it. I've probably had harder days in my life, but I've not had a harder seven-week period with sustained activity. But I think it was really good for me. If it had been too easy, I might have just said, "Well, this is nothing special." I really did see I was earning something and that my classmates who stayed really wanted to be here. This was the kind of people I wanted to go to school with, form friendships with, and work with in the Coast Guard in the future—people who were dedicated to what they were doing and were willing to take on those sacrifices for greater rewards and opportunities down the road.

As can be imagined, swabs will occasionally balk at making the sacrifices to which they agreed on R-Day. Adrenaline wears off, exhaustion sets in, and they begin to question not only their own decisions, but the commands of their cadre. For small indiscretions, a short round of incentive training is generally all that is required to get a swab back on course, as 2/C Jake Rendon confirms:

Little problems we try to correct with little IT sessions. It's called FIT. Say somebody takes eyes out of the boat. You say, "Quick, twenty pushups! Is it going to happen again?" They say, "No, sir!" We move on. So you're trying to address stuff really quickly. If the company is struggling as a whole, we have a five-minute IT session with the whole company. Say we need to address a respect issue or everybody's goofing off. We get the whole company together, and we try to address it as a company. We take care of it real quick. It happened; move on, forget about it. We try to motivate them to want to fix what they're doing. Yelling only goes so far. I remember, as a swab, that you get to a point where it didn't matter. You have to get them to want to motivate themselves.

Sometimes, however, individual swabs may require more than a quick IT session. Losing motivation, their attitudes might begin to harden, their performance to taper. When this becomes a larger problem than IT can solve, cadre have other tools at their disposal, such as sending the swab to PEP. Rendon continues:

PEP is the Performance Enhancing Platoon. It's usually for kids with attitude problems, the ones who stand out in a bad way. It's basically an entire swab summer in two hours. You break them down in the first few minutes physically; it's physically very grueling. You break them down in the beginning, and you address the problems that they're having. You tell them, "If you want to be here, you need to start showing it." In the last ten to fifteen minutes, you really try to motivate them. You start building them up again. You tell them, "You can do this. You can do better. I know you can. We need to see improvement." So physically, it's very tough, even as cadre, because you have to do everything they do. It's really swab summer in two hours. I did it yesterday, and I thought it went very well, at least with the swab I was pepping. I could really see where he was broken down in the beginning. He was struggling, and then towards the end, you could tell he was really getting motivated, he wanted to be here, he was sounding off. So even in those short two hours, I could see some change. Physically, it's really tough, but it works for most kids. For some, it doesn't, but hopefully it worked yesterday. We did have a kid where it didn't work yesterday. He just wasn't getting it. He came back and he still had attitude that he wrote about in his thoughts, and that made me angry. It's tough. It just doesn't click with some people, so we send them back to the command table at dinner. Who knows? Maybe another PEP. It's hard to tell, so you just play it by ear.

Even the best swabs can find themselves "on the PEP train," as it is called. As tough as it is, most exit the ride reenergized, as did 4/C Doctolero:

I'm terrible at pushups, and I got in trouble a lot. I actually got pepped. It was awful. Awful. But I felt so accomplished after, be-cause I didn't give up. There were a bunch of people who didn't want to do it, and they quit. I just kept pushing through it. I surprised myself. I was like, "What? I can do this? It's crazy." The physical part was a challenge for everybody, you know?

Even when I got pepped, it sucked at the moment, but honestly, I'm glad I did it. PEP was not something that I want to do again, but it reminded me why I'm here. In the middle of the summer, it's just like, "Why am I here? I just want to go home. This is miserable. My friends are in college having fun and partying and being normal, and I'm here getting yelled at like a dog." PEP actually motivated me again to want to be here.

Swabs chat on the deck of the cutter *Eagle*, the Coast Guard's sail training vessel. The number of women joining the service has been on the increase over recent years.

Women in the Coast Guard

Women have played an important role in the Coast Guard throughout its history. The Lighthouse Service, one of the Coast Guard's predecessors, began employing female lighthouse keepers as early as the 1830s. The most famous of those keepers was Ida Lewis, who is credited with having saved no fewer than eighteen lives. Her 1881 rescue of two soldiers who had fallen through harbor ice earned congressional attention, and she became the first female to receive a Gold Lifesaving Medal. Lewis made her last rescue at the age of sixty-three.

2/C Laroche shoulders a full sea bag while overseeing her swabs' performance.

first two Coast Guard cutters with active-duty, mixed-gender crews sailed, each with a dozen women on board, and by 1978, every job available to men in the Coast Guard was also available to women, something no other service could boast until 2013. Lieutenant Commander Michael Thomas of the Admissions Department is proud of the lead the Coast Guard has taken in the recruitment of women:

We're around 30 percent every year in each class. Of all the service academies, the Coast Guard seems to draw more females, although I think Navy is making a late run at us. Since we've accepted women at the Academy, any job is available to females. We don't have restrictions like "You can do everything but this or that." They become general line officers like the males. I think that makes us very attractive as a service.

Female representation has risen steadily over the years. This summer, fully 37 percent of the Academy's incoming students were young ladies—a record high—and women now comprise nearly 15 percent of active-duty Coast Guard personnel. For Lieutenant Kehlenbach, females have always been a part of her Coast Guard experience:

It was not uncommon to have other women in the unit. My first unit had two other females. They tried not to send females to units by themselves, so I was the third female at my unit. I was always very fortunate to have senior female leadership. I had female chiefs when I was at Group Portland. My commanding officer was a female, so I haven't had the experience of not having senior female leadership in my career. There are still some female firsts that have yet to be achieved. For me, it's commonplace, but I have peers that are firsts, such as the first African American female engineer who graduated from the Academy. She is here now as an instructor. It is pretty neat that there are still female firsts, but for me, it's commonplace to have a large portion of the crew be female. In Alaska, while I was there, we had two female ensigns arrive, and looking back, I thought it was pretty neat that now I'm the more senior female in the mentor/role model position. I've never run into any problems as a female.

Despite this long and distinguished record of service, the Coast Guard Academy, like all of the bigger military academies in the United States, did not admit women until 1976, with the first female cadets graduating four years later. The following year, the

Today, there are still more males than females at the Academy, but 2/C Durand finds the imbalance unimportant:

You do notice that there are fewer girls. I've never had a problem with it. You do notice sometimes with someone in a head position that you'll say, "Oh my gosh, that's a woman." But it's really just because there are fewer of us. I really don't think it's that big of a deal here.

Durand's shipmate 2/C Jennifer Patron feels much the same about her own experience:

The ratio of females to males is about 30:70 here. I think the experience for us is the same. I've never felt anything different because I am a woman, or even because I'm a Hispanic woman. Nobody has ever said anything or done anything or even insinuated that I'm different. There was something that Admiral Stosz said that I noticed. She was addressing a crowd, and she was very proud that they introduced her as our superintendent and not as the first woman to be superintendent, and that's kind of the way it is here. They don't say, "Here comes the Hispanic female." I'm very proud of being Mexican, and I'm part of clubs like the Compañeros Council and things like that which celebrate my ethnicity. There are various things to celebrate it, but it's only if you want to. It's very fair, very equal.

Of course, female swabs do associate some summer annoyances specifically with the behavior of their male counterparts. 4/C Doctolero sums up how she often felt during the summer's training:

I guess they seriously do think we are inferior. They don't want to listen to our ideas. It happened a couple of times during swab summer. A girl would say something, and they were like, "Ahh, that's so stupid." A guy would say the exact same thing, and all of a sudden, it was the best idea in the world. I'd say, "She just said that!" And they would be like, "She didn't say it like this. This is better!" It was the same exact thing, and you find that in school as well. I'm good at math, and for some reason, nobody thinks I can be smart in math. So my friend, he was sitting next to me, and I was like, "Oh, if you ever need help in math, you can come to me." And he

was like, "Really?" The teacher said, "We only have two As in the class." I said, "Maybe it's me!" And he said, "Rhea, it's not going to be you." And when we got them back, who got the A? He was like, "Oh, wow!" It's fun to prove people wrong, I guess.

4/C Brosnan concedes that the boys may have been physically stronger, but she is confident that the ladies more than held their own across all activities. According to Brosnan, the sexes' respective skills actually complemented each other nicely.

During swab summer, there was definitely a difference, physically. The guys are generally a lot stronger and a lot faster; but then again, you have to stay with the group. I'm totally for girl power—girls are strong and everything—but physically, the guys are stronger. But when it came to other things—you know, they time you for everything, like taking quick showers, changing into new clothes, or head and water breaks, the girls were always the first back on the bulkhead. We were always the fastest. When it came to the physical stuff, the guys definitely had us beat, though. It definitely worked out. The girls seemed to be a lot more serious with things. Maybe we weren't the fastest, but we were running as hard as we could, whereas the guys didn't really need to run as hard as they could. They were able to goof off a little bit, which was good for us, especially because they provided comic relief. We'd be on the bulkhead, and they'd try to make us laugh, and you're not allowed to show any emotion. They tried to balance us out. They were like, "Take it easy!" The girls were more focused; it definitely balanced and worked out.

Although Brosnan felt that the boys were not always giving the girls a fair shake, she never thought they were being malicious. What trainers, cadre, and female swabs alike often had to push against were the young men's tendency to use brawn alone to overcome all obstacles:

The guys in my company are all real good guys—trust me when I say that—real good guys. But they definitely didn't listen to the girls when it came to ideas or anything like that. I wasn't used to people not taking me seriously. Another thing was physical strength. They were like, "Oh, you're a girl. You can't do it." They don't mean it in a degrading way; they just mean, "Well, I'm a guy, so yeah, naturally I'm stronger. I'll go first and do it, and then I'll help you over." But it's funny: a lot of the things that we had to do were designed so that you didn't really need to be that strong. Especially our last challenge, where you had to bring everybody over the wall. You didn't really need to be that strong to lift the person up. But they were like, "Okay, strong guys go first." I remember being up there and thinking, "Guys, it's not hard. It's really not that hard!" The cadre actually asked us this: "Does anybody really feel like they've been underestimated?" And everyone stuck out their paw: "Yeah, I feel like I've been underestimated here." It was interesting to see how many people had their paws out. It made me think, "Wow, what can you do that I don't know?"

As might be expected, male swabs see the relationship slightly differently. 4/C Wood paints a rosier picture:

I think that's where we became more of a team. Where the girls couldn't do something, the guys would help and do stuff for them. When the girls were good at certain things, they would help us guys. That's where we really became a company; we helped each other when people weren't good at something in particular.

Lingering teenage gender rivalries aside, women have made steady inroads since their acceptance into the Academy's ranks. Rear Admiral Sandra Stosz is perhaps the finest evidence of that. She was not only the first female Academy graduate to achieve flag rank, but also the first female to be placed in charge of any military academy in the United States.

Stosz was born in Takoma Park, Maryland, and spent her childhood in nearby Ellicott City, during which time her father worked for the Navy as a civilian. Close in age with her three brothers, she notes the influence they had on her:

I was raised as a tomboy, and I always loved the outdoors. I always wanted to be something that had to do with science: a biologist, ornithologist, a zoologist. Anything that ended in -ologist interested me—even a paleontologist for a while. When I was a

kid, I always thought I was going to go to college and become a scientist; I wanted to do something outdoorsy. Then, in 1976, I was a junior in high school, and the Baltimore Sun ran a feature article on the Naval Academy opening its doors to women under the Defense Authorization Bill. In 1976, all service academies were required by law to open their doors to women, so I went ahead and applied. It sounded like a wonderful opportunity, a life of adventure at sea.

Even though I thought I wanted to be a scientist, I think what I was looking for was something exciting and adventuresome. The idea was being able to go to sea not just as an adventure, but as a chance to serve the country—and oh, by the way, it provided a free education. You've got to figure that I was born and raised during the time of the oil shock of the mid '70s, a pretty big economic downturn. You couldn't get jobs anywhere. I had done farm labor as a kid to try to earn money to make ends meet. The idea of a free education was beyond belief, and owing five years afterwards didn't seem like anything, so I applied to the Naval Academy.

The Naval Academy required a senatorial nomination; it's very political. My mother found a friend of hers who knew a retired Maryland state senator, and they set me up with a courtesy meeting with him so he could put in a good word for me with Senator Sarbanes. Then I had an interview with Senator Sarbanes and I got a nomination to the Naval Academy. Meanwhile, my guidance counselor told me there was a Coast Guard Academy. We didn't know between us, but it sounded like a small Navy, so I applied here and was quickly accepted. My mother said, "Well, you'd better send in your fee, a couple of hundred bucks to accept and take that bird in the hand." The Naval Academy was right close to home; it was big and famous, and everybody had heard of it, but I sent my money into the Coast Guard Academy, and I never looked back. I came here to visit and liked the small, New England college feel, so I ended up coming here.

For Stosz, the early days of coeducation at the Academy were no walk in the park:

I was in the third class of women admitted to the Academy. Even though I give the Coast Guard such credit, there wasn't any stirring in the culture yet to accept women. Wonderful men like Admiral Tom Wetmore, the assistant superintendent when women were integrated, did a great job with all the fundamental stuff—providing bathrooms and ordering women's uniforms—but for the men who were here, especially that last class of men, their entire ethos and identity was tied up with being the last class without women. That was what they latched onto as something that mattered to them in an amazing way, which made it tough on us. Everywhere they went, that was their thing: they were the last class without the scourge of women. We were outcasts, and nobody wanted us here. The senior people were great, but out of the cadets themselves, it seemed like not many of them wanted us here. The officers and all of the people trying to make it work were doing the best they could.

By the time I graduated four years later, there were women in all of the classes, and women had graduated through. When I graduated in 1982, it was a very different atmosphere; it was more like high school. By the time I graduated, most of the new kids coming in, the 4th class cadets, didn't know what it was like, because women had always been there in their minds. The atmosphere might not have had all the kinks worked out, but it was a lot further along. When I first came in, for instance, there were no women's sports. We had to start our own teams and work our way through that. I joined sailing, because that was one of the few things you could do that was coed. I had always been a basketball person, a track person, and a swimmer in high school, but there were no teams like that here for women. Sailing is not the best exercise, so despite being an active person, I started to gain weight. I went and swam on the men's team here for one winter, just to keep in shape, because I wasn't going to be able to compete with men. The coach, to his credit, let me work out with the men and swim on the team, so to speak. I of course didn't swim in the meets, but lots of people reached out and tried to integrate us. However, without sports, logistics, and with the cultural attitude, it was a different kind of environment for a while.

Rear Admiral Sandra Stosz, superintendent of the U.S. Coast Guard Academy.

Ultimately, Stosz persevered and graduated on schedule. She had entered the Academy with twenty-nine sister cadets; only ten survived the four-year trial. The operational Coast Guard would, of course, present its own challenges, but Stosz found that integration process easier:

In the field, I was the first woman on a few of my ships and the only woman on a couple for a while, but I think it was easier, because you actually have control if you are a minority in a situation. I really think that if you choose to be positive, then you can go on board and break the ice. I was the first female assigned to the Coast Guard cutter CLOVER, out of Eureka, California. She was a medium-endurance cutter at the time, and I was the operations officer. I was a lieutenant, and the men just didn't know what to make of it. I'll give you an example. Back in those days, there was a tradition of using the ship's bell, which was normally used to mark time and ring the captain aboard or to announce there was a woman coming on board. Because there hadn't been women assigned to ships, the quarterdeck watch would just ring the bell and say on the 1MC, "Lady guest arriving." That way, the guys below decks would know there's a woman coming aboard—usually a wife or girlfriend—to visit their husband or friend on duty. Guys in those days would just throw a towel around themselves in transit around the ship between the showers and the berthing areas, and that's why it was done.

When I was first assigned, I reported aboard, and I was in my uniform. I could see the quarterdeck watch grabbing that bell, and I could see him getting those big eyes, because I am a permanent party now. He's looking at me, and he's looking at the bell and looking back at me, and he's wondering whether he should ring the "Lady guest arriving," and he does: "Now, lady guest arriving." All I did was go over to him and say, "You know, it's going to be a long three years if every time I come across the brow you pipe me as a lady guest." He just needed me to tell him that. I didn't take offense at it or anything.

I was the operations officer, so I was in charge of that quarterdeck shack. I quickly noticed that my guys, in the morning, would be reading. I looked at what they were reading, and it was something like Penthouse. I went into the quarterdeck shack, and there were publications strewn around, so I said, "You know, this isn't the appropriate kind of reading material to have on the quarterdeck. We've got people from the public coming and going, and it's not the right image. They scrambled to put it away, and they responded well. They just didn't know what was expected, so I thought, "You know, they don't know about me, and I have all the power here, because I can help educate them as to what it's like having a woman on board." It's no mystery, but if you've never had a woman on board, you don't know. It worked out really well, and after a while, on that ship, the guys would confide in me on those quiet midwatches. When there was nothing going on, they'd say, "Ma'am, we're glad you're on board. Now, when we see you coming on the mess deck, we can tell people to stop cussing, because Miss Stosz is on board." They were using me as top cover to clean up the act. When I was on the mess deck and heard cussing, I could say, "Hey! That's not appropriate. Would you say that to your mother or your wife?" People started to understand it was not appropriate.

You treat them respectfully, because most of them don't mean it intentionally. In those days, it was just ignorance. I could have easily just withdrawn to my stateroom and been offended. Instead, I did a mission of outreach to educate people. I tried to earn their respect. I didn't go on there thinking just because I was a lieutenant I had instant respect; I tried to be a really competent operations officer and navigator. I tried to wear my uniform well, so when I held my guys accountable, I was setting the example. People always say to me that it must have been awful and hard to be the only woman aboard a ship. I tell them, "No, it can be an opportunity if you seize it and actually look forward positively to how you can make a difference." It is better to change behaviors and earn their respect, not just presume it's going to be there for you and then be disappointed when you come on like a prima donna. You're going to get exactly what you're looking for, so I went on board looking to earn respect and to help that crew understand that it wasn't scary to have a woman on board, and that's exactly what I got. You get what you look for, and I wish I could teach more people that.

Swabs take a summer math exam. With the Academy's emphasis on science, technology, engineering and math, it is important to keep skills sharp over the long summer.

Academics

Swab summer is a grueling experience, one fraught with challenges both physical and mental. The 4th class school year puts it to shame. The fixed freshman schedule requires cadets to take an extraordinary number of credit hours, and there is no shortage of other obligations beyond the academic load they bear. Cadets attend military trainings, participate in athletics, and complete hundreds of hours of community service. On top of all that, many somehow find time for extracurriculars—joining the band, acting in plays, or engaging in religious activities.

In preparation for the 4th class year, swabs take several summer classes. Math and science dominate the freshman and sophomore curricula, so the Academy wisely mandates a summer math course to keep swabs' skills from melting away in the heat. Another significant amount of classroom time is devoted to understanding the Coast Guard's core values. Whereas civilian students might find the thought of summer math repugnant, swabs generally welcome the break. 4/C Kyle Wood found his summer studies useful:

I'm definitely learning a lot, so that's good. It gives us a good foundation for the school year, because I already know the school year is going to be rough with all the classes, military trainings, and sports together. That's going to be a lot more than it is now, so it's good to have that foundation in math to go into the school year with. I have a reading class, and that's fun, too. We're learning a lot there. I like all the honor trainings, too. I think it's important to instill those values, to really teach what they mean and not just say them, because people can view them in many different ways. When you really sit down and explain exactly what they are, there is no excuse not to follow them, so that's good. They seem very obvious to me. I was raised that way, so everything they're teaching I try to uphold, and I think I do. I feel like it's pretty obvious, and hopefully they'll go into more detail about some things during the school year. Everything is good, and I can really tell it helps.

As the summer progresses, however, the classes become more difficult—if only because physical demands are beginning to take their toll. 4/C Rheanastasia Doctolero had this to say as a swab:

I like them, but the only thing is I'm so exhausted from my day, it's hard to stay awake. I drink water like crazy in my classes, and I'm always standing up; it's really hard to stay awake. It's not that they are boring. The training we went to yesterday was really good. The speaker was really good, he was very interesting, and I still couldn't stay awake, so I know it's not the class. It's me now; I'm just exhausted. I have to say the adrenaline I had the first two weeks is slowly wearing away. I can see this when I discuss it with my other shipmates; it's not as fun as it was. It's becoming the same routine, and now I'm just dragging through it. I remember

they told me when you hit the fourth week, it's going to be hard. I thought they were saying it was going to be physically hard, or they're going to be throwing more stuff at us. It's not even that; I'm just tired of doing it, you know?

4/C Frederick Higgins found at the time that math class had a positive effect, even on his nutrition:

It's a pain to stay awake, but they're beneficial, as they're supposed to be. Everybody enjoys the math class because we get to eat and sort of relax, so everybody enjoys math class. It also gives us homework to do, so the cadre have to give us time to do homework, which allows us to eat more, so we all enjoy math class.

Dr. Richard Freeman is a civilian professor at the Academy who teaches electrical engineering during the academic year. He is also one of the swab-summer math instructors and jokes that this extra duty helps to keep his own math skills sharp. Originally from Chicago, Freeman attended Iowa State University, majoring in computer engineering. After graduation, he worked for AT&T before returning to his alma mater both to teach and to earn his PhD. Some seven or eight years later, Freeman assumed a teaching position at Valparaiso University, a small liberal-arts school in Indiana. He initially came to the Coast Guard Academy in 2008 to fill a yearlong position but ended up staying, finding the new experience refreshing:

There were huge differences in the students. Number one, the students here have to come to class. They have to be dressed, so you don't have students coming to class in pajamas and flip-flops—no fuzzy slippers. In addition to that, they're on time, they're respectful, and if not, there are mechanisms to address problems. From a student perspective, that's how things look. From a faculty perspective, from the institution's perspective, we are expected to have office hours. At other universities, if I had office hours, fine, but if I was off doing something else, oh well. Here, there is an expectation that you will have office hours; you are going to be available to cadets if you're not in class or working on something, and that's fine. It's very student-centric here, and I think that's really important. We've got kids to basically commit nine years of their life at least. Four years at the Academy and five years active duty, and if they want to go aviation, we're talking another four or five years. They're committing a major chunk of their life without really knowing a whole lot about what they want to do, so I think it's important that we're available and really work with them as much as we can.

The Academy is all about growth, both in experience and in knowledge. Even over the short course of the summer, Freeman notices significant student development in the classroom:

I see some big changes over the summer. The first time I have contact with them is day number four. They start with R-Day; they report in on Monday, they're sworn-in, and they start the indoc process. Tuesday, they take their math placement exam, and Thursday, they come to class for the first time. That first day is pretty tough. Some of them are thinking, "Oh my god! What did I get into? Do I really want to stay here? I didn't know this was what I was signing up for." Some of them are prior enlisted, and they may be a little hesitant about coming into the classroom; others are fairly comfortable. Some have gone through ROTC or gone through the prep school program and are less worried. They have done the military side of it, so they know what they're supposed to be doing militarily, and they have an idea of what they're supposed to be doing in the classroom, and it's just a matter of speed. I'm trying to get them up to learning at university speed. That first day, they are so disoriented, so I usually have them give their name, where they're from, what they are thinking about for a major, and their impressions of their experience so far.

By the end of the summer, they have a sense of the indoc process. They're actually starting to come together as a company, as a team, as peers; they know what they're doing. They were talking at the end of the class today: "Well, maybe we should do this differently. We've only got X amount of time to do this, and we keep missing it by ten or fifteen seconds, so instead of you holding the door, somebody else should hold the door, because . . ." They're getting much better at figuring out what's going on and how should

they respond, but they're also pretty worn out, so having class today at 8:00 A.M. isn't bad. It's when they have class at the end of the day that they have a real problem. In summers past, they've been on the obstacle course, lunch, swimming, and then they had to come to class in an air-conditioned room where they're sitting down. Nobody's yelling at them, and it becomes really easy for them to relax. The next thing you know, they're out. I kind of feel bad for the cadre, too, because whatever the swabs are going through, the cadre are going through it with them. They actually have to be awake before them and up after them, and they're running around all day trying to keep everything on schedule and on track. It's tough on them, but even with them, you see growth. You see them grow from "Okay, I survived swab summer. I survived the 4th class year, I survived the 3rd class year." Sometimes, they're a little cocky after that, and I think the experience of actually having to command, to actually have to be the training cadre, is very good for them. They're taking on a lot of responsibility. You see them growing into that, as well. Some of them actually start to learn what their management styles are. They start to learn that yelling at cadets might not work after a while, because they get used to it; they almost become desensitized. Almost. But for the most part, I like working with the cadre, because I see that growth in them. At the end of the class, they are here, and it's "Sir, did you have any problems?" Some of them I had when they were swabs. I've had them for swab math and have had them in class here in the department. It's interesting to see that growth.

Freeman also found the Academy's faculty much different from those in civilian schools:

If you broke the faculty down, you would have your permanent, commissioned teaching staff. Those are officers permanently assigned here. They will retire from here after thirty years or so in the Service. You have your rotators, who are in for three or four years—rotating, active-duty officers—and then you have the civilians who fall into one or two categories, either tenure track or non-tenured track. It's interesting, because even amongst the civilian faculty there's a pretty good mix—some who have had careers were astronauts. This past year, Dan was up on the International Space Station. He retired from the active-duty Coast Guard, went back to NASA, and was the space-station commander for a few months, so you get people on that end. We get officers from aviation billets, prevention billets, and other billets from within the Coast Guard. Their job is to come here, teach, and generate interest in what it is they do within the Service. Aviation is probably the easiest one; it doesn't take much to convince some cadets they should be interested in flying. We also have officers from safety and prevention; they work in-sector. They do safety inspections of vessels, and they also work with manufacturers on new designs requiring safety approval from the Coast Guard.

Although the Academy may not be the only institution that attracts bright students, cadets generally face tougher lives than their civilian counterparts:

The students who go into engineering anywhere are just as bright, but these students are also committed to military service. One thing I can say about them here is that they are way, way oversubscribed in terms of their academics, their military, and their athletic obligations. We have cadets that are really, really busy with very little free time. When you think about your average university, you have some students who are oversubscribed, but a lot of them aren't. They're thinking, "Okay, I'm done with class today. I'm going to go play Xbox. I'm going to do this. I'm going to do that." They do some of that here, but for the most part, they have those three things with which they need to be concerned. They're making sure they're keeping up academically, athletically, and militarily.

Freeman notes that it can be easy to forget how young these cadets are:

I think part of the challenge is remembering that even though they have accepted this obligation, they're still eighteen-, nineteen-, and twenty-year-olds, and they do what eighteen-, nineteen-, and twenty-year-olds are going to do. Sometimes, they don't exercise good judgment. A lot of times, it's not that we're going to kick them out because they're out of uniform, they failed to salute, or

Dr. Richard Freeman teaching a summer math class.

in the military and some of us that haven't—so it's very different. In our section, we've got twelve faculty; five of them are rotators. The rotators are coming from other duty stations within the Coast Guard. When I first got here, Captain Dan Burbank was here, and he was at that time one of two active-duty Coast Guardsmen who something small like that. It's usually pretty big things. If a cadet's not making it academically, is not making it militarily, those are really the two biggies. There's an academic review board, and it's made up of more than just the dean's division. It's more than just an academic review; it's the company officers, advisors, and even coaches sitting in, so it's some of everything. It's those three legs. They may say, "Yes, this cadet may have had a problem with this particular class, so what do we do? If this is somebody we want to retain, what's the plan?"

Even on the academic side, we do early warnings. At other universities, a midterm report is purely optional. So as a faculty member, if I had someone who wasn't doing well at midterm, I could let them know, but it wasn't required. Here, there is an expectation. We report a grade for every cadet at midterm, and if we're looking at someone who's in the D and F range, there's a report we can fill out that explains what's going on with the cadet. It lists that cadet's quiz grades, exam grades, and homework grades—in general, what's going on with that cadet and what do we think we can do to help that cadet pull that grade up. That report goes to the advisor, the company officer, and it's shared with the coaching staff. Maybe you have a cadet who's way too involved with a sport, and he may, unfortunately, need to leave that sport and do something else.

Once they graduate, cadets usually find themselves in high-technology settings. Many of their science and engineering classes are designed to help them understand the sophisticated ships and aircraft on which they are likely to work:

During the fall, I teach electrical circuits and rotating machines, a course we call EC & M. It's a combination of circuit analysis (both alternating and direct current), three-phase alternating current power, and motors. That course is also taught to the other three engineering disciplines with the idea of: what happens when this cadet graduates and is commissioned? They might be a student engineer on a cutter somewhere. Understanding how to generate electric power or understanding circuits is a must; they have to pick up these skills. I also teach a course called PECS, or Principles of Electronic Communication Systems. It's a technology

The cadre also spend time with swabs off the field and in the classroom, helping to prepare them for the upcoming academic year.

course for the non-engineers, the other majors. We try to get them to understand how the technology works. You go on the bridge of a cutter, and there are multiple radios. Why are there so many different radios? Why can't we just have one radio and communicate with everybody in the world? Well, it doesn't work that way. In PECS, we get into the how and the why. It's there to help them understand the technology behind the procedures. You can learn the procedures; you go to trainings, and you learn this is what you do. PECS gets them to understand why they have to do what they do.

Freeman is constantly amazed by the growth and leadership opportunities that officers provide cadets, even on the simplest occasions:

One of things I've learned here at the Academy is there are lots of times when officers look to the firsties to take care of a situation. I recall my first year here, there was a 4th class orientation course, and they needed some chaperones, so I went. It was interesting, because one of the officers, a Navy exchange officer, is waiting; the buses are lined up, and we're about ready to go. He walks up and asks the firstie, "What's going on?" The firstie replies, "Sir, *everyone is all accounted for, blah, blah, blah, blah. Here's what's going on with the box lunch, blah, blah, blah, blah." The officer says, "Okay, you take care of it." So instead of telling the firstie what to do, it's just "You take care of it." A couple of firsties got together and said, "Okay, I've got my pickup; we can do this. We'll make sure we get the rest of the lunches, we'll get them in my truck and drive them out." Taken care of. It's that increasing sense of responsibility that is so important.*

In an age where many young adults leave civilian collages with little focus, Freeman remarks on the maturity cadets possess when they exit the Academy:

Along the way you see multiple switches turn on. By the time they're firsties, they carry themselves differently, they look differently. You can look at firsties and say, "I can see an officer." With the 4th class, well . . . Someone will say, "Oh, so and so did something," and you'll think, "Oh, that was dumb!" Then, you remember they're still young—still young, but still a lot of expectations. I had a cadet come up to me and ask if she could take the final exam early, because her ship was going to be in Australia and they had to make sure they didn't miss movement. They think ahead. Sometimes, the cadets are that organized; they're that aware of their responsibilities, and they take their responsibilities seriously. Of course, sometimes they struggle with it, but when I think back to the time I was in college, I know I struggled with a lot of the same things: maturing, being responsible, doing this, and doing that. If I had read the material, I might decide to skip class. Or so and so is going somewhere exciting, and it's Friday afternoon, so I'll skip class. They don't have that option here, and even when they do miss class on an excusal, they have to keep up.

Freeman is also routinely impressed with students' academic prowess:

Typically, I see it when you put them into a project situation, such as when you give them the capstone project firsties must complete. This is a year-long project in electrical engineering. They really do take on sometimes as much or more than you're willing to give. Sometimes, they're not quite sure how to start a project, but once

you get them going, they pick it up and run with it. Sometimes, I get very surprising results. I had one project where we were trying to build an alternative communication system. We got to the point where we were going to have to have somebody build the system. We know how much it costs. We're going to need two of them at least, and it's going to take about a month to build, and then we can start testing. It was really a year-long feasibility study. It was a very interesting project, because once we got them rolling, the firsties really took to it. I think they took that project as far as they could take it, given time and budget restraints. What they handed over in their final report was: 1) Here's who you need to talk to. 2) Yes, it's more than feasible. 3) For this amount of money, for this amount of time, you can have these systems built and start testing. So there are some projects that go very well, some that don't go so well, but I think all of them get something out of it.

It's obvious that the officers in the faculty have made a real impression on Freeman and that he finds working with them refreshing. He notes the passion they bring to their jobs, a passion he often finds missing in civilian teaching environments:

I've been engaging officers in conversation and asking them, "When did you realize you made the right decision?" Each of these officers will tell you the exact moment, exactly when it clicked and they said, "Yeah!" It could be something like: "It was the first time I had to airlift someone off a ship because he had a severely broken leg. He had to get to the hospital, it was bad weather, a real hairy landing. The family thanked us a couple of weeks later," to "The first time I did a boarding and this happened or that happened." I think if you talk to most of the officers, they can tell you when that point occurred, when they knew they had made a great decision.

Teaching cadets has itself been extremely fulfilling for Freeman, engendering in him a sense of pride in having helped form the next generation of officers:

Graduation is always a nice moment. It's a very nice moment, because sometimes you can look and say, "Wow! I remember when that kid . . . I didn't think that kid was going to make it because she didn't understand this or he just didn't understand that . . ."

When you see them graduate, it's very rewarding. I love what I do. There's a sense of serving your country, in an odd sort of a way; someone has to do this job, someone has to train them. The Cadet Division takes care of the military training. Our job is to make them thinkers—to bring that additional dimension—and it's exciting. It's great to take a group of cadets to someplace like Sikorsky Helicopter and walk with them down the assembly line and have the workers just stop. They see uniforms, and they just stop. You can tell they have pride in what they do, and I feel that same thing. You can go and teach somewhere and not be fulfilled. At the end of the year, no matter what's happened, when you go to graduation, it is exciting. There's a lot of pride in being able to look back at some of these kids and say, "I remember the first day of swab math,

and I didn't think that kid was going to make it." And now, they've graduated and are commissioned officers. So you see that growth. At many universities, you don't always see that.

It's special. It's a very special place. I think each place I've worked, the three universities, have all been unique, but this, by far, falls way outside of the normal academic environment. Outside of the whole sense of pride in helping to educate young, future officers, this is a good bunch of people to work with. People come in with different experiences, and it really is an opportunity to interact with people in a way that you probably don't get to elsewhere. It really is very rewarding.

Crew prepare to head to sea with a deckload of buoys aboard the USCG Cutter *Ida Lewis*. Buoy tenders are also known as "black hulls".

Into the Fleet

Cadets spend their last three summers training in the operational fleet. The hands-on, real-world experience, be it aboard ship or in-sector, gives cadets a taste of what is to come. Commander Jeffrey Haukom is the Academy's cadet training officer. As such, he oversees all aspects of the cadets' military training, from basic indoctrination to mandatory trainings in areas such as civil rights and sexual harassment. As Haukom points out, cadets are training, in one fashion or another, just about every waking moment over the course of four years:

It's a lot to talk about. I could unfold our two-hundred-week continuum and show you everything we do to progressively build up these people—the positions and the challenges that we give them. For example, we give cadets a set of specific training modules. This week, the 1st class cadets are working on their Officer Professional Military Education module number one. We give a scenario to them; it's a case study taken from an actual Coast Guard unit. We tell them to think about yourself as an ensign: You're the morale officer on a Coast Guard cutter, and you are in charge of the morale budget in the Navy Motion Picture Association movies. You've got a lot of money and resources at your disposal that are pilferable and have to be accounted for in a certain way. There are procedures to follow, and the person you relieved didn't do such a good job. Here are some of the challenges you face. Here are the references; you're welcome to read them. Tell us how you would handle this particular challenge. They write a paper, they talk about it with their company officer and company chief, and we actually end up grading them on it. Just as you have a grade point average for your academic courses, you've got a military precedence average for your military training. The things that we do here feed into that. We even schedule things like social etiquette training. Everything that has to do with their professional growth outside of the classroom and off the athletic field I've got something to do with at some point. I work with company officers and the commandant of cadets, and we try to shepherd these young people into the right direction, fostering an environment here in Chase Hall that allows for their professional growth.

While much of his work focuses the training cadets receive at the Academy, Haukom also places cadets into the summer trainings they receive elsewhere:

During the summer, we focus on their professional military skills, particularly for 1st, 2nd, and 3rd class cadets. I spend a lot of the academic year monitoring all of the training that I just described, and simultaneously, I'm reaching out to the fleet and looking for underway operational opportunities for the cadets. Basically, I'm going out to the area schedulers, the district schedulers, and say-ing, "How many vacant cutter racks do you have this summer? I've got 260 1st class cadets who need to get underway and get some operational training, and I've got X number of 3rd class cadets who need to get underway." And it's not just on cutters; we send them to sectors and air stations, providing a variety of experiences for them. A couple of new experiences we provide for them are in the marine-safety field. We're actually sending them out on commercial vessels with Coast Guard officers to do vessel inspections. They will get underway with these vessels—everything from large container ships and cruise ships to tugboats on the Mississippi. While on board, they will inspect every aspect: their navigational systems, safety systems, and their engineering systems.

Haukom is always looking to expand cadets' horizons. Given the Coast Guard's global presence, he is often sending them far from U.S. shores:

We recently started a program with the Jewish Institute for National Security Affairs. We sent three cadets to Israel to work with some West Point cadets. It's a cultural interaction and exchange where they met with Israeli defense-force members and toured Israel, spending a lot of time focused on what Israel is, where they are, and the defense challenges they face. They were able to interact with their counterparts and look at the differences and similarities. It was really interesting, especially for some of our government majors following that international relations track.

The 1st class cadets went to cutters, academic internships, and regimental-leadership staff positions here at the Academy, where they actually spent half the summer running the corps that remains on board. We sent some of them ocean racing. We had three cadets ride the Japanese Coast Guard training vessel KOJIMA from Honolulu to Baltimore through the Panama Canal, so we're looking at these international opportunities as well—and that's just the 1st class. I send the 3rd class cadets out to cutters, small-boat stations, and aboard EAGLE over the summer. A major piece of my challenge is finding units and racks on cutters who will open up and provide them the right kind of training. We don't just send them out there with airline tickets and say, "Meet the cutter here at this pier," although that in and of itself is a challenge when you have over 500 cadets moving to cutters which are being rerouted due to operational tasking changes. What we try to provide is the best kind of guidance and structured training we can. We don't simply rely on the units to just build us an officer, so part of my job is to continually remain abreast of fleet operations, policies, systems, training requirements, and liaise with the fleet—talk about what new navigation systems are out there and what they are using now. I'm constantly asking them how are they training their officers and what they find works best.

Haukom also arranges those portions of the cadre's hectic schedules that are not exclusively dedicated to indoctrinating swabs:

They have three weeks of leave during the summer, and when they're not being cadre, they're running through a series of professional military trainings that are typically about a week in length. They have range training, where they qualify with the basic service pistol. They have a week on T-boats, the tugboats we have here at the Academy for ship-handling training. Then they move to ROTR, where they learn all about the nautical rules of the road, the navigation rules, and hopefully they pass their actual exam, which is a commissioning requirement. They have cadre prep week, where they get together with their cadre section. They make all their plans and they dust off the playbook in terms of what we taught them during 100th Week before they even started the summer period. They have CATP, the Cadet Aviation Training Program. This is a week at an air station where they get time in the flight simulator and flights on real aircraft, maybe a hoist in a helicopter from the water, and they take part in the Coastal Sail Training Program over a two-week period.

While cadets are spending fleet time performing real-life tasks, they are still training and have specific goals to meet for the summer. This situation poses a challenge both for the cadets themselves and for the personnel aboard their host vessels. To ensure that both parties benefit, Haukom has created a document detailing the unique relationship that they must forge together:

Every year, I put together the CSTM, the Cadet Summer Training Manual. This is the training curriculum for 1st and 3rd class cadets in the operational fleet. Every cadet gets a copy of this, and every unit gets a copy of this, so that everyone is on the same page in terms of our enabling and our terminal performance objectives. A terminal performance objective may be, for example, having a 1st class cadet attain their Quartermaster of the Watch qualification. In order to do this, there are several steps or tasks, enabling objectives, they have to meet. We lay these all out in the CSTM, and we give them credit for however many tasks and qualifications they satisfactorily complete. We tie the tasks and quals, the enabling objectives and terminal performance objectives, to an assessment criteria. It's a point-based system we model after the officer evaluation reports we receive as officers. Instead of an OER, it's a CER, or cadet evaluation report. It looks a little bit like an officer evaluation report. Half of it is about their character, leadership, and attitude. The other half covers how many tasks they completed, how many qualifications they earned, how many special evolutions they participated in, and their conduct.

Part of it is for them to sit down with the officers and reflect on their growth and development. They actually get points for that. Did they sit down with an officer once a week and talk about their "light bulb" moment? What dawned on them that week as a future Coast Guard leader? What did they see during our fleet operations that made them go, "Now I get it. I see why you did that, and that makes sense to me now." We ask them to tie that in with the character and leadership training they received at the Academy— see if they can bring it full circle now that they've seen it in a performance-based environment.

This is another one of my big challenges: making sure our training objectives align with those of the fleet and that we can accurately assess and hold our cadets accountable. This manual is their guidance for the summer, for both the cadets and the fleet. I send a similar document to just fleet officers who are training our cadets. The copy of the CSTM sent to officers is my playbook behind the scenes; cadets don't see that version. It's our regulations and expectations. This is what we expect of you, the unit, and of the cadets. Here are the cadet regulations. Here's what they can and can't do. You have agreed to take these cadets on board, and we really appreciate that, but with that comes some responsibility. We expect you to treat our cadets in the appropriate manner. 1ˢᵗ class cadets should be viewed as junior break-in officers. 3ʳᵈ class cadets are viewed more like junior enlisted. These are the tasks they should be assigned. They should be assigned to the appropriate level in the chain of command. A supervisor for a 3ʳᵈ class cadet might be a 2ⁿᵈ class petty officer. The supervisor for a 1ˢᵗ class cadet is probably going to be an ensign or a lieutenant, junior grade, and we really do expect you, as the command cadre, to spend some time with these cadets. Talk to them, listen to them. When you evaluate and you fill out the CER on them, sit them down, have a face-to-face, and don't wait until the last day. Have periodic counseling sessions to keep them apprised of their progress in your eyes regarding your expectations; don't make it a surprise for them. In other words, treat them as you would your junior officers. So that's the challenge I have, trying to maintain those expectations and ensure our training objectives are met in a productive and a fair way.

To ensure that the Academy meets its training objectives, Haukom reviews the summer's reports and evaluates the individual cadets' performance upon their return in late August:

The last couple of weeks, I've been spending all of my time going through cadet evaluation reports and having some very frank meetings with cadets who did not do very well this summer. I am also making the appropriate people aware of deficiencies so they can keep an eye on the progress of these cadets throughout this next year and beyond. By the right people, I mean company officers, company chiefs, nautical science instructors, and even the commandant of cadets. We debrief all of the cadets as they return. We want to hear all the great things they did, as well as all the things that maybe weren't so great, and try to help them make sense of those experiences. Unfortunately, we do get cadets who come back and say, "You know, my unit didn't seem quite right, the

Commander Jeffrey Haukom

way they operated—a little bit different than what we learned in our leadership classes here. For example, they did this and that, and I don't really know why they did that." My role is to listen to what they are telling me and help make sense of it. I can say, "Well, have you considered the reason they did it this way was because of X,Y, and Z?" In some cases, I follow up with the units to find out what's going on there.

In some cases, we run into situations where a particular person in a leadership role didn't do the best job with the cadets they could have, so we talk about that. We ask, "What did you learn? What would you have done differently?" I get them to tell me what they didn't like and what they did. "What would have been more effective? Have you considered this? Have you considered that?" In some cases, it boils down to maybe that guy was just a jerk. Well, that happens. This is the real world and you're going to run into these people. Show them it's a learning opportunity, and chalk it up to experience. You may not have had a fantastic time, but at least you know the type of leader you don't want to be and why. That is by far and away the exception to the experience our cadets get in the fleet—probably less than 1 percent.

By and large, they come back, and I love to sit down with them. We get them together in groups of about thirty, about a company-sized group. 1st class and 3rd class we do separately; it's kind of a guided discussion. I say, "I want to hear about your summer. I want to hear about the good, the bad, and everything in between, and, particularly, any core value things, positive or negative, that you witnessed out there: Honor, respect, devotion to duty. Train-

Cadre also spend a week of their summer at a Coast Guard air station.

ing objectives. What worked, what didn't work? Let's hear some of the great sea stories. Let's hear about some of the challenges, and maybe we can make some amendments to this Cadet Summer Training Manual. Maybe we can change some of the tasks, quals, objectives, or maybe the assessment criteria to better reflect reality and provide a more level playing field for next summer's cadets. Logistics: Did you run into any logistical problems? Physically getting from here to there?" We are trying to improve, so we guide the discussion, and we open it up, and the cadets take off. Some of it I don't like to hear, because it's "Yeah, well this policy didn't work well," but it's good for me to hear so I can make some changes. For the most part, these cadets come up with some great suggestions.

As many cadets attest, enthusiasm for Academy life often wanes by the end of the first academic year. The long grind following a difficult summer can leave 4th class students struggling to remember why they ever accepted their appointments in the first place. Haukom sees the summer programs as offering cadets important reminders of what they have to look forward to:

It's so great to see these cadets come back. The vast majority of them are energized. The 3rd class cadets come back with their first taste of the operational Coast Guard. They just went through their 4th class year, which was extraordinarily challenging for them, and it's like, "Yup. Now I remember why I joined the Coast Guard. They let me actually get on the boat on a search and rescue case, talk on the radio, and I was talking to real boats. We were saving lives!" The 1st class cadets tend to come back talking about their first taste of what it's like to be a junior officer in the fleet, the quals they earned, and the leadership responsibilities they were given. They get collateral duties and projects. Perhaps they were the project officer for a change-of-command ceremony. That's significant. They dealt with all kinds of people and had a budget. You can see it on their face when they come back: "Now, I get it!"

For Ensign Michael Klakring, one summer's experience at sea was so enjoyable that he considered postponing his existing plans:

The third summer, I went to a buoy tender in Oregon. I really wanted to go to flight school the whole time, but I realized things might not go the way I wanted them to, so I decided to check out some boats. I liked the black hulls, the buoy tenders, so I checked them out. It was a blast, and it almost had me thinking I could go to a boat first and then apply to flight school. I finally decided to go to flight school, but it was a blast. It was nice to see that afloat side, even for that short time. It was nice just to get a taste of it.

Buoy tending is fun. because there's always work to do. There is a schedule, and you always know exactly what you're going to do when you go out, as opposed to the white hulls. I haven't been on a white hull, but my understanding is that you go out, and maybe you find something, and maybe you don't. You just kind of sail in circles and see what you can find—different missions, different tastes, for sure. On a black hull, it's a small crew on a big boat, so everybody knew each other. It's really hard work, but you can see the results right there, every day. You can do that, and there's also law-enforcement stuff; they have boarding teams who go off the buoy tenders, as well. It's a multi-mission platform.

Cadre 2/C Ryan Babb recounts the summer he shared with his class aboard the Eagle:

It was a great experience. I did that for five weeks. We sailed from New London all the way to Waterford, Ireland, across the north Atlantic—nineteen days at sea. That was pretty interesting, and then we sailed to Hamburg, Germany, where she was built, for the seventy-fifth birthday of EAGLE. From there, we sailed to London, England. From that point, I flew back to the United States and then to the law-enforcement cutter SHERMAN in San Diego, which was a 378' cutter. I participated in what is known as a "south pat," or southern patrol. We basically went along Mexico, up and down the coast, looking for drug trafficking. So I got to go all over during 3rd class summer. It was a really interesting experience—to be underway on a cutter, doing what the actual Coast Guard does.

Although there was always the possibility for friction between the cutter's crew and the visiting cadets, Babb found it easy to avoid:

A lot of people are skeptical of cadets and what we're all about. At first, in my experience, they didn't really like us. We showed them we could work and were willing to listen to them, because they are more expert at what they do than we could ever be. We tried to learn from them. A lot of the enlisted personnel I worked with took me under their wings, taught me what they knew, and let me work with them, which was really nice. It took a while for the enlisted and the cadets on my boat to get used to each other, but by the end, we were working pretty well together. The reception can be rough, but as long as you show that "I'm here to work, I'm here to help, and I'm here to learn from you," people are much more willing to accept us. Being a follower is very important. Sometimes, these people have had bad experiences with cadets, and I completely understand their point of view.

On the SHERMAN, I participated on the engineering side. I tried to get security qualified, which is where you make rounds of the cutter and make sure all the engineering systems, mechanical and electrical, are running properly. The engineers are a group of people who don't get the credit and acknowledgement they deserve. While they're down there sweating, the people on deck get the public's eye. After engineering, I did various other things, such as helping to clean up from a tank that started spewing oil. I got to work on changing oil filters, and that was really cool, because a cutter's oil filters are huge. After that, I moved to the deck force, and I got to learn and become qualified in helm, or driving the boat, and how to be a lookout. We had done that on EAGLE, but it's different between cutters, because they are two different types. I learned what takes place on the bridge and the thought process of the officer of the deck. It's something that I would like to do. I liked engineering, but I think I would rather go deck. I also did a little bit of mess cooking, which was probably my favorite part of the summer, because it was something I could really get my hands on, really participate in, and actually help the crew: washing dishes, making the food, setting tables, and things like that—serving the officers. That was the most hands-on experience I consistently got all summer, and that was pretty awesome. I liked getting to work *with these people. You gain their respect and their trust, and you get to serve them.*

For 2/C Joseph Trump, field experience taught him just how relevant the school year really was to his future life:

For me, it was an easy transition as far as knowledge goes, because at the end of 4th class year, there's this thing called the 4th class indoctrination board. We get a big packet of information that you have to learn before you're tested on it by the board. If you actually learn all that information and retain it, it makes 3rd class summer really easy. You learn the distress signals, day shapes, light configurations for boats, and those kinds of things. When you go out to the fleet, those are the things you need to get qualified in: helm, lookout, and things like that. I have a pretty good memory, and I think that stuff is pretty interesting, so on EAGLE, I got qualified on helm and lookout like that. When I went to the 210' in Oregon, I again qualified in helm and lookout in a day, so the crew liked me, because I was able to get into the rotation and they didn't have to stand watch as often. The more people understand that the things they do here are really to set them up for success and not just waste their time, the better experience they will have out in the fleet. Some people don't really get that at first. I didn't really think about that at the time; I just thought it was interesting, and it worked out that way. As far as the experience in the fleet compared to here, it's two completely different Coast Guards. The fleet is a lot more relaxed. When you're on watch, it's very serious, but with personal things, it's more relaxed. You have other jobs to do, but there's no reason to freak out about them; as long as they get done in a timely manner and correctly, it's okay. I love the fleet. I can't wait to graduate, and I can't wait to get out and do that kind of stuff. I like it here, too, but it's definitely a lot different than the fleet. That's what the summers are for.

Swabs move into a stress position after once again displeasing their cadre.

Survival: Swab Strategies

After the initial shock of R-Day, most swabs begin piecing together a strategy to help them survive the summer. Prepsters and those students who attended introductory programs offered by the Academy generally have an easier start, but even they occasionally struggle. While the indoctrination process is dead serious, there is a game-like element to the undertaking, and once swabs realize this, life becomes at least moderately easier. As 4/C James Hegge notes, the swab's role is simple:

Pretty much, the basic thing is, "Yes, sir! No, sir! No excuse, sir! Aye aye, sir!" Unless they ask for something else, you pretty much can't go wrong with that. Everyone pretty much gets it: basic response. They won't yell at you for it. If they ask you for something

When swabs are once again expected to take care of and think for themselves at summer's end, many discover that they are slightly out of practice. 2/C Ryan Babb found his first academic year tougher than the summer because of this:

In swab summer, the swab can pretty much turn their brain off and just follow directions, and if you follow directions, most of the time you will be completely fine. During the school year, you have to think constantly. You're up really late, depending upon how quickly you can get your homework done. The shock and awe is still there, and there are a lot more things to worry about. That's when teamwork really kicks in, because you need your shipmates.

4/C Rheanastasia Doctolero developed a strategy to maintain a comforting sense of home throughout the summer:

In the little free time we did have, I made sure I wasn't ever alone, especially being away from home. At home, life is very close-knit, very lovey-dovey. When you say hello, you kiss people on the cheek. And I like hanging out with people. During the day here, you don't have that social interaction, so at nighttime, we always hung out in groups. My dad would send me little games to play with my friends. Have you ever heard of BeanBoozled? It's a jelly-bean game. They'll give you two of the same colored jelly beans that can be two different flavors. They could be toothpaste, or they could be blueberry. A white one could taste like baby wipes or coconut. So we did that, and it was a lot of fun—little things just to keep us going. That was a big part of it: just hanging out with people, feeling kind of normal, I guess.

Not every strategy proved effective. Part of the fun in the cadre's mission is to find fault, and at that they are remarkably adept. For 4/C Sheila Bertrand, nothing she did seemed to escape their criticism in the early portion of the summer:

How long can you go without getting yelled at? Not very long. By the time you get yelled at, you're about done with that strategy, and you go the next day and try a different one, and it still doesn't work. So you've just got to do what they tell you to do—trust in what they do and what they say.

A member of the cadre demonstrates the squat with her swabs.

else, then you might offer up another answer. Don't come up with some oddball excuse. You know what they want, you know what you did. Don't lie, don't try to change the subject, don't try to push the blame off yourself, because, most likely, it will just get you in worse trouble.

For 4/C Jake Carlton, his visits to cadet counselors and his ability to tune things out are what helped him through the process. Like many, he also tried to tackle challenges one at a time:

I just focused on the task we were doing, like when the cadre went in and destroyed our rooms and we had to work as a team to accomplish a goal. I enjoyed those parts. It made me look at the better side of swab summer, the more enjoyable aspects that helped me balance out the negative parts—constantly getting yelled at, staring at a wall, being braced up, and all that. I'm really good at blocking it all out, listening but not really letting it affect me. That's why I went to the counselors, just as a time to let loose, because that's really the only time they give you. I went maybe once a week or so. I just went to the cadet counselors. They aren't military, and their files are closed; no one else sees them besides the cadet counselors, and then, after seven years, they toss them. The counseling was a good thing, and I'd recommend people take advantage of them if they have homesickness or other problems.

4/C Kyle Woods would simply try to beat the cadre at their own game:

You always wanted to outwork the cadre. They have to do a lot of the exercises with you, so if you can beat them, they stop, just because they can't go anymore. That was always a challenge, because they were in pretty good shape. It was always hard, but it was fun just to try to beat them.

4/C Frederick Higgins found comfort in adopting a better-him-than-me mentality:

As bad as it sounds, I would just listen to other people getting in trouble, and I would just think, "Well, at least I'm not that kid." That was for the in-the-moment type of situations. I didn't really write home or anything; I just slept and made fun of other people. That sounds bad, but it wasn't making fun of them; it was just, like, "I could be this kid," weighing out a better or worse situation. "It could always be worse"—that was what I was thinking.

One of the cadre's objectives is to get swabs to work together as a team. The cadre are such effective teachers that the swabs quickly learn to use teamwork to thwart them. 2/C Cathy Durand recalls one survival technique they used early in her swab summer experience:

Bathroom time is definitely a bonding experience. That's basically the only time you have to talk to each other, when you are in the bathroom. I'm very bad at remembering names, but one girl could remember all of them, so she was always the first girl to leave the bathroom. She could say the names, and we could all say them after her. You form little tricks amongst yourselves to help you get by. Throughout the whole summer, we're told, "You guys need to work as a team. If one person fails, you all fail." One of the first things we are told is: "You are no longer an individual. You are a company." One of the biggest things from the summer is teamwork. You bond pretty quickly: with your roommate, probably the first night; with your whole company, probably less than a week. You know everyone.

2/C Babb also recalls taking advantage of breaks to strategize:

During the head and water breaks, depending on the amount of time we were given, we would all congregate and talk about what we were doing wrong, what we needed to fix, and what we had to watch out for. That's really a time to catch your breath and talk to your shipmates. You'd be like, "Hey, I need help with this," or, "I can help you with this," or, "Everybody make sure you have such and such an item." There's a lot of camaraderie that forms, just trying to get through the summer. There are certain things that you can't really work on with other people during the school year, but during swab summer, you're pretty much allowed to work on anything and everything with your shipmates, except for indoc exams and things like that. The biggest thing during swab summer you learn is that teamwork and camaraderie.

4/C Koachar Mohammad and his fellow swabs quickly passed along tips to help their shipmates, and in turn, his company performed at a higher level:

We learned little tricks here and there: how to shower faster or how to fill up the water bottles faster; how to learn information, like the indoc. If one of us learned a trick, we'd tell everybody: how to make your rack or how to put your pants on faster—little techniques like that. We'd share them with everybody.

As a swab, 4/C Doctolero had trouble regurgitating indoc under pressure, but she could follow a shipmate's lead. She explains that the classroom was the only safe place for them to pass on their respective survival strategies to their male counterparts:

I can say it in my head all day. If you ask me the Academy rules, I can list them off or I can write them down as fast as possible, but when they're in my face and I'm on the spot, my tongue gets tied, so I can never answer them on time. But overall, we are doing pretty good. One person will usually start it off, the indoc, and then everybody else will catch on—"Oh, that's what it is,"—and then we all fall into unison. We're getting better at working together. We're not exactly perfect yet, of course. During classes, we get to communicate with each other, but when we're with the cadre, of course, we can't talk. The only time we can talk is in the bathroom, but we're segregated, girls and boys, so when we are in the class-room, the girls can talk with the boys and say, "Hey, we did this. You guys should do this, too." So it's getting better.

A weekly event called the "formal room-and-wing inspection" provides swabs the chance to work together to solve a common problem. The inspection is a test of every swab's ability to fo-cus on minute details. Nothing is overlooked; cadre examine each room with something like a fine-tooth comb, and rooms that fail to meet the standard are "tossed." As a swab, 4/C Sheila Bertrand quickly found a solution to this new challenge:

Last week, we had formal room-and-wing after I spoke with you. The cadre came through and tore our rooms apart. It literally looked like a hurricane had gone into every room. So we're all trying to get them perfect this morning so they don't get torn up again. One person's room they didn't really touch. He was a prep-ster though, so he knew what they wanted. I'm going to have him look at our room before we say we're done, make sure everything's in place. We're trying to work on the team-building thing—every-one helping each other. It's been pretty good. We're getting a lot

more times made, and it's a lot more fun to figure out how to work as a team and stuff like that. Hopefully, we can keep it up.

As the summer moves forward, swabs began to see progress within their companies. As a swab, 4/C Frederick Higgins attested:

It's all right. I'm kind of under the radar. I don't get in too much trouble. I'm personally just trying to help out my fellow shipmates. I'm not saying I'm perfect or anything, but I'm not having as much trouble as others. As a group, we're getting closer. We're making more and more of our times, and compared to other companies, it seems like we're a little farther along. I feel like we're finally start-ing to jell, and probably by the end of this week, we'll be making almost all of our times—shower times and things like that. People are making fewer silly mistakes that basically slow everything down.

4/C Scooter Finney's company also began to jell, even working together to pick up their injured classmates' slack:

We still have several people on chits, so when we're trying to make times, they're always a little bit slower. As a company, we all care about each other. In terms of a fluid, single body, we're not there at all. We have a lot of work to do, but we're certainly better than we were. As far as communication goes, we know how to talk to each other, and we're all friendly. I think we're coming along.

We always had to make all the timed evolutions, and if you got back first, you would get IT'd by yourself, so we were always help-ing one another out. We came up with new strategies for shower-ing faster. There were showers that we took as a company in under five minutes. That's going into our rooms, changing, going into the shower, showering, going back to our rooms, changing again, and getting back to the bulkhead. We thought of strategies, and I'll give you one example. The class of 2016 was divided into three parts, three groups who went on EAGLE. People who couldn't go on EAGLE for medical reasons were distributed to companies that weren't on EAGLE at the time. We got someone who had a broken hand, a broken wrist, or something like that, but essentially, he had one useless hand. We always had to change really fast, do everything extremely fast. We had all these evolutions, and we had a person who couldn't even put on his own socks, so we would go and get changed really fast, and everyone would go to his room and help him change. It was that type of teamwork that allowed us to get him ready and out on the bulkhead. We had to move his entire room, too. All of that goes to show that if you get to know how to play the system, you can get by. We never performed effortlessly or seamlessly, but we made it, so that means something, I guess.

4/C Doctolero's company was able to work together even when relationships were strained:

I think company-wide morale is pretty good. There are tensions. Sometimes this makes the mission harder, and sometimes it makes it easier, because everybody is avoiding each other and just getting things done. There are always some shipmates willing to help the others. As far as that goes, actually, everybody's always willing to help. I think we're coming better together as a team. If we see a shipmate struggling, we're more willing to help them now. It's become more of a family. I'm a little faster than my roommate, so I'll finish things earlier and help her, or she'll help me, because I'm always forgetting my cover. She'll be like, "Rhea, where's your cover?" She helps me remember my uniform, I help her stow her stuff, so we're a good team. I think the company is getting there. We have to get better on our times, but we're pretty good. I'm happy with my company.

4/C Bertrand found daily progress to be hit or miss, but one day's problems never rolled into the next:

Some days, when we got in trouble the day before, we were like, "All right guys, we gotta do it right today. Just try your best everyone: 100 percent." Some days it would work, and some days it wouldn't. It was just, "Bad day yesterday; let's start off again today." Our cadre were big believers in the thought that "Every day is a new day; let's start off fresh." I don't believe we ever got dropped or IT'd for something we did the day before. Some nights they did it late, but the next day was a brand-new page.

4/C Wood's company got off to a very slow start. They began to

Swab Sheila Bertrand strains to hold her rifle at arm's length.

see dramatic improvement only after cadre had the swabs reflect on the reasons they had chosen to attend the Academy:

In the beginning, we weren't really working together very well, but then, towards the end of the summer, we all got to know each other and helped each other out and cared for each other more.

An athletic coach explains the need to think before acting when solving problems.

We started working more as a team, and we almost ended up winning Honor Company, because we became so close and everybody was doing their part. Last semester, we came in second for Honor Company, so we've been doing pretty good since the end of swab summer. It was gradual. There was a point where they set us all down and talked to us. They made us think about why we wanted to come here, and everybody realized that everybody—no matter that we came from different places, different backgrounds—everybody was here for the same reason. We all wanted to help other people.

As Companies begin to work together, they receive fewer punishments. In 4/C Hegge's eyes, the resulting drop in stress levels was one of the best side effects of teamwork:

We're finally starting to get it together and not getting in trouble as much. It makes life much nicer—less yelling, less IT, fewer problems in general, which really helps. We're not doing badly, but we can definitely do a lot better. We've still got problems to work out. I imagine we'll get rid of them sometime in the next couple of weeks. We've had three people drop out. One person dropped out on the first day—just decided this was not what she or he wanted. The second one, I don't know why he dropped out. The other one, although I would have loved to have seen him turn around and

succeed at this, was causing problems. I don't like saying it, but now that he's not here, things will probably go a bit smoother for a while. We all have our problems, and we all make mistakes every now and again, but some of us were making a lot more of them than others. The fifth law of the Navy states, "On the strength of one link in the cable, dependeth the might of the chain. Who knows when thou may'st be tested, so live that thou bearest the strain." This really holds true for the entire company. If one of us is messing up, it's going to affect the entire company and hold us all back. So if one is having trouble, we really need to help him as much as we can. Your roommate should be the first person you go to asking for help. After that, if they can't help you, you just go and find somebody you know who can.

The various achievements of each company are logged throughout the summer. One overall goal is to win the position of Honor Company within the corps. As Regimental Commander Andrew Ray notes, this tribute is awarded three times during the year:

Honor Company is rated by regimental staff. There's an Honor Company in the fall, spring and summer. During the school year, the criteria are a little different. It's drill, intercompany sports, your wins, losses, and other things. During the summer, it's really all swab- and aimster-oriented: their average scores for indoc tests, their weekly form in the wings, how they performed at the weekly drill, inspection, and how they wear their uniforms. Sea Trials, the culminating event of the summer, plays a large role in determining Honor Company. That's the final test: How did everyone come together as a team? How did they succeed under pressure? They're tired, mentally and physically, and that plays into it. There are a whole lot of aspects that will be recorded throughout the summer on a daily basis. There is an Honor Company board so that you can see who is in that position. Everything is tallied, percentages are done, and the new Honor Company is announced at the change-of-command ceremony at the end of the summer or for every new term or semester. It's a pretty big deal. Of course, some people are like, "Honor Company? Whatever!" and they roll their eyes. There are, unfortunately, those cadets here, but we also have cadets here who see Honor Company as an indicator of how well we perform and how well people followed us in our leadership roles.

At the end of this particular summer, Foxtrot was named Honor Company. 4/C Higgins relates his experience as a member of Foxtrot:

We're doing better. Yesterday, we had a pretty good day. We made the majority of our times in general, and we're finally working as a team. Every cadet has the best interests of the company before themselves now, so that helps a lot. Everybody tries to help each other. Everybody seems to have their bad days—some just seem to have more consecutive bad days than others do—but we all try to help each other as best we can. During free times, not that we really had many, people would joke around. We became friends in general, and I'm assuming that's how people coped. Apparently, we were a good company, because we got Honor Company for swab summer, but for me, personally, I just felt like we had a bunch of really good individuals who could take care of themselves. We did assess each other's strengths and weaknesses and tried to help each other.

As all of the students I interviewed attest, swabs struggle for much of the summer to learn to work effectively as a team. 2/C Babb explains why this should come as no surprise:

Too many chiefs and not enough Indians. That can happen a lot here. The first thing taught to you in swab summer and your 4th class year is how to be a follower. You have these 250 new leaders who are coming into the class—250 leaders who have developed their leadership skills throughout high school and are all coming to the same place—and the first thing you teach them is how to be a follower. Then, you work your way up through the followership continuum. You start with a sheep, which is somebody who has low critical thinking and is a passive person. You move up to a yes person, who mindlessly agrees to do and complete the task. Then,

you move to a disgruntled follower, who is somebody who has high critical thinking, can think independently, but is passive and won't really act, because they are disgruntled. Next is an effective follower, who is someone who is both active and will participate, actively engaging in things and noticing if something is going wrong and willing to fix it themselves; independent and critical thinking is high. You go through those stages during swab summer and figure out what works, and you build yourself a foundation of followership.

4th class year is all followership with a little bit of leadership sprinkled in. For example, there is something called a "4th Class of the Week." This person is the liaison to the upperclass for all the 4th class in their company for that week. That's your chance to learn some leadership skills and take on some responsibility. From that point, since you've built a followership foundation, you start to come into your own leadership style. From there, the 1,200 cadets who were leaders can all be leaders at different points in time for different things. There is a lot of variety in leadership styles, with people on many different levels in terms of confidence in leadership. There are definitely a lot of differences between people's leadership abilities and what they've learned and how they've learned; it all comes down to their background. There are those people who were born to command, born to lead, and they do take charge, but those people often need to learn when to step back and be a follower, giving somebody else a chance to learn. This is a huge learning curve for a lot of people. A lot of people have also learned when they need to step up. Honestly, that's where a lot of people grind gears with each other—learning that give-and-take. It's probably one of the tougher things at the Academy. The academics are extremely hard, and sometimes the physical part can be pretty tough, but learning leadership and having the necessary self-awareness to become a better leader, that's really what this institution is grinding into us.

USCG Cutter *Eagle* at her berth in New London, just south of the Coast Guard Academy. *Eagle* operates as both a training vessel and an emissary for the nation.

USCG Cutter *Eagle*

At the end of the summer, swabs board *Eagle* for their first experience at sea as part of the Coast Guard. *Eagle* is, in many ways, the Service's flagship, known around the world. For most cadets, this is their first real oceangoing experience, and for nearly all, their first time on a sailing ship of this scale. As the ship can only accommodate 153 cadets at one time, swabs are sent aboard in three waves. The first group meets the *Eagle* in Nova Scotia and sails her to Portland, Maine. The second group takes her from there to Newport, Rhode Island. The last group sails her offshore before heading back to her berth along New London's waterfront.

The *Eagle* is 295' long with a beam, or width, of 39'. The bottom of her keel is some 17' below the ocean's surface, and her steel hull displaces over 1,800 tons. Although she has a single diesel engine to push her along when needed, her main propulsion consists of over 22,000 square feet of sail, allowing her to reach a maximum speed of 16 knots, or 18.4 miles per hour. She—and ships are always referred to in the feminine—is a barque, a term that denotes the particular arrangement of her sails. While it is the fashion today to call all large sailing vessels "tall ships," sailors disdain this practice and always refer to a vessel with the specific name that identifies its rig. The barque rig has three masts; it is square rigged on the foremast and on the mainmast, but it is fore-and-aft rigged on the mizzenmast. Full-rigged vessels are square rigged on all three masts, giving them more sail surface area and, thus, more speed. To handle the added canvas, however, requires a larger crew. The barque rig was developed to balance the need for crew and speed.

Eagle is an impressive sight to behold, but her beauty belies a darker past. She was launched in 1936 as the *Horst Wessel* near Hamburg, Germany. Built by the Nazis as a sail-training ship, she took her name from a martyred Nazi thug, and Adolf Hitler himself attended her launching ceremony. When the Allied forces defeated Germany, her fortunes brightened; she was taken by the United States as part of war reparations and was commissioned into the Coast Guard in 1946.

Ed Lowe, USCG Retired, is the last living member of the Coast Guard crew that was sent to Germany at the end of World War II to bring the *Eagle* home. Despite his ninety-two years of age, Lowe recalls the adventure as if it were yesterday. The crew found the ship in Bremerhaven, driven into the banks of the Elbe River. Although she managed to escape the widespread destruction that the city suffered at the end of the war, she was not exactly in Bristol fashion:

A forty-five-member German crew was on the ship. It was right across the river. The ship was rotten, dirty, and streaked with rust. What was left of the sails were flapping, and she was leaning over in the muddy river. Somebody said, "That's what we're getting? That thing? Does the skipper know this?" One guy said, "The best you can do is jack up the whistle and put a new boat under it." All the sails were rotten, all the rigging was rotten. The shrouds, the steel cables holding up the masts, were rusted. The paint was a mess. There was nobody there but the six of us. We kept waiting for the cadets, but we never got any word.

The Coast Guard's plan was to pick the best of the three sister sailing vessels that had survived the war, put her back into shape, and sail her home with the help of Academy cadets. After the mission to acquire a sail-training vessel went before Congress, the head office sent a telegram:

On a wire that came through, it said, "You will receive no money, no authorization, and no bodies. Bring it home anyhow."

With no help or money on the way, Lowe and his shipmates began preparing the vessel to sail home. She would need new sails, rigging, and electrical and mechanical systems, as well as a new engine. Lowe was ordered not to board the vessel again unless carrying badly needed materials, but he immediately ran into problems locating suitable replacements. With much of Germany flattened, citizens were tight-lipped about the locations of supplies that they so desperately needed themselves. Because there were submarine pens at Bremen, however, Lowe concluded that there must have been local supply depots that kept the fleet in action. Eventually, he stumbled across them. Driving around with a Navy friend one day, he came across a road that led into a forest:

Oil tanks had been built during the war to put the fuel in they were going to get from Romania until the Allies bombed the fields. The tanks were never used—brand-new, underground tanks. We got on top of one of the tanks and came across a hatch. While we were trying to open it, out in the distance, somebody decided it was a good day to go out pot-shooting. Bang! Wheeeeeew . . . and down the valley the bullet went! Boy did I fall on the ground in a hurry. We were there for a little while and decided to try again. We got it open, and there was a ladder going straight down, and it was just loaded. It was a bonanza.

Returning with an armed guard, they found what they needed for the ship:

There was one guard. It took a little doing, and the guard didn't like it, so I told one of the men to stay and watch him, and we went in. We found electrical cables, conduit, and I took anything that I thought we would need that we would have to buy: sheet metal, wire rope, just about anything. It's hard to describe. That's the way it went, and it worked out pretty good.

Eventually, their labor problems were resolved as well. About forty new enlisted personnel from the Coast Guard's training center in Cape May were sent over with a handful of officers. These men, along with the German crew that was already aboard the ship, provided enough hands to cross the Atlantic. After acquiring the necessary materials, Lowe figures they only had about a month to do the work:

On the 15th of May, both crews were mustered in the waist of the ship. McGowan read his orders, giving the ship its new name. Immediately after that, he took command. We finished our work and departed the 30th of May. We had tugboats accompany us, because we were advised we would have to be towed; they hadn't had time to remove all of the mines from the area around the Cliffs of Dover. From Germany down to Falmouth, we were in a mined area, and a sailboat couldn't make it. We stayed in Falmouth for four days and then went to Madeira for three or four days before heading across.

After surviving an immense hurricane, the *Eagle* eventually arrived in New York harbor with tattered sails. Since then, she has been the Coast Guard's sail-training vessel, and thousands of cadets have enjoyed their first experience at sea aboard her.

Captain Raymond Pulver had only just assumed command of the *Eagle* at the beginning of this particular swab summer. No stranger to her decks, Pulver had spent time on her as both a cadet and an officer. Born in Carmel, New York, he spent most of his early life in Rhode Island. Although the state is known for its maritime heritage, Pulver did not think about a career on the sea until high school. His father had attended the Academy for two years, and the stories he told intrigued Pulver enough to apply:

If I remember correctly, my parents didn't even know I applied. I got into the Academy, and I sat down with my parents, and I said, "I want to give it a shot." I've never looked back from that point on. I graduated in 1987. It was one of the smallest classes at the Academy; there were some budget challenges at the time. We entered about 250, 260 folks and graduated less than 130.

After graduation, Pulver dove into his career, always advancing and taking on new challenges. His first assignment, aboard a ship, sent him south:

I was very fortunate, as I received my first choice. It was the late '80s—Miami Vice and all that—great stuff going on in the enforcement side of the drug trade, and I wanted to get involved in all that. I became Ensign Pulver on the Coast Guard cutter DAUNTLESS and spent two years there. We had about a half a dozen drug busts while I was on board. I was then fortunate enough to get a command of my own patrol boat off Hatteras, where I spent two and a half years patrolling the Onslow Bay and Raleigh Bay area off Hatteras and North Carolina. It was mostly search and rescue. We had about ten large cases in that two-year period. In addition to that, we did some law enforcement, fisheries enforcement, and boating safety. It's amazing how many different missions we got involved in. We also got involved with the out-load. That was during the first Gulf War, and the Cape Fear River was out-loading at that point, so we did security there. That was part of the homeland security mission, securing our ports. We were doing that in the early '90s, working with Marines, working with Coast Guard reservists, working with Coast Guard active duty. As a lieutenant, junior grade, in command of a patrol boat running those forces on the river, it was certainly a challenge, but again, the Coast Guard was so good to offer that to me and one other lieutenant, junior grade. I'm sure those early responsibilities the Coast Guard gave us wet our whistle to stay in the Service. It was a great responsibility for two twenty-four-year-old kids, and we're very proud to have done our job securing that river.

I left there and went up to a command and operations center, where you make the decisions on operations. You dispatch the assets, sort of like a 911 operator for the ocean. That, again, was eye-opening, because you're not just doing your patrol boat/cutter missions; you are now doing prevention missions, oil response, and dealing with personnel casualties within the Service. That, again, was eye-opening—just a tremendous tour.

From there, I went to a high-endurance cutter as the third in command. During the Cuban exodus, I was very involved with the thirty-seven thousand Cubans in the water. I was both the assistant and what's called the J3, or the operations officer. I didn't really work for the cutter; I worked for a larger staff on the cutter at that time, and we brought all those people to safety. From there, my next patrol went to Europe after the former Soviet Union stepped out and all of those countries opened up. The U.S. military was trying to get U.S. vessels there, and they wanted the Coast Guard to go in. Coast Guard cutter DALLAS was that asset. We spent a hundred days over in Eastern Europe. We had an amazing tour there—so many different countries, so many different responsibilities given to that cutter, an instrument of peacetime cooperation and missions I had not yet been involved with.

From there, the Coast Guard invested in me (and hopefully in the Service) and sent me to grad school. I got a double math degree up at Cornell University and went into workforce planning at headquarters. I did the forecasting of our human-resources capital and calculated where we needed to place people. It really opened my eyes to the business side of the Coast Guard and how our government works internally. I was fascinated by that, and that experience came back later to help me with my last job. From there, I went to Coast Guard cutter barque EAGLE as her executive officer. I came here and had a great time working for Captain Ivan Luke. It was extraordinary. It was all about getting cadets that experience on the sea and how important it was—that first experience—and now, I'm pleased to be back here in that same role. After leaving the EAGLE, I became the assistant commandant of cadets at the Academy. I had the privilege of leading a corps of over a thou-

A swab stands the bow watch as the sun begins to set.

sand cadets and watching them develop into the leaders they are today. It's wonderful to see these great rescues, to see what these young lieutenants are doing—young patrol-boat skippers, people in Iraq, people doing prevention and keeping our ports safe. All those people were cadets or officer candidates who I sailed with on EAGLE or had the privilege to lead as cadets. To see their growth ten years later and see the responsibilities they've taken on, it's extraordinary. It's wonderful feedback for me on how important those years were.

Captain Raymond Pulver teaches a crewmember to use a sextant.

cessful there. We had great, great aviation and intelligence—just a great conglomerate of assets being put together. We ended up with several drug seizures. That program itself has been extraordinary, working those assets together and stopping hundreds of tons of cocaine every year from entering Central America, where they break it down. Our commandant talks about how the Coast Guard removes more cocaine than all of the rest of continental United States law enforcement agencies together. It's an amazing amount of cocaine we stop in those transit zones. This really talks about the value of our Coast Guard to our nation.

From there, I worked on modernization. The Coast Guard was modernizing, and with my resources background, it seemed to be the right assignment as I left the cutter BEAR. The person I worked for actually became the commandant of the Coast Guard. He brought me up, and I was his congressional affairs chief for the past two years. I worked the Hill, again, applying different experiences from operations, organization, and the command center—the breadth of what the Coast Guard does—and applied that knowledge with an operational twist on the Hill. Our job was basically to educate, making sure Congress knew what we were doing and its importance. It was a fascinating job, and it brought me here to being the commanding officer of barque EAGLE.

Pulver has always found his role as a Coast Guard officer stimulating, but like any military position, it can take a toll on one's family life:

The Coast Guard is always looking to groom people for those next assignments, so they move their officers around pretty quickly. That is part of the military-services mentality. Fortunately, I've had a very patient wife and a wonderful family, and that's worked out real well for all of us. My kids have lived in five or six states, and my wife has not only been around the East Coast, but she's visited me in different countries. It's been a really neat opportunity for us. You have to embrace the lifestyle, because if you don't embrace it, you have to leave it. It's a demanding lifestyle. You move a lot. It's tough to really be integral with a community, because you come in for three years and then you leave, so those have been some of

I was privileged after that to go to the Coast Guard cutter BEAR, a 270' cutter. I had a wonderful crew. We worked very hard and did a whole bunch of fisheries boardings off the mid-Atlantic during one patrol. We spent most of our time in the deep Caribbean chasing go-fasts. We employed an interdiction squadron of helicopters which were embarked on our cutters, and our job was to stop the go-fasts bringing in cocaine. We were fortunate to be suc-

the challenges, but our family and our extended family have been strong for us. I wouldn't have turned down those opportunities and experiences for my family for anything at this point, but there were some tough times. You know, with eleven years at sea—and by the time I get through with this, it will have been some thirteen or fourteen years at sea—I've missed some events, too. Again, that's the patience and understanding of a family so important for a Coast Guard career.

Despite the *Eagle*'s unique propulsion system, her daily operations are governed by the same principles as are all other Coast Guard vessels:

About ten or fifteen years ago, after a safety study on EAGLE, they determined that we should work for the same operational commander as all the other major cutters in the fleet, the Atlantic Area Commander. We go through the same thing all the other major cutters go through, from damage control to navigation, and that holds the standard. The reality is—with the exception of your mission and your propulsion system—we try to meet the same fleet standards. EAGLE goes through the same maintenance cycles and the same inspections, from administrative to safety compliance.

Where it gets different, I would say, is in its mission. On my last cutter, my job was to put officers on a drug boat or put a rescue team on a rescue case. My job was to be in the right spot and get those teams off the ship where they could affect something. The mission on EAGLE is different. I go port to port, and my job is to put training on target (our cadets and officer candidates), and the target is inside the ship, so instead of having boarding teams, I have training teams. We train all day and night. We have it scheduled so we are always training, either on watch or off watch. We cycle through our training objectives, from damage control to seamanship, from medical to navigation—you name it. That is our primary mission, but how we operate as a cutter and how we operate day to day is, hopefully, fleet standard.

Aside from serving as a training platform for both cadets and officer candidates, the *Eagle* plays another significant role within the Service:

We also have a public-relations function. When we do get to port, it's a whole new world. To go into a port and have one or two hundred people or more come to the port because America's tall ship is there is a real privilege. We are ambassadors of our nation when we go abroad. I've seen where the lines to get on board the ship are five to ten hours long. People will line up the night before, because they haven't seen the ship, so from our perspective, that's a great honor and a privilege, and we take that privilege seriously. We try to give every visitor a positive image of our nation and our Coast Guard.

The *Eagle* may be like no other cutter in the Service, yet Pulver feels he has the experience required to handle this unusual ship:

We're a little bit of a one-off from the rest of the fleet, but all the cutters I've been on prepared me for this. Working external affairs has prepared me for this job. Working as the dean of students and understanding the cadet and officer candidate programs has helped me with this job. Working at a command center across all missions, workforce planning, and how our workforce fits together—all those things, including the five sea tours, have helped prepare me for this job. When I say that, I say marginally prepared me for it, because until you're in it, you don't fully understand what it is. It's an extraordinary opportunity, and I appreciate the Coast Guard giving me the responsibility of EAGLE for these three years.

Not only is the *Eagle* unique because of its reliance on sails for propulsion, but its crew size also differs considerably from that of a standard fleet asset. She simply requires many more hands to operate than other cutters do:

Our permanent crew is fifty-seven. Actually, compared to a major cutter, I have the least amount of people. We bring in volunteers from throughout the Coast Guard who join us in the summer to get us up to about eighty, and it makes sense. We don't need eight or nine cooks when we are in port; we need them when we're underway. By the time we fill up with doctors, extra medical staff, cooks, a few extra engineers, some extra trainers, damage control, and seamanship personnel, we get up to about eighty folks, and we be-

come a crew. After that, we can get up to 153 trainees on board, so you get up to 240 people on board. The Coast Guard doesn't have other vessels with 240 people on board. There are a lot of people working, but I need all those hands to handle sail. I need to be able to handle sail day and night with people on watch all the time, as well as to fulfill the primary mission of getting our cadets and our officer candidates to sea. EAGLE is an unbelievable platform for providing that underway experience, where cadets are integral to the operation of the cutter. We need them all to work hard while they're on board so we can get from point A to B and, in between, get them a little training. From turning off the navigation gear and having them use a sextant to find the next island to hauling on lines to raise the yards, from doing the navigation briefs to doing the collaterals on board, the cadets or the officer candidates are going to do all of that, and our job is to coach them.

Our goal is to have them learn as much as possible. They have training sessions in damage control, seamanship, and all of the rest. When you add that all up, my goal when they walk off is to have them surprised at how much they've learned. There are no classrooms on board; everything is hands-on. At the end of the five or six weeks, I want them to feel more comfortable, more confident in this environment. Those are all objectives. I want them to walk away and feel proud of what they were able to accomplish, no different from cadet Pulver in 1984 when he sailed on EAGLE himself. We're all-in to expose them to as much as possible. We keep them busy. We feed them well, we work them hard, and when they walk away, they walk away proud, and that's great. It's a maritime service, and I want them to be proud no matter where they serve in the Coast Guard, on or off cutters. I want them to have the experience of being on the water and being successful, and that, hopefully, is what EAGLE provides.

Swabs can only accomplish so much in the one week they spend aboard the *Eagle*. The real growth occurs when cadets come aboard for a more extended period between their 3rd and 2nd class years:

They figuratively and literally learn the ropes over that five-, six-week period. When they come on board, they're new to it. Within

a week or two, they start understanding how things work. By the third or fourth week, they've got all their qualifications done, and by the time they leave, they walk away confident that they can perform on board. A lot of them come back as 2nd class or 1st class cadets, and I put them in leadership roles. When the upperclass come on board, they're an integral part of the EAGLE wardroom.

They help with the mission, and they make that transition. They definitely get a lot of time at sea, and they get a lot of time to learn to qualify at watch stations. A lot of them will go into the crew-watch qualifications and get those quals. Even 3rd class cadets will get those qualifications, and that takes a lot of effort. They absolutely do grow during their five to six weeks on board. I think they learn a lot here, but I'm not sure they are aware of everything they learn while on board. That's the magic of it; they walk away with confidence and an understanding and a liking for the sea and its lore, which is in the Academy mission statement. I think when they all leave here, they're leaving as able seaman—able to handle lines, understand watch routines, and understand what it means to be afloat. I see them grow over the five or six weeks, and the same is true for the upper-class cadets that come on board.

On EAGLE, they get disconnected. They're not up on the Internet every night, and they get a chance to concentrate on this thing called a maritime profession. When they first come on board, the upperclass are insecure leaders; they're not sure what they're doing is right. By the time they leave, they understand their job, they understand how it fits into the ship's routine and how important every single job is on the cutter. Every job is equally important on a cutter. That's why I love cutters: everything is important. There are no days off for anybody, including the cadets. I think when they leave here, they leave with great confidence, and they can help run a command. When they become ensigns on their next tour, they've done everything an ensign should do. I call it the complete ensign experience. They've driven a ship, they've done collaterals, they've been given projects, they've led people, and they've had to work in a wardroom, where everything doesn't always come together easily. That's how it's going to be at their next unit, so I'm glad they're getting this experience when they come on board.

As I accompanied this summer's swabs on their trip from Portland to Newport, I noticed that the command style on board seemed professional but relaxed. I asked Pulver whether this style was typical on board cutters or was, instead, a reflection of the *Eagle's* specific mission as a training platform for cadets. He replied that it was neither; rather, it had more to do with what he refers to as the command climate:

There are times when the tone changes, but if our junior officers and senior cadets are doing a great job leading, our crew is doing a great job teaching, and we're being safe on board, maybe you don't have to do the Captain Bligh thing. It doesn't have to be an oppressive environment. It's very positive on board. I'm very proud of how positive it is. That said, we have our moments. If someone's being unsafe or someone decides to do something unsafe aloft, there will be times that they are not as comfortable. I personally believe that the sea provides risk and stress automatically and people will certainly rise to the occasion. I'm convinced all people come on board to be successful. Maintaining stress at a level where it's destructive is unnecessary and actually works against the goals. My outlook is the same with the weather. If there's a storm coming, I like to ride the outside of the storm so we can get great sailing and great ship-handling, but if we go to the eye of that storm and its twenty-foot seas and everyone's sick and no one can train, it defeats the purpose. So there is that balance between positive attitude and having everybody know what's right and what's wrong. We have our moments, unfortunately, when something goes wrong and we have to address it, and that's not normally in that same, casual tone.

We try to provide this leadership laboratory as well, which means that cadets make mistakes. They're going to be given leadership roles, and they're going to make mistakes with them. As long as they're growing from it and the cutter and personnel are safe, I'm good with that. At moments, we'll make people a little uncomfortable when they make mistakes, but I hope it never becomes oppres-

Swab Stephanie O'Gara clearly enjoys her view from the height of the main top.

sive, unless they're just not giving their best effort. If people give their best effort, they're going to find a nice environment here.

Command climate is emphasized. We like the fact that we have unbelievable retention in the Coast Guard. You talk to leadership folks, and, normally, the most influential person that you have in

Aboard the USCG Cutter *Eagle*

Clockwise: A swab climbs through the fog to the main top. Few sails are set as little wind exists to propel the vessel.

A good breeze drives *Eagle* on her course south from Portland, Maine, to Newport, Rhode Island.

Eagle's triple helm allows crew to control the vessel in the heaviest of weather. In case of problems, there is an additional emergency helm farther aft.

Clockwise: Swabs must work with the permanent crew to get the ship from one port to the next. Nearly every job aboard a sailing vessel requires teamwork, making *Eagle* the perfect training platform for cadets.

A sailor walks out on the footropes hanging beneath the yard. For safety's sake, once in position, crew snap themselves into place with safety lines linked to their climbing harnesses.

Sailing vessels are some of the most beautiful man-made creations found at sea. The geometry of *Eagle's* sails provides endless photographic opportunities.

This page, clockwise: Two crewmembers and cadre 2/C Lena Ludewig (center) climb aloft.

Swabs eat lunch below decks. Food for snacks between meals is always available. Besides fruit, sweets, and assorted drinks, large boxes of Saltines are always available to help queasy swabs overcome their seasickness.

The entire crew must work together to set certain sails. Here swabs and enlisted crew hoist the topsail yard to its final height.

Opposite page, clockwise: Crew sweat some running rigging on a blustery day. Swabs get their first duties at sea as Coast Guard members onboard *Eagle*.

Swabs climb the windward shrouds to reach the upper yards where work awaits them.

Swabs learn basic shipboard firefighting techniques as part of their training while aboard Eagle. They learn to quickly don firefighting suits and handle high-pressure hoses such as this.

Opposite page: Cadets climb shrouds to reach the topgallant yard. *Eagle* has over six miles of running and standing rigging.

This page, clockwise: Swab Ardy Effendi points towards a school of dolphins headed for the ship.

Swabs work with enlisted crew to prepare meals aboard ship, sometimes for as many as 240 people.

The crew musters on deck to hear the general plan for the day.

This page, clockwise: Swabs stand watch on the bow on a foggy morning.

A swab leans against the rail while standing watch in the stern.

Swabs line the rail after finishing a work detail. Their days aboard the ship allow for more rest than they get at the Academy.

Opposite page, clockwise: Swab Hailey Thompson lends scale to *Eagle's* massive spars.

Swab Melissa Keeley dons a safety harnesses before going aloft.

Eagle can reach a speed of seventeen knots under sail alone.

218

your life is the person who you work directly for, as opposed to thinking that the captain or the admiral or the commandant of the Coast Guard are going to really influence you. It's more immediate. If you empower people, you make the appropriate command climate: everyone knows the objectives, there is a lot of communication, people are heard when they want to be heard, and people have an opportunity to speak. In our Service, people come to work, and they like the mission. They like what they're doing, and they feel they and their families are taken care of.

Does every cutter have the same leadership philosophy? I will say this: our bosses stress command climate. They want a positive command climate. They want a place where everyone feels they're heard, but they also want discipline in the fleet at the same time, and I think it's the responsibility of the commanding officer to be able to mesh those two. Our wardroom and our chief's mess have a command style, because we talk about this. There is an active conversation on how we maintain a positive command climate. Having our customers on board at all times, the trainees, is interesting, too. I know command climate means a lot to the Coast Guard, up to the point of losing discipline. There is a balance there, and it's okay for it to be positive on board.

The relative sizes of the various departments on board the *Eagle* may differ from those on board other large cutters in the fleet. The basic organization, however, remains the same, reflecting what Pulver calls a plug-and-play system:

We have a very traditional organization on board, as with all our cutters. There is an executive officer who manages the daily routine. We have department heads. In this case, we have a support-and-supply department head who owns the storekeepers, the yeoman, the cooks, the medical, and all those groups who are in support. We have an engineering department that is responsible for the power plant and all hotel services on board. We have a deck and an operations department that's combined as an operations department, but deck is a big piece of it, obviously, on EAGLE. They're responsible for the navigation, getting from point to point, and also responsible for the sails and all the sail-handling. Within

that, there is a chief's mess, where we have one chief from each of those departments permanently assigned. We then have the 1st class mess, which is the senior enlisted level. At that point, we basically have every division. At the first class petty officer level, we get into electricians and MKs, machinery technicians, and food subsistence. There are damage controlmen, main prop, and the auxiliary. They're all in that 1st class mess. We have two warrants on board, one for the main propulsion and one for the sailing rig. They are essential to us, too. In the ops department, there is the mainmast, the foremast, and the mizzenmast. The mizzenmast also does all of our navigation work. When the cadets are on board, the way we have it worked out right now is: the senior cadet at each mast runs the cadets on that mast, and they report to the department head directly. So one mast, interestingly enough, will be associated with engineering. Yes, they'll work the sail, but those upper-class cadets work for the engineer and will do engineering collaterals as well. We try to fully integrate the trainees into that organization. It puts more on those senior cadets to be part of the wardroom, working with the chief's mess and mentored by them, so they can be successful. And that's no different than your first cutter. I was adopted by the chief's mess, and I had an officer from the year ahead of me help me out greatly as I worked for my ops boss, so it's not a different model. That's why I like it so much. We have this organization, and it's plug and play. We can have a crew of fifty-seven, and yet underway, we can have over 240 people on board, and they all fit into their niche. You don't have to manage by individuals; you manage by project or division, and the people fall in where they're supposed to be, because they understand the organization.

Because the *Eagle* represents the swabs' first time at sea as members of the United States Coast Guard, Pulver wants it to be a positive experience:

For the 4th class, the objective is to indoctrinate them on life at sea. When they leave, we want them to be comfortable being on the ship. There is much less training, because we only have a week. We try to get them excited about things like nautical history. We do some seamanship, we do some damage control. We do that in the first few days, and then they stand their watch. They have a competition on Thursday known as the EAGLE Olympics, which reinforces what they have learned, and then we are back in port by Friday. It's a short week, but it's a great week that exposes them to life at sea and what they'll be doing the next summer. They then head back to continue their indoctrination into the Coast Guard at Chase Hall. It's just one week here of the seven, but it's an important piece of that puzzle.

For the most part, swabs are enthusiastic about their first trip on *Eagle*. 4/C Rheanastasia Doctolero found the change of pace refreshing:

I think I liked the EAGLE because it wasn't swab summer. I definitely enjoyed myself, because I felt like an adult. It was kind of cool to be given responsibility; you're holding duty shifts and standing watch. There were some duties that were awful, like if you have the 4:00 A.M. to 8:00 A.M. shift, you don't get to sleep after it, so it's a really, really long day. Those are the worst. You're tired, and you've got to stay up and do the duty, but it was definitely a good experience. I personally liked the aspect of working in the same position as the people I'll be leading when I'm an officer. It was totally different from anything I've ever done. Going up to the top and helping set the sails, going into the engine room and checking the engine and stuff—we got to do that this summer. I was pretty excited. It's pretty cool, sailing your own boat. I got to drive and learn how to use different navigation tools. It was a really great experience. Some people hated it, but I loved it, and I'm glad I didn't get seasick. Whether or not you get seasick determines whether or not you like EAGLE.

Katie Brosnan loved every aspect of the week at sea:

EAGLE was awesome. I loved EAGLE. It was so great, and I think a lot of it was just because I got to talk to a lot of other kids from other companies I didn't know before. You got to do crazy things like climbing up the rigging to the royals and letting down the sails. That was really great. You see dolphins jumping out of the water. It was also better than swab summer, because you could get some

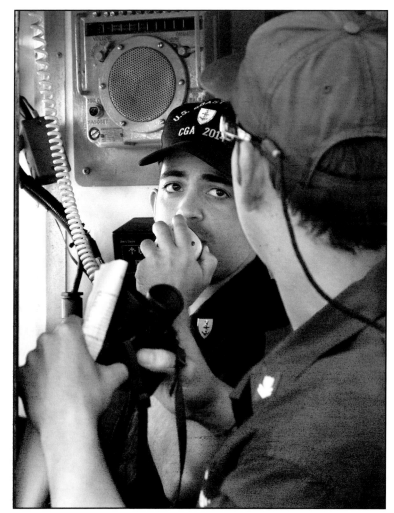

2/C Pablo Ortiz operates one of the *Eagle's* many radios.

sleep. We got to talk to a lot of enlisted people. I thought that was really good, because one day we'll be officers leading them, and you know that they have way more experience than you do. You'll be fresh out of the Academy, and yet you'll be in charge of them, and they'll probably have twenty years' experience on you. I made it a point to be super respectful to the enlisted people and really try to learn everything they're doing, really try to be a sponge in that

I didn't get as seasick, surprisingly, as many people did. I got a little bit nauseous, but I sat down and did okay, but a lot of people ended up vomiting. For swab summer, I definitely liked it. I'd rather have been on EAGLE for the amount of time that I was in swab summer. Just to be on EAGLE wasn't that much fun. I could see how a Coast Guard unit or an actual cutter that is doing real Coast Guard work would be a lot more interesting than just sailing on a boat, especially the sail stations. I didn't really enjoy that, but I'd take that over being in swab summer. It was the best part of swab summer.

One evening, the *Eagle* ran into some rough weather. High winds and rain sent many queasy swabs to the rails of the ship as she pounded through seas under a full press of canvas. Because the ship began to head off course, the crew doused the sails and used her engine to run her directly into the wind. Since the only experience the swabs had aloft was setting sails on a calm, sunny day, I assumed it would be the permanent enlisted crew who would furl the sails in the stormy night. I was mistaken, as 4/C Katie Brosnan attests:

They got us from the engine room to help with the sails. I love climbing, so I thought it was great. It was crazy. That's another thing: You have a harness, right? You see pictures, and you think, "Oh, they have a harness." But you're not clipped in all the time. You're only clipped in when you stop! "Oh, don't worry. You have a harness!" It's like we're seven! It's not hooked in. When you're holding onto the sails, if you let go, you're gone, so we were holding on so tight. Oh man, that was scary, but fun. But I can tell people, "Yeah, I took in sails in a storm on a square rigger." That was awesome.

4/C Fred Higgins was also called to furl sail in the storm:

It was a night where it was raining pretty hard and really blowing. I was up there. It was very eerie because the foghorn was blowing and you could see fog going through the sails and you felt the rain. While you're up there, you're just doing what you need to do, but it was kind of scary on the way going up. Once you take your mind

Eagle sailing in light airs off the New England coastline.

environment and soak up everything. A lot of the enlisted people are really nice and tried to show me everything. They were excited, because they like their job and want to tell you everything.

While he preferred *Eagle* to training at the Academy, Koachar Mohammad's response to the experience was less enthusiastic:

off the fact that you're rolling on the sea and up a hundred feet in the air, it's not too bad. It's something that you like to talk about when you're not up there. I enjoyed it.

EAGLE was fun per se. It was something that wasn't like the rest of swab summer, so that part was enjoyable. During the first day, they trained us on what would we would be doing for EAGLE. You got out of it what you wanted by just asking crewmembers about what was going on. During the day, if there weren't sail stations, which is when basically everybody goes up on deck and helps raise and lower sails, we would be doing our duties—like mess cook, where we would cook, or engine or deck watch. They split people up into different places below deck. I believe the purpose was to learn things at sea—how life is in the fleet, but also, to think about your crew. Since we were the crew, we saw how it felt to be the person doing all the stuff that you wouldn't typically be doing as an officer. If you weren't on duty, you were basically sitting around, but of course somebody would always ask, "Are you doing anything?" If your answer was no, they'd say, "Then, go clean that or go do this."

Some swabs claim to have suffered from boredom while aboard the *Eagle*. 4/C Scooter Finney does not see how that could have been possible:

In my opinion, boredom is not something that should be a reality. People talk about being bored, and that's shameful in a sense. We got to sit around and we got to sleep. It was great! We hadn't had that in almost two months, and we were free in a big sense, and that was enough for me. We got more sleep. I mean, we had to wake up at random times, but if you were up late, they let you sleep in. There was little to be complained about in that regard, in my opinion.

I thought it was great. The way I approach life in general is that if you go into something with the right attitude, you'll have fun, and I did just that. I didn't get seasick. I spent time on small boats when I was young, so I did my time with seasickness back then. The sailing could have been better. We went from Newport to New London,

so we just went out, went in circles, and came in. There was no wind, so it lacked excitement, but it was still really cool. I've never been on a ship like that. Every means for survival is on the ship; essentially, it's a city by itself, a floating town. I got to climb up in the rigging, and I really enjoyed that. I saw dolphins. It was all really fun, and it was my first taste of life at sea. All in all, that's my favorite thing I've done so far.

4/C Kyle Wood, who approaches life with much the same mindset as his shipmate Finney, also found his time aboard the *Eagle* exhilarating:

We were on the first leg with EAGLE. It was a lot of fun. It was exciting to get out there and see what EAGLE is like. It was a good experience. It was mostly calm, and we saw some dolphins and whales and stuff. It was cool. You have to work, but it was fun working. We had deck watch, lookout, and got to go up the masts and furl the sails. I didn't ever find it boring, because there was always something you could find to do, even if no one was telling you what to do. I always found something I was able to do.

As a 1st class cadet, Breanna Hite has had both the swab and the 3rd class experiences aboard the *Eagle*. She sees the vessel as an important training platform for cadets:

It is a part of the operational Coast Guard, but it's not so operational that if you don't do something right you're in big trouble. Everybody takes turns standing watches and you try to get qualifications. The crew on EAGLE is primarily enlisted personnel, and as future officers, we're going to have to deal a lot with enlisted members of the Coast Guard, and we are going to be their leaders, so it's good for us to have some interaction with them that we don't usually have here during the school year at the Academy. The cadets, with the help of the enlisted, do everything on the boat: set the sails, set sea details, navigate, cook, and stuff like that. This probably isn't one of the goals of the Academy, but I personally think during those six weeks on EAGLE you are able to interact with a lot more with your classmates than you would on a daily basis at the school. You make a lot more friends that maybe you didn't have during your first year here. I think that's an awesome experience. You're going to be with these people for three more years at the Academy.

2/C Joseph Trump feels much the same way:

The EAGLE is a pretty significant part of swab summer. Although many people would disagree, I think the EAGLE is one of the most important aspects of being a cadet. You learn so much on EAGLE that you don't know you've learned and that you can't learn anywhere else. I just finished reading a book called BARQUE Of SAVIORS. It's mostly about the transition of EAGLE from the German navy to the Coast Guard, but it has a quote I really liked. I haven't memorized it verbatim, but it says the aim of sail training is to get you away from the mediocrity of learning how to just survive in the world—how to just get a job and just live. It helps you to see what life really is about, and you can't do that in a classroom. It's such a different life. You learn a lot about yourself, you learn a lot about the people you're with, and you learn a lot about the world: the weather, the places that you go, and the interaction between humans and nature. You don't get that on a powered vessel. I think the EAGLE is the best cutter we have.

Swabs paddle three rafts roped together back to the Academy after having first run to Mamacoke Island, north of the school.

Sea Trials

Perhaps the most memorable day of swab summer is the last. Having survived seven weeks of indoctrination, swabs face one final challenge before the summer is officially secured: Sea Trials. Sea Trials is a grueling, all-day affair of physical, mental, and emotional tests during which swabs are judged on everything they learned over the course of the summer. Although swabs must perform as individuals, this no-holds-barred, bare-fisted slugfest can only be survived with help from shipmates.

As with all major events at the Academy, rumors of what Sea Trials will bring spread through the eight companies like wildfire, fueled, in part, by cadre. Swabs can never quite pinpoint the exact source of the information they have received, yet they are surprisingly well informed. Of course, many swabs have brothers or sisters who have passed through the Academy or older friends who have leaked some choice details. When asked how he found out about Sea Trials, 4/C Scooter Finney replied:

Rumors. Rumors are somehow created, and I don't understand how people know, but we knew. We knew that we were waking up around three, three thirty. I don't know how people found out about that, but once one person knew, they told everybody, so we knew it was coming.

This particular summer, the cadre from one company repeatedly warned swabs that the circus was coming to town. 4/C Frederick Higgins:

You knew Sea Trials was going to happen; you just didn't know when it was going to happen or what would happen. Everybody was asking about it right up to it. Swabs would ask, "Sir, what's going to happen for Sea Trials?" They would answer, "What are Sea Trials?" In our company, they called Sea Trials "Disneyland." They were like, "This Friday, we're all going to Disneyland! We're going to have so much fun!" They were pretty clear about letting us know we'd find out when we got there.

Regardless of how much or how little swabs actually knew about Sea Trials, they all realized it was coming, and most of them feared its arrival—the cadre made sure of that. The cadre from one company went so far as to plant a fake schedule for their swabs to find, thereby simultaneously testing the swabs' honor by seeing whether they would return the found document. The swabs did so (and saw through the ruse). When the day finally does arrive, it begins both early and ominously. 4/C Koachar Mohammad remembers the first moments clearly:

That night, I couldn't really sleep, because I knew it was going to come. I feel like before Sea Trials actually started, like ten minutes

before, a lot of us were awake, because we knew it was going to come. The cadre started playing music. It started out as soft, quiet music from Batman. It was that scary music leading up to something that's really bad that's about to happen. They were playing that, and then out of nowhere, the sirens go off, and they kicked doors in and came into our rooms. This was the first time they ever came into our rooms during the summer while we were in bed. They started IT'ing us inside our rooms. That was the first time that happened, too. Then, they changed the music. The sirens were going off, lights were flashing, and they changed the music to heavy metal and played it really loud. That was pretty funny.

4/C Katie Brosnan was asleep when the assault began. The music entered her dreams, turning them into nightmares:

On Saturday morning, they woke us up at like three in the morning or whatever. The new Batman had come out, and they played the soundtrack from the movie. It was funny, because I was asleep, but you know how when you're asleep you can hear music? They were playing a heartbeat noise, and you hear the noise, and you think it's your own heartbeat. It was so creepy. Then, all of a sudden, it turns into a siren, and they're yelling, "Get up!" It was crazy, but at that point, it was exciting. It was like, "Yeah! Sea Trials! It's almost over! I've just got to get through today! Even if I completely bomb today, twenty-four hours will pass and it's over!"

Like his fellow swabs, 4/C Finney knew the day was coming, and yet its actual commencement was still a complete shock:

It was the single most physically challenging day of my life. Period. I'm not sure how much you've heard about this, but we sleep on top of our racks, with our racks already made, because reveille goes on for, I think, thirty seconds. By the end of it, they expect us to be on the bulkhead, dressed and ready. So I sleep in gym shorts and a gym shirt, and I always had my socks right next to me. I put my socks on, hop down, put my shoes on, and run out, every morning. They were opening doors and yelling at people. Before I even had one sock completely on, I was on the ground doing pushups— and this was at 3:30 A.M. Within ten seconds of waking up, I was doing pushups to the point where I couldn't do any more pushups, and then, the whole day continued with that intensity.

Most of the trials revolve around the same types of challenges the swabs have faced all summer—marching, running, obstacle courses, swimming—but this day is unique in its non-stop intensity. Further increasing the challenge is the additional requirement that swabs carry fully loaded sea bags throughout the day, never letting them touch the earth. Once the swabs have been rousted from their bunks and thoroughly IT'd in the barracks, whole companies pour from Chase Hall, flowing down the Hill to drown the football field in a wash of blue. As the sun will not be up for hours, the entire corps drilling on the field is illuminated only by the harsh sodium lights above, which cast black shadows on the too-green plastic turf under their feet. A continual din of shouted orders and responses adds the last surrealistic touch to the scene. Company officers view the scene from the top of the bleachers, discussing any problems they already see forming. The adrenaline rush that the swabs felt on R-Day returns as they quickly learn that there will be no pleasing the cadre this day. Row upon row of swabs line the white yard lines that slash across the field.

All of the swabs wear orange and yellow reflective vests, distinguishing them from their leaders throughout the day. A single member of the cadre, holding a bullhorn to his mouth, begins directing an interminable set of calisthenics as others scrutinize the swabs, seeking out any error. Any swab failing to perform is torn from the group and sent to the sidelines, where waiting cadre pounce, happy to provide personalized attention. The workout is brutal, and only when the swabs seem about to break does it suddenly end. Exhausted companies reform on the perimeter of the field as breakfast arrives in cardboard boxes. Cadets stand in ranks as they devour the meal, swabs and cadre alike weighted down by the large green sea bags they shoulder. Swabs must square this meal, as they do all others. One company's swabs figure out that if they all turn ninety degrees, they can rest their breakfast cartons on their shipmates' packs, easing the task of wolfing down the morning's energy allowance. It is the day's first real show of teamwork.

4/C Brosnan believes her cadre were some of the toughest on the field:

We had to carry our sea bags around all day, and you couldn't let them touch the deck. I remember we were eating a snack, or having lunch, and you had to eat it standing up. It was us and another company beside us. The other company's cadre said to their swabs, "Okay, you guys can have a break. You can put your sea bags down while you eat." And we were over standing at attention with our sea bags on. What I really respected about our cadre during Sea Trials was all of them had sea bags and they carried them the whole day, too—and they had textbooks in their sea bags, not just their uniforms, boondockers, and all the stuff we had. They packed it to the max, carried it around all day, and they ran with us. We definitely got yelled at a lot, definitely got screamed at and told we weren't honorable and all that stuff, but at the end of the day, they ran Sea Trials with us, and that meant a lot. It definitely meant a lot. Yeah, the cadre were pretty good.

The swimming trial was the most difficult for many swabs—especially those who were not strong swimmers in the first place, such as 4/C Rheanastasia Doctolero:

The only time I struggled was in swimming, because I cannot swim for my life. I almost drowned like twice. That was bad. It was rough, it was long, it was dark. I couldn't see anybody, and no one could see me. It was terrible. It was literally just swimming for an hour. There was one part where we had a medicine ball and we had to keep it out of the water for like five or ten minutes, something like that. That was just tough, because I can barely swim with my own weight, let alone with a five-pound medicine ball. There was another part where you had to see how many lengths of the pool you could swim in a certain amount of time. We had to swim from one end and back, and they keep counting, but I'm a slow swimmer. We also had Karama from Rwanda, and he doesn't know how to swim, either. This was his first time touching water when he got here, so we had some of the weakest swimmers. They were trying to help us, but somebody trying to help me accidentally pushed me under. That was tough. I did not like that part at all.

Swab Emily Quallen stands at attention, fully loaded with the day's gear.

4/C Brosnan usually feels comfortable in the water, yet she too found the swimming trial to be the most difficult, both mentally and physically:

Swimming was really scary. It was safe, because, obviously, you have all the cadre along the pool and they are all lifeguard-certified, so the situation is safe. If anything is really going to go wrong, they'll jump in. I'm not a super-strong swimmer, but I'm very comfortable in the water, and I can stay afloat. I'm not going to drown, but there were some kids who couldn't swim. They couldn't swim back and forth across the pool or get their pants off to use as a flotation device. Two guys were having a lot of trouble with it. I swam over, and I had to do his pants for him. I told him, "All right, all you need to do is stay afloat." He was freaking out. That was really scary for me, because it was real; it wasn't just like, "Oh, I can't do one more pushup." The lights went on and off. Then, they were spraying you with water, and there were crazy noises and stuff. I ended up putting him on his back, and I was holding his chin up with my thumb. I'm not a rescue swimmer; I don't know what I'm doing. And I had to go back and forth across the pool. I was just swimming with him back and forth across the pool. I was like, "Guys, I need help!" Some people came and helped me, and we were trying to keep him afloat, because you couldn't go back to the other side until everyone was across. So it's not like I could just keep him afloat while everybody else went back and forth. We had to take him with us.

Because I was swimming so much, using so much energy because I was probably not using the right technique, my calf cramped up, and then I couldn't swim. Someone else took the guy, and one of the other guys swam over to me, took my leg, and bent it to massage my calf. I'm like, "Okay, I'm good," and he went right on to the next guy.

So it was things like that—how my shipmates saw that I had cramped. They just came right over, no problem, fixed my leg, and went back onto swimming back and forth. It was good, but it was definitely scary. There was another kid, too, who was having trouble swimming, and some of my other shipmates had him taken care of. That night, we had carry-on that meal. The cadre told us that incident really freaked them out. They thought they were going to have to jump in to save us.

As swabs struggle individually with the physical strains of the day, they also struggle to work as a team—much as they have throughout the summer. When 4/C Doctolero found a lack of company-wide support, she teamed up with a friend:

That day was long and painful. That was such a very long day. A lot of people didn't realize that teamwork was such a big part of it, and a lot of people were trying to be that super swab: "Let me do it by myself." Me and this one guy, his last name is Hemi, we formed this team where we were like, "Okay, I'm going to have your back; you're going to have mine." We would hold our sea bags together. Everything we did, we both carried the weight, so it was so much easier. Other people were trying to do it by themselves, and they were struggling. We weren't even tired; we were good.

Doctolero felt the company's weaknesses really showed during the rafting trial:

There was a lot of arguing involved. We learned the hard way that we are not very good at working as a team. We're good in small groups of teams, but not when acting as one large team. There were times where we just went around in circles—we didn't even make it back—and our cadre were mad at us, because all we did was argue. Nobody wanted to listen, and everyone thought they had the best idea in the world.

There are humorous incidents throughout the day (although it is doubtful swabs see them as such). During the rafting trial, swabs must paddle three unwieldy rafts, which are joined together by line, down the Thames River. As the wind and tide rise in strength throughout the day, the chore becomes much more difficult. 4/C Brosnan tells what happened to her own mini-fleet:

We paddled back, but because it got stormy, we got nowhere. It was funny: on the whole Thames River—the entire river, nice and big, nice and wide—there was, I think, one pole. I'm pretty sure there's just one pole in the entire Thames River, and we managed to wrap around it. That was bad. But you couldn't go downstream really; you couldn't do it, even if we were synchronized. The current was just way too strong.

Like all things, Sea Trials must end eventually, and when it does, it is as if a light has been switched off, leaving the whole summer in the dark past. For swabs, everything seems to change when this one day ends and swab summer is officially secured. Cadre go from tyrannical taskmasters to friends, mentors, and shipmates. The feeling swabs have about the conclusion of the summer is uniform: elation. 4/C Jake Carlton, with the summer now a comfortable semester behind him, looks positively back on the test:

Sea Trials was pretty physical and intense, but it was a good challenge. I think I actually liked it. It was difficult—the first half of the morning. I definitely had problems because of the humidity and heat that day, but you feel good once you've finished Sea Trials. You feel good. It's like, "I get to go to sleep?" The next morning was awesome. The rest of the time was ours. We got our phones back, and we could call home. I called home, "Mom, I'm alive!" I called my dad, and he was like, "Yeah, I knew you could do it. I can say it now: 'I told you so.'" The next morning was awesome, because we still had a cals session just for stretching, because we spent sixteen hours, pretty much nonstop, on Sea Trials. We did the stretches, and then we pretty much plopped on the ground for five minutes and did the star stretch, where you just throw out your arms and lay there on the ground. The cadre were all just sitting off in the distance talking while we were doing it. Swab summer was over, and they weren't yelling at us anymore.

While 4/C Brosnan was thrilled and relieved knowing that swab summer was over and was able to thoroughly enjoy the final evening's activity:

It was good to have that "It's over!" feeling—definitely a real sense of accomplishment. At the end of the day, they had us impersonate our cadre. So Sea Trials is over, and that night, you have a meeting on the bulkhead, and you're allowed to relax and chill out, and we were asked to impersonate our cadre. You couldn't tell them who the cadre were; we would just act like them, and they would have to guess. It was so funny; they would know exactly who we were mimicking. We would mimic some of their quirks and some of the things they used to do. Some of them do a particular hand motion,

Sea Trials

Clockwise: 2/C Alyssa Turner gets her troops moving.

The morning begins well before sunrise. Swabs pack their sea bags and meet on the football field where the longest day of the summer begins.

Echo Company follows their guidon as they carry a raft around the track.

Clockwise: Swabs head down a waterfront dock where they will perform a drug search aboard one of the Academy's training boats.

Swab Joseph Rizzardi reports exactly where he found this suspicious bag aboard the vessel he searched. Swabs often found themselves tongue-tied, not yet knowing the proper maritime nomenclature.

Swabs are stopped between the day's major events to do extra pushups and sit-ups.

Swab Ryan O'Neill strains to complete the number of crunches he has to do to finish this particular task.

Teamwork makes the day easier, although swabs often forget this foundational principal during this stressful day.

Swabs and their gear must all go over this wall on the obstacle course. Sea Trials is considered the final exam, and swabs will have to pull from all of the summer's lessons to finish the day.

Clockwise: 2/C Moore drives a swab to complete his task. By the end of the summer, even the cadre are looking to end the yelling.

Swabs paddle their raft back towards the Academy in the late afternoon. On this particular day, a tremendous lightning storm forced an early end to the day's activities.

Hotel Company heads down the docks in the early morning haze.

some of them stomp their feet, you know? It was all in good humor, though, and we asked them to imitate some of us. They'd imitate some of us, and we were like, "Oh, we're so stupid!" It was pretty silly, but that was a lot of fun that night. It was a good night, and that was the end of Sea Trials.

She found that the transition from swab back to human being posed a linguistic challenge:

It was hard not calling yourself in the third person, to switch back to the use of "I," because you had been using "Swab So-and-So" for so long. You had to really think about what you were going to say, because you don't use "I" or "me" or "we" during the summer. Whenever swabs talk, it's this long, drawn-out sentence that no one really understands. You use big words, and you don't know really where you're going with it. We all used super big words in the beginning, and we didn't always know what we were saying.

Like Brosnan, 4/C Scooter Finney felt a sense of accomplishment at the end of Sea Trials:

It was pretty difficult, and it was more chaotic than all the other days, too. It was tough, but it was also the most satisfying day of swab summer—definitely. That was our last week of swab summer, because we had EAGLE the last week. At the end of the day, the regimental commander of the summer talked to us and said, "You're not swabs anymore. You can relax"—right there, right when we were finished with our march, so it was like something from a movie, I guess. It was great, but it was hard.

For 4/C Kyle Wood, whose enthusiasm for the entire summer never flagged, Sea Trials was the icing on the cake:

That was probably my favorite day, actually. It was really hard, but you could see all the stuff you've worked for come together. There were challenges for us as a team, and you could see us overcoming the challenges. You could see your work accomplishing something, instead of just working, working, working and not seeing any results. We actually got to see results during Sea Trials, and I enjoyed that. The start was really bad. You got dropped as soon as you were out your door that morning. They were yelling at you the

whole time, telling you to pack your bags and stuff. We had to pack all the clothes and stuff we needed. Some of it we didn't need; it was just in there to make our bags heavier. Most of the things were stuff we would need throughout the day. I didn't know what hit me. It was hard to sleep that night anyway. It was stunning. All of the tasks were hard, but they were all fulfilling once you did them. We didn't get to do the rafting because of the weather; they cut it short. It felt really good when it was over; I really felt accomplished. It was one of those things where you worked so hard and it was finally over. It just felt good that you accomplished something. We ate in the wardroom that night, but we had carry-on, so we got to talk to the cadre. It was exciting.

Although Sea Trials was certainly rough, the daily grind had been in many ways more difficult for 4/C Doctolero:

It felt good; just being done with everything was just a great feeling. We had the death march at the end of Sea Trials. That was one of the hardest things ever. You know you will be done after this super long walk, but you still have on these heavy boots and your bag, and you're just dying. But Sea Trials wasn't exactly the worst. We kind of dragged through it. It was tough, yeah, it was super tough, but I wouldn't say that was the worst. I can't really say there was a worst day, because there were many equally bad days. Just waking up in the morning was so tough. The first thing you thought was, "Man, my day just started, and I have to go through all this." Cals in the morning was the absolute worst thing. If there was any part of the summer I hated the most, it was cals. You woke up, and you ran around, and they made us do all this exercise. You're like, "I just woke up. I didn't have a good sleep. I'm tired. I can't brush my teeth, because you give me two minutes in the bathroom." It was just awful, waking up and working out for an hour. You're just sitting there, counting down and thinking, "Oh my God, when is this going to end?" That's all I did: watch my watch. There was no one set, bad day. There was definitely no one day where I thought, "Oh my God, this is terrible." It was just the morning. Once you got over cals in the morning, it wasn't smooth sailing, but it was "Yes, I'm done with that!" Cals was brutal. And I lived in the hurt locker because I can't do pushups. And every time I couldn't do pushups, they'd call me out, and I would go to the hurt locker. I'm still pretty bad. I just took my PFE, and I got to twenty-five pushups. I'm proud of myself, because I started off doing sixteen. I'm moving up slowly. Somebody told me I can't be great at everything. I'm still hoping to reach that forty-eight mark, maxing it out. That would be cool. Forty-eight pushups for girls is maxing out; maybe I'll get there one day. I maxed out everything else, so not being able to do a lot of pushups didn't really hurt me; it would just be nice to be able to do them.

What she really enjoyed was the return to some type of normalcy after the day's end:

That was pretty tough, but it was nice knowing you were done. You could get some real sleep, you could take naps after four o'clock. It was nice to be able to just dictate your own life again and not be treated like a baby. That was the worst thing. Your senior year, your parents give you all this liberty and freedom, and then it's all taken away in one instant. That was nice to get a little bit of it back. You still don't have all of your freedoms—you still have your rules and your restraints—but it was nice to feel somewhat normal. Looking back, Sea Trials, or just swab summer in general, was just a great experience. I would not take it back for the world. I probably would not want to do it again, but I'm glad I did it. It's just something you can't really explain to people. I told my friends some of the things we were doing, and they were like, "What? That's crazy. Why are you doing that?" It's pretty cool to think I did this, or that I walked around all day with a fifty-pound bag on my back. I did pushups with a fifty-pound bag. It's pretty cool, some of things that we've done. I've been able to stand. It's made me mentally stronger. It's pretty awesome.

Portrait of an Officer

Captain Ernie Cummings, now retired, grew up near the Academy on a farm on Lantern Hill. According to local legend, the hill was often used as a makeshift lighthouse, guiding ships into the mouth of the Mystic River. When his father died at a young age, his mother sold the farm they operated and moved the family to Mystic, the town where her ancestors had first settled. Decades earlier, her father had brought velvet-making machines from Germany to the area, establishing the Rossie Mill on the Mystic River. In the intervening years, the First World War had interrupted the supply of parts for the cantankerous German looms. Now, as the Second World War was nearing an end, the velvet mills breathed their last. At the close of the war, his mother moved the family once again, this time to New York, with the hope of placing her children into better schools. His mother remarried, and his new stepfather believed the Academy would provide her three sons not only with an excellent education but with a meaningful career path after graduation. When Cummings entered the Academy in the summer of 1958, it was a very different place than it is today:

We got sworn in, and, of course, there was no parade or anything. We were all put in Mac Hall, McAllister Hall, which is a small auditorium, and after the superintendent swore us in, he said, "Look at the person on your left and the person on your right. Only one of you will be here for graduation." They knew how many they were going to lose. Some of my classmates washed out. We had some interesting ones that washed out as I guess you do in every college, university, or Academy, where it's just not for them.

We were not allowed to put in for leave, I believe, until Thanksgiving. There were a number who had to leave because of medical deficiencies and whatnot, but for the most part, people lasted for quite a while. Over the four years, however, we lost an awful lot of people. We started out with almost 300 and ended up graduating, I think, ninety-two. The biggest thing was academics—failure to meet the standard in academics. There were some conduct problems, of course, and there were some people who found out this wasn't for them, and it was probably good that they found that out early. Now, Congress has changed this. Congress said, "Hey, Coast Guard! You're throwing too many people out. You're costing us money. Rethink it."

Cummings quickly discovered that having an older brother at the Academy was not necessarily helpful. Whenever his brother John had command, Cummings was expected to work harder than his shipmates:

And it went on all summer, where every time I went to go sailing, because John also taught sailing, he would say, "Hey, Cummings, you know how to sail. Go on a work detail instead." That summer, I never got to go sailing, because he would send me on work details. He was living at home with my mother who lived in Misquamicut at the time. My birthday was in July, and my mother sent me over a birthday cake with him to give to me. Well, he and the other summer ensigns ate it and told me how good it was. That's the way that went. Unfortunately, they hadn't told me anything useful about swab summer. It was very different. Here I was, looking forward to the summer, and all of a sudden, I'm at the Academy in June, the beginning of July. Truthfully, I kind of enjoyed it. Well, I enjoyed the whole Academy. We all graduated with a BS in engineering. Everybody took exactly the same courses; there were no tracks where you could go into different majors.

Just before graduation, 1st class cadets were given the opportunity to choose their first assignment within the fleet. Because there were limited openings, not everyone received his first choice:

Back in those days, they did things differently when you graduated. Billet night, nowadays, goes by where you stand in your class rankings. In my day, everybody had the same shot at a billet. The billets would come out of Washington, and the Academy would publish them. You would see, let's say, four ships in California in the San Francisco Bay area with twelve billets on them. So first, you would put in for San Francisco, and when you got down to twelve people, then you would go for particular billets in that area. I put in for San Francisco, and I don't remember how many billets were available, but more cadets signed up than were billets available, so we drew cards to see who would get them, with the highest cards winning. My two of spades did not cut it.

An unpopular port that year was New York, so I ended up in New York. But I had a great time there. I had a great first ship. It was the MACKINAC and mainly did ocean station patrols, search and rescue, and things like that. I had a great time and spent almost two years on her, and then I got command of a 95' boat out of Rockaway, New York. It was very interesting, especially for that time in our history. We're talking about the early '60s; that's when all the '60s movements were coming on. We used to go over to The Bitter End in New York quite frequently, where Judy Collins, Joan Baez, and all the folk singers started out. It was good times. We didn't make much money, of course; it was $222.80 a month. Of course, it bought a lot more in those days. When you go out to sea for a month, a month and a half, and then you get back in again, you have almost two months' pay to go out and have a good time with in the city.

Swabs Ashley Dumont and Frederick Higgins on the waterfront.

The '60s were a tumultuous time in American history. Like all American military services, the Coast Guard played a vital role during the Vietnam War. By the end of the war, some eight thousand Coast Guardsmen aboard nearly sixty vessels had patrolled the coasts and rivers of Southeast Asia. Cummings was among those who served:

I volunteered for that. A lot of my classmates went, and we took the 82's over to Vietnam. They were put on the decks of freighters and taken to Subic Bay. We outfitted them in Subic Bay, and then, they went across the South China Sea to Vietnam. To begin with, they were mainly river patrols, at least in our division. We were in the Soai Rap and the Long Tau Rivers leading up to then-Saigon, now Ho Chi Minh City. The Navy didn't have a platform to fill that requirement in the rivers at that time, so they asked the Coast Guard if they could send some of their patrol boats over, and that's how we got to go over there.

When asked whether he and his shipmates had felt like sitting ducks, hemmed in by dense tropical forests along the riverbanks, Cummings had this to say:

Well, when you're that age, you feel impervious. It was exciting. I extended my time there for a period of a couple of months and then went back to the Groton training center, which is now the University of Connecticut extension. The ice patrol is still there. I was there not too, too long when a vacancy developed over at the Academy waterfront, and I was detailed to take that job. I was chief of the small-craft branch and head sailing coach at the Academy. After a few years there, I requested to go back to Vietnam again, this time on a buoy tender. We took care of all of the aids to navigation throughout Vietnam and Thailand. Maybe I was young and idealistic, and in those days, we all thought this was the thing to do. Times had certainly changed from my first tour in Vietnam. When you came back the first time, if you walked into a bar with your uniform on, you couldn't buy a drink; everybody would buy them for you. The second time, life had changed a little bit. Attitudes had changed, and you wouldn't walk into a bar with your uniform on. When I came back the second time, I was stationed in the San Francisco Bay area.

Upon returning to the States, Cummings once again took command of a Coast Guard vessel. From there, his career continued to take him to places and positions he had never dreamed as a swab:

It was a great place and a great tour of duty. It was a reserve training vessel out of Alameda, California. I was the CO of that. That got decommissioned, and I was sent to be the XO of a new unit called the Vessel Traffic Systems. There was a bad accident underneath the Golden Gate Bridge—a couple of tankers ran into each other—and after that, they decided maybe we had better control traffic. This was a pilot program on vessel traffic control, and that was very interesting. I left there after a couple of years, I guess, and was detailed to the Navy War College in Newport, Rhode Island. I spent a year at the War College and left there to go to Astoria, Oregon, as CO of a buoy tender. Left there to be CO of the base group San Francisco, and stayed there for five years. Went back

to New Bedford to be CO of the VIGILANT, a 210' cutter. When I left there—and this sounds crazy—I was detailed to the Army War College in Carlisle, Pennsylvania. It's a senior war college, and you study strategy, tactics, international relations, and things like that. I studied there for a year.

With eight children, moving as often as he did posed a number of challenges for his family:

Of the kids, one or two of them hated it; the rest of them thrived on it. It all depends on the personality of the child. I moved twenty-two times. I had one daughter who went to three different first grades: one in the Philippines, one in California, and one in Rhode Island. That's tough on them, and that created a funny story. We got a call from the school; the teacher wanted to have a teacher-parent conference. We couldn't figure out why, because she had excellent marks. She was doing very well, and she had a good personality. We got there, and the teacher said all of that; she was doing great. She was one of her star students, but she had one problem. We asked what it was, and she said, "She can't tell right from left." I started laughing and said, "I tell you what: ask her about port and starboard." We had to stop using port and starboard and use right and left. I still have trouble with right and left. My wife laughs at me.

The constant change of address may have been difficult on the children, but it did not dissuade one of his sons from attending the Academy nor another from joining the Marines. As Cummings was completing his tour at the Army War College, his career took another surprising turn:

I got a call from headquarters near the end of my tour at the Army War College, and they asked me if I would be interested in a ship called the EAGLE. I said, "Sure," and I went. The EAGLE is normally a two-year job; I stayed there for five years. I tell everybody that's because I'm a slow learner. The decision was made to send the EAGLE to Australia for the Australian centennial, and the superintendent of the Academy wanted me to stay on board, because we were going to go independent. It's a long trip, and it was going to take almost a year, so headquarters left me there for the trip down and the return trip back. I started on the EAGLE in 1983. I had a sailing background, and I was head of the waterfront. I also, when I was at the Academy, made a number of trips as a junior officer on the EAGLE, so I did have EAGLE experience. I've had some pretty good jobs. The commandant, Admiral Papp, said being the captain of the EAGLE is the best job he'd ever had in the Coast Guard—and he's the commandant! Most officers probably don't even aspire to being the CO of the EAGLE, because it's limited right now to experience. Usually, an XO will fleet up after another command or another assignment in between XO and CO. That limits the pool of candidates.

Cummings feels that the experience cadets get aboard a sailing vessel such as the *Eagle* cannot be replicated aboard other cutters in the fleet:

On EAGLE, they get to know the sea and how it works—how the currents, tides, and the wind affect the vessel you're on. There's no better way to learn it than using the sails to harness that wind and to use the tides to your best advantage. This is the best platform to learn it on, rather than a power boat where you can just say, "Ahead one third." You've got to think ahead, plan things out on this vessel. The goal of the Academy is to develop young men and women to be our future officers, and the EAGLE itself demands teamwork. You can immediately pick out the leaders who are going to be able to get their classmates and underclassmen to sail the vessel and complete the tasks assigned. It's an amazing platform for that. You can just watch them grow and gain both self-esteem and self-respect. They're really great. The cadets nowadays are so much smarter than I ever was. They know so much more. They're just really great people.

Once back from Australia, Cummings returned to his alma mater for his next tour of duty:

I left EAGLE after five years and was stationed at the Academy as the head of the professional studies department. Then, I said, "Help! Let me out of here! I've been here for six years. Send me to Alaska." I went up to Alaska and got a great job as the CO of the largest Coast Guard facility in the world—in Kodiak, Alaska. That was a lot of fun. Went from there to being the chief on the commandant's staff for international affairs. I stayed there about a year and asked to move again. There was a great job coming up with the Armed Forces Inaugural Committee: President Clinton's inauguration. The head of security for the inauguration and all of the events surrounding the inauguration is usually a Coast Guard officer. I asked for that job, and they gave it to me, and my last year I spent over there. After that, I came back to the Academy for a day to retire off the EAGLE, so that was my career. Thirty years in service.

Cummings displays an extraordinary enthusiasm for both the operational Coast Guard and the Academy, and like every officer I interviewed, he finds the transformation that cadets undergo miraculous:

Swab summer is great. I find it amazing you can take this young woman or this young man in at nine o'clock in the morning on Reporting Day, and by four o'clock in the afternoon, they've completely transformed them. They give their parents a little parade, and then they say goodbye. What a transformation—and that's only the beginning of it. You take that young man or young lady in June or July, and look at them again at the end of August, and they're completely different people. The Coast Guard has so many good people—very few that I would speak of without some sort of reverence.

The entire corps of cadets, having returned from their summer assignments, stands ready for the Change of Command and Shoulder Board ceremony.

Moving Up

Sea Trials finishes with a long forced march, swabs still carrying their fully loaded packs at the end of the most punishing day of their lives. This particular summer, some companies must forgo the march due to the arrival of a tremendous lightning storm in the late afternoon. Many swabs welcome this early reprieve; others feel cheated of their final triumph. The storm, in many respects, seems fitting. Just as the tempest on R-Day foretold the tumultuous months ahead, this one cleanses the swabs of the summer's sweat, washing each one's slate clean. At the storm's conclusion, swabs and cadre stand together as shipmates.

It is by now August, and the school year approaches. Cadets who were scattered throughout the fleet for the summer return to the Academy to tell their tales. The campus springs back to life as a thousand cadets bustle about on individual missions. To formally welcome the battle-worn swab-summer survivors into their ranks, a formal ceremony will be held on Washington Parade Field.

The day chosen for the ceremony is beautifully sunny and warm. Parents are welcome, but the Academy does not fuss over this simple transition, and Bear Drive remains largely empty. As I look up the drive toward Chase Hall, a sea of cadets in sharply pressed uniforms swings into view. Swabs have changed noticeably in the two months since their swearing-in ceremony, but the differences between them and the upperclassmen are still striking. The upperclassmen simply stand taller, displaying a confidence and ease the swabs have yet to acquire. Seeming as comfortable in their uniforms as they are in their own skins, they are truly young officers in the making. Like most military ceremonies, this one gets underway to the sounds of martial music. The Coast Guard Band leads the Color Guard onto the parade field, followed by a thousand cadets in shades of blue. They march out onto the field and down its length, arraying themselves by company in front of Hamilton Hall, a sight that would surely impress even the most jaded.

To kick things off, a speech is made, welcoming swabs into the corps as 4th class cadets. The change-of-command ceremony follows, during which regimental command of the corps passes from one firstie to another. Last comes the shoulder-board ceremony, during which swabs receive their first shoulder boards in recognition of their having survived swab summer. These shoulder boards, which are deep blue and feature small shields, must successfully weather a full academic year before they may support their first gold stripes. Traditionally, each cadet chooses a cadre member with whom he feels a connection to attach this new sign

Swabs ask their favorite cadre to award them with their first shoulder boards.

of rank. The entire shoulder-board ceremony is surprisingly simple and quick, almost an afterthought.

When the ceremonies are complete, the corps marches back up Bear Drive and disperses throughout Chase Hall, once again leaving the campus quiet. Cadets spend the next week getting ready for the academic semester. Paperwork is completed, books gathered, and the new cadets leave behind what they thought would be the hardest chapter in their lives. By the end of the first semester, few still give the summer much thought, buried as they are beneath an avalanche of work.

241

Alpha Company in formation on the Washington Parade Field. When the summer ends, academic pursuits quickly assume the primary role in cadet's lives.

Life Beyond

As fall approaches, the heat and humidity of summer fade away and the Academy grounds come to life with cadets scurrying to and from class. Although the newly minted 4th class cadets maintain vestiges of their low status, the campus begins to feel more like the quintessential New England college. The role each class plays within the corps changes with the end of swab summer. Though the 2nd class cadets' role as cadre falls behind, their responsibilities towards the 4th class do not. 2/C Jake Rendon describes his new obligations:

242

When the school year starts, you are still in that leadership role: making sure they're doing their job, making sure their uniform looks good, making sure their respect is still there and they don't forget everything they learned during swab summer. But there's no more yelling, no more making them do pushups and squats. I wouldn't call it friendship, because you are still a mentor, but you can talk to them a little bit: "How is your day going? How's the school year? How are your classes?" We need to be there to talk to them if they need it on a more personal level, but you're still there as a mentor, making sure they're doing their jobs.

The 4th class cadets also assume new roles, as 2/C Ryan Babb notes:

Their job will change completely from swab summer into the 4th class year. They'll be responsible for academics and things like the cleanliness of the wing area. They take out trash, and they do clocks, which is where they stand outside of a clock in the passageway and they yell when formation will be. For example, they would shout, "Sir or ma'am: There are now ten minutes to go until this afternoon's meal formation. This afternoon's meal formation will be held at fair- or foul-weather parade. Uniform for this afternoon's meal formation will be blah, blah, blah . . ." Then, they have to spout indoc. They need to memorize three meals in advance, the movies playing at the Waterford 9 Cinema down the street, the happenings in sports at the Academy, and days to go until important events.

2/C Joseph Trump explains the organization of the corps of cadets, as well as the work he will do with the 4th class cadets he has been assigned:

We have eight companies, and each company is broken into three departments. Each department has a number of divisions. During the school year, each division usually has one firstie, one 2nd class, one or two 3rd class, and one or two 4th class. It's that division's responsibility to make sure that everyone in the division is doing well; they're all supposed to help each other. Most of the focus is on helping the 4th class. The 3rd class in that division are the direct supervisors of the 4th class. First semester, I was lucky; I had probably the best 4th class ever. She didn't need help with anything. Her uniform looked fantastic, her grades were better than mine; I didn't have anything to do. My second-semester 4th class were really great, and I really liked both of them, but they both struggled academically, and one of them struggled a lot with the military aspect, as well. It was my responsibility to see they were getting the academic help they needed, and if they couldn't find it themselves, I was supposed to try to find it for them. As far as the military side of it goes, I would inspect their room probably once every couple of weeks just to make sure everything was good. They were really good at keeping their rooms neat, so that wasn't much of a concern, but I would take a look at their uniforms in formation every day. Even though it wasn't swab summer, it was still something that we expect from them. It's not quite as important as during the summer, but they still need to do it.

The 1st class is in charge of making sure everyone is doing what they are supposed to be doing. Each division has a job they do, and they also make sure that job is taken care of. It's mostly the 3rd and the 4th interacting, because once you get to be a 3rd, it's expected that you can figure out how to get your own help with things. If you really need help, you can go to a 2nd class, but you're expected to be autonomous at that point. 4th aren't really expected to know how to do anything, because they just got here. If a 3rd can't figure out how to help them, he can go up to the 2nd class and say, "I can't figure out how to help my 4th. Can you do anything?" And if they can't, the firstie can, because they have a lot of firstie power. Good firsties are really, really great. I've had fantastic firsties all four semesters. I think it's a really good system, and it works really well to get people help when they need it. The chain-of-command system we have is really good. It also works the other way, as well. If a 4th gets into trouble, then you can try to fix it at the lowest level. They'll say, "I did this wrong. Can you help me?" The 3rd, if it's above them, will go to the 2nd, and so on.

As Trump explains, part of the goal is to help the 4th class cadets keep their heads above water during this their most difficult year:

Once they get through swab summer, we focus on trying to keep as many of them here as we can. Academics are really the main focus. I thought 4th class year was fairly easy, fairly stress-free, because as a 4th class, you have no responsibilities beyond the academics and a little military training. Swab summer is really stressful, but 4th class year is stressful on its own. As upperclassmen, our focus is to try to help them. Swab summer is to help them without them knowing we're helping them, where for the 4th class year, we are supposed to help them. The 3rd class are really supposed to focus as much energy as they can on getting their 4th class to be successful throughout the whole year—and, especially, academically. If your shoes aren't that shiny and your uniform doesn't look all that great but your academics are really, really good, you'll be okay. If your uniform is spectacular and you have the greatest brace in the world and you're an outstanding military cadet and you're failing all of your classes, you're going to get disenrolled. That's the stress I think the school year provides. We take a lot of credits in our 4th class year. I think I took twenty-one credit hours. My girlfriend went to the University of Central Florida, and she took something like ten. The course load by itself is pretty stressful. Swab summer is more of a physical and a psychological stress; the school year is more stressful mentally.

Lieutenant LuAnn Kehlenbach notes that leadership roles and positions constantly change, giving cadets the chance to grow as individuals:

Each class has its own personality, and that personality changes over time, because each year, they have a different mission. The sophomores are being role models, the juniors are being mentors, and seniors are being leaders. You could argue that they're all being leaders, but in that continuum, they each have their own role. As a class, some step up sooner than others. Some are interested in other things; it depends on what they make a priority. I think that could be said of every high-school class and at every institution; there are some personalities that come out. In addition to the formal leadership within the regiment, there are also class presidents, you know, so there are informal leaders within the class, as well.

When asked whether it is up to the officers to bestow leadership roles on the cadets, Kehlenbach replied:

I think it happens both formally and informally. There are those who may have never held a leadership position but are leaders of their peers. There are a lot of opportunities here. On the athletic field, there are team captains. There is also a hierarchy within the corps, so there are leadership positions within the company they apply for, and there is an interview process for those positions. That's across all eight companies. In addition to that, there are the regimental positions, so there are eight 1st class cadets who lead the regiment, and they apply and are interviewed for those positions, also, so it's a little bit of both. Sometimes, you encourage those you know could do it if they applied themselves. Maybe they have no interest in doing it, but that's part of our role as staff—to help mentor them into wanting to seek additional responsibility.

Kehlenbach adds that there are academic leadership roles, as well:

Academically, there is a cadet mentoring program and a peer mentoring program, so there is both formal and informal. Some people are really good at a particular topic, so they will help with that topic, and then there are others who, just within their division, make sure their underclass know who to go to for help, even if it's not them. They may not be good at math, but they know who is, so they can send them to the right person for additional help. The faculty is also available for additional help. They have nightly tutoring sessions they can attend as well, so there is a lot of support. At night, you might go by a study room and find a group of cadets working together. They have to rely on their shipmates not just here but after they graduate. Networking is extremely important, because something might be happening on your cutter that you'd never seen before, but you can reach out to your classmates who are in the same position you are, and maybe they've had that experience, or they've had that collateral duty, so they know what the references are, they know what the memo is supposed to say. It's important they keep those good relationships not only here, but after they leave.

Looking back, 2/C Cathy Durand remembers clearly how difficult her first semester was:

It's tough. My high school prepared me a lot for college in general, but it's still more work than you ever expect when you leave high school—although I feel that may be true for any college. The combination of it being freshman year and being here is a lot, though. The 3rd class year is definitely better. On top of academics, you still have a lot of things that just 4th have to deal with. You're still bracing up, you're still squaring meals, you're still taking out trash, so it's definitely the hardest year here.

I think I had maybe twenty credits my first semester here, so it's a lot. My first semester I had SED, which is an engineering class, history, English, Calc II, a health class, a gym class, chemistry, and chem lab. Everyone has to take chemistry your 4th year, and everyone has to take physics your 3rd year. Everyone has to go through Calc II, even if you're a government major. There are a lot of required classes. I took Calc II in high school, got a five on my AP test, but still didn't pass the validation test over the summer, so I retook Calc II—although seeing it again made it an easier class for me. I hadn't seen chemistry since sophomore year, but I had taken AP Physics in high school, so that helped me a lot this year. Even if you don't get to validate the classes, just having taken them in high school helps a lot. During your sophomore year, you can start to get into your major's classes. I validated Physics I, so second semester, I took Physics II. There were two major classes each semester I took, and each had a lab. First semester, I had government, probability, statistics, and differential equations. Last semester, I had absolutely no humanities courses; it was all math and science.

Although the first academic year is ever arduous, 2/C Jennifer Patron feels that the quality and dedication of the teaching staff ensure that cadets are given every opportunity to succeed:

During swab summer, they force you to go to bed at ten so they can make sure you're rested. It's funny, because I remember the cadre always saying ten o'clock was going to be the earliest bedtime

2/C Joseph Trump

you would ever have, and that was true. I remember staying up late at night working on my chemistry homework. It was difficult, but because of prep school, I had a little more confidence. The good thing, though, academically—and it goes throughout the four

Swab Kochar Mohammad on the deck of *Eagle*.

You still have your support, no matter what phase you're going through. The teachers are both military and civilian, and it's funny, because the civilian teachers only have a glimpse of what you're going through. Some of the officers who teach you know what's going on; they've done it, or they've heard enough about it. It's good though; you get along with all of them, and they're all very helpful. All the teachers here have been phenomenal.

You do get a lot of help from the classes above, too. Within Chase Hall, the cadets' little world, they set up tutor programs, and everyone helps each other if they need it. We set up study groups. Usually, a group of 4th and then one upperclass will help a bunch of them. We're very supportive, because no one wants to see anyone leave, so we do help each other out. Sometimes, it gets very difficult, because the workload for each person is large, but the upperclass can acknowledge and remember how they felt when they first got to the Academy. During my 4th class year, my 3rd was extremely helpful. He helped me out more than I could have asked for. I was very grateful for his help and his attention in making sure he was there for me. The days I would get really frustrated with one of my classes, he was like, "It's okay; it happens to everyone." The fact they can associate with you makes it better. It is very important to have that 4th and upperclass relationship—always being professional but making sure they can relate.

To Patron, support is the key to making it through, whether it comes from peers, teachers, or family. She attributes her own continued motivation to the strong ties she maintains to her parents and her siblings.. The Coast Guard's belief in the importance of family helps:

I think having really strong support, regardless of what phase you are in, is very important. I have my family, and my family is very, very important to me. We all lived in Italy back in 2009, and when I found out I was coming to the Academy after prep school in 2010, my family packed all their things, and they actually came here. That was huge for me, because I wouldn't be where I am without my family. My sister has been a big support; she's always there. She's my friend and my sister. The same with my brother; he's my

years—is that the teachers are very helpful and they are very open. They're not afraid to sit there with you, and if it takes an hour, it takes an hour. That's something I learned in prep school and I took care of almost immediately. I went to see my teachers, and that helped out a lot, but it was still hard. Chemistry, for instance, or calculus—they were still very hard, but the teachers are very open. It's difficult, but you have the support, just like in swab summer.

little motivator. He looks up to me, and I always want to do the right thing for him, my mom, and my dad. My dad helped me a lot, as well. He has gone through the military, too, but he worked his way up and worked very hard to be where he is, and I'm working my way. My mother is the support. She tells me all the little things and details about home. That's what I'm very grateful for, and I wouldn't make it through the Academy without my family. I am very fortunate. They currently live in Newport, Rhode Island, so we're all very close to each other. That's the good thing about the Academy; they always understand family is important. If I route a special and request that I would like to go home and see my family, if there are no military obligations, then there is no reason they will tell me no. They are very supportive. That's been a big thing.

Like nearly every cadet, Patron has times encountered waters so rough that they caused her resolve to waver:

A lot of it is picking yourself back up and getting through it. Each day brings a new challenge. I think the biggest challenge I went through was physics, so it was an academic challenge for me. People have different challenges. That was very hard, because no matter how hard I worked, no matter how hard I studied (and I would spend hours with the teacher), it just didn't sink in. It was very, very frustrating for me. That's when your classmates and your shipmates come in and let you know they're going through it, too. Nonetheless, I was still very angry—all these emotions, like, "Why am I doing this?" That was just last semester. After all I went through with prep school, 4th year and first semester of 3rd year, you would think I'd be okay, but that second semester really got to me. I was like, "I've done everything right so far. How come I'm struggling so much?" So that was very difficult for me, but you have the support and the people who help you, so that really made it better with time. The good news is I'm starting to transition into my government classes. Once you start getting into what you like and what you're interested in, it gets better. I've been pretty happy. There have been days where I think, "Oh, this is hard." For the most part, I'm very happy to wake up in the morning, put on my uniform, and just go along with my day, and there's not a day where

I wish I was doing something else. I don't want to be sleeping in and staying up late and partying. I want to be here. If that means hard work, that's what it means. I think the thing is because it is so difficult, if you want to be here, you'll end up staying here. If you don't want to be here, you'll drop out on your own. It's not because the Academy did it to you; it's something you did or something you didn't work hard enough for. For the most part, if you really want to be here and you really want to work hard, you'll get through. I'm a firm believer of that, because I work hard every day to make sure that I'm ready, working towards graduation and moving on into the fleet.

The cadets I had followed over the summer generally confirm that the first semester proved incredibly challenging. Some students excelled, while others floundered. 4/C Rheanastasia Doctolero found that the cadre's warnings had been right on target:

I'm tired. I sleep a lot less. I think it's harder than swab summer just because of the simple fact that your schedule isn't dictated to you. You don't have a set thing to do every hour, every minute of the day. They do semi-micromanage your time, but not as much as they did during swab summer.

My first semester was good, but I got caught up in helping other people rather than helping myself. I tutor a lot, so I'd be up until two, three in the morning trying to help people study. I kind of pushed myself to the side, although I did well considering I wasn't focused on myself. Even my sponsor mom (she's a lieutenant commander here) said, "Rhea, I saw your grades. Wow! If only you focused on yourself, what could you have gotten? You probably would've had a 4.0!" I was like, "Yeah, yeah, but I like to help people." At my old school, they said I had this motherly instinct; I just want to nurture everybody. I like to help people, but this semester, I learned I have to take time for myself, too. The first semester, that's when you fall into your routine. You stumble a little bit, but I had a pretty good semester. I had navigation, navigation labs, calculus, English, and swimming. I also had chemistry and chem lab. I did not like chemistry at all; chemistry is like the worst class ever. Last semester I tried cheerleading and found I'm not a cheerleader. I faked it. Fake it till you make it! I smiled, I jumped, I cheered around, "Yeah!" but it's not my thing. I thought I could try new things, so I tried cheerleading. I've always done track and cross-country, so next year, I'm definitely doing cross-country. I might try something new in the spring, like soccer, or the rifle team sounds cool. Maybe I'll try the pistol team. I might do those kinds of things.

4/C Jake Carlton breezed through his first semester's academics despite the heavy course load:

I had SE, or Statics and Engineering Design, general chemistry, calculus, my U.S. Coast Guard History class, my Leaders in U.S. History class, chem lab, English, and swimming. I was in "rock swimming," because during swab summer I had the "Chase Hall crud," a nasty cough that passed around a lot during swab summer. I had it during the test, and I couldn't breathe during one lap of the swim, so I had to stop and catch my breath. I said, "Yeah, I've been sick, and I've been coughing up some crap." They said I could retake it a little later, but I never got a chance to retake it, so I got stuck in rock swimming, which I didn't mind once we got into it a little bit more. I realized how much I didn't know about swimming, the actual strokes to use, so I was kind of glad I was in rock swimming and learned how to do it correctly. I tested out of it and went into the normal swimming class and passed that at the end of the semester with an A. We also had a fitness and wellness class, too.

Carlton finished the first semester with a 3.62 grade point average. He earned two stars to wear on his uniform—gold for his academic achievements and silver for his military ones—an impressive feat for any cadet.

4/C Koachar Mohammad also earned a gold star for his first-semester academics while meeting all of his military and athletic obligations. When asked to compare the academic year to swab summer, he said:

I think, in some ways, it was more challenging—academically, definitely frustrating. There are some nights where you don't really get much sleep. I ended up doing actually rather well. I got a gold star. That was pretty hard to do, but I did it. I ended up with a 3.34, but I worked hard. It was difficult, especially with football. There were nights where I didn't start homework until really late. The beginning of the semester was the hardest, getting into the routine. The teachers tell you to do all this, but you know you really don't have to do all this. You have to do some of it, and you have to figure that out for yourself.

4/C Sheila Bertrand preferred the academic semester to swab summer, though she found it more difficult than she had predicted it would be. Like the majority of her peers, she had been a high achiever in high school:

All of the classes at our high school were honor classes, and everyone had to take them. I was in AP Calculus, so that was the highest math class. We had to take Latin from middle school through high school, and I was in a college-credit Latin class, based on the UConn Latin class, so I have a college credit for that. All of my other classes were standard honor classes. For my electives, I had piano, creative writing, and digital photography. For my core classes, I had anatomy and physiology, British literature, Advanced Latin Empire, which was the college course, AP Calculus, and philosophy. I also did sports all year round. It was a public school, but it was a magnet school. Probably 95–100 percent of each grade goes to a four-year college.

What new cadets discover their first academic year is undoubtedly similar to what they would have found at any competitive civilian university: the workload is greater is greater than it was in high school; the pace, more demanding. Bertrand found her first semester very difficult, as she continued to grapple with the adjustment to Academy life:

I actually got put on academic probation. I passed all of my classes except for one, and if you're a 4th and you fail one class or don't pass, you get put on ac-pro. So I'm on that, but it's just one semester. I just need a 2.5 and I'll be off it, so I'm definitely working to get off this semester. It was in calculus. Academics were by far the hardest for me. I feel the people who went to private school or boarding school were most prepared. I went to an inner-city public school. I just felt like there was so much that I had yet to learn, so from the beginning I felt like I was playing a little bit of catch-up, and then, when I got my midterm grades, I felt like I was playing extreme catch-up. I felt like I was running a two-mile race and I was a mile behind. Figuring out how to get help was a struggle for me, in the sense that in high school, everyone came to me for help. I knew how to help people; I just didn't know which method would actually help me. I had to figure out what kind of learner I was. Before, in high school, I could just take some notes and pass the test. Now, I had to figure out if I needed someone to do the work in front of me or if I needed to go through it and do it myself. I wasn't sure if I needed to sit down with someone one-on-one and do it with them, or whether I just needed to sleep and hear it in my headphones. For different subjects, it took different things, and it took a while to figure that out.

Bertrand may have struggled, but help was never far away:

Teachers are incredibly helpful here. The biggest problem, if I didn't understand the teacher I had, was finding another teacher who taught the subject who was also willing to help me. The writing center, the reading center—they're great. They'll help you with your papers—any paper. I had two wonderful teachers: Lieutenant Geyer and Commander St. George. I wouldn't have passed chemistry this year without them. I walked in and pulled off a C+ on the final and brought my grade to a C from an F, just off the one test. I couldn't have done that without them. Like math, I came really close to passing, but I wouldn't have been anywhere near there if it wasn't for Lieutenant Commander Steinhouse. The teachers are amazing. Lieutenant Commander Steinhouse isn't my teacher. She won't be my teacher next semester, and she probably won't ever be my teacher while I'm here, but she stayed after for hours to help me after work, and she has little kids. She has a family, but she would stay after to help me and one of my friends so we could pass our tests. She helped us do the best we could.

Bertrand lays out her punishing academic, military, and athletic schedule, which is typical for 4th class cadets:

Cadets must maintain their physical health throughout the four academic years.

I took Statics and Engineering Design, Calculus I, Chemistry I, Chem Lab, U. S. Coast Guard History, Leaders in U.S. History, and Intro to College Communications, which was an English class. We had 4th class skills development, but that lasted like half a semester. We take swimming and Health and Wellness I. I was a cheerleader in the fall, and I'm playing lacrosse this spring. This semester, I'll take Calc I again, Chem II, Chem II lab, Fundamentals of Navigation, Fundamentals of Navigation lab, Macroeconomics, English, and Speech Composition, I believe it's called.

I get up at five thirty. During school, if I don't have a clock to do in the morning, I can get up at six o'clock if I can change in ten minutes. I get up, and clocks are at 0610. 0620 is formation. We leave breakfast at 0640, and we take out trash from our assigned areas. 0700 to 0800 is the military training period, 0800 to 1600 are class periods, and 1600 to 1800 is for sports. Between 1700 to 1900 is dinner, and 1800 through the rest of the night is yours. Ten o'clock is taps, but you don't need to be in bed by then. During the school year, I wasn't usually getting to bed until 2:00 A.M.; I was up pretty late doing homework and stuff.

4/C Katie Brosnan explains some of the differences between her swab experience and her first semester:

The academic year is a different kind of stress. Before you can become a leader, you have to be a follower, and swab summer is your following period. During the summer, you can just be brain-dead, you know? You just follow orders. When the school year comes around, it's all on you. You have to do it yourself, and you have to be able to think for yourself. You have to have a good attitude. The academic load is so much. It's so much. It's a lot of work, and staying on top of it all is tough. You have to prioritize what's important to you and what can't wait. I found out what was important to me, whereas in high school, I never really had to give anything up. But I like that a lot; I know what's important to me now. If I was ever unsure, I'm not now. I like that. I like finding out that stuff about myself.

I actually got a gold star for academics, so that was pretty good. I was surprised. I was like, "Wow! Cool!" So I get to wear it on my uniform. There's a lot of other awards to be won. You can get gold, silver, blue, and bronze. A gold star is for academics; a silver star is for military performance. I was put up for a silver star, but only 20 percent of your company can get it, so even if you're eligible, you might not get it. A blue star is for physical, so if you score above a 270 on a PFE, you get a blue star; I'm not in the running for that! A bronze star is if you increase your GPA by, I think, .5. That's kind of cool: goals you can work towards. Then, you have your pistol and rifle qualifications. You can get expert on it, or you can be a sharpshooter, and those are real military ribbons. When you become an officer, you still wear them, and that's kind of cool. They give you these opportunities—no time to do them, but they're out there.

Brosnan was unaware of the physical toll her first semester was taking until she got home for Christmas break:

I had winter break, which was three weeks, and it was a really, really relaxing break. The whole time, I had lots of rest, and I saw some friends from high school, which was really good, but I slept a lot. I slept for days, but they say that's normal. I thought something was wrong with me, like I had mono or something. I'd sleep twelve hours, and I'd nap all day. I did get up out of bed sometimes and go see my friends. I had a lot of fun, though. I also saw some of my friends from the Coast Guard; all of us from New York got together and had a nice day.

When asked whether her friends attending traditional colleges understand her new life, Brosnan had this to say:

It was definitely hard to explain to them—just little things in talking to them, I guess. I'll be using dialect or language they don't quite understand, but they don't really say anything. I guess they don't understand some of the stresses involved; like when I say, "Oh, I can't do that, because I'll get bagged," they say, "So?" They don't know what that means. Some of the stresses they can't really wrap their heads around. It's one of those things you have to live to appreciate, so I totally understand why they don't get it right off the bat. I still love them to death, because, you know, I grew up with them. They know a lot about me that some of my Coast Guard friends don't know, and I don't have to explain to them who I am;

they already know. In the Coast Guard, I'm still developing that bond.

After swab summer, you trust your company so much and it's weird, because they don't really know that much about you and you don't really know all that much about them, so it's this weird bond. It's definitely unique. You know they'd do anything for you, and you'd do the same for them in a heartbeat, but we're getting to know each other; I like it a lot.

Brosnan's chats with her friends from home have given her new perspective on the path she has chosen:

I *always ask, "How is real college?" You know how sometimes you doubt the Academy a little bit? "Why am I here? Why am I doing this?" Well, I talked to some of my high school friends, and they seem to be having a good time, but they're a little lost, some of them—not as focused. I know some of the things you do (as a 4th, especially) seem trivial, but then at the end, you know there is a bigger picture. You know at the end of the day you're going to be serving your country and it's going to be worth it. You know, some of my college friends, they don't really have the big picture yet, which is kind of scary. I guess as freshmen, in either a service academy or a regular college, we're still trying to figure things out.*

Wherever Brosnan turns, she finds reassurance that her decision to attend the Academy was the right one:

Our first lieutenant is really good. He gave us this speech, and he said, "You know, we're all in this together. It's the Coast Guard family, and we've got to stick together."—which is really great. I want to be a part of the Coast Guard family. He stressed family and having a lot of pride in what we do. You know, as 4th class, we have to take out the trash, and we have to clean the hallways and all the common spaces. We also have to greet all upperclass when we pass them. I was taking out the trash one day, you know, squaring with the trash bag, and a firstie came by. I said, "Good morning, sir!" He held open the door for me, and I said, "Thank you, sir!" He looked at me, and he said, "Thank you. You're doing a really good thing for your country. I don't know if you know it right now, but you're doing a really good thing." I was like, "Thanks!" It's just little things like that. He didn't need to say that. I'm just 4th class, and he's a firstie. He doesn't even need to speak to me, but just the fact he went out of his way to say that—that's what gives you hope in this place, because there are people who are like that. That means a lot. It's really important.

When one swab forgets his *Running Light*, his entire company learns the consequences of not checking their shipmates before leaving the barracks.

Advice for Incoming Swabs

In the months since swab summer, the students I trailed have had time to reflect on what made their experiences a success. Here is their advice to future cadets.

4/C Kyle Wood believes a rosy outlook makes all the difference:

Keep a positive attitude. Always find the bright side in things, always look at how it's helping you. And if you don't complain about everything, it will go really fast, and you'll end up having fun as you go through it. Just keep a good attitude, no matter what.

4/C Koachar Mohammad recommends keeping a low profile:

No matter how well prepared you are, you're still going to make mistakes. Do what they tell you to do, and try not to ask questions. Don't stick out. I think that's where I had problems; I stuck out. I would ask a question when I had a question. Just don't stick out. If nobody knows what to do, then just copy what everybody else is doing. There were definitely people who were less noticeable than others for whatever reason. Try to lay under the radar; it can be very hard at times.

4/C Sheila Bertrand suggests developing a thick skin:

I took it personally, so I think that's why I had such a rough time. I guess in high school, I wasn't really used to being told, "You're wrong. You're wrong. You're wrong." I had almost perfect grades, I was vice president of my class, I played sports and was captain of three teams. I was never anywhere that I had to fight for my survival. When I came here and they tell you everything you're doing is wrong even when you're right, you take it personally. The key is in just how fast you figure out not to take it personally, and it probably took me five out of the seven weeks to figure it out.

4/C Rheanastasia Doctolero extols the virtues of a firm body and an open mind:

Make sure you're in shape. We have people coming in who didn't do a pushup in their life. They have all the brains in the world, but in swab summer, brains don't get you far. You've got to make sure you work out before you come. Come with an open mind. If you come here with this "I'm going to be the best" mentality or "This place sucks" mentality, it's not going to work. Just keep an open mind. Yeah, you want to be the best, but swab summer isn't about being the best. It's about learning to cooperate and learning to work with people. You really have to be open-minded about everything. You're going to do things you don't want to do, you're going to deal with people you don't want to deal with, and you have to be able to adjust to the situation. If you want to be the best and you're partnered with the worst, you can't just leave him, you know? Come with an open mind, and you'll get through it. Everyone's done it. That's what also got me through: everybody's done it. It's not like I'm doing something foreign or they're putting me through extra punishment.

4/C James Hegge prescribes a dash of levity and a dollop of teamwork:

You can't take everything quite as seriously as the cadre are saying. If you do, it's real easy to just break and not be able to make it. You have to be able to see how this is serious but, also, it's just training. You need to have fun with it. If you don't, it's going to break you. They literally say they will try to break you and send you home. It is their job to get rid of those that should not be here, who are going to slack off and not do what they're supposed to. Honestly, the Coast Guard does not want people who will not take their jobs seriously. When the cadre are yelling at you, they're doing their job. They'll say you are the worst swab in the entire regiment. It may or may not be true, but if you believe it's true, it will get to you, it will break you. One of the easiest things to do is to just work as a team. If you work as an individual, they will literally come down harder on you than they will on anyone else. They don't need individuals; they need people working together as a team.

4/C Frederick Higgins assures future cadets that the key to success is incredibly simple:

Listen to what they're yelling about. Just don't think. Don't take anything personally. It will make sense in the end.

Swabs learn to work together to surmount obstacles placed in their path. Picked for their leadership qualities, many initially find it difficult to follow another's lead.

Change

Swab summer is, of course, a learning process for swabs and cadre alike. Less obvious is that it is a learning process for the Coast Guard Academy as well. As any institution should, the Academy scrutinizes the effectiveness of the summer training, seeking to better its performance in the future. When cadre are given their first real leadership role during the summer, individual performance varies considerably. Many falter for a short period as they learn to handle their new responsibilities, but most quickly adapt, taking on more nuanced leadership postures as the weeks progress. Some, however, never manage to settle; even worse, a few seem to channel Captain Bligh. These latter leadership choices are not optimal, and officers who currently oversee the summer process hope to improve it. Commander Jeffrey Haukom recalls that during his boot-camp experience at Officer Candidate School, officers yelled at him ceaselessly—but only up to a point:

I could always sense there was someone looking at me, and if I so much as bent my head the wrong way, I was going to get yelled at. It was the initial shock and awe, but you start picking it up, you start learning the rules. At OCS, I noticed the volume was dropping. I no longer felt I was surrounded by six officers all trying to find my deficiencies. I got that sense: "Okay, I must be doing something right here." They gave us more autonomy; we started having more leadership roles. It's a bit like apples and oranges, though, when you start comparing OCS and swabs. A good part of my class were already senior enlisted people who had been in the Coast Guard for ten years, so this isn't really apples to apples, but I think the philosophy merits some consideration, and that is something we're looking at this off-season. I've had this conversation with the commandant of cadets, who had this conversation with the superintendent, and we are all looking toward improving a process that I think already works quite well. But I do think there is room for improvement, and that will, perhaps, yield not only a better training environment for the swabs but for the cadre, as well.

The training that recruits receive at OCS is conducted by experienced personnel, who generally know when to ease up and allow trainees to have more autonomy. Members of the cadre, however, are more likely to forget their mission, become overzealous, or attempt to solve every problem with incentive training. Although cadre have many tools at their disposal, the hammer may seem the simplest to wield. Haukom believes that the key to improving cadre performance lies within the core value of respect:

I think we're in a better position, given our size in relation to the other service academies, to really focus more on the individual. That's one of the things we constantly remind our cadre: "Yes, they're swabs, and yes, we have to transform civilians into mili-tary members, but they're also someone's son and daughter and brother and sister." We are going to get them to do what we want them to do, and it's not always going to be pleasant for them, but we are going to treat them with respect. There will be no hazing, and we're not ever going to put their safety in jeopardy of any kind. We have a layered defense against that ever happening. We have people watching the cadre, and then people watching them, and so we've been successful in that regard. Once the swabs make it through and now they're 4th class cadets, then our challenge is to treat them as such and foster their development so they maintain that interest and desire, which can be difficult to maintain when you're saddled with a full academic load. This is their first college semester, and the classes are hard. A lot of these people in high school were the top dog; things came easily to them. They were in the top 5 percent of their class. Not only is it the next level of academic work here, but there is more. They also have military training and athletics and all this other stuff, so it's a whole new challenge for them. Our challenge is to keep them on track and keep them motivated, which is why I love to debrief the 3rd class cadets after their first operational summer. For so many of them, that summer is just "Boom!" They get out there, and they get the salt air in their face, and they remember why it is they joined. They redouble their efforts to excel.

Haukom is happy with the summer's outcome. Still, he wishes to straighten those sections of track that threaten derailment:

I am very happy with their performance and the final product. That said, we are actually putting together a working group to analyze the overall strategy of swab development. We actually sent some people to West Point to see how they do it. We are looking at cadre who are still hoarse by the end of the summer and the swabs who are still getting yelled at during the last week. Maybe there is a valid reason for both, but what we're going to look at is going into the swab-summer process with a developmental strategy in mind that might suggest: "We know we are doing our job as cadre because the swabs are doing their job as swabs if the volume goes down over time, if we're not yelling as much." Because, if you think about it, you probably shouldn't have to be yelling as much. The initial week, two weeks, there's going to be a lot of yelling. It's going to be loud, and I think that's fine. The mission is to take these civilian teenagers and turn them into members of the military.

As an officer candidate, I remember being scared to death, which is good. Fear is a great motivator, and it taught me that military tenant: you don't question orders. You're given an order, you carry it out. You don't make excuses; you do it. You certainly don't question it, and that's a difficult thing for some civilians, particularly some young teenage civilians, to grasp. They need that in-your-face: "Oh, you're gonna do it, or you're going to be doing a lot of pushups. We're going to make you want to do it." So I think these guys and gals have done a fantastic job accomplishing their mission, instilling that initial indoctrination sense of urgency while doing it safely without crossing that line. They've been able to indoctrinate the swabs and turn them into military members in a safe fashion. So is there room for improvement? That's where I think we need to look. If the swabs are accomplishing their mission, coming together as a team, learning what they need to learn, and becoming military members, maybe we should start giving them a little bit of responsibility—if not responsibility, at least the reward of not being yelled at on each and every turn. I think the philosophy merits some consideration, and that is something we're looking at this off-season.

I think it goes back to learning styles. We've certainly got empirical data that suggests people learn differently. Some people need to be kept on top of, and some people just shut down under this pressure. That's what we're going to analyze this off-season. What's that happy medium? Certainly, we're still going to use shock and awe initially, but we're going to need to look for opportunities to back off, and that's where we will make that transition, allowing the swabs to feel that sense of accomplishment: "Hey, we are coming together as a team. We are doing something right. They're not yelling at us as much!" I think that's going to be effective for most of them, if not all of them. I hope we will see an exponential increase in morale and, then, performance.

There are many people who just start to tune out with constant yelling, but when you show them that respect, that "You've been here a while, we've yelled at you, you've shown some improvement; now, I'm going to speak to you like a human being, but you're still going to carry it out," I just think it's going to speed the development of both the swab and the cadre. I think the cadre are going to realize they don't have to be jerks. They can feel like they've done a pretty good job when they see the results. That's what we are going to focus heavily on in this off-season, and then, it will be a matter of introducing it to the next group of cadre during 100th Week. We've already got some ideas about how we might insert this training and what we might look at doing to get the message to them. This isn't your father's cadre experience anymore. This isn't even the one you saw. And if you find you are still yelling during the last week of the summer until you're hoarse, you might have to stop and ask, "What are we doing wrong?"

Despite periodically having to deal with cadets who do not make the grade, Haukom clearly loves his work at the Academy:

I wanted to come back here to be the cadet training officer because I really loved working with cadets. There's just something about working with these extremely talented, intelligent, and motivated young people—taking them from high-performing high-school graduates. But let's be clear: they're teenagers still, and they look and act like teenagers in many ways, but in just a short four-year process, turn them into military officers performing at a high level. Before you know it, they're qualified to stand a bridge watch and they're making decisions. It's just amazing to see that transformation. The position I'm in now is unique and rewarding for me, because a lot of the people I'm working with now who are on staff here as lieutenants were my students when they were cadets and I was a lieutenant. So it's great when they come back now and I get to hear all their experiences. It's very rewarding to see the fruits of your labor in the flesh. I love it here.

By one semester into this particular school year, the idea that change might be coming to the swab-summer experience had already filtered down through the ranks to the 4th class students. I found their reactions surprising. Most considered the thought of changing swab summer heretical. Despite the many difficulties and criticisms they had when immersed in the process themselves, once it was over, they saw little need for improvement. Were they suffering from Stockholm syndrome, or did they think it only fair that future swabs suffer as they had? In my mind, these remain open questions.

Mistakes made by cadre can be seen as part of the learning process. After all, few people take up the reins of command without stumbling under their sudden pull. Of broader importance, though, is what they learn from the experience and how they strive to improve in the future. It was clear to me by the end of the summer that both swabs and cadre were able to learn from good and bad experiences, with relatively few exceptions.

There is no doubt that the boot-camp experience creates bonds not easily broken, nor that the obstacles swabs must overcome make them stronger. 4/C Kyle Wood was as enthusiastic at the end of the summer as he was at the start:

I came in knowing what was going to happen, and I really didn't find anything surprising, so I just kept a good attitude, and it helped me, I'm sure. It was good. I'd say the hardest part of the summer was just being away from my family and not being able to talk to them. I guess that's why they do it. Because of that, you lean on your shipmates and all your other classmates, and you grow stronger with them, and that helps build teamwork, so it was good.

I enjoyed meeting everybody and growing closer to all of my classmates, and just knowing that I got through the summer with them was pretty big. I think the summer was very effective. I think we learned teamwork in working with all types of people, no matter where they came from, what their background was, or what they were like. We learned to get along and accomplished a lot. I think that helped us and will help us throughout our Coast Guard careers. The summer pushes you a lot, and you learn what you can push yourself to do. You learn you can do a lot more than you think you can.

There were many swabs who seemed enjoy the summer thoroughly. 4/C Scooter Finney remembers only one point at which he lost patience with the process:

I think I went into it with the correct mentality. I feel like I didn't take most of it personally, or any of it. I only remember one specific time when it really, mentally, got to me. I was really upset. That was one dinner where we had somebody that was on the summer regimental staff sitting with us. We were eating burritos, and you can't look at your food, of course, and you have to take small bites, and the whole time she was just pestering us. I couldn't eat, and it was spilling all over me, and, I don't know, it just got to me. I got really irritated. I got really frustrated, and at that point, I just left. I didn't even finish my food. I was just mad. I don't know why, but it just got to me. Other than that, I maintained a pretty stable, happy attitude the entire time. A lot of it was fun. I would honestly say that I had a good time during swab summer. It was easier than the school year. In whole, I enjoyed it; there was a lot of cool stuff that we got to do.

Finney likens portions of the indoctrination process to a game, albeit one with quite serious objectives:

I would say that any boot-camp program is a game, in the sense that your superiors essentially mess with you. You can't do anything right, and for the most part, you're not granted any compliments. The aim is to make you more humble, show you that you have a lot to learn, which I think it did. But then, the summer is over, and you see how the cadre are really just normal people. They had to fill that role over the summer, so in many senses, it's a game. They did yell at us a lot, but in some regards, it was all for show, because their objective was to make us understand what the Coast Guard does and make us conform to the military lifestyle. There were times when they weren't yelling at us; they were just speaking to us plainly, explaining why we were here and why it was important. They would ask us why we wanted to be here, what we were doing here. There were times when they facilitated our reflection on what we wanted out of it all, and that was helpful, too; they weren't always yelling at us. It was funny: The other day, we

*were talking to one of the chaplains, and I said, "It's just a game."
He said, "No, it's not a game. It's honor, respect, and devotion to
duty." That was the first time I thought about that aspect. I swore
to defend the Constitution of the United States. That's a big deal.*

Finney very much enjoyed the summer, though he missed certain
freedoms:

*It had to be the fact that I couldn't do what I wanted—in the sense
that it was nice and sunny outside, and I had a river and an ocean
and a forest around me, and yet I had to march around and wear a
shirt and wear shoes and get haircuts—so, I guess, the conformity
aspect of it all, the fact that I couldn't be free. I would describe
myself as a free spirit, and I had to conform to military life, so that
was hard, but going through it all, wearing uniforms and things
like that, I've realized how little a part of myself clothing is, or
hair. It's not that big of a deal. It's not me; it just isn't.*

Despite these few issues, Finney never once doubted his decision
to join the Coast Guard:

*Never. There wasn't a point where I thought of quitting. There
wasn't a point where I regretted my decision to come, and, as I said
before, the concern I had was whether or not I'd be able to make
it. The day before R-Day, somebody said it would be the hardest
thing I'd ever have to do. So that's when I really thought how hard
it could be, and I would say it wasn't that bad. It could have been
harder. It could have been physically harder, and they could have
been outright verbally abusive, which they weren't allowed to do,
so I'd say every aspect of it could have been more intense.*

Some five months later, he still appreciations the summer's value:

*I would say, as a whole, it definitely did a lot for me. I think one
of the biggest things was making you go through the transition
from civilian to military life. In that regard, I think it was very effective. Everything was extremely regimented, and everything was
extremely easy to mess up. Going into the school year, things relax
a lot more, so in that sense, it was very helpful with all the random military stuff: waking up, squaring corners, eating, and such.
Now, people don't yell at you, so it's easier now in that sense, and*

*it showed us how to do things very quickly and efficiently, which is
something I think I could be a lot better at. I think everyone could
be better at that, but it showed us the ways in which you can utilize
time, and it showed us that it was necessary.*

4/C Koachar Mohammad admits that he had many doubts throughout the summer months, yet he emerged confident that he and his
shipmates had made great strides toward cooperating effectively:

*I think we definitely improved. I wouldn't say that we did it to per-
fection, but we did very well—extremely well when compared to
the beginning. In the beginning, we tried to act like a company, but
there were small things. For example, they would make somebody
exercise, IT them basically, and everybody else just stood there
studying their RUNNING LIGHT. At some point, they said, "Everybody get down with him." We had just let him do the work all by
himself. By the fourth or fifth week, as soon as they IT'd somebody,
everybody would be down there with them without being told, because we were taking it on as a team. I think the challenges we had
during the summer—like the teamwork courses, the teambuilding
exercises—I think they definitely helped. We needed to involve the
whole group, and if there was one person dragging behind, we
needed to help him. It needed a team effort, and if not, we'd end
up basically not succeeding. Everybody had their own strengths;
where one person would be lagging, in the next area, he could be
succeeding and helping others. The attitude was that everybody
really wanted to work together to get through it. Everybody had a
cooperative attitude.*

On several occasions, Mohammad even toyed with the idea of
quitting, though the thought was never more than a fleeting indul-
gence:

*During the first week, I thought about quitting, but I never really
thought about actually going through with it. I went to speak with
the chaplain once to tell her how I felt. Basically, I was having a
really tough time. I spoke with her, and she told me, "Well, you
have to decide. Is this something you want to do? Is this something
you're willing to put up with so that you can become an officer?"
After that, I realized how much I wanted to do it, but almost ev-*

ery day, you think, "I don't deserve this. Why am I here? I'm a normal person. What makes them better than me?" Before I knew it, however, the days just went by, and seven or eight weeks had been done, and swab summer was over. During the summer, they tell you not to take it personally. Even before I came here, people told me, "Never take it personally," but something about it really makes you want to take it personally. Now that it's over, of course, I hold no grudges, but at the time, emotions made it mentally challenging. I definitely let my emotions get in the way sometimes. Sometimes, you think you might be doing something right, or even if you are doing something right, they say you're wrong. If they say you're wrong, then you're wrong. You can get pretty emotional; it can make you pretty upset. I've talked to recruits that want to come here, and they've asked me about it. I tell them how it is and give them the best tips that I can, but I always tell them, "I can't really tell you how it is. Until you go through it, you can't really understand."

Mohammad does not necessarily feel that the summer prepared him for the academic year, per se; nonetheless, he is adamant that the experience was vital:

I realized, ironically, that it develops character and it develops an appreciation. I don't think you can get the values of honor, respect, and devotion to duty without swab summer. Before I came here, I was telling everybody, "Oh yeah. Honor, respect, and devotion to duty. They don't have to do all that. They can just tell us to follow these values." But honestly, without this training, how many people would still cheat, how many people would still steal, and how many people would be deceitful? I definitely think it taught us a lot. I don't think it prepared me for academics at the Academy, because it didn't have anything to do with academics, but it had everything to do with the military and what the Coast Guard stands for.

Despite any difficulties, Mohammad feels good about his decision to tough it out for the future:

I think I made the right decision, although sometimes it's really tough. Like right now, especially, coming back from break, it's like, "Oh, why did I come back?" It's definitely hard. The academic

Swab Katie Brosnan

semesters are very difficult. All you want to do is sleep sometimes, and you can't do that. When the weekends come around, you're like a zombie. The first year is the hardest—that's what they say. They say the academics get harder, but 4th class academics are hard alone, plus you have all these other duties. You still can't look around, you can't look at your food—it just makes this place more difficult. What's coming around in the future should be better.

4/C Katie Brosnan summed up the single biggest takeaway from swab summer in one word:

Teamwork. I think they wanted me to learn that I can't go through this whole Coast Guard thing by myself, I can't do it alone, and I think they also wanted me to step back and evaluate what's important to me. Obviously, I think they wanted me to get fit and learn to work as a team. I think that's part of it—and also, to learn how people see you. The point isn't to run the fastest. For me, it wasn't, anyway. It was like, "Great. You can run that fast, but do you turn around and go back for the slowest person?"

259

Throughout the summer, Brosnan had looked forward to its end. But at the conclusion of the last day, she found herself ambivalent about what lay in store:

I remember when swab summer was secured, when it was over. They had us all in the quad, and they said, "Swab summer is secured!" and everyone was so happy. But I was thinking it was kind of funny: over swab summer, you don't actually think. The cadre do the thinking for you, and you just have to follow directions. Your brain just stops working. For me, that was definitely scary, and I noticed that happening. When the school year started up, I was like, "Oh, shoot! Now, it's all on me! Now, I have to be the one. Can I get to class on time?" Obviously, you get to where you need to go, but now, you can't get into trouble, because now, it's not just "Drop and give me ten!" Now, you're going to get punished for it, and if you rack up enough class I, class II, and class III demerits, you get kicked out, you know? So when swab summer was secured,

I was like, "Oh, shoot. Now it really starts." But then, I'm sure when I graduate I'll be like, "Oh, shoot. Now, it really starts!"

Five months later, no ambivalence remains:

I definitely feel good about my decision to come here. Even on my lowest days here, when I'm feeling just horrible, I know that I want to be in the Coast Guard. That definitely does help. It's not over yet, obviously. I'm just going to keep trucking through, I guess. I haven't even had my 3rd class summer yet, so I'm excited about that. I've met a lot of good people, and I've found out a lot about myself, which I don't think I would have had I gone to a civilian college. I found out what's important to me. I like it here. People are good. I know it's something I want to do—finish it, you know? I definitely have a lot more respect for servicemen and -women and what they have to go through.

While swabs often feel the summer will never end, it is just a short hike on the long road ahead of them. In two years' time, they will stand as cadre in front of new recruits.

The Coast Guard Officer

The ultimate goal the Academy holds before each cadet is for him or her to become a leader of character. Swab summer only marks the first small step along that path. Even after four challenging years, graduates are still nearer the beginning of their journey than the end, and the best officers retain a commitment to continual personal growth throughout their careers. The process is both demanding and competitive, and those who fail to achieve find themselves quickly left behind. To understand the immensity of the challenge that officers face, just consider the tiny fraction of women and men who manage to earn their captain's bars. There

Swabs learn many new ways to strengthen their arms over the summer.

are nearly 50,000 people in the Coast Guard, yet only about 400 active-duty officers hold the rank of captain—fewer than 1 percent.

So what qualities go into the making of a stellar Coast Guard officer? Although nothing so complex can be reduced to a simple checklist, the answers given by Coast Guard personnel are enlightening. Most interestingly, the longer an officer has served in the Coast Guard, the more likely his response to this question will align with the responses given by his or her colleagues. Put more simply, as officers' careers progress, they tend to reach the same conclusion about what makes a great leader. The irony is that swabs are given the answer on their very first day. But filled as they are with youthful enthusiasm, they do not yet see the ocean for the waves. As long as swabs focus their attention on each individual comber threatening to swamp them, they miss the overall pattern governing the ocean's surface. The formal and experiential training they are to receive over the course of their careers will eventually bring clarity. Wisdom, it seems, really does come with age.

Students entering the Academy come for a host of reasons. Common to all is their desire to serve, their vision of a greater good, and their capacity to see beyond themselves. That these are their motivations is most refreshing to hear, especially in a world where the rich and famous are revered for their financial status rather than for their depth of character. Although all swabs clearly articulate their desire to be part of something larger than themselves, most have given significantly less thought to the qualities that officers should possess. Many of their visions of an officer have been ripped straight from the silver screen: a tall, steely-eyed, cool-as-a-cucumber leader whose troops will gladly follow her to hell and back. I asked a number of swabs before R-Day what qualities an officer should possess. What follows is a smattering of their responses:

I think staying calm under pressure.

Tactfulness and having people understand that you're in charge. Intelligence, experience, and also being able to listen to those who know more than you so that you won't necessarily make the same mistakes.

Mental and physical toughness.

I think they would also have to be pretty quick. There are situations where you'll have to be able to think quickly. You can't stall; that could cost a life—yours or someone else's. There are consequences for hesitance. You have to be quick on your feet.

Someone who doesn't collapse under stress, knows what they are doing, and is smart enough to do it in the situations that come up.

Someone who can get the enlisted below them to do what needs to be done. They have to be smart and well-liked. Probably calm, and not likely to freak out when things happen.

They either need to be a charismatic leader or lead by example. They need to show their men that they are ready to do what needs to be done—not just put them in harm's way and say, "You need to do this," and then just sit back and watch.

I think you have to be a leader, but a leader from behind who is pushing everyone to the front, versus a leader from the front yelling at everyone behind.

They have to live by the rules they are yelling at other people to follow. They have to live by those exact rules, and if they're not, they're being hypocritical. They have to be very smart in what they say to other people and be able to motivate people, versus leaving those people that may be behind, behind.

I definitely have to say keeping an open mind. You can't just say, "My way or the highway." You have a lot to learn from other people, and I think that's very important. Being able to listen to other people is big, respecting everyone's differences.

As cadets mature, they develop more nuanced conceptions of what makes an officer great. By the time they are cadre, they may retain some of their earlier beliefs, but training at the Academy has them thinking along additional lines. Core values begin to appear in their thinking. 2/C Evan Rothfeld:

Having those core values and internalizing them—honor, respect, and devotion to duty—that's the key part. But it's going beyond the "Let's get through this place." It's trying to perfect everything. I think that's what it comes down to: try to be the best. If you're taking an engineering class, try to be the best in that engineering class; try to get an A+. If you're doing something physical, try to be the best in that. I think Coast Guard officers need to be perfect, not just average.

1/C Breanna Hite, in her last year at the Academy, realizes that there is no one formula. Yet she sees adaptability and respect for others as having primary importance:

I don't think there are a set list of things that make you a perfect leader, but I think one thing that's really important is to know who you are leading and how different people respond in different ways to leadership. You can't lead everybody the same way. I think that's a very important quality: to be observant and see how you might change your leadership style for different people you're leading. I think in order to be respected as a leader, you have to respect your followers and be open to feedback and to change. Somebody once

told me, "In order to be a good leader, you first must be a good follower," and I definitely agree with that. I don't think everyone is born a leader. Maybe not everyone has had past leadership experiences when they report in on R-Day, but I think you become a leader while you're here. You definitely receive opportunities for higher leadership here. I don't know that everybody who graduates is ready for what's out there, but I think they will quickly become ready once they're in the real fleet. I'm not there yet, but I think if they don't make the cut in the fleet, it won't go much further than that.

At the top of the cadet chain of command, 1/C Andrew Ray stresses the value in being personable and approachable:

Personable. I think no matter what position you hold, from an ensign with a division of ten and three collateral duties to a CO in charge of an entire cutter, you need to actually take the time to meet and know your people. Being personable gets you so much farther. Everyone talks about being squared away, and time management is enormous. Being able to manage your time, knowing what your responsibilities are, getting your work done in a timely way is huge. When things get behind, they just start to pile up. That's the real world.

Approachable. As friendly as you are, however, you still have to be ready to lay the law down, be ready to discipline. You need to walk that fine line where you're approachable, personable, friendly to everyone, whether they are a seaman or an XO, but when the time comes and things get serious, be able to lay the law down. There's a book out there written by a retired navy captain called IT'S YOUR SHIP, a phenomenal book. It talks about his leadership style and how he took command of a boat and transformed that boat into the highest-performing boat in the Pacific Ocean. There's a chapter called "Look for Results, Not Salutes." That's what I think it's all about. You don't want people to respect you just based on your bars, what you have on your shoulder.

Ensign Collin Shembry, who only recently graduated, learned as much about being an officer during his summers afloat as he did at the Academy:

I think at the beginning, I didn't have any idea or concept of what a good officer should be. That just wasn't what I was concerned with; I was focused on being a good swab or being a good 4th class. In your 4th class year, they start training you to assume the next responsibility. How are you going to be a good 3rd class? So you started preparing for that. As a 3rd class, you start saying, "Hey, how am I going to be a good cadre?" It's during the 2nd and 1st class years they start saying, "These are the traits of good officers. This is how an officer should be." This is where they really start training you for that. A lot of it comes from the examples and experience. If you've ever been micromanaged, you know it's ineffective and it just makes you angry.

The summers out in the fleet are where we gain a lot of experience. I've been on three cutters out there. The VIGOROUS: got to see good things out of the ensigns and a really great commanding officer who ended up coming here for OCS. I think he just became a captain and left for somewhere else. I was on the WALNUT in Hawaii and the BERTHOLF, which I took from Hawaii to San Francisco, so I got to see a whole bunch of different leadership styles, like the ops officer on the WALNUT who said, "I am placing full trust in you until you prove to me you're not deserving. As long as you do your job and you're forthcoming and honest, I will continue to trust you, and we'll have a good relationship. But if you lie to me or try to hide something, that trust goes away, and your life will get harder." While that seems like a bold stand in the beginning, it is very reasonable and makes a lot of sense. Moving over to one of the other cutters, the XO would see something he didn't like and just walk right by you, not saying anything. Maybe that was just a rank thing. Maybe he felt as the XO, he didn't have to be the one coming down on every little nitpicky detail. But I feel if you walk by something and you see that it's not right, it's pretty easy to just say, "Hey, you need to be wearing the OD blouse on top of your shirt." It's like, "Aye aye, sir! Got it." Delegating it out and hearing about it three days later seems a bit crazy. It bred a very weird command climate and a lot of unhappy folk on board that cutter.

Merle Smith, who in 1966 became the first African American to graduate from the Academy, feels that two key attributes are flexibility and perseverance:

I think a lot of it is fortitude. You don't give up. They train you to be able to do anything, and the expectation is that whatever they throw at you, you can handle. It doesn't matter what your specialty was, and so I think they still put people out who have all of those character traits. I think that's what the Coast Guard is really about: to train people where they can throw anything at them. They're smart enough, they're tough enough, they'll do it. We have so many different functions we perform. You don't hear anybody say, "I was never trained for that." I have a bumper sticker on the back of my car that says, "U.S. Coast Guard. Been there, done that."

Captain Bryan Finch, the Academy's chaplain, was long an officer in the Navy. He has seen firsthand what it takes to be an officer in both Services. Like Smith, he sees elasticity as the hallmark of a Coast Guard officer:

Coast Guard officers who are truly great are those who can keep themselves focused on the mission and, at the same time, be multitasked to do various other functions, as well. The Coast Guard is about the size of the New York Police Department; the bench is not very deep, so they must be Semper Gumby, always flexible, in everything they do. They must have the ability to take on different types of roles quickly, without a lot of time for protracted training modules. It's not like the Air Force or some of the other services. They have to respond, and their underway time is every day, every hour, and every minute. They face emergencies. Life is not static; life is dynamic, and so they have to be as well. Their challenges are phenomenal, as are their abilities to move into different theaters, whether its overseas operations, icebreaking, or whatever. A good Coast Guard officer keeps full focus on the mission. I think those who have been able to do that and keep that focus have been the most successful. They're also such good humanitarians. They're very understanding and far more compassionate than a lot of the other military branches. I had a colonel in the Marine Corps tell me one time, "You know, I wanted my daughter to go the Coast

Guard Academy because it takes more to save a life than it does sometimes to take it away." He was very proud that his daughter came to the Coast Guard.

I think with the Coast Guard, they love the Service, and I think that's one reason they have the high retention level they do. They love their mission. It's not the Navy; it will never be the Navy, and the Navy can never be them. There is some overlap, but the Coast Guard does what it does the best, and it does it 24/7. Another thing the Coast Guard does is power down to the most junior person on the deck and give them tons of responsibilities, tons of duties, tons of chances to excel, which I think is just phenomenal. The Navy is so hierarchical and so structured that this doesn't happen. In the Coast Guard, they step up; they start taking on leadership roles even as cadets. They don't sit around and wait for some $2.25 rank epaulets to tell them they're in charge; they just grab the reins, and they go for it.

Each day you wake up, you can go and make a difference—maybe in a family's life, maybe assisting a community, maybe in a country's interaction—maybe you can make a difference. You don't know how that package is going to come around; you just know you've got to be there to make that difference, and I think that is what gets them up in the morning and keeps them going. It gives them the excitement and the desire to stay the course, because they see they're making a difference. I don't know what we'd do without them, from the draught-stricken Mississippi to Somalia with its pirates to wherever in the world you chose to go, they're making some kind of impact, and that's really phenomenal. It's a comforting thought that something's working.

USCG Motor Life Boat 47274 heading back to her berth in Point Judith, RI.

Dr. Erik Wingrove-Haugland believes in the ultimate importance of just a few key traits:

It's hard to pick out the most important characteristics for a Coast Guard officer, and, naturally, I lean towards the ones that I'm working on: honesty and integrity. These are really crucial things. I'd like it for those things to be taken as a baseline, as a given. After that, I would probably say: the willingness to question yourself, *the willingness to always be asking, "Am I doing the right thing?" Like with the cadre: "I'm yelling. How's that working? Why isn't it working better? What else can I do that might be more effective?" The Coast Guard's missions are much more nebulous than the standard missions of the Department of Defense. The combat mission is certainly complicated but relatively straightforward. Our missions have much more judgment involved in carrying them*

265

Over a thousand officers in the making head back to Chase Hall after the Change of Command ceremony officially ends the summer's work.

out successfully. Even the definition of what makes it successful: clear in some cases, such as search and rescue; but in ship inspections, law enforcement, marine environmental safety, it's much more qualitative than quantitative, so the willingness to always be questioning themselves is a crucial skill for a Coast Guard officer. Our missions evolve, and so we need Coast Guard officers to be able to evolve, and if they can be constantly questioning themselves, be asking, "How can I be doing this better?" then regardless of the mission, regardless of the expectations, they're going to be more successful. I think with military officers, especially with the amount of authority that military officers get, where they get into trouble is when they start to have the attitude that they know everything, not questioning that their way is the way. They should

periodically question themselves and even have doubts. They don't necessarily have to do it publicly by expressing doubts about themselves to others, but it's important to have them.

Lieutenant Greg Batchelder concedes that the Academy cannot possibly teach everything it takes to be an officer in the little time it has each cadet. Rather, most practical knowledge must be picked up in the fleet. According to Batchelder, the Academy must impart one lesson in particular:

The most important thing they learn here is how to take care of other people. The competence, the specialty, whether they're going to sector, afloat, or flight school, they're going to learn after they leave here. Yes, it helps to have some background and some idea of what you're getting into, but one thing is the same up front: you're going to have people working for you. You could be the most competent ship-driver 1ˢᵗ class cadet leaving here ever, and if you can't manage people and take care of them, you're going to fail. You may think you know everything now, and you may know everything they've taught you—you have a 4.0, and you've aced everything—but as soon as you get out there, you are going to find there are things you don't know. You need your chief, you need your BM1, even your non-rates. In helicopter operations, for example, where are those glow sticks you have to have on board at night—even if you knew everything about helicopter operations and how to run them, if you didn't know where those glow sticks were, you couldn't run those operations. The newest non-rate is probably the one who knows where they are, because he was the one asked to put them away.

If you can't take care of those people, then they're not going to take care of you, and I think that's what I try to teach them. Some people get it, and some people have a chip on their shoulder: "I'm going to be an officer. They work for me." Well, that's the wrong attitude. They need to learn how to take care of people. They have to take care of their needs at work, for their development, their advancements, their promotions, getting them to where they want to go professionally, and they've got to take care of their home life. If they work twenty-four hours a day and have a terrible home life, it's going to show up at work. People will be coming to them. Knowing how to manage those expectations and lead those people is the first step to becoming successful. If you take care of them and their needs, and you're totally incompetent in your job, they will teach you and train you and get you to where you should be. But if you can't take care of them, they're not going to help you out at all. Getting cadets to understand that is a giant task.

Many officers cite experience as the best teacher when it comes to defining their own command styles. Lieutenant James Bendle draws inspiration from the best of the officers under whom he has served:

Humility is what I like to talk about, and I talk about that a lot. A good officer is a very humble officer. You know, if you're good, people know it pretty quickly. You don't need to beat your chest and say, "I'm the best." The best officers I've served with have been incredibly humble. They did all the right things. Following doctrine and policy is something I always bring the students back to, and I often talk about how important that is.

At the core of a successful officer, Commander Haukom sees character above all else. As nearly every officer mentioned, without integrity, nothing else matters:

I guess we provide the foundation of basic military skills and character development. We need to ensure when cadets walk across that stage and receive their diploma and their commission, preparing to head out to their first operational unit, we're confident in their core values—their honor, their respect, and their devotion to duty. We've worked with them now for four years, and we are confident they have that solid, core-values foundation. They've got the character and the basic building blocks of leadership to go out and do good things. A few years back, there was a popular term floating around these passageways: the "service-ready ensign." That meant different things to different people. Some people took it literally as "They are ready"—as soon as they cross that stage, send them to that Coast Guard cutter and give them the mid-watch. That's not going to happen. We don't have the time here to give them a bachelor of science degree, ensure their athletic, physical, and spiritual development, while honing all of their character, leadership, core-values development, and their professional skills to the point where they are going to walk on board, meet the captain, and stand a watch. You can't do it. By definition, the captain has to gain faith and confidence in them, and that's going to take a little bit of time right there, but we can provide the basic foundations of character and leader development. The core values are there.

We bring in professors, officers, coaches, nautical science instructors, and chaplains, and everybody comes together as a team to

267

ensure a cadet is well-rounded, holistic, steeped in the basic tenants of our core values, that they've got those fundamental building blocks of character and leadership and they've got the basic military skills. They've successfully completed the four nautical science courses, they've successfully completed at least sixteen weeks of operational training at Coast Guard units, they've passed the rules-of-the-road test. We look at these things, we check them off, and that is what makes me confident in delivering an ensign to a unit and saying, "This is your new apprentice leader. They excelled here, they studied here. They've got the basic skills to begin breaking in, standing a watch. We feel they are going to succeed in standing that watch, because we are confident they have met all the requirements of a break-in leader. They've demonstrated they've got the character and leadership traits to step on board and perform well. They have the foundation on which to build. We can attest to their basic core values right now, and they're only going to get better."

I don't need to have them leave here knowing they are already a great ship driver or that they know how to diagram the electrical system of the cutter. They are going to learn that, and that's fine, but they have to have the core values down. The fundamentals—that's what they learn here. It's not just the ship driver, and it's not just the leader; it's both ends and everything in between.

Honor is one of our core values. We not only have a lot of training, but they're challenged along the way throughout the whole 200 weeks. The four years they're here, they're naturally placed in situations where we hold them accountable. We don't play around with honor. Even if a cadet doesn't cheat but helps cover for another who did the result is the same: they're both gone.

We have a system here we use to track cadet progress in general: academics, military training, conduct. I can login and bring up a cadet record, and I was looking at one the other day in the process of reviewing his summer performance. I like to look and see what else they've done. We've actually got a meeting later today (it's called a "suitability-for-service" hearing) for a cadet who had a

particularly poor summer experience. If you look back on their history and they really haven't done a fantastic job, to use nautical terms, we are going all-stop: Let's take a fix. Let's see what we need to do to remediate them. Do we have time to do it? With one of these guys, I'm not sure. We might just have to make a tough decision and say, "Thank you for your time." I'm not sure at this time, from what I've seen, that this guy has that solid foundation of honor, respect, and devotion to duty—the type of character and leadership traits required to walk on board and begin learning how to lead people or stand a watch. Honor never sleeps; it's always on watch. After four years, we've usually got a pretty good sense of the person's character and can attest they have the basic foundation to go out and start learning how to really be a Coast Guard officer, both in terms of leadership and the professional skillset of their chosen career path.

We need the foundations. We need the core values in place as an officer. Even if they didn't do all that well in their military skills training or their nautical science courses, is there still something to build on there? One of the cases I'm looking at now had to do with a cadet on a cutter this summer where he didn't do so well. He didn't stand a very taut watch—just didn't do that well. So I asked a ton of follow-up questions of the CO and the XO, and they painted the picture of a guy who didn't show up for his watch, someone they always had to go looking for. So now I'm getting into his character. It's okay if you don't know the right answer—we don't expect you to always know it necessarily—but we do expect you to be on time, learn, and put forth an effort. This kid was a little bit shy in that capacity; he couldn't get any one down very well. But if I see a cadet who is trying hard, doing the best he can, an honorable cadet, but squeaking by academically, if they have that foundation, squeaking by might be good enough. You may have heard the term "anchorman," the person who graduates last in their class? You've got the valedictorian, the honor grad, and then you've got the anchorman, our Service anchor, just sitting on the bottom—the kind of person I just described—you know, trying really hard and an honorable person who really wants to succeed but just can't really bring it all together to get that A in class every time? They can get the C. What's interesting is that it's shocking to look at the number of senior officers and even admirals who were themselves anchormen in their class.

We had a guy, an interesting case, who is on a plane today heading up to Kodiak, Alaska. He was a 1st class cadet, a fantastic guy: motivated, always a positive attitude, got along with his classmates. The underclass knew they could go to him for guidance and good advice. He was always that guy showing up first with a smile on his face, saying, "What can I do to help?" He's the kind of guy you want as your best friend. He just had trouble with grades. He had that basic foundation; there was no doubt about it. He had it. The other requirement is you have to maintain a grade point average to get a degree. We have other requirements here, as well—you have to pass your nautical science classes, you have to pass your rules-of-the-road test—but this guy struggled pretty much universally with the academics (great at everything else he did here).

Due to academic circumstances, he was unfortunately not able to continue here. I know the academic division, the dean, and his staff worked with him, gave him various opportunities and counseling, but it just wasn't in the cards. However, he had demonstrated just so much character, exemplified our core values in everything else he did, and he wanted to be in the Coast Guard. He said, "Well, if I can't be an officer, I still want to be in the Coast Guard. Can I enlist?" We said, "Well, sure, you can go to a recruiter, but give us a few minutes." So we worked with headquarters, the Office of Enlisted Personnel, and found a deal where he could get credit for the work he has already done in three years at the Coast Guard Academy—the various nautical science courses he took and the professional military training. He could actually apply that to a special program that allowed him to not only skip boot camp but enter the Coast Guard enlisted force as a 3rd class petty officer rather than as a seaman. He is the kind of guy who everybody on staff here immediately said, "Hey, what can I do to help this guy?" It took a lot, but we put together a package and today this guy is on a plane heading to Kodiak, Alaska, to report on board

The Coast Guard Academy mascot Objee as he stands near the Honor Wall.

Coast Guard cutter *ALEX HALEY* as a 3rd class boatswain's mate. That just underscores how much value we place in the core values, character, and leadership development. That's the foundation, and if you can't get the academic piece, we still want you somewhere in the Coast Guard. One promotion and he can apply to OCS.

As the commanding officer of the *Eagle*, Captain Wes Pulver notes many qualities that are common to the most successful officers. He begins with the basics, then moves on to the essential philosophy that underpins any leadership position:

That's a tough question, actually, because we're such a diverse Service. I think a desire to be around the maritime community is important. No matter what job we do, we serve the American public. I think a matter of service is important—the desire to serve. I've admired people who can balance all the responsibilities with a smile, balance their position with empathetic discussions with their crew or with whomever they work. Great communication skills, great leadership skills, operational desire, interest in the maritime environment—those are all things that are important.

I will say the most important characteristics are the Coast Guard's core values of honor, respect, and devotion to duty. When the Coast Guard came out with this, I was a junior officer, and I thought it was kind of cliché, but I will tell you openly that everyone from the newest non-rate to the commandant and everyone in between believes in those values. When people don't have those values, they don't fit the Service mold real well, and they move on. Honor, respect, devotion to duty—those are three really high standards, and when you first hear them, you're like, "That's easy!" Not always. Always being honorable is a challenge. Being asked a question and having to give an answer is sometimes uncomfortable. Devotion to duty—what does that mean? If you take that to the full extent, it's having twelve, fourteen years at sea and being away from your family, or it's standing watch on Christmas, or it's putting yourself in harm's way for others. Look at some of the rescues carried out by Coast Guard men and women last winter. It's extraordinary. It's getting to the oil-pollution spill and making sure it's cleaned. This value of respect—treating other people in the same way you would like to be treated—that is an internal thing. I always ask people their leadership philosophy. What is it? That core value of respect—the fact that when a new non-rate walks on board, I'm going to treat that person with respect. They volunteered to be in the Service, they're volunteering to serve afloat, they have a desire to be successful. I do believe everybody joins to be successful. They earn my respect just for signing on the dotted line.

You start looking at those core values and what they mean to the organization. They weren't written down before the early '90s, but you look back over the history of our Service, back to 1790, and I think we've always had them. I think it's really important for our Service to have these core values as a common frame of reference. I think that's what we try to do here, and maybe that's back to the command environment. You look at those core values, and they start setting a climate that's respectful, positive, and all those things. We have our moments when people fall from the core values, and we resolve them, and we resolve them swiftly. But if you look at organization with core values—and it doesn't matter if you're on a cutter, a small-boat station, a sector, or headquarters—inculcating people with those core values is a powerful thing. I'm convinced it's part of the success of our Service. There is that saying that when everyone else comes in, we go out. Why do we do that? The mission, the drive to help others. Devotion to duty—why do we do that? Sometimes you have to ask yourself, but as a Service, we are continually doing it, and what a Service to be affiliated with.

I will say everyone approaches it differently. We have those same attributes, but we are a very diverse and eclectic organization, and I think that adds to our strength, too. I might approach something completely differently than the person sitting at the desk next to me, and that is more strength for the Service, not less. Diversity, whether it's in thought, background, or whatever that diversity is, I think that's part of the strength of our Service.

I get excited and passionate. I am excited about these young men and women who come on board. Once in a while, people say this generation isn't as good. I disagree. They're not just good; they're better. I can't wait to see what they're able to do. I get to see that from ten years ago. There are kids I sailed with, those kids I was at the Academy with, and the junior enlisted here as well; they are driven and motivated. They want to be successful, and they want to believe in something. I think our Service gives them that something to believe in. It's powerful.

At the end of the day, as a service, we work really hard. I think we believe in what we do. It's nice to be in this Service. I believe in every mission we do. That's awesome. To be affiliated with the institution of the U.S. Coast Guard is a real privilege. As an organization, I'm very proud to be in it, very proud to be part of it. When my time is up and I move on, I will be very proud to have given those years of my life to this organization and to this nation. Between stopping drugs, rescuing folks, helping with our engagement around the world, I've been privileged to do this, and it feels really great.

As the Academy's superintendent, Rear Admiral Sandra Stosz has strong opinions about what qualities make an effective officer. The search for future officers possessing those qualities begins in the Admissions Department:

We are looking for people who are leaders, who have character, who have demonstrated an ability to do the right thing and make the tough decisions; people who will intervene in a situation where they see something wrong being done; people who are communicative, who can get along, who can work as a team. We want people who can rise above and who really want to make a difference. Those are some of the foundational qualities we look for in the essay questions. The qualities we look for do change a little over time, but there are some foundational ones that remain.

Stosz prefers to avoid oversimplification, but when time is of the essence, she gives cadets what she terms her quick recipe for success:

The simple version, when there is little time and I want something to stick, is this: hard work plus perseverance will equal success. Hard work and perseverance—that combination is powerful. You see it on the sports field, you see it in the classroom, you see it getting through tough times. The hard work is important, because you've got to do that; nothing comes easy or free. Perseverance is important, as well—especially nowadays. This generation tends to work really hard until they hit a barrier, but they fall back easily. They turn around and try something else until they hit a barrier and fall back again. You need to persevere.

Stosz sees cadets' time at the Academy as a journey—one whose completion requires both motivation and direction. Most importantly, she warns that cadets must always be guided by a moral compass:

Honor, respect, devotion to duty. That is such a bull's-eye here at the Academy, a front-and-center requirement: honor, respect, devotion to duty, core values, leader of character, moral compass. Certainly, not all the hard work and perseverance in the world pays off if you're headed in the wrong direction. The young people here are in a four-year journey of self-discovery; they are going to be leaders of character. There are two components of leadership they learn here. First, they learn how to be a follower. When they are 4th class cadets, they're learning how to be good followers; it's called leading self. Leading others is the next task they get. The young people here need to have an element of passion. They need to find their passion, find what makes them really just sizzle here, find what makes them want to get up in the morning and go and be a cadet. If they don't find that passion, they're going to have a hard time making it, because they're going to find themselves adrift. Without that passion and purpose, they are going to have a hard time aligning that hard work and perseverance. They have to have a goal, and they have to head there guided by a moral compass. Even with a passion, it's easy to fall off course without a moral compass, without that north star. The core values are your compass; it's how you perform, how you present yourself, it's how well you're prepared. I always mention core values, especially the respect piece. Respect is so powerful. Sometimes, if you have a full understanding of respect, the honor and the devotion to duty takes care of itself.

No stranger to authority, Stosz makes a careful distinction among three sources of power. One, in particular, should be tapped only sparingly:

It's too easy to hide behind and lead from a position of power. A lesson I have for senior people is that you've got three kinds of power: you've got this positional power [pointing to the stripes on her sleeve], you've got professional power, and you have personal power. You should only use the positional power when everything else fails. Everywhere you go to lead in the Coast Guard, show up at that unit with the full expectation that your first mission is to earn the respect and the trust of that crew, not to simply use these stripes. You earn that through your personal and your professional power—how well you do your job, how well you interact, communicate, and lead those people. Do that successfully, and you won't need the stripes, the crows, or whatever the devices are.

In the Coast Guard, they're not going to be so concerned about whether you've got an admiral's stripe or a petty officer's stripe; they're going to try to help you as a fellow human being and a fellow Coast Guardsman.

In the end, Stosz believes that the qualities expected of officers can be found right there in the language of each of the promises that cadets make along the way.

These are found in our mission statement that hangs on the wall there, the oath of office that they take, and in the commission they receive. If you look at the wording in all three of those documents, they hold the great qualities that young 4th class cadets need to start thinking about. If you read the commissioning language, it speaks of the president reposing special trust and confidence in the fidelity, abilities, and integrity of those he commissions into the Coast Guard. These are powerful words: "special trust and confidence in the fidelity, abilities, and integrity." So are you worthy of that commission? Will you be worthy to raise your hand and take that oath to protect and defend the Constitution? Those are the virtues and the values they need to internalize before they can graduate from here.

When the swabs all swore the oath of office on R-Day, they were handed the key to becoming great officers. What they heard sound-ed quite straightforward, an easy recipe for success. What they began to understand as the summer progressed was that putting simple theories into practice often proves incredibly complex. To Lieutenant Kehlenbach, the formula for success as an officer of the United States Coast Guard is easy to say but takes a lifetime to learn:

I think you just have to stick to our core values: honor, respect, and devotion to duty. Having that foundation, getting everybody to accept those core values and letting those values be what guides their daily activities, I think that's what it takes. It's not just about being a good student. It's not just being a good athlete or performing militarily. It's about the whole package. As you drive into the Academy, you see those banners: Developing Leaders of Character Since 1876. While we may be a college, I believe we are here to develop officers. Even though they will leave here with a degree, to me, that's not as important as their character.

And so swab summer ends where it began, with honor, respect, and devotion to duty. Swabs begin their arduous journey during their first summer, hemmed in by a seemingly insurmountable bluff. Only a single path, straight and narrow, cuts across its rocky face. The cadets' four-year ascent presents new challenges, new experiences, and new opportunities, each expanding the boundaries of what they discover themselves capable. The path is not for everyone. Difficult and steep, many will turn many back to search for less demanding routes. Those who summit, however, are rewarded with a view of ships sprinkled across the vast, blue ocean below, ships patiently waiting for their new ensigns.

Acknowledgments

I would like thank the United States Coast Guard for allowing me to pursue this project. From the moment personnel in Washington gave the project a green light, every single person I met and spoke with not only welcomed me to the Academy, but went well out of his or her way to assist me with my work. I discovered that the men and women of the Coast Guard live their lives practicing the very ideals they instill in the Academy's cadets. Not coming from a military family, I confess to my initial trepidation in pursuing this work. The summer I spent following the cadets who appear in this book and interviewing the officers charged with their education quickly became one of the most refreshing experiences of my life. I left the campus with a profound respect and admiration for them as individuals, for the work they do, and for the service they provide to our nation. By the end of my time at the Academy, I had become one of its biggest fans.

I want to thank all of the officers and personnel at the Academy for their help and guidance. Despite their busy lives, they all made time to help me understand their mission. I am deeply indebted to Admiral Sandra Stosz, not only for giving me free reign of the campus, but also for taking the time to talk with me about the institution. I owe a special debt to Lieutenant LuAnn Kehlenbach (now Lieutenant Commander Kehlenbach) for guiding me through the intricacies of the institution and military life, as well as for providing me with all of the information and schedules I required. Lieutenant Commander Michael Thomas (now Commander Thomas) also went well out of his way to ensure I saw what I needed to see. While my original request was simply to interview him, he directed me to others who could help with the project and made sure I could follow swabs onto the *Eagle* for a five-day voyage. For his help I am forever grateful. Thanks also to Senior Chief Tony McDade for keeping me on track and helping me whenever roadblocks appeared. These officers clearly exemplify the highest ideals of the United States Coast Guard.

I want to thank PA3 Diana Honings for getting me headed in the right direction at the very start, and all of the cadets who allowed me to interview them before, during, and after swab summer. They generously allowed me to gather their impressions during what were undoubtedly some of the most stressful days of their lives, and I appreciate their willingness to add to their already considerable load. I thank the cadre for allowing me to follow them around with my camera while they performed their duties, and every cadet who stopped to ask if they could help me get somewhere or find an office. From what I observed on a daily basis, the future of the United States Coast Guard is in the best of hands.

I want to thank my good friend Captain Carl Tjerandsen, Retired, for all of his insight and encouragement, and especially for his willingness to read the first draft of the manuscript and provide me with insightful feedback. His intimate knowledge of the Academy and astute observations guided me throughout the long process of creating this book. I would be hard pressed to find a better friend.

Finally, I wish to thank my wife Sue for humoring me as I pursue my unending list of projects. Without her, none of them would have come to fruition, and I marvel at her patience and capacity to endure them. She has always been, and always will be, the guiding light of my life.

Sincerely,

Markham Starr   2013

Additional Books
by
Markham Starr

Building a Greenland Kayak

•

On Oceans of Grey: Portrait of a Fishing Port

•

Against the Tide: The Commercial Fishermen of Point Judith

•

The Catboat: A Photographic Album

•

Voices from the Waterfront: Portrait of the New Bedford Fishing Industry

•

Down on the Farm: The Last Dairy Farms of North Stonington

•

Finest Kind: The Lobstermen of Corea

•

End of the Line: Closing the Last Sardine Cannery in America

•

Barns of Connecticut

•

In History's Wake: The Last Trap Fishermen of Rhode Island

MarkhamStarrPhotography.com
CatboatAlbum.com